Building RESTful Python Web Services

Create web services that are lightweight, maintainable, scalable, and secure using the best tools and techniques designed for Python

Gastón C. Hillar

BIRMINGHAM - MUMBAI

Building RESTful Python Web Services

First published: October 2016

Production reference: 2221116

Published by Packt Publishing Ltd.
Livery Place
35 Livery Street
Birmingham
B3 2PB, UK.
ISBN 978-1-78646-225-1

www.packtpub.com

Credits

Author

Gastón C. Hillar

Reviewer

Elmer Thomas

Commissioning Editor

Aaron Lazar

Acquisition Editor

Reshma Raman

Content Development Editor

Divij Kotian

Technical Editor

Gebin George

Copy Editor

Sneha Singh

Project Coordinator

Sheejal Shah

Proofreader

Safis Editing

Indexer

Rekha Nair

Graphics

Jason Monteiro

Production Coordinator

Melwyn Dsa

About the Author

Gastón C. Hillar is Italian and has been working with computers since he was eight. He began programming with the legendary Texas TI-99/4A and Commodore 64 home computers in the early 80s. He has a Bachelor's degree in Computer Science from which he graduated with honors, and an MBA from which he graduated with an outstanding thesis. At present, Gastón is an independent IT consultant and freelance author who is always looking for new adventures around the world.

He has been a senior contributing editor at Dr. Dobb's and has written more than a hundred articles on software development topics. Gaston was also a former Microsoft MVP in technical computing. He has received the prestigious Intel® Black Belt Software Developer award eight times.

He is a guest blogger at Intel® Software Network (`http://software.intel.com`). You can reach him at `gastonhillar@hotmail.com` and follow him on Twitter at `http://twitter.com/gastonhillar`. Gastón's blog is `http://csharpmulticore.blogspot.com`.

He lives with his wife, Vanesa, and his two sons, Kevin and Brandon.

Acknowledgments

At the time of writing this book, I was fortunate to work with an excellent team at Packt Publishing , whose contributions vastly improved the presentation of this book. Reshma Raman and Aaron Lazar allowed me to provide them ideas to develop this book and I jumped into the exciting project of teaching how to use many popular web frameworks to develop RESTful Web Services with Python 3.5. Divij Kotian helped me realize my vision for this book and provided many sensible suggestions regarding the text, the format and the flow. The reader will notice his great work. It was great working with Divij in another book. In fact, it is the third book in which I was able to work with Reshma and Divij. It's been great working with them in another project and I can't wait to work with them again. I would like to thank my technical reviewers and proofreaders, for their thorough reviews and insightful comments. I was able to incorporate some of the knowledge and wisdom they have gained in their many years in the software development industry. This book was possible because they gave valuable feedback.

Gebin George did a wonderful job when the book moved into the production stage. He has made all the necessary adjustments to generate the final version of the book with an outstanding layout. Gebin made the book easy to read in its different versions and made sure I was happy with the results. A book like this one with so many tables, figures, pieces of code, commands and sample outputs requires skilled people with eye for detail during all the stages. I was fortunate to have Gebin onboard. I would like to thank my technical reviewers and proofreaders, for their thorough reviews and insightful comments. I was able to incorporate some of the knowledge and wisdom they have gained in their many years in the software development industry. This book was possible because they gave valuable feedback.

I usually start writing notes about ideas for a book when I spend time at software development conferences and events. I wrote the initial idea for this book in San Francisco, California, at Intel Developer Forum 2015. One year later, at Intel Developer Forum 2016, I had the chance to discuss with many software engineers the book I was finishing and incorporate their suggestions in the final drafts.

The entire process of writing a book requires a huge amount of lonely hours. I wouldn't be able to write an entire book without dedicating some time to play soccer against my sons Kevin and Brandon, and my nephew, Nicolas. Of course, I never won a match. However, I did score a few goals.

About the Reviewer

Elmer Thomas completed a B.S. in Computer Engineering and a M.S. in Electrical Engineering at the University of California, Riverside. His focus was on Control Systems, specifically GPS navigation systems, spending several years serving as a research assistant, building software and hardware for self driving cars at U.C. Riverside and Berkeley, resulting in *2 co-publications*: *Aided Integer Ambiguity Resolution Algorithm* and *Data Fusion via Kalman Filter: GPS & INS*. During the final years of his Masters program, he added a few mentors, partners and some business skills through the Tuck Executive Program at Dartmouth to his repertoire and co-founded several companies with varying degrees of success over the next 7 years. During this time he helped hundreds of business profit while achieving over 50 awards from local and state government for service in the community.

While building businesses, Elmer served on various boards to help foster growth in local business communities in Riverside and Orange County, including the Riverside Technology CEO Forum, the TechBiz Connection, OCTANe and TriTech. Next, he began serving at SendGrid, an email API and Service Company, as one of the first 5 employees in a now 300+ employee company on the verge of going public. Service began as the web development manager, and then he moved into a product development role while helping build out a quality assurance program. After spending 2 years traveling to over 50 events, speaking, teaching and mentoring as a Developer Evangelist within the Send Grid marketing department, Elmer then served as the Hacker in Residence on the community team at SendGrid. In that role he mentored over 50 startups, many belonging to accelerators such as Techstars and 500 Startups, and hundreds of developers through live consulting and development of productivity content and software.

He currently serves as the Developer Experience Engineer at SendGrid, leading, developing and managing SendGrid's open source community, which includes over 24 active projects across 7 programming languages. These open source projects process hundreds of millions of emails per day for our customers. He also serves as Vice President of the Council for the Advancement of Black Engineers, drawing from experience as chapter president of the National Society of Black Engineers while a student at U.C. Riverside, supporting our mission to increase the number of culturally responsible Black Engineers with PhD's, post-doctoral training and professional engineering registrations.

As member of the board of directors for Operation Code, he helps equip military veterans and their families with programming knowledge through mentorship to help veterans create new career paths in software development. Through his volunteer work with the Girls Scouts of San Gorgonio Council, Elmer focuses on helping bring STEM experiences to girls, specifically within the age groups between 9 and 14 years old, including his own 11 year old daughter, who is now a Girl Scout cadette. To help serve his local community, he is a member of the board of directors of his local HOA. He is considered a social media influencer, driving 100s of millions of visits to various web pages. He is known as ThinkingSerious on various social networks.

Elmer's passions include family time with his wife, and 2 daughters, reading, writing, watching videos, especially in virtual reality, developing software and creating in general, especially in the area of personal development and productivity through quantification techniques. I would like to thank my wife Linda and daughter Audrey for their patience and quiet time for me to complete this review.

More detail can be found at his blog, `ThinkingSerious.com`.

www.PacktPub.com

For support files and downloads related to your book, please visit www.PacktPub.com.

Did you know that Packt offers eBook versions of every book published, with PDF and ePub files available? You can upgrade to the eBook version at www.PacktPub.com and as a print book customer, you are entitled to a discount on the eBook copy. Get in touch with us at service@packtpub.com for more details.

At www.PacktPub.com, you can also read a collection of free technical articles, sign up for a range of free newsletters and receive exclusive discounts and offers on Packt books and eBooks.

https://www.packtpub.com/mapt

Get the most in-demand software skills with Mapt. Mapt gives you full access to all Packt books and video courses, as well as industry-leading tools to help you plan your personal development and advance your career.

Why subscribe?

- Fully searchable across every book published by Packt
- Copy and paste, print, and bookmark content
- On demand and accessible via a web browser

Table of Contents

Preface

REST (Representational State Transfer) is the architectural style that is driving modern web development and mobile apps. In fact, developing and interacting with RESTful Web Services is a required skill in any modern software development job. Sometimes, you have to interact with an existing API and in other cases, you have to design a RESTful API from scratch and make it work with **JSON (JavaScript Object Notation)**.

Python is one of the most popular programming languages. Python 3.5 is the most modern version of Python. It is open source, multiplatform, and you can use it to develop any kind of application, from websites to extremely complex scientific computing applications. There is always a Python package that makes things easier for you to avoid reinventing the wheel and solve the problems faster. The most important and popular Cloud computing providers make it easy to work with Python and its related Web frameworks. Thus, Python is an ideal choice for developing RESTful Web Services. The book covers all the things you need to know to select the most appropriate Python Web framework and develop a RESTful API from scratch.

You will work with the three most popular Python web frameworks that make it easy to develop RESTful Web Services: Django, Flask, and Tornado. Each web framework has its advantages and tradeoffs. You will work with examples that represent appropriate cases for each of these Web frameworks, in combination with additional Python packages that will simplify the most common tasks. You will learn to use different tools to test and develop high-quality, consistent and scalable RESTful Web Services. You will also take advantage of object-oriented programming, also known as OOP, to maximize code reuse and minimize maintenance costs.

You will always write unit tests and improve test coverage for all of the RESTful Web Services that you will develop throughout the book. You won't just run the sample code but you will also make sure that you write tests for your RESTful API.

This book will allow you to learn how to take advantage of many packages that will simplify the most common tasks related to RESTful Web Services. You will be able to start creating your own RESTful APIs for any domain in any of the covered Web frameworks in Python 3.5 or greater.

What this book covers

Chapter 1, *Developing RESTful APIs with Django*, in this chapter we will start working with Django and Django REST Framework, and we will create a RESTful Web API that performs **CRUD (Create, Read, Update and Delete)** operations on a simple SQLite database.

Chapter 2, *Working with Class-Based Views and Hyperlinked APIs in Django*, in this chapter we will expand the capabilities of the RESTful API that we started in the previous chapter. We will change the ORM settings to work with a more powerful PostgreSQL database and we will take advantage of advanced features included in Django REST Framework that allow us to reduce boilerplate code for complex APIs, such as class based views.

Chapter 3, *Improving and Adding Authentication to an API with Django*, in this chapter we will improve the RESTful API that we started in the previous chapter. We will add unique constraints to the model and update the database. We will make it easy to update single fields with the PATCH method and we will take advantage of pagination. We will start working with authentication, permissions and throttling.

Chapter 4, *Throttling, Filtering, Testing and Deploying an API with Django*, in this chapter we will take advantage of many features included in Django REST Framework to define throttling policies. We will use filtering, searching and ordering classes to make it easy to configure filters, search queries and desired order for the results in HTTP requests. We will use the browsable API feature to test these new features included in our API. We will write a first round of unit tests, measure test coverage and then write additional unit tests to improve test coverage. Finally, we will learn many considerations for deployment and scalability.

Chapter 5, *Developing RESTful APIs with Flask*, in this chapter we will start working with Flask and its Flask-RESTful extension. We will create a RESTful Web API that performs CRUD operations on a simple list.

Chapter 6, *Working with Models, SQLAlchemy, and Hyperlinked APIs in Flask*, in this chapter we will expand the capabilities of the RESTful API that we started in the previous chapter. We will use SQLAlchemy as our ORM to work with a PostgreSQL database and we will take advantage of advanced features included in Flask and Flask-RESTful that will allow us to easily organize code for complex APIs, such as models and blueprints.

Chapter 7, *Improving and Adding Authentication to an API with Flask*, in this chapter we will improve the RESTful API in many ways. We will add user friendly error messages when resources aren't unique. We will test how to update single or multiple fields with the PATCH method and we will create our own generic pagination class. Then, we will start working with authentication and permissions. We will added a user model and we will update the database. We will make many changes in the different pieces of code to achieve a specific security goal and we will take advantage of Flask-HTTPAuth and passlib to use HTTP authentication in our API.

Chapter 8, *Testing and Deploying an API with Flask*, in this chapter we will set up a testing environment. We will install nose2 to make it easy to discover and execute unit tests and we will create a new database to be used for testing. We will write a first round of unit tests, measure test coverage and then write additional unit tests to improve test coverage. Finally, we will learn many considerations for deployment and scalability.

Chapter 9, *Developing RESTful APIs with Tornado*, we will work with Tornado to create a RESTful Web API. We will design a RESTful API to interact with slow sensors and actuators. We will defined the requirements for our API and we will understand the tasks performed by each HTTP method. We will create the classes that represent a drone and write code to simulate slow I/O operations that are called for each HTTP request method. We will write classes that represent request handlers and process the different HTTP requests and configure the URL patterns to route URLs to request handlers and their methods.

Chapter 10, *Working with Asynchronous Code, Testing, and Deploying an API with Tornado*, in this chapter we will understand the difference between synchronous and asynchronous execution. We will create a new version of the RESTful API that takes advantage of the non-blocking features in Tornado combined with asynchronous execution. We will improve scalability for our existing API and we will make it possible to start executing other requests while waiting for the slow I/O operations with sensors and actuators. Then, we will set up a testing environment. We will install nose2 to make it easy to discover and execute unit tests. We will wrote a first round of unit tests, measure test coverage and then write additional unit tests to improve test coverage. We will create all the necessary tests to have a complete coverage of all the lines of code.

What you need for this book

In order to work with the different samples for Python 3.5.x, you will need any computer with an Intel Core i3 or higher CPU and at least 4 GB RAM. You can work with any of the following operating systems:

- Windows 7 or greater (Windows 8, Windows 8.1 or Windows 10)
- macOS Mountain Lion or greater
- Any Linux version capable of running Python 3.5.x and any modern browser with JavaScript support

You will need Python 3.5 or greater installed on your computer.

Who this book is for

This book is for web developers who have working knowledge of Python and would like to build amazing web services by taking advantage of the various frameworks of Python. You should have some knowledge of RESTful APIs.

Conventions

In this book, you will find a number of text styles that distinguish between different kinds of information. Here are some examples of these styles and an explanation of their meaning.

Code words in text, database table names, folder names, filenames, file extensions, pathnames, dummy URLs, user input, and Twitter handles are shown as follows: "If no game matches the specified id or primary key, the server will return just a 404 Not Found status."

A block of code is set as follows:

```
from django.apps import AppConfig
class GamesConfig(AppConfig):
    name = 'games'
```

Any command-line input or output is written as follows:

```
python3 -m venv ~/PythonREST/Django01
```

 Warnings or important notes appear in a box like this.

 Tips and tricks appear like this.

Reader feedback

Feedback from our readers is always welcome. Let us know what you think about this book-what you liked or disliked. Reader feedback is important for us as it helps us develop titles that you will really get the most out of. To send us general feedback, simply e-mail feedback@packtpub.com, and mention the book's title in the subject of your message. If there is a topic that you have expertise in and you are interested in either writing or contributing to a book, see our author guide at www.packtpub.com/authors.

Customer support

Now that you are the proud owner of a Packt book, we have a number of things to help you to get the most from your purchase.

Downloading the example code

You can download the example code files for this book from your account at http://www.packtpub.com. If you purchased this book elsewhere, you can visit http://www.packtpub.com/support and register to have the files e-mailed directly to you.

You can download the code files by following these steps:

1. Log in or register to our website using your e-mail address and password.
2. Hover the mouse pointer on the **SUPPORT** tab at the top.
3. Click on **Code Downloads & Errata**.
4. Enter the name of the book in the **Search** box.
5. Select the book for which you're looking to download the code files.
6. Choose from the drop-down menu where you purchased this book from.
7. Click on **Code Download**.

Once the file is downloaded, please make sure that you unzip or extract the folder using the latest version of:

- WinRAR / 7-Zip for Windows
- Zipeg / iZip / UnRarX for Mac
- 7-Zip / PeaZip for Linux

The code bundle for the book is also hosted on GitHub at `https://github.com/PacktPubl ishing/Building-RESTful-Python-Web-Services`. We also have other code bundles from our rich catalog of books and videos available at `https://github.com/PacktPublishing/`. Check them out!

Errata

Although we have taken every care to ensure the accuracy of our content, mistakes do happen. If you find a mistake in one of our books-maybe a mistake in the text or the code- we would be grateful if you could report this to us. By doing so, you can save other readers from frustration and help us improve subsequent versions of this book. If you find any errata, please report them by visiting `http://www.packtpub.com/submit-errata`, selecting your book, clicking on the **Errata Submission Form** link, and entering the details of your errata. Once your errata are verified, your submission will be accepted and the errata will be uploaded to our website or added to any list of existing errata under the Errata section of that title.

To view the previously submitted errata, go to `https://www.packtpub.com/books/conten t/support` and enter the name of the book in the search field. The required information will appear under the **Errata** section.

Piracy

Piracy of copyrighted material on the Internet is an ongoing problem across all media. At Packt, we take the protection of our copyright and licenses very seriously. If you come across any illegal copies of our works in any form on the Internet, please provide us with the location address or website name immediately so that we can pursue a remedy.

Please contact us at `copyright@packtpub.com` with a link to the suspected pirated material.

We appreciate your help in protecting our authors and our ability to bring you valuable content.

Questions

If you have a problem with any aspect of this book, you can contact us at `questions@packtpub.com`, and we will do our best to address the problem.

1
Developing RESTful APIs with Django

In this chapter, we will start our journey towards RESTful Web APIs with Python and four different Web frameworks. Python is one of the most popular and versatile programming languages. There are thousands of Python packages, which allow you to extend Python capabilities to any kind of domain you can imagine. We can work with many different Web frameworks and packages to easily build simple and complex RESTful Web APIs with Python, and we can also combine these frameworks with other Python packages.

We can leverage our existing knowledge of Python and its packages to code the different pieces of our RESTful Web APIs and their ecosystem. We can use the object-oriented features to create code that is easier to maintain, understand, and reuse. We can use all the packages that we already know to interact with databases, Web services, and different APIs. Python makes it easy for us to create RESTful Web APIs. We don't need to learn another programming language; we can use the one we already know and love.

In this chapter, we will start working with Django and Django REST Framework, and we will create a RESTful Web API that performs **CRUD (Create, Read, Update, and Delete)** operations on a simple SQLite database. We will:

- Design a RESTful API to interact with a simple SQLite database
- Understand the tasks performed by each HTTP method
- Set up the virtual environment with Django REST framework
- Create the database models
- Manage serialization and deserialization of data
- Write API views
- Make HTTP requests to the API with command-line tools
- Work with GUI tools to compose and send HTTP requests

Designing a RESTful API to interact with a simple SQLite database

Imagine that we have to start working on a mobile App that has to interact with a RESTful API to perform CRUD operations with games. We don't want to spend time choosing and configuring the most appropriate **ORM (Object-Relational Mapping)**; we just want to finish the RESTful API as soon as possible to start interacting with it via our mobile App. We really want the games to persist in a database but we don't need it to be production-ready, and therefore, we can use the simplest possible relational database, as long as we don't have to spend time making complex installations or configurations.

Django REST framework, also known as DRF, will allow us to easily accomplish this task and start making HTTP requests to our first version of our RESTful Web Service. In this case, we will work with a very simple SQLite database, the default database for a new Django REST framework project.

First, we must specify the requirements for our main resource: a game. We need the following attributes or fields for a game:

- An integer identifier
- A name or title
- A release date
- A game category description, such as *3D RPG* and *2D mobile arcade*.
- A `bool` value indicating whether the game was played at least once by a player or not

In addition, we want our database to save a timestamp with the date and time in which the game was inserted in the database.

The following table shows the HTTP verbs, the scope, and the semantics for the methods that our first version of the API must support. Each method is composed by an HTTP verb and a scope and all the methods have a well defined meaning for all games and collections.

HTTP verb	Scope	Semantics
GET	Collection of games	Retrieve all the stored games in the collection, sorted by their name in ascending order
GET	Game	Retrieve a single game
POST	Collection of games	Create a new game in the collection
PUT	Game	Update an existing game

HTTP verb	Scope	Semantics
DELETE	Game	Delete an existing game

In a RESTful API, each resource has its own unique URL. In our API, each game has its own unique URL.

Understanding the tasks performed by each HTTP method

In the preceding table, the GET HTTP verb appears twice but with two different scopes. The first row shows a GET HTTP verb applied to a collection of games (collection of resources) and the second row shows a GET HTTP verb applied to a game (a single resource).

Let's consider that http://localhost:8000/games/ is the URL for the collection of games. If we add a number and a slash (/) to the preceding URL, we identify a specific game whose id or primary key is equal to the specified numeric value. For example, http://localhost:8000/games/12/ identifies the game whose id or primary key is equal to 12.

We have to compose and send an HTTP request with the following HTTP verb (POST) and request URL (http://localhost:8000/games/) to create a new game. In addition, we have to provide the **JSON (JavaScript Object Notation)** key-value pairs with the field names and the values to create the new game. As a result of the request, the server will validate the provided values for the fields, make sure that it is a valid game and persist it in the database.

The server will insert a new row with the new game in the appropriate table and it will return a 201 Created status code and a JSON body with the recently added game serialized to JSON, including the assigned id or primary key that was automatically generated by the database and assigned to the game object.

```
POST http://localhost:8000/games/
```

We have to compose and send an HTTP request with the following HTTP verb (GET) and request URL (http://localhost:8000/games/{id}/) to retrieve the game whose id or primary key matches the specified numeric value in the place where {id} is written.

For example, if we use the request URL `http://localhost:8000/games/50/`, the server will retrieve the game whose id or primary key matches `50`.

As a result of the request, the server will retrieve a game with the specified id or primary key from the database and create the appropriate game object in Python. If a game is found, the server will serialize the game object into JSON and return a `200 OK` status code and a JSON body with the serialized game object. If no game matches the specified id or primary key, the server will return just a `404 Not Found` status:

```
GET http://localhost:8000/games/{id}/
```

We have to compose and send an HTTP request with the following HTTP verb (`PUT`) and request URL (`http://localhost:8000/games/{id}/`) to retrieve the game whose id or primary key matches the specified numeric value in the place where `{id}` is written and replace it with a game created with the provided data. In addition, we have to provide the JSON key-value pairs with the field names and the values to create the new game that will replace the existing one. As a result of the request, the server will validate the provided values for the fields, make sure that it is a valid game and replace the one that matches the specified id or primary key with the new one in the database. The id or primary key for the game will be the same after the update operation. The server will update the existing row in the appropriate table and it will return a `200 OK` status code and a JSON body with the recently updated game serialized to JSON. If we don't provide all the necessary data for the new game, the server will return a `400 Bad Request` status code. If the server doesn't find a game with the specified id, the server will return just a `404 Not Found` status.

```
PUT http://localhost:8000/games/{id}/
```

We have to compose and send an HTTP request with the following HTTP verb (`DELETE`) and request URL (`http://localhost:8000/games/{id}/`) to remove the game whose id or primary key matches the specified numeric value in the place where `{id}` is written. For example, if we use the request URL `http://localhost:8000/games/20/`, the server will delete the game whose id or primary key matches `20`. As a result of the request, the server will retrieve a game with the specified id or primary key from the database and create the appropriate game object in Python. If a game is found, the server will request the ORM to delete the game row associated with this game object and the server will return a `204 No Content` status code. If no game matches the specified id or primary key, the server will return just a `404 Not Found` status.

```
DELETE http://localhost:8000/games/{id}/
```

Working with lightweight virtual environments

Throughout this book, we will be working with different frameworks and libraries, and therefore, it is convenient to work with virtual environments. We will work with the lightweight virtual environments introduced in Python 3.3 and improved in Python 3.4. However, you can also choose to use the popular `virtualenv` (https://pypi.python.org/pypi/virtualenv) third-party virtual environment builder or the virtual environment options provided by your Python IDE.

You just have to make sure that you activate your virtual environment with the appropriate mechanism when it is necessary to do so, instead of following the step explained to activate the virtual environment generated with the `venv` module integrated in Python. You can read more information about PEP 405 Python Virtual Environment that introduced the `venv` module at https://www.python.org/dev/peps/pep-0405.

Each virtual environment we create with `venv` is an isolated environment and it will have its own independent set of installed Python packages in its site directories. When we create a virtual environment with `venv` in Python 3.4 and greater, pip is included in the new virtual environment. In Python 3.3, it was necessary to manually install pip after creating the virtual environment. Notice that the instructions provided are compatible with Python 3.4 or greater, including Python 3.5.x. The following commands assume that you have Python 3.5.x installed on macOS, Linux, or Windows.

First, we have to select the target folder or directory for our virtual environment. The following is the path we will use in the example for macOS and Linux. The target folder for the virtual environment will be the `PythonREST/Django` folder within our home directory. For example, if our home directory in macOS or Linux is `/Users/gaston`, the virtual environment will be created within `/Users/gaston/PythonREST/Django`. You can replace the specified path with your desired path in each command.

```
~/PythonREST/Django
```

The following is the path we will use in the example for Windows. The target folder for the virtual environment will be the `PythonREST/Django` folder within our user profile folder. For example, if our user profile folder is `C:\Users\Gaston`, the virtual environment will be created within `C:\Users\gaston\PythonREST\Django`. You can replace the specified path with your desired path in each command.

```
%USERPROFILE%\PythonREST\Django
```

Now, we have to use the `-m` option followed by the `venv` module name and the desired path to make Python run this module as a script and create a virtual environment in the specified path. The instructions are different depending on the platform in which we are creating the virtual environment.

Open a Terminal in macOS or Linux and execute the following command to create a virtual environment:

```
python3 -m venv ~/PythonREST/Django01
```

In Windows, execute the following command to create a virtual environment:

```
python -m venv %USERPROFILE%\PythonREST\Django01
```

The preceding command doesn't produce any output. The script created the specified target folder and installed pip by invoking `ensurepip` because we didn't specify the `--without-pip` option. The specified target folder has a new directory tree that contains Python executable files and other files that indicate that it is a virtual environment.

The `pyenv.cfg` configuration file specifies different options for the virtual environment and its existence is an indicator that we are in the root folder for a virtual environment. In OS and Linux, the folder will have the following main sub-folders—`bin`, `include`, `lib`, `lib/python3.5` and `lib/python3.5/site-packages`. In Windows, the folder will have the following main sub-folders—`Include`, `Lib`, `Lib\site-packages`, and `Scripts`. The directory trees for the virtual environment in each platform are the same as the layout of the Python installation in these platforms. The following screenshot shows the folders and files in the directory trees generated for the `Django01` virtual environment in macOS:

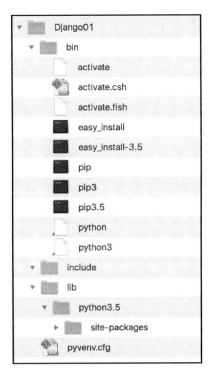

The following screenshot shows the main folders in the directory trees generated for the virtual environments in Windows:

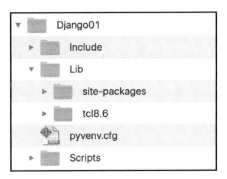

After we activate the virtual environment, we will install third-party packages into the virtual environment and the modules will be located within the `lib/python3.5/site-packages` or `Lib\site-packages` folder, based on the platform. The executables will be copied in the `bin` or `Scripts` folder, based on the platform. The packages we install won't make changes to other virtual environments or our base Python environment.

Now that we have created a virtual environment, we will run a platform-specific script to activate it. After we activate the virtual environment, we will install packages that will only be available in this virtual environment.

Run the following command in the terminal in macOS or Linux. Note that the results of this command will be accurate if you don't start a different shell than the default shell in the terminal session. In case you have doubts, check your terminal configuration and preferences.

```
echo $SHELL
```

The command will display the name of the shell you are using in the Terminal. In macOS, the default is `/bin/bash` and this means you are working with the bash shell. Depending on the shell, you must run a different command to activate the virtual environment in OS or Linux.

If your Terminal is configured to use the `bash` shell in macOS or Linux, run the following command to activate the virtual environment. The command also works for the `zsh` shell:

```
source ~/PythonREST/Django01/bin/activate
```

If your Terminal is configured to use either the `csh` or `tcsh` shell, run the following command to activate the virtual environment:

```
source ~/PythonREST/Django01/bin/activate.csh
```

If your Terminal is configured to use either the `fish` shell, run the following command to activate the virtual environment:

```
source ~/PythonREST/Django01/bin/activate.fish
```

In Windows, you can run either a batch file in the command prompt or a Windows PowerShell script to activate the virtual environment. If you prefer the command prompt, run the following command in the Windows command line to activate the virtual environment:

```
%USERPROFILE%\PythonREST\Django01\Scripts\activate.bat
```

If you prefer the Windows PowerShell, launch it and run the following commands to activate the virtual environment. However, notice that you should have scripts execution enabled in Windows PowerShell to be able to run the script:

```
cd $env:USERPROFILE
PythonREST\Django01\Scripts\Activate.ps1
```

After you activate the virtual environment, the command prompt will display the virtual environment root folder name enclosed in parenthesis as a prefix of the default prompt to remind us that we are working in the virtual environment. In this case, we will see (Django01) as a prefix for the command prompt because the root folder for the activated virtual environment is Django01.

The following screenshot shows the virtual environment activated in a macOS El Capitan terminal with a bash shell, after executing the previously shown commands:

As we can see in the preceding screenshot, the prompt changed from Gastons-MacBook-Pro:~ gaston$ to (Django01) Gastons-MacBook-Pro:~ gaston$ after the activation of the virtual environment.

The following screenshot shows the virtual environment activated in a Windows 10 Command Prompt, after executing the previously shown commands:

As we can notice from the preceding screenshot, the prompt changed from
`C:\Users\gaston\AppData\Local\Programs\Python\Python35` to `(Django01)`
`C:\Users\gaston\AppData\Local\Programs\Python\Python35` after the activation of
the virtual environment.

It is extremely easy to deactivate a virtual environment generated with the previously explained process. In macOS or Linux, just type `deactivate` and press Enter. In a Windows command prompt, you have to run the `deactivate.bat` batch file included in the Scripts folder (`%USERPROFILE%\PythonREST\Django01\Scripts\deactivate.bat` in our example). In Windows PowerShell, you have to run the `Deactivate.ps1` script in the `Scripts` folder. The deactivation will remove all the changes made in the environment variables.

Setting up the virtual environment with Django REST framework

We have created and activated a virtual environment. It is time to run many commands that will be the same for either macOS, Linux or Windows. Now, we must run the following command to install the Django Web framework:

```
pip install django
```

The last lines of the output will indicate that the `django` package has been successfully installed. Take into account that you may also see a notice to upgrade `pip`.

```
Collecting django
Installing collected packages: django
Successfully installed django-1.10
```

Now that we have installed Django Web framework, we can install Django REST framework. We just need to run the following command to install this package:

```
pip install djangorestframework
```

The last lines for the output will indicate that the `djangorestframework` package has been successfully installed:

```
Collecting djangorestframework
Installing collected packages: djangorestframework
Successfully installed djangorestframework-3.3.3
```

Go to the root folder for the virtual environment-Django01. In macOS or Linux, enter the following command:

```
cd ~/PythonREST/Django01
```

In Windows, enter the following command:

```
cd /d %USERPROFILE%\PythonREST\Django01
```

Run the following command to create a new Django project named gamesapi. The command won't produce any output:

```
django-admin.py startproject gamesapi
```

The previous command created a gamesapi folder with other sub-folders and Python files. Now, go to the recently created gamesapi folder. Just execute the following command:

```
cd gamesapi
```

Then, run the following command to create a new Django app named games within the gamesapi Django project. The command won't produce any output:

```
python manage.py startapp games
```

The previous command created a new gamesapi/games sub-folder, with the following files:

- __init__.py
- admin.py
- apps.py
- models.py
- tests.py
- views.py

In addition, the gamesapi/games folder will have a migrations sub-folder with an
__init__.py Python script. The following diagram shows the folders and files in the
directory trees starting at the gamesapi folder:

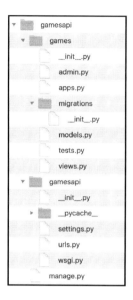

Let's check the Python code in the apps.py file within the gamesapi/games folder. The
following lines shows the code for this file:

```
from django.apps import AppConfig


class GamesConfig(AppConfig):
    name = 'games'
```

The code declares the GamesConfig class as a subclass of the django.apps.AppConfig
class that represents a Django application and its configuration. The GamesConfig class just
defines the name class attribute and sets its value to 'games'. We have to add
games.apps.GamesConfig as one of the installed apps in the gamesapi/settings.py
file that configures settings for the gamesapi Django project. We built the preceding string
as follows-app name + .apps. + class name, which is, games + .apps. + GamesConfig. In
addition, we have to add the rest_framework app to make it possible for us to use Django
REST Framework.

The `gamesapi/settings.py` file is a Python module with module-level variables that define the configuration of Django for the `gamesapi` project. We will make some changes to this Django settings file. Open the `gamesapi/settings.py` file and locate the following lines that specify the strings list that declares the installed apps:

```
INSTALLED_APPS = [
    'django.contrib.admin',
    'django.contrib.auth',
    'django.contrib.contenttypes',
    'django.contrib.sessions',
    'django.contrib.messages',
    'django.contrib.staticfiles',
]
```

Add the following two strings to the `INSTALLED_APPS` strings list and save the changes to the `gamesapi/settings.py` file:

- `'rest_framework'`
- `'games.apps.GamesConfig'`

The following lines show the new code that declares the `INSTALLED_APPS` strings list with the added lines highlighted. The code file for the sample is included in the `restful_python_chapter_01_01` folder:

```
INSTALLED_APPS = [
    'django.contrib.admin',
    'django.contrib.auth',
    'django.contrib.contenttypes',
    'django.contrib.sessions',
    'django.contrib.messages',
    'django.contrib.staticfiles',
    # Django REST Framework
    'rest_framework',
    # Games application
    'games.apps.GamesConfig',
]
```

This way, we have added Django REST Framework and the `games` application to our initial Django project named `gamesapi`.

Creating the models

Now, we will create a simple `Game` model that we will use to represent and persist games. Open the `games/models.py` file. The following lines show the initial code for this file, with just one import statement and a comment that indicates we should create the models:

```
from django.db import models

# Create your models here.
```

The following lines show the new code that creates a `Game` class, specifically, a `Game` model in the `games/models.py` file. The code file for the sample is included in the `restful_python_chapter_01_01` folder:

```
from django.db import models


class Game(models.Model):
    created = models.DateTimeField(auto_now_add=True)
    name = models.CharField(max_length=200, blank=True, default='')
    release_date = models.DateTimeField()
    game_category = models.CharField(max_length=200, blank=True,
default='')
    played = models.BooleanField(default=False)

    class Meta:
        ordering = ('name',)
```

The `Game` class is a subclass of the `django.db.models.Model` class. Each defined attribute represents a database column or field. Django automatically adds an auto-increment integer primary key column named `id` when it creates the database table related to the model. However, the model maps the underlying `id` column in an attribute named `pk` for the model. We specified the field types, maximum lengths and defaults for many attributes. The class declares a Meta inner class that declares a ordering attribute and sets its value to a tuple of string whose first value is the `'name'` string, indicating that, by default, we want the results ordered by the `name` attribute in ascending order.

Then, it is necessary to create the initial migration for the new `Game` model we recently coded. We just need to run the following Python scripts and we will also synchronize the database for the first time. By default, Django uses an SQLite database. In this example, we will be working with this default configuration:

```
python manage.py makemigrations games
```

The following lines show the output generated after running the preceding command.

```
Migrations for 'games':
  0001_initial.py:
    - Create model Game
```

The output indicates that the `gamesapi/games/migrations/0001_initial.py` file includes the code to create the `Game` model. The following lines show the code for this file that was automatically generated by Django. The code file for the sample is included in the `restful_python_chapter_01_01` folder:

```python
# -*- coding: utf-8 -*-
# Generated by Django 1.9.6 on 2016-05-17 21:19
from __future__ import unicode_literals

from django.db import migrations, models


class Migration(migrations.Migration):

    initial = True

    dependencies = [
    ]

    operations = [
        migrations.CreateModel(
            name='Game',
            fields=[
                ('id', models.AutoField(auto_created=True,
primary_key=True,
                serialize=False, verbose_name='ID')),
                ('created', models.DateTimeField(auto_now_add=True)),
                ('name', models.CharField(blank=True, default='',
                 max_length=200)),
                ('release_date', models.DateTimeField()),
                ('game_category', models.CharField(blank=True, default='',
                 max_length=200)),
                ('played', models.BooleanField(default=False)),
            ],
            options={
                'ordering': ('name',),
            },
        ),
    ]
```

The code defines a subclass of the `django.db.migrations.Migration` class named `Migration` that defines an operation that creates the `Game` model's table. Now, run the following python script to apply all the generated migrations:

```
python manage.py migrate
```

The following lines show the output generated after running the preceding command:

```
Operations to perform:
  Apply all migrations: sessions, games, contenttypes, admin, auth
Running migrations:
  Rendering model states... DONE
  Applying contenttypes.0001_initial... OK
  Applying auth.0001_initial... OK
  Applying admin.0001_initial... OK
  Applying admin.0002_logentry_remove_auto_add... OK
  Applying contenttypes.0002_remove_content_type_name... OK
  Applying auth.0002_alter_permission_name_max_length... OK
  Applying auth.0003_alter_user_email_max_length... OK
  Applying auth.0004_alter_user_username_opts... OK
  Applying auth.0005_alter_user_last_login_null... OK
  Applying auth.0006_require_contenttypes_0002... OK
  Applying auth.0007_alter_validators_add_error_messages... OK
  Applying games.0001_initial... OK
  Applying sessions.0001_initial... OK
```

After we run the preceding command, we will notice that the root folder for our `gamesapi` project now has a `db.sqlite3` file. We can use the SQLite command line or any other application that allows us to easily check the contents of the SQLite database to check the tables that Django generated.

In macOS and most modern Linux distributions, SQLite is already installed, and therefore, you can run the `sqlite3` command-line utility. However, in Windows, if you want to work with the `sqlite3.exe` command-line utility, you will have to download and install SQLite from its Web page-http://www.sqlite.org.

Run the following command to list the generated tables:

```
sqlite3 db.sqlite3 '.tables'
```

Run the following command to retrieve the SQL used to create the `games_game` table:

```
sqlite3 db.sqlite3 '.schema games_game'
```

The following command will allow you to check the contents of the games_game table after we compose and send HTTP requests to the RESTful API and make CRUD operations to the games_game table:

```
sqlite3 db.sqlite3 'SELECT * FROM games_game ORDER BY name;'
```

Instead of working with the SQLite command-line utility, you can use a GUI tool to check the contents of the SQLite database. DB Browser for SQLite is a useful multiplatform and free GUI tool that allows us to easily check the database contents of an SQLite database in macOS, Linux and Windows. You can read more information about this tool and download its different versions from http://sqlitebrowser.org. Once you installed the tool, you just need to open the db.sqlite3 file and you can check the database structure and browse the data for the different tables. You can use also the database tools included in your favorite IDE to check the contents for the SQLite database.

The SQLite database engine and the database file name are specified in the gamesapi/settings.py Python file. The following lines show the declaration of the DATABASES dictionary that contains the settings for all the database that Django uses. The nested dictionary maps the database named default with the django.db.backends.sqlite3 database engine and the db.sqlite3 database file located in the BASE_DIR folder (gamesapi):

```
DATABASES = {
    'default': {
        'ENGINE': 'django.db.backends.sqlite3',
        'NAME': os.path.join(BASE_DIR, 'db.sqlite3'),
    }
}
```

After we executed the migrations, the SQLite database will have the following tables:

- auth_group
- auth_group_permissions
- auth_permission
- auth_user
- auth_user_groups
- auth_user_groups_permissions
- django_admin_log
- django_content_type
- django_migrations
- django_session

- games_game
- sqlite_sequence

The games_game table persists in the database the Game class we recently created, specifically, the Game model. Django's integrated ORM generated the games_game table based on our Game model. The games_game table has the following rows (also known as fields) with their SQLite types and all of them are not nullable:

- id: The integer primary key, an autoincrement row
- created: datetime
- name: varchar(200)
- release_date: datetime
- game_category: varchar(200)
- played: bool

The following lines show the SQL creation script that Django generated when we executed the migrations:

```
CREATE TABLE "games_game" (
    "id" integer NOT NULL PRIMARY KEY AUTOINCREMENT,
    "created" datetime NOT NULL,
    "name" varchar(200) NOT NULL,
    "release_date" datetime NOT NULL,
    "game_category" varchar(200) NOT NULL,
    "played" bool NOT NULL
)
```

Django generated additional tables that it requires to support the Web framework and the authentication features that we will use later.

Managing serialization and deserialization

Our RESTful Web API has to be able to serialize and deserialize the game instances into JSON representations. With Django REST Framework, we just need to create a serializer class for the game instances to manage serialization to JSON and deserialization from JSON.

Django REST Framework uses a two-phase process for serialization. The serializers are mediators between the model instances and Python primitives. Parser and renderers handle as mediators between Python primitives and HTTP requests and responses. We will configure our mediator between the Game model instances and Python primitives by creating a subclass of the rest_framework.serializers.Serializer class to declare the fields and the necessary methods to manage serialization and deserialization. We will repeat some of the information about the fields that we have included in the Game model so that we understand all the things that we can configure in a subclass of the Serializer class. However, we will work with shortcuts that will reduce boilerplate code later in the next examples. We will write less code in the next examples by using the ModelSerializer class.

Now, go to the gamesapi/games folder folder and create a new Python code file named serializers.py. The following lines show the code that declares the new GameSerializer class. The code file for the sample is included in the restful_python_chapter_01_01 folder.

```python
from rest_framework import serializers
from games.models import Game


class GameSerializer(serializers.Serializer):
    pk = serializers.IntegerField(read_only=True)
    name = serializers.CharField(max_length=200)
    release_date = serializers.DateTimeField()
    game_category = serializers.CharField(max_length=200)
    played = serializers.BooleanField(required=False)

    def create(self, validated_data):
        return Game.objects.create(**validated_data)

    def update(self, instance, validated_data):
        instance.name = validated_data.get('name', instance.name)
        instance.release_date = validated_data.get('release_date',
instance.release_date)
        instance.game_category = validated_data.get('game_category',
instance.game_category)
        instance.played = validated_data.get('played', instance.played)
        instance.save()
        return instance
```

The GameSerializer class declares the attributes that represent the fields that we want to be serialized. Notice that they have omitted the created attribute that was present in the Game model. When there is a call to the inherited save method for this class, the overridden create and update methods define how to create or modify an instance. In fact, these methods must be implemented in our class because they just raise a NotImplementedError exception in their base declaration.

The create method receives the validated data in the validated_data argument. The code creates and returns a new Game instance based on the received validated data.

The `update` method receives an existing `Game` instance that is being updated and the new validated data in the `instance` and `validated_data` arguments. The code updates the values for the attributes of the instance with the updated attribute values retrieved from the validated data, calls the save method for the updated `Game` instance and returns the updated and saved instance.

We can launch our default Python interactive shell and make all the Django project modules available before it starts. This way, we can check that the serializer works as expected. In addition, it will help us understanding how serialization works in Django. Run the following command to launch the interactive shell. Make sure you are within the `gamesapi` folder in the Terminal or command prompt:

```
python manage.py shell
```

You will notice that a line that says (`InteractiveConsole`) is displayed after the usual lines that introduce your default Python interactive shell. Enter the following code in the Python interactive shell to import all the things we will need to test the `Game` model and its serializer. The code file for the sample is included in the `restful_python_chapter_01_01` folder, in the `serializers_test_01.py` file:

```
from datetime import datetime
from django.utils import timezone
from django.utils.six import BytesIO
from rest_framework.renderers import JSONRenderer
from rest_framework.parsers import JSONParser
from games.models import Game
from games.serializers import GameSerializer
```

Enter the following code to create two instances of the Game model and save them. The code file for the sample is included in the `restful_python_chapter_01_01` folder, in the `serializers_test_01.py` file:

```
gamedatetime = timezone.make_aware(datetime.now(),
timezone.get_current_timezone())
game1 = Game(name='Smurfs Jungle', release_date=gamedatetime,
game_category='2D mobile arcade', played=False)
game1.save()
game2 = Game(name='Angry Birds RPG', release_date=gamedatetime,
game_category='3D RPG', played=False)
game2.save()
```

After we execute the preceding code, we can check the SQLite database with the previously introduce command-line or GUI tool to check the contents of the `games_game` table. We will notice the table has two rows and the columns have the values we have provided to the different attributes of the `Game` instances.

Enter the following commands in the interactive shell to check the values for the primary keys or identifiers for the saved `Game` instances and the value of the `created` attribute includes the date and time in which we saved the instance to the database. The code file for the sample is included in the `restful_python_chapter_01_01` folder, in the `serializers_test_01.py` file:

```
print(game1.pk)
print(game1.name)
print(game1.created)
print(game2.pk)
print(game2.name)
print(game2.created)
```

Now, let's write the following code to serialize the first game instance (`game1`). The code file for the sample is included in the `restful_python_chapter_01_01` folder, in the `serializers_test_01.py` file:

```
game_serializer1 = GameSerializer(game1)
print(game_serializer1.data)
```

The following line shows the generated dictionary, specifically, a `rest_framework.utils.serializer_helpers.ReturnDict` instance:

```
{'release_date': '2016-05-18T03:02:00.776594Z', 'game_category': '2D mobile
arcade', 'played': False, 'pk': 2, 'name': 'Smurfs Jungle'}
```

Now, let's serialize the second game instance (`game2`). The code file for the sample is included in the `restful_python_chapter_01_01` folder, in the `serializers_test_01.py` file:

```
game_serializer2 = GameSerializer(game2)
print(game_serializer2.data)
```

The following line shows the generated dictionary:

```
{'release_date': '2016-05-18T03:02:00.776594Z', 'game_category': '3D RPG',
'played': False, 'pk': 3, 'name': 'Angry Birds RPG'}
```

We can easily render the dictionaries hold in the `data` attribute into JSON with the help of the `rest_framework.renderers.JSONRenderer` class. The following lines create an instance of this class and then calls the `render` method to render the dictionaries hold in the data attribute into JSON. The code file for the sample is included in the `restful_python_chapter_01_01` folder, in the `serializers_test_01.py` file:

```
renderer = JSONRenderer()
rendered_game1 = renderer.render(game_serializer1.data)
```

```
rendered_game2 = renderer.render(game_serializer2.data)
print(rendered_game1)
print(rendered_game2)
```

The following lines show the output generated from the two calls to the `render` method:

```
b'{"pk":2,"name":"Smurfs Jungle","release_date":"2016-05-
18T03:02:00.776594Z","game_category":"2D mobile
arcade","played":false}'
b'{"pk":3,"name":"Angry Birds RPG","release_date":"2016-05-
18T03:02:00.776594Z","game_category":"3D RPG","played":false}'
```

Now, we will work in the opposite direction: from serialized data to the population of a Game instance. The following lines generate a new `Game` instance from a JSON string (serialized data), that is, they will deserialize. The code file for the sample is included in the `restful_python_chapter_01_01` folder, in the `serializers_test_01.py` file:

```
json_string_for_new_game = '{"name":"Tomb Raider Extreme
Edition","release_date":"2016-05-18T03:02:00.776594Z","game_category":"3D
RPG","played":false}'
json_bytes_for_new_game = bytes(json_string_for_new_game ,
encoding="UTF-8")
stream_for_new_game = BytesIO(json_bytes_for_new_game)
parser = JSONParser()
parsed_new_game = parser.parse(stream_for_new_game)
print(parsed_new_game)
```

The first line creates a new string with the JSON that defines a new game (`json_string_for_new_game`). Then, the code converts the string to `bytes` and saves the results of the conversion in the `json_bytes_for_new_game` variable. The `django.utils.six.BytesIO` class provides a buffered I/O implementation using an in-memory bytes buffer. The code uses this class to create a stream from the previously generated JSON bytes with the serialized data, `json_bytes_for_new_game`, and saves the generated instance in the `stream_for_new_game` variable.

We can easily deserialize and parse a stream into the Python models with the help of the `rest_framework.parsers.JSONParser` class. The next line creates an instance of this class and then calls the `parse` method with `stream_for_new_game` as an argument, parses the stream into Python native datatypes and saves the results in the `parsed_new_game` variable.

After executing the preceding lines, `parsed_new_game` holds a Python dictionary, parsed from the stream. The following lines show the output generated after executing the preceding code snippet:

```
{'release_date': '2016-05-18T03:02:00.776594Z', 'played': False,
'game_category': '3D RPG', 'name': 'Tomb Raider Extreme Edition'}
```

The following lines use the `GameSerializer` class to generate a fully populated `Game` instance named `new_game` from the Python dictionary, parsed from the stream. The code file for the sample is included in the `restful_python_chapter_01_01` folder, in the `serializers_test_01.py` file.

```
new_game_serializer = GameSerializer(data=parsed_new_game)
if new_game_serializer.is_valid():
    new_game = new_game_serializer.save()
    print(new_game.name)
```

First, the code creates an instance of the `GameSerializer` class with the Python dictionary that we previously parsed from the stream (`parsed_new_game`) passed as the `data` keyword argument. Then, the code calls the `is_valid` method to determine whether the data is valid. Notice that we must always call `is_valid` before we attempt to access the serialized data representation when we pass a `data` keyword argument in the creation of a serializer.

If the method returns `true`, we can access the serialized representation in the `data` attribute, and therefore, the code calls the `save` method that inserts the corresponding row in the database and returns a fully populated `Game` instance, saved in the `new_game` local variable. Then, the code prints one of the attributes from the fully populated `Game` instance. After executing the preceding code, we fully populated two Game instances: `new_game1_instance` and `new_game2_instance`.

 As we can learn from the preceding code, Django REST Framework makes it easy to serialize from objects to JSON and deserialize from JSON to objects, which are core requirements for our RESTful Web API that has to perform CRUD operations.

Enter the following command to leave the shell with the Django project modules that we started to test serialization and deserialization:

```
quit()
```

Writing API views

Now, we will create Django views that will use the previously created `GameSerializer` class to return JSON representations for each HTTP request that our API will handle. Open the `games/views.py` file. The following lines show the initial code for this file, with just one import statement and a comment that indicates we should create the views.

```
from django.shortcuts import render

# Create your views here.
```

The following lines show the new code that creates a `JSONResponse` class and declares two functions: `game_list` and `game_detail`, in the `games/views.py` file. We are creating our first version of the API, and we use functions to keep the code as simple as possible. We will work with classes and more complex code in the next examples. The highlighted lines show the expressions that evaluate the value of the `request.method` attribute to determine the actions to be performed based on the HTTP verb. The code file for the sample is included in the `restful_python_chapter_01_01` folder:

```
from django.http import HttpResponse
from django.views.decorators.csrf import csrf_exempt
from rest_framework.renderers import JSONRenderer
from rest_framework.parsers import JSONParser
from rest_framework import status
from games.models import Game
from games.serializers import GameSerializer


class JSONResponse(HttpResponse):
    def __init__(self, data, **kwargs):
        content = JSONRenderer().render(data)
        kwargs['content_type'] = 'application/json'
        super(JSONResponse, self).__init__(content, **kwargs)


@csrf_exempt
def game_list(request):
    if request.method == 'GET':
        games = Game.objects.all()
        games_serializer = GameSerializer(games, many=True)
        return JSONResponse(games_serializer.data)

    elif request.method == 'POST':
        game_data = JSONParser().parse(request)
        game_serializer = GameSerializer(data=game_data)
        if game_serializer.is_valid():
```

```
                game_serializer.save()
                return JSONResponse(game_serializer.data,
                status=status.HTTP_201_CREATED)
            return JSONResponse(game_serializer.errors,
            status=status.HTTP_400_BAD_REQUEST)


    @csrf_exempt
    def game_detail(request, pk):
        try:
            game = Game.objects.get(pk=pk)
        except Game.DoesNotExist:
            return HttpResponse(status=status.HTTP_404_NOT_FOUND)

        if request.method == 'GET':
            game_serializer = GameSerializer(game)
            return JSONResponse(game_serializer.data)

        elif request.method == 'PUT':
            game_data = JSONParser().parse(request)
            game_serializer = GameSerializer(game, data=game_data)
            if game_serializer.is_valid():
                game_serializer.save()
                return JSONResponse(game_serializer.data)
            return JSONResponse(game_serializer.errors,
            status=status.HTTP_400_BAD_REQUEST)

        elif request.method == 'DELETE':
            game.delete()
            return HttpResponse(status=status.HTTP_204_NO_CONTENT)
```

The JSONResponse class is a subclass of the django.http.HttpResponse class. The superclass represents an HTTP response with a string as content. The JSONResponse class renders its content into JSON. The class defines just declare the __init__ method that created a rest_framework.renderers.JSONRenderer instance and calls its render method to render the received data into JSON save the returned bytestring in the content local variable. Then, the code adds the 'content_type' key to the response header with 'application/json' as its value. Finally, the code calls the initializer for the base class with the JSON bytestring and the key-value pair added to the header. This way, the class represents a JSON response that we use in the two functions to easily return a JSON response.

The code uses the `@csrf_exempt` decorator in the two functions to ensure that the view sets a **Cross-Site Request Forgery (CSRF)** cookie. We do this to make it simple to test this example that doesn't represent a production-ready Web Service. We will add security features to our RESTful API later.

When the Django server receives an HTTP request, Django creates an `HttpRequest` instance, specifically a `django.http.HttpRequest` object. This instance contains metadata about the request, including the HTTP verb. The `method` attribute provides a string representing the HTTP verb or method used in the request.

When Django loads the appropriate view that will process the requests, it passes the `HttpRequest` instance as the first argument to the view function. The view function has to return an `HttpResponse` instance, specifically a `django.http.HttpResponse` instance.

The `game_list` function lists all the games or creates a new game. The function receives an `HttpRequest` instance in the `request` argument. The function is capable of processing two HTTP verbs: GET and POST. The code checks the value of the `request.method` attribute to determine the code to be executed based on the HTTP verb. If the HTTP verb is GET, the expression `request.method == 'GET'` will evaluate to `True` and the code has to list all the games. The code will retrieve all the `Game` objects from the database, use the `GameSerializer` to serialize all of them, and return a `JSONResponse` instance built with the data generated by the `GameSerializer`. The code creates the `GameSerializer` instance with the `many=True` argument to specify that multiple instances have to be serialized and not just one. Under the hoods, Django uses a `ListSerializer` when the `many` argument value is set to `True`.

If the HTTP verb is POST, the code has to create a new game based on the JSON data that is included in the HTTP request. First, the code uses a `JSONParser` instance and calls its parse method with request as an argument to parse the game data provided as JSON data in the request and saves the results in the `game_data` local variable. Then, the code creates a `GameSerializer` instance with the previously retrieved data and calls the `is_valid` method to determine whether the `Game` instance is valid or not. If the instance is valid, the code calls the `save` method to persist the instance in the database and returns a JSONResponse with the saved data in its body and a status equal to `status.HTTP_201_CREATED`, that is, `201 Created`.

TIP

Whenever we have to return a specific status different from the default `200 OK` status, it is a good practice to use the module variables defined in the `rest_framework.status` module and to avoid using hardcoded numeric values.

The `game_detail` function retrieves, updates or deletes an existing game. The function receives an `HttpRequest` instance in the `request` argument and the primary key or identifier for the game to be retrieved, updated or deleted in the `pk` argument. The function is capable of processing three HTTP verbs: `GET`, `PUT` and `DELETE`. The code checks the value of the `request.method` attribute to determine the code to be executed based on the HTTP verb. No matter which is the HTTP verb, the function calls the `Game.objects.get` method with the received `pk` as the `pk` argument to retrieve a Game instance from the database based on the specified primary key or identifier, and saves it in the `game` local variable. In case a game with the specified primary key or identifier doesn't exist in the database, the code returns an `HttpResponse` with its status equal to `status.HTTP_404_NOT_FOUND`, that is, `404 Not Found`.

If the HTTP verb is `GET`, the code creates a `GameSerializer` instance with `game` as an argument and returns the data for the serialized game in a `JSONResponse` that will include the default `200 OK` status. The code returns the retrieved game serialized as JSON.

If the HTTP verb is `PUT`, the code has to create a new game based on the JSON data that is included in the HTTP request and use it to replace an existing game. First, the code uses a `JSONParser` instance and calls its parse method with request as an argument to parse the game data provided as JSON data in the request and saves the results in the `game_data` local variable. Then, the code creates a `GameSerializer` instance with the Game instance previously retrieved from the database (`game`) and the retrieved data that will replace the existing data (`game_data`). Then, the code calls the `is_valid` method to determine whether the Game instance is valid or not. If the instance is valid, the code calls the `save` method to persist the instance with the replaced values in the database and returns a `JSONResponse` with the saved data in its body and the default `200 OK` status. If the parsed data doesn't generate a valid Game instance, the code returns a `JSONResponse` with a status equal to `status.HTTP_400_BAD_REQUEST`, that is, `400 Bad Request`.

If the HTTP verb is `DELETE`, the code calls the `delete` method for the Game instance previously retrieved from the database (`game`). The call to the `delete` method erases the underlying row in the `games_game` table, and therefore, the game won't be available anymore. Then, the code returns a `JSONResponse` with a status equal to `status.HTTP_204_NO_CONTENT` that is, `204 No Content`.

Now, we have to create a new Python file named `urls.py` in the `games` folder, specifically, the `games/urls.py` file. The following lines show the code for this file that defines the URL patterns that specifies the regular expressions that have to be matched in the request to run a specific function defines in the `views.py` file. The code file for the sample is included in the `restful_python_chapter_01_01` folder:

```
from django.conf.urls import url
from games import views

urlpatterns = [
    url(r'^games/$', views.game_list),
    url(r'^games/(?P<pk>[0-9]+)/$', views.game_detail),
]
```

The `urlpatterns` list makes it possible to route URLs to views. The code calls the `django.conf.urls.url` function with the regular expression that has to be matched and the view function defined in the views module as arguments to create a `RegexURLPattern` instance for each entry in the `urlpatterns` list.

We have to replace the code in the `urls.py` file in the `gamesapi` folder, specifically, the `gamesapi/urls.py` file. The file defines the root URL configurations, and therefore, we must include the URL patterns declared in the previously coded `games/urls.py` file. The following lines show the new code for the `gamesapi/urls.py` file. The code file for the sample is included in the `restful_python_chapter_01_01` folder:

```
from django.conf.urls import url, include

urlpatterns = [
    url(r'^', include('games.urls')),
]
```

Now, we can launch Django's development server to compose and send HTTP requests to our unsecure Web API (we will definitely add security later). Execute the following command:

```
python manage.py runserver
```

The following lines show the output after we execute the preceding command. The development server is listening at port 8000 .

```
Performing system checks...
System check identified no issues (0 silenced).
May 20, 2016 - 04:22:38
Django version 1.9.6, using settings 'gamesapi.settings'
Starting development server at http://127.0.0.1:8000/
Quit the server with CONTROL-C.
```

With the preceding command, we will start Django development server and we will only be able to access it in our development computer. The preceding command starts the development server in the default IP address, that is, 127.0.0.1 (localhost). It is not possible to access this IP address from other computers or devices connected on our LAN. Thus, if we want to make HTTP requests to our API from other computers or devices connected to our LAN, we should use the development computer IP address, 0.0.0.0 (for IPv4 configurations), or :: (for IPv6 configurations) as the desired IP address for our development server.

If we specify 0.0.0.0 as the desired IP address for IPv4 configurations, the development server will listen on every interface on port 8000. When we specify :: for IPv6 configurations, it will have the same effect. In addition, it is necessary to open the default port 8000 in our firewalls (software and/or hardware) and configure port-forwarding to the computer that is running the development server. The following command launches Django's development server in an IPv4 configuration and allows requests to be made from other computers and devices connected to our LAN:

```
python manage.py runserver 0.0.0.0:8000
```

If you decide to compose and send HTTP requests from other computers or devices connected to the LAN, remember that you have to use the development computer's assigned IP address instead of localhost. For example, if the computer's assigned IPv4 IP address is 192.168.1.106, instead of localhost:8000, you should use 192.168.1.106:8000. Of course, you can also use the host name instead of the IP address. The previously explained configurations are very important because mobile devices might be the consumers of our RESTful APIs and we will always want to test the apps that make use of our APIs in our development environments.

Making HTTP requests to the API

The Django development server is running on localhost (127.0.0.1), listening on port 8000, and waiting for our HTTP requests. Now, we will compose and send HTTP requests locally in our development computer or from other computer or devices connected to our LAN. We will use the following different kind of tools to compose and send HTTP requests throughout our book.

- Command-line tools
- GUI tools
- Python code
- JavaScript code

 Notice that you can use any other application that allows you to compose and send HTTP requests. There are many apps that run on tablets and smartphones that allow you to accomplish this task. However, we will focus our attention on the most useful tools when building RESTful Web APIs.

Working with command-line tools – curl and httpie

We will start with command-line tools. One of the key advantages of command-line tools is that we can easily run again the HTTP requests after we built them for the first time, and we don't need to use the mouse or tap the screen to run requests. We can also easily build a script with batch requests and run them. As happens with any command-line tool, it can take more time to perform the first requests compared with GUI tools, but it becomes easier once we performed many requests and we can easily reuse the commands we have written in the past to compose new requests.

Curl, also known as cURL, is a very popular open source command-line tool and library that allow us to easily transfer data. We can use the curl command-line tool to easily compose and send HTTP requests and check their responses.

If you are working on either macOS or Linux, you can open a Terminal and start using curl from the command line. If you are working on any Windows version, you can easily install curl from the Cygwin package installation option, and execute it from the Cygwin terminal. You can read more about the curl utility at http://curl.haxx.se. You can read more about the Cygwin terminal and its installation procedure at http://cygwin.com/install.html.

Open a Cygwin terminal in Windows or a terminal in macOS or Linux, and run the following command. It is very important that you enter the ending slash (/) because /games won't match any of the patterns specified in urlpatterns in the games/urls.py file. We are using the default configuration for Django that doesn't redirect URLs that don't match any of the patterns to the same URLs with a slash appended. Thus, we must enter /games/, including the ending slash (/):

```
curl -X GET :8000/games/
```

The preceding command will compose and send the following HTTP request-GET http://localhost:8000/games/. The request is the simplest case in our RESTful API because it will match and run the views.game_list function, that is, the game_list function declared within the games/views.py file. The function just receives request as a parameter because the URL pattern doesn't include any parameters. As the HTTP verb for the request is GET, the request.method property is equal to 'GET', and therefore, the function will execute the code that retrieves all the Game objects and generates a JSON response with all of these Game objects serialized.

The following lines show an example response for the HTTP request, with three Game objects in the JSON response:

```
[{"pk":3,"name":"Angry Birds
RPG","release_date":"2016-05-18T03:02:00.776594Z","game_category":"3D
RPG","played":false},{"pk":2,"name":"Smurfs
Jungle","release_date":"2016-05-18T03:02:00.776594Z","game_category":"2D
mobile arcade","played":false},{"pk":11,"name":"Tomb Raider Extreme
Edition","release_date":"2016-05-18T03:02:00.776594Z","game_category":"3D
RPG","played":false}]
```

As we might notice from the previous response, the curl utility displays the JSON response in a single line, and therefore, it is a bit difficult to read it. In this case, we know that the `Content-Type` of the response is `application/json`. However, in case we want to have more details about the response, we can use the `-i` option to request curl to print the HTTP response headers. We can combine the `-i` and `-X` options by using `-iX`.

Go back to the Cygwin terminal in Windows or the Terminal in macOS or Linux, and run the following command:

```
curl -iX GET :8000/games/
```

The following lines show an example response for the HTTP request. The first lines show the HTTP response headers, including the status (`200 OK`) and the `Content-type` (`application/json`). After the HTTP response headers, we can see the details for the three `Game` objects in the JSON response:

```
HTTP/1.0 200 OK
Date: Tue, 24 May 2016 18:04:40 GMT
Server: WSGIServer/0.2 CPython/3.5.1
Content-Type: application/json
X-Frame-Options: SAMEORIGIN
[{"pk":3,"name":"Angry Birds
RPG","release_date":"2016-05-18T03:02:00.776594Z","game_category":"3D
RPG","played":false},{"pk":2,"name":"Smurfs
Jungle","release_date":"2016-05-18T03:02:00.776594Z","game_category":"2D
mobile arcade","played":false},{"pk":11,"name":"Tomb Raider Extreme
Edition","release_date":"2016-05-18T03:02:00.776594Z","game_category":"3D
RPG","played":false}]
```

After we run the two requests, we will see the following lines in the window that is running the Django development server. The output indicates that the server received two HTTP requests with the `GET` verb and `/games/` as the URI. The server processed both HTTP requests, returned status code 200 and the response length was equal to 379 characters. The response length can be different because the value for the primary key assigned to each game will have an incidence in the response length. The first number after `HTTP/1.1."` indicates the returned status code (`200`) and the second number the response length (`379`).

```
[25/May/2016 04:35:09] "GET /games/ HTTP/1.1" 200 379
[25/May/2016 04:35:10] "GET /games/ HTTP/1.1" 200 379
```

The following image shows two terminal windows side-by-side on macOS. The Terminal window at the left-hand side is running the Django development server and displays the received and processed HTTP requests. The Terminal window at the right-hand side is running `curl` commands to generate the HTTP requests.

It is a good idea to use a similar configuration to check the output while we compose and send the HTTP requests. Notice that the JSON outputs are a bit difficult to read because they don't use syntax highlighting:

```
(Django01) Gastons-MacBook-Pro:gamesapi gaston$ python manage
.py runserver 0.0.0.0:8000
Performing system checks...

System check identified no issues (0 silenced).
May 30, 2016 - 18:42:07
Django version 1.9.6, using settings 'gamesapi.settings'
Starting development server at http://0.0.0.0:8000/
Quit the server with CONTROL-C.
[30/May/2016 18:42:14] "GET /games/ HTTP/1.1" 200 379
[30/May/2016 18:42:25] "GET /games/ HTTP/1.1" 200 379
```

```
(Django01) Gastons-MacBook-Pro:bin gaston$ curl -X GET :8000/
games/
[{"pk":3,"name":"Angry Birds RPG","release_date":"2016-05-18T
03:02:00.776594Z","game_category":"3D RPG","played":false},{"
pk":2,"name":"Smurfs Jungle","release_date":"2016-05-18T03:02
:00.776594Z","game_category":"2D mobile arcade","played":fals
e},{"pk":11,"name":"Tomb Raider Extreme Edition","release_dat
e":"2016-05-18T03:02:00.776594Z","game_category":"3D RPG","pl
ayed":false}](Django01) Gastons-MacBook-Pro:bin gaston$
(Django01) Gastons-MacBook-Pro:bin gaston$ curl -iX GET :8000
/games/
HTTP/1.0 200 OK
Date: Mon, 30 May 2016 18:42:25 GMT
Server: WSGIServer/0.2 CPython/3.5.1
X-Frame-Options: SAMEORIGIN
Content-Type: application/json

[{"pk":3,"name":"Angry Birds RPG","release_date":"2016-05-18T
03:02:00.776594Z","game_category":"3D RPG","played":false},{"
pk":2,"name":"Smurfs Jungle","release_date":"2016-05-18T03:02
:00.776594Z","game_category":"2D mobile arcade","played":fals
e},{"pk":11,"name":"Tomb Raider Extreme Edition","release_dat
e":"2016-05-18T03:02:00.776594Z","game_category":"3D RPG","pl
ayed":false}](Django01) Gastons-MacBook-Pro:bin gaston$
(Django01) Gastons-MacBook-Pro:bin gaston$
```

Now, we will install HTTPie, a command-line HTTP client written in Python that makes it easy to send HTTP requests and uses a syntax that is easier than curl (also known as cURL). One of the great advantages of HTTPie is that it displays colorized output and uses multiple lines to display the response details. Thus, HTTPie makes it easier to understand the responses than the curl utility. We just need to activate the virtual environment and then run the following command in the terminal or command prompt to install the HTTPie package:

```
pip install --upgrade httpie
```

The last lines for the output will indicate that the `django` package has been successfully installed.

```
Collecting httpie
  Downloading httpie-0.9.3-py2.py3-none-any.whl (66kB)
Collecting requests>=2.3.0 (from httpie)
  Using cached requests-2.10.0-py2.py3-none-any.whl
Collecting Pygments>=1.5 (from httpie)
  Using cached Pygments-2.1.3-py2.py3-none-any.whl
Installing collected packages: requests, Pygments, httpie
Successfully installed Pygments-2.1.3 httpie-0.9.3 requests-2.10.0
```

In case you don't remember how to activate the virtual environment that we created for this example, read the following section in this chapter- *Setting up the virtual environment with Django REST framework.*

Now, we can use an `http` command to easily compose and send HTTP requests to `localhost:8000` and test the RESTful API built with Django REST framework. HTTPie supports curl-like shorthands for localhost, and therefore, we can use `:8000` as a shorthand that expands to `http://localhost:8000`. Run the following command and remember to enter the ending slash (/):

```
http :8000/games/
```

The preceding command will compose and send the following HTTP request: GET `http://localhost:8000/games/`. The request is the same one we have previously composed with the curl command. However, in this case, the HTTPie utility will display a colorized output and it will use multiple lines to display the JSON response. The preceding command is equivalent to the following command that specifies the GET method after `http`:

```
http GET :8000/games/
```

The following lines show an example response for the HTTP request, with the headers and the three Game objects in the JSON response. It is indeed easier to understand the response compared with the results generated when we composed the HTTP request with curl. HTTPie automatically formats the JSON data received as a response and applies syntax highlighting, specifically, both colors and formatting:

```
HTTP/1.0 200 OK
Content-Type: application/json
Date: Thu, 26 May 2016 21:33:17 GMT
Server: WSGIServer/0.2 CPython/3.5.1
X-Frame-Options: SAMEORIGIN
[
    {
        "game_category": "3D RPG",
        "name": "Angry Birds RPG",
        "pk": 3,
        "played": false,
        "release_date": "2016-05-18T03:02:00.776594Z"
    },
    {
        "game_category": "2D mobile arcade",
        "name": "Smurfs Jungle",
        "pk": 2,
```

```
        "played": false,
        "release_date": "2016-05-18T03:02:00.776594Z"
    },
    {

        "game_category": "3D RPG",
        "name": "Tomb Raider Extreme Edition",
        "pk": 11,
        "played": false,
        "release_date": "2016-05-18T03:02:00.776594Z"
    }
]
```

We can achieve the same results by combining the output generated with the curl command with other utilities. However, HTTPie provides us exactly what we need to work with RESTful APIs. We will use HTTPie to compose and send HTTP request, but we will always provide the equivalent curl command.

The following image shows two Terminal windows side-by-side on macOS. The terminal window at the left-hand side is running the Django development server and displays the received and processed HTTP requests. The Terminal window at the right-hand side is running HTTPie commands to generate the HTTP requests. Notice that the JSON output is easier to read compared to the output generated by the curl command:

We can execute HTTPie with the -b option in case we don't want to include the header in the response. For example, the following line performs the same HTTP request but doesn't display the header in the response output, and therefore, the output will just display the JSON response:

```
http -b :8000/games/
```

Now, we will select one of the games from the preceding list and we will compose an HTTP request to retrieve just the chosen game. For example, in the previous list, the first game has a pk value equal to 3. Run the following command to retrieve this game. Use the pk value you have retrieved in the previous command for the first game, as the pk number might be different:

```
http :8000/games/3/
```

The following is the equivalent curl command:

```
curl -iX GET :8000/games/3/
```

The previous commands will compose and send the following HTTP request: GET http://localhost:8000/games/3/. The request has a number after /games/, and therefore, it will match '^games/(?P<pk>[0-9]+)/$' and run the views.game_detail function, that is, the game_detail function declared within the games/views.py file. The function receives request and pk as parameters because the URL pattern passes the number specified after /games/ in the pk parameter. As the HTTP verb for the request is GET, the request.method property is equal to 'GET', and therefore, the function will execute the code that retrieves the Game object whose primary key matches the pk value received as an argument and, if found, generates a JSON response with this Game object serialized. The following lines show an example response for the HTTP request, with the Game object that matches the pk value in the JSON response:

```
HTTP/1.0 200 OK
Content-Type: application/json
Date: Fri, 27 May 2016 02:28:30 GMT
Server: WSGIServer/0.2 CPython/3.5.1
X-Frame-Options: SAMEORIGIN
{
    "game_category": "3D RPG",
    "name": "Angry Birds RPG",
    "pk": 3,
    "played": false,
    "release_date": "2016-05-18T03:02:00.776594Z"
}
```

Now, we will compose and send an HTTP request to retrieve a game that doesn't exist. For example, in the preceding list, there is no game with a `pk` value equal to `99999`. Run the following command to try to retrieve this game. Make sure you use a `pk` value that doesn't exist. We must make sure that the utilities display the headers as part of the response because the response won't have a body:

```
http :8000/games/99999/
```

The following is the equivalent curl command:

```
curl -iX GET :8000/games/99999/
```

The preceding commands will compose and send the following HTTP request: `GET http://localhost:8000/games/99999/`. The request is the same than the previous one we have analyzed, with a different number for the `pk` parameter. The server will run the `views.game_detail` function, that is, the `game_detail` function declared within the `games/views.py` file. The function will execute the code that retrieves the `Game` object whose primary key matches the `pk` value received as an argument and a `Game.DoesNotExist` exception will be thrown and captured because there is no game with the specified `pk` value. Thus, the code will return an HTTP 404 Not Found status code. The following lines show an example header response for the HTTP request:

```
HTTP/1.0 404 Not Found
Content-Type: text/html; charset=utf-8
Date: Fri, 27 May 2016 02:20:41 GMT
Server: WSGIServer/0.2 CPython/3.5.1
X-Frame-Options: SAMEORIGIN
```

We will compose and send an HTTP request to create a new game.

```
http POST :8000/games/ name='PvZ 3' game_category='2D mobile arcade'
played=false release_date='2016-05-18T03:02:00.776594Z'
```

The following is the equivalent curl command. It is very important to use the `-H "Content-Type: application/json"` option to indicate curl to send the data specified after the -d option as `application/json` instead of the default `application/x-www-form-urlencoded`:

```
curl -iX POST -H "Content-Type: application/json" -d '{"name":"PvZ 3",
"game_category":"2D mobile arcade", "played": "false", "release_date":
"2016-05-18T03:02:00.776594Z"}' :8000/games/
```

The previous commands will compose and send the following HTTP request: POST `http://localhost:8000/games/` with the following JSON key-value pairs:

```
{
    "name": "PvZ 3",
    "game_category": "2D mobile arcade",
    "played": false,
    "release_date": "2016-05-18T03:02:00.776594Z"
}
```

The request specifies `/games/`, and therefore, it will match `'^games/$'` and run the `views.game_list` function, that is, the `game_detail` function declared within the `games/views.py` file. The function just receives `request` as a parameter because the URL pattern doesn't include any parameters. As the HTTP verb for the request is POST, the `request.method` property is equal to `'POST'`, and therefore, the function will execute the code that parses the JSON data received in the request, creates a new Game and, if the data is valid, it saves the new Game. If the new Game was successfully persisted in the database, the function returns an HTTP 201 Created status code and the recently persisted Game serialized serialized to JSON in the response body. The following lines show an example response for the HTTP request, with the new Game object in the JSON response:

```
HTTP/1.0 201 Created
Content-Type: application/json
Date: Fri, 27 May 2016 05:12:39 GMT
Server: WSGIServer/0.2 CPython/3.5.1
X-Frame-Options: SAMEORIGIN
{
    "game_category": "2D mobile arcade",
    "name": "PvZ 3",
    "pk": 15,
    "played": false,
    "release_date": "2016-05-18T03:02:00.776594Z"
}
```

Now, we will compose and send an HTTP request to update an existing game, specifically, the previously added game. We have to check the value assigned to pk in the previous response and replace 15 in the command with the returned value. For example, in case the value for pk was 5, you should use `:8000/games/5/` instead of `:8000/games/15/`.

```
http PUT :8000/games/15/ name='PvZ 3' game_category='2D mobile arcade'
played=true release_date='2016-05-20T03:02:00.776594Z'
```

The following is the equivalent curl command. As happened with the previous curl example, it is very important to use the `-H "Content-Type: application/json"` option to indicate curl to send the data specified after the `-d` option as `application/json` instead of the default `application/x-www-form-urlencoded`:

```
curl -iX PUT -H "Content-Type: application/json" -d '{"name":"PvZ 3",
"game_category":"2D mobile arcade", "played": "true", "release_date":
"2016-05-20T03:02:00.776594Z"}' :8000/games/15/
```

The previous commands will compose and send the following HTTP request: PUT `http://localhost:8000/games/15/` with the following JSON key-value pairs:

```
{
    "name": "PvZ 3",
    "game_category": "2D mobile arcade",
    "played": true,
    "release_date": "2016-05-20T03:02:00.776594Z"
}
```

The request has a number after `/games/`, and therefore, it will match `'^games/(?P<pk>[0-9]+)/$'` and run the `views.game_detail` function, that is, the `game_detail` function declared within the `games/views.py` file. The function receives `request` and `pk` as parameters because the URL pattern passes the number specified after `/games/` in the `pk` parameter. As the HTTP verb for the request is PUT, the `request.method` property is equal to `'PUT'`, and therefore, the function will execute the code that parses the JSON data received in the request, creates a `Game` instance from this data and updates the existing game in the database. If the game was successfully updated in the database, the function returns an `HTTP 200 OK` status code and the recently updated `Game` serialized serialized to JSON in the response body. The following lines show an example response for the `HTTP` request, with the updated `Game` object in the JSON response:

```
HTTP/1.0 200 OK
Content-Type: application/json
Date: Sat, 28 May 2016 00:49:05 GMT
Server: WSGIServer/0.2 CPython/3.5.1
X-Frame-Options: SAMEORIGIN
{
    "game_category": "2D mobile arcade",
    "name": "PvZ 3",
    "pk": 15,
    "played": true,
    "release_date": "2016-05-20T03:02:00.776594Z"
}
```

In order to successfully process a PUT HTTP request that updates an existing game, we must provide values for all the required fields. We will compose and send an HTTP request to try update an existing game, and we will fail to do so because we will just provide a value for the name. As happened in the previous request, we will use the value assigned to pk in the last game we added:

```
http PUT :8000/games/15/ name='PvZ 4'
```

The following is the equivalent curl command:

```
curl -iX PUT -H "Content-Type: application/json" -d '{"name":"PvZ 4"}'
:8000/games/15/
```

The previous commands will compose and send the following HTTP request: PUT
http://localhost:8000/games/15/ with the following JSON key-value pair:

```
{
    "name": "PvZ 4",
}
```

The request will execute the same code we explained for the previous request. Because we didn't provide all the required values for a Game instance, the
game_serializer.is_valid() method will return False and the function will return an
HTTP 400 Bad Request status code and the details generated in the
game_serializer.errors attribute serialized to JSON in the response body. The
following lines show an example response for the HTTP request, with the required fields
that our request didn't include values in the JSON response:

```
HTTP/1.0 400 Bad Request
Content-Type: application/json
Date: Sat, 28 May 2016 02:53:08 GMT
Server: WSGIServer/0.2 CPython/3.5.1
X-Frame-Options: SAMEORIGIN
{
    "game_category": [
        "This field is required."
    ],
    "release_date": [
        "This field is required."
    ]
}
```

When we want our API to be able to update a single field for an existing resource, in this case, an existing game, we should provide an implementation for the PATCH method. The PUT method is meant to replace an entire resource and the PATCH method is meant to apply a delta to an existing resource. We can write code in the handler for the PUT method apply a delta to an existing resource, but it is a better practice to use the PATCH method for this specific task. We will work with the PATCH method later.

Now, we will compose and send an HTTP request to delete an existing game, specifically, the last game we added. As happened in our last HTTP requests, we have to check the value assigned to pk in the previous response and replace 12 in the command with the returned value:

```
http DELETE :8000/games/15/
```

The following is the equivalent curl command:

```
curl -iX DELETE :8000/games/15/
```

The preceding commands will compose and send the following HTTP request: DELETE http://localhost:8000/games/15/. The request has a number after /games/, and therefore, it will match '^games/(?P<pk>[0-9]+)/$' and run the views.game_detail function, that is, the game_detail function declared within the games/views.py file. The function receives request and pk as parameters because the URL pattern passes the number specified after /games/ in the pk parameter. As the HTTP verb for the request is DELETE, the request.method property is equal to 'DELETE', and therefore, the function will execute the code that parses the JSON data received in the request, creates a Game instance from this data and deletes the existing game in the database. If the game was successfully deleted in the database, the function returns an HTTP 204 No Content status code. The following lines show an example response for the HTTP request after successfully deleting an existing game:

```
HTTP/1.0 204 No Content
Date: Sat, 28 May 2016 04:08:58 GMT
Server: WSGIServer/0.2 CPython/3.5.1
Content-Length: 0
X-Frame-Options: SAMEORIGIN
Content-Type: text/html; charset=utf-8
```

Working with GUI tools – Postman and others

So far, we have been working with two terminal-based or command-line tools to compose and send HTTP requests to our Django development server-cURL and HTTPie. Now, we will work with **GUI (Graphical User Interface)** tools.

Postman is a very popular API testing suite GUI tool that allows us to easily compose and send HTTP requests, among other features. Postman is available as a Chrome App and as a Mac App. We can execute it in Windows, Linux and macOS as a Chrome App, that is, an application running on top of Google Chrome. In case we work with macOS, we can use the Mac App instead of the Chrome App. You can download the versions of the Postman App from the following URL-`https://www.getpostman.com`.

You can download and install Postman for free to compose and send HTTP requests to our RESTful APIs. You just need to sign up to Postman and we won't be using any of the paid features provided by Postman cloud in our examples. All the instructions work with Postman 4.2.2 or greater.

Now, we will use the **Builder** tab in Postman to easily compose and send HTTP requests to `localhost:8000` and test the RESTful API with this GUI tool. Postman doesn't support curl-like shorthands for localhost, and therefore, we cannot use the same shorthands we have been using when composing requests with HTTPie.

Select **GET** in the dropdown menu at the left-hand side of the **Enter request URL** textbox, and enter `localhost:8000/games/` in this textbox at the right-hand side of the dropdown. Then, click **Send** and Postman will display the Status (**200 OK**), the time it took for the request to be processed and the response body with all the games formatted as JSON with syntax highlighting (**Pretty** view).

The following screenshot shows the JSON response body in Postman for the HTTP GET request:

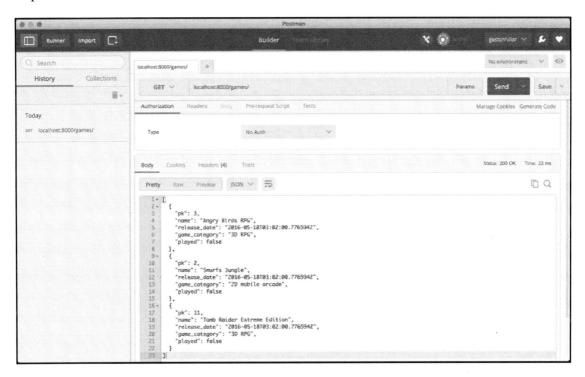

Click on **Headers** at the right-hand side of **Body** and **Cookies** to read the response headers. The following screenshot shows the layout for the response headers that Postman displays for the preceding response. Notice that Postman displays the **Status** at the right-hand side of the response and doesn't include it as the first line of the Headers, as happened when we worked with both the cURL and HTTPie utilities:

Now, we will use the **Builder** tab in Postman to compose and send an HTTP request to create a new game, specifically, a POST request. Follow the next steps:

1. Select **POST** in the drop-down menu at the left-hand side of the **Enter request URL** textbox, and enter `localhost:8000/games/` in this textbox at the right-hand side of the dropdown.

2. Click **Body** at the right-hand side of **Authorization** and **Headers**, within the panel that composes the request.

3. Activate the **raw** radio button and select **JSON (application/json)** in the dropdown at the right-hand side of the **binary** radio button. Postman will automatically add a **Content-type** as **application/json** header, and therefore, you will notice the **Headers** tab will be renamed to **Headers (1)**, indicating us that there is one key-value pair specified for the request headers.

4. Enter the following lines in the textbox below the radio buttons, within the **Body** tab:

```
{
    "name": "Batman vs Superman",
    "game_category": "3D RPG",
    "played": false,
    "release_date": "2016-05-18T03:02:00.776594Z"
}
```

The following screenshot shows the request body in Postman:

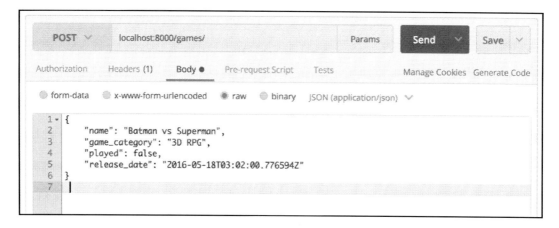

We followed the necessary steps to create an HTTP POST request with a JSON body that specifies the necessary key-value pairs to create a new game. Click on **Send** and Postman will display the Status (`201 Created`), the time it took for the request to be processed and the response body with the recently added game formatted as JSON with syntax highlighting (**Pretty** view). The following screenshot shows the JSON response body in Postman for the HTTP POST request.

 If we want to compose and send an HTTP PUT request with Postman, it is necessary to follow the previously explained steps to provide JSON data within the request body.

One of the nice features included in Postman is that we can easily review and again run the HTTP requests we have made by browsing the saved **History** shown at the left-hand side of the Postman window. The History pane displays a list with the HTTP verb followed by the URL for each HTTP request we have composed and sent. We just need to click on the desired HTTP request and click **Send** to run it again. The following screenshot shows the many HTTP requests in the **History** pane and the first one selected to send it again.

JetBrains PyCharm is a very popular multiplatform Python IDE (short for Integrated Development Environment) available on macOS, Linux and Windows. Its paid Professional version includes a REST Client that allows us to test RESTful Web services. In case we work with this version of the IDE, we can compose and send HTTP requests without leaving the IDE. You don't need a JetBrains PyCharm Professional version license to run the examples included in this book. However, as the IDE is very popular, we will learn the necessary steps to compose and send an HTTP request for our API using the REST Client included in this IDE.

Now, we will use the **REST Client** included in PyCharm professional to compose and send an HTTP request to create a new game, specifically, a POST request. Follow the next steps:

1. Select **Tools** | **Test** RESTful Web Service in the main menu to display the REST Client panel.
2. Select **POST** in the HTTP method dropdown menu in the REST Client pane.
3. Enter `localhost:8000` in the **Host/port** textbox, at the right-hand side of the dropdown.
4. Enter `/games/` in the **Path** textbox, at the right-hand side of the **Host/port** textbox.

5. Make sure that the **Request** tab is activated and click on the add (**+**) button at the bottom of the **Headers** list. The IDE will display a textbox for the name and a dropdown for the value. Enter `Content-Type` in **Name**, enter `application/json` in **Value** and press Enter.

6. Activate the **Text:** radio button in **Request Body** and click the **...** button, on the right-hand side of the **Text** textbox, to specify the text to send. Enter the following lines in textbox included in the **Specify the text to send** dialog box and then click on **OK**.

```
{
    "name": "Teenage Mutant Ninja Turtles",
    "game_category": "3D RPG",
    "played": false,
    "release_date": "2016-05-18T03:02:00.776594Z"
}
```

The following screenshot shows the request built in PyCharm Professional **REST Client**:

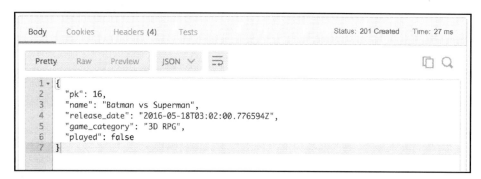

We followed the necessary steps to create an HTTP POST request with a JSON body that specifies the necessary key-value pairs to create a new game. Click on the submit request button, that is, the first button with the play icon at the upper-left corner of the **REST Client** pane. The REST client will compose and send the HTTP POST request, will activate the **Response** tab, and display the response code **201 (Created)**, the time it took for the request to be processed, and the content length at the bottom of the pane.

By default, the REST client will automatically apply JSON syntax highlighting to the response. However, sometimes, the JSON content is displayed without line breaks and it is necessary to click on the reformat response button, that is, the first button in the **Response** tab. The REST client displays the response headers in another tab, and therefore, it just displays the response body in the **Response** tab. The following screenshot shows the JSON response body in the REST client for the HTTP POST request:

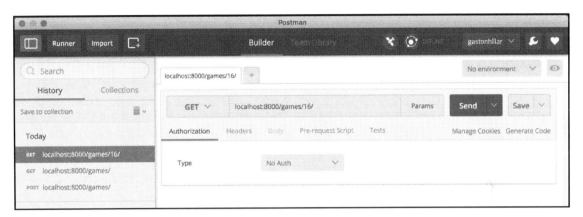

If we want to compose and send an HTTP PUT request with the REST Client included in PyCharm Professional, it is necessary to follow the previously explained steps to provide JSON data within the request body.

In case you don't work with PyCharm Professional, run any of the following commands to compose and send the HTTP POST request to create the new game:

```
http POST :8000/games/ name='Teenage Mutant Ninja Turtles'
game_category='3D RPG' played=false
release_date='2016-05-18T03:02:00.776594Z'
```

The following is the equivalent `curl` command:

```
curl -iX POST -H "Content-Type: application/json" -d '{"name": "Teenage
Mutant Ninja Turtles", "game_category": "3D RPG", "played": "false",
"release_date": "2016-05-18T03:02:00.776594Z"}' :8000/games/
```

Telerik Fiddler is a popular tool for Windows developers. Telerik Fiddler is a free Web debugging proxy with a GUI but it only runs on Windows. Its main Web page promotes it as a multi-platform tool, but at the time this book was published, the macOS and Linux versions were completely unstable and their development abandoned. We can use Telerik Fiddler in Windows to compose and send HTTP requests, among other features. You can download Fiddler for Windows from the following URL-`https://www.telerik.com/download/fiddler`.

Stoplight is a popular powerful API modeling tool that allows us to easily test our APIs. Its HTTP request maker allows us to compose and send requests and generate the necessary code to make them in different programming languages, such as JavaScript, Swift, C#, PHP, Node, and Go, among others. You can sign up to work with Stoplight at the following URL-`http://stoplight.io`.

We can also use apps that can compose and send HTTP requests from mobile devices to work with the RESTful API. For example, we can work with the iCurlHTTP App on iOS devices such as iPad and iPhone-`https://itunes.apple.com/us/app/icurlhttp/id611943891?mt=8`. In Android devices, we can work with the HTTP Request App-`https://play.google.com/store/apps/details?id=air.http.request&hl=en`.

The following screenshot shows the results of composing and sending the following HTTP request with the iCurlHTTP App: `GET http://192.168.1.106:8000/games/`. Remember that you have to perform the previously explained configurations in your LAN and router to be able to access the Django development server from other devices connected to your LAN. In this case, the IP assigned to the computer running the Django Web server is `192.168.1.106`, and therefore, you must replace this IP with the IP assigned to your development computer.

At the time this book was published, the mobile apps that allow you to compose and send HTTP requests do not provide all the features you can find in Postman or command-line utilities.

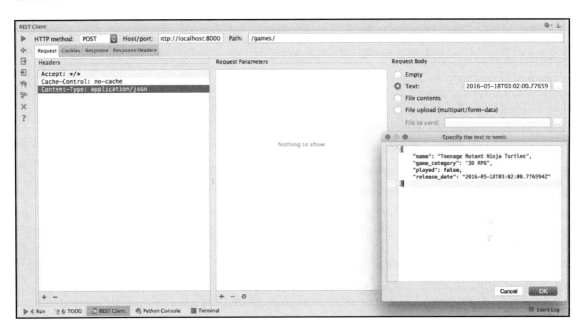

Test your knowledge

1. If we want to create a simple `Player` model that we will use to represent and persist players in Django REST framework, we can create:
   1. A `Player` class as a subclass of the `djangorestframework.models.Model class`.
   2. A `Player` class as a subclass of the `django.db.models.Model class`.
   3. A Player function in the `restframeworkmodels.py` file.

2. In the Django REST Framework, serializers are:
   1. Mediators between the model instances and Python primitives.
   2. Mediators between the view functions and Python primitives.
   3. Mediators between the URLs and view functions.

3. In the Django REST Framework, parsers and renderers:
    1. Handle as mediators between model instances and Python primitives.
    2. Reset the board.
    3. Handle as mediators between Python primitives and HTTP requests and responses.

4. The `urlpatterns` list declared in the urls.py file makes it possible to:
    1. Route URLs to views.
    2. Route URLs to models.
    3. Route URLs to Python primitives.

5. HTTPie is a:
    1. Command-line HTTP server written in Python that makes it easy to create a RESTful Web Server.
    2. Command-line utility that allows us to run queries against an SQLite database.
    3. Command-line HTTP client written in Python that makes it easy to compose and send HTTP requests.

Summary

In this chapter, we designed a RESTful API to interact with a simple SQLite database and perform CRUD operations with games. We defined the requirements for our API and we understood the tasks performed by each HTTP method. We learned the advantages of working with lightweight virtual environments in Python and we set up a virtual environment with Django REST Framework.

We created a model to represent and persist games and we executed migrations in Django. We learned to manage serialization and serialization of game instances into JSON representations with Django REST Framework. We wrote API views to process the different HTTP requests and we configured the URL patterns list to route URLs to views.

Finally, we started the Django development server and we used command-line tools to compose and send HTTP requests to our RESTful API and analyzed how each HTTP request was processed in our code. We also worked with GUI tools to compose and send HTTP requests.

Now that we understand the basics of Django REST Framework, we will expand the capabilities of the RESTful Web API by taking advantage of the advanced features included in the Django REST Framework, which is what we are going to discuss in the next chapter.

2
Working with Class-Based Views and Hyperlinked APIs in Django

In this chapter, we will expand the capabilities of the RESTful API that we started in the previous chapter. We will change the ORM settings to work with a more powerful PostgreSQL database and we will take advantage of the advanced features included in Django REST Framework that allow us to reduce the boilerplate code for complex APIs, such as class-based views. We will:

- Use model serializers to eliminate duplicate code
- Work with wrappers to write API views
- Use the default parsing and rendering options and move beyond JSON
- Browse the API
- Design a RESTful API to interact with a complex PostgreSQL database
- Understand the tasks performed by each `HTTP` method
- Declare relationships with the models
- Manage serialization and deserialization with relationships and hyperlinks
- Create class based views and use generic classes
- Work with endpoints for the API
- Create and retrieve related resources

Using model serializers to eliminate duplicate code

The GameSerializer class declares many attributes with the same names that we used in the Game model and repeats information, such as the types and the max_length values. The GameSerializer class is a subclass of rest_framework.serializers.Serializer, it declares attributes that we manually mapped to the appropriate types and overrides the create and update methods.

Now, we will create a new version of the GameSerializer class that will inherit from the rest_framework.serializers.ModelSerializer class. The ModelSerializer class automatically populates both set of default fields and a set of default validators. In addition, the class provides default implementations for the create and update methods.

 In case you have any experience with Django Web Framework, you will notice that the Serializer and ModelSerializer classes are similar to the Form and ModelForm classes.

Now, go to the gamesapi/games folder and open the serializers.py file. Replace the code in this file with the following code, that declares the new version of the GameSerializer class. The code file for the sample is included in the restful_python_chapter_02_01 folder:

```
from rest_framework import serializers
from games.models import Game


class GameSerializer(serializers.ModelSerializer):
    class Meta:
        model = Game
        fields = ('id',
                  'name',
                  'release_date',
                  'game_category',
                  'played')
```

The new GameSerializer class declares a Meta inner class that declares two attributes: model and fields. The model attribute specifies the model related to the serializer, that is, the Game class. The fields attribute specifies a tuple of string whose values indicate the field names that we want to include in the serialization from the related model.

There is no need to override either `create` or `update` methods because the generic behavior will be enough in this case. The `ModelSerializer` superclass provides implementations for both methods.

We have reduced the boilerplate code that we didn't require in the `GameSerializer` class. We just needed to specify the desired set of fields in a tuple. Now, the types related to the game fields are included only in the `Game` class.

 Press *Ctrl + C* to quit Django's development server and execute the following command to start it again:

```
python manage.py runserver
```

Working with wrappers to write API views

Our code in the `games/views.py` file declared a `JSONResponse` class and two function-based views. These functions returned `JSONResponse` when it was necessary to return JSON data and a `django.Http.Response.HttpResponse` instance when the response was just of an HTTP status code.

No matter the accepted content type specified in the HTTP request header, the view functions always provide the same content in the response body-JSON. Run the following two commands to retrieve all the games with different values for the `Accept` request header-`text/html` and `application/json` :

```
http :8000/games/ Accept:text/html
http :8000/games/ Accept:application/json
```

The following are the equivalent curl commands:

```
curl -H 'Accept: text/html' -iX GET :8000/games/
curl -H 'Accept: application/json' -iX GET :8000/games/
```

The preceding commands will compose and send the following HTTP request: `GET http://localhost:8000/games/`. The first command defines the `text/html` value for the `Accept` request header. The second command defines the `application/json` value for the `Accept` request header.

You will notice that both the commands produce the same results, and therefore, the view functions don't take into account the value specified for the `Accept` request header in the HTTP requests. The header response for both commands will include the following line:

```
Content-Type: application/json
```

The second request specified that it will only accept `text/html` but the response included a JSON body, that is, `application/json` content. Thus, our first version of the RESTful API is not prepared to render content other from JSON. We will make some changes to enable the API to render other contents.

Whenever we have doubts about the methods supported by a resource or resource collection in a RESTful API, we can compose and send an HTTP request with the OPTIONS HTTP verb and the URL for the resource or resource collection. If the RESTful API implements the OPTIONS HTTP verb for a resource or resource collection, it provides a comma-separated list of HTTP verbs or methods that it supports as a value for the `Allow` header in the response. In addition, the response header will include additional information about other supported options, such as the content type it is capable of parsing from the request and the content type it is capable of rendering on the response.

For example, if we want to know the HTTP verbs that the games collection supports, we can run the following command:

```
http OPTIONS :8000/games/
```

The following is the equivalent curl command:

```
curl -iX OPTIONS :8000/games/
```

The previous command will compose and send the following HTTP request: OPTIONS `http://localhost:8000/games/`. The request will match and run the `views.game_list` function, that is, the `game_list` function declared within the `games/views.py` file. This function only runs the code when the `request.method` is equal to `'GET'` or `'POST'`. In this case, `request.method` is equal to `'OPTIONS'`, and therefore, the function won't run any code and won't return any response, specifically, it won't return an `HttpResponse` instance. As a result, we will see the following Internal Server Error listed in Django's development server console output:

```
Internal Server Error: /games/
Traceback (most recent call last):
  File
"/Users/gaston/Projects/PythonRESTfulWebAPI/Django01/lib/python3.5/site-
packages/django/core/handlers/base.py", line 158, in get_response
    % (callback.__module__, view_name))
```

```
ValueError: The view games.views.game_list didn't return an HttpResponse
object. It returned None instead.
[08/Jun/2016 20:21:40] "OPTIONS /games/ HTTP/1.1" 500 49173
```

The following lines show the header for the output that also includes a detailed HTML document with detailed information about the error because the debug mode is activated for Django. We receive a `500 Internal Server Error` status code:

```
HTTP/1.0 500 Internal Server Error
Content-Type: text/html
Date: Wed, 08 Jun 2016 20:21:40 GMT
Server: WSGIServer/0.2 CPython/3.5.1
X-Frame-Options: SAMEORIGIN
```

Obviously, we want to provide a more consistent API and we want to provide an accurate response when we receive a request with the `OPTIONS` verbs for either a game resource or the games collection.

If we compose and send an HTTP request with the `OPTIONS` verb for a game resource, we will see the same error and we will have a similar response because the `views.game_detail` function only runs the code when the `request.method` is equal to `'GET'`, `'PUT'`, or `'DELETE'`.

The following commands will produce the explained error when we try to see the options offered for the game resource whose id or primary key is equal to 3. Don't forget to replace 3 with a primary key value of an existing game in your configuration:

```
http OPTIONS :8000/games/3/
```

The following is the equivalent curl command:

```
curl -iX OPTIONS :8000/games/3/
```

We just need to make a few changes in the `games/views.py` file to solve the issues we have been analyzing for our RESTful API. We will use the `@api_view` decorator, declared in `rest_framework.decorators`, for our function-based views. This decorator allows us to specify the HTTP verbs that our function can process. If the request that has to be processed by the view function has an HTTP verb that isn't included in the string list specified as the `http_method_names` argument for the `@api_view` decorator, the default behavior returns a `405 Method Not Allowed` status code. This way, we make sure that whenever we receive an HTTP verb that isn't considered within our function view, we won't generate an unexpected error as the decorator handles the response for the unsupported HTTP verbs or methods.

Under the hoods, the `@api_view` decorator is a wrapper that converts a function-based views into a subclass of the `rest_framework.views.APIView` class. This class is the base class for all views in Django REST Framework. As we might guess, in case we want to work with class-based view, we can create classes that inherit from this class and we will have the same benefits that we analyzed for the function-based views that use the decorator. We will work with class-based views in the forthcoming examples.

In addition, as we specify a string list with the supported HTTP verbs, the decorator automatically builds the response for the OPTIONS HTTP verb with the supported methods and parser and render capabilities. Our actual version of the API is just capable of rendering JSON as its output. The usage of the decorator makes sure that we always receive an instance of the `rest_framework.request.Request` class in the `request` argument when Django calls our view function. The decorator also handles the `ParserError` exceptions when our function views access the `request.data` attribute that might cause parsing problems.

Using the default parsing and rendering options and move beyond JSON

The `APIView` class specifies default settings for each view that we can override by specifying appropriate values in the `gamesapi/settings.py` file or by overriding the class attributes in subclasses. As previously explained, the usage of the `APIView` class under the hoods makes the decorator apply these default settings. Thus, whenever we use the decorator, the default parser classes and the default renderer classes will be associated with the function views.

By default, the value for the DEFAULT_PARSER_CLASSES is the following tuple of classes:

```
(
    'rest_framework.parsers.JSONParser',
    'rest_framework.parsers.FormParser',
    'rest_framework.parsers.MultiPartParser'
)
```

When we use the decorator, the API will be able to handle any of the following content types through the appropriate parsers when accessing the `request.data` attribute:

- `application/json`
- `application/x-www-form-urlencoded`
- `multipart/form-data`

When we access the `request.data` attribute in the functions, Django REST Framework examines the value for the `Content-Type` header in the incoming request and determines the appropriate parser to parse the request content. If we use the previously explained default values, the Django REST Framework will be able to parse the previously listed content types. However, it is extremely important that the request specifies the appropriate value in the `Content-Type` header.

We have to remove the usage of the `rest_framework.parsers.JSONParser` class in the functions to make it possible to be able to work with all the configured parsers and stop working with a parser that only works with JSON. The `game_list` function executes the following two lines when `request.method` is equal to `'POST'`:

```
game_data = JSONParser().parse(request)
game_serializer = GameSerializer(data=game_data)
```

We will remove the first line that uses the `JSONParser` and we will pass `request.data` as the data argument for the `GameSerializer`. The following line will replace the previous lines:

```
game_serializer = GameSerializer(data=request.data)
```

The `game_detail` function executes the following two lines when `request.method` is equal to `'PUT'`:

```
game_data = JSONParser().parse(request)
game_serializer = GameSerializer(game, data=game_data)
```

We will make the same edits done for the code in the `game_list` function. We will remove the first line that uses the `JSONParser` and we will pass `request.data` as the data argument for the `GameSerializer`. The following line will replace the previous lines:

```
game_serializer = GameSerializer(game, data=request.data)
```

By default, the value for the `DEFAULT_RENDERER_CLASSES` is the following tuple of classes:

```
(
    'rest_framework.renderers.JSONRenderer',
    'rest_framework.renderers.BrowsableAPIRenderer',
)
```

When we use the decorator, the API will be able to render the following content types in the response, through the appropriate renderers, when working with the `rest_framework.response.Response` object:

- `application/json`
- `text/html`

By default, the value for the `DEFAULT_CONTENT_NEGOTIATION_CLASS` is the `rest_framework.negotiation.DefaultContentNegotiation` class. When we use the decorator, the API will use this content negotiation class to select the appropriate renderer for the response based on the incoming request. This way, when a request specifies that it will accept `text/html`, the content negotiation class selects the `rest_framework.renderers.BrowsableAPIRenderer` to render the response and generate `text/html` instead of `application/json`.

We have to replace the usage of both the `JSONResponse` and `HttpResponse` classes in the functions with the `rest_framework.response.Response` class. The `Response` class uses the previously explained content negotiation features, renders the received data into the appropriate content type, and returns it to the client.

Now, go to the `gamesapi/games` folder and open the `views.py` file. Replace the code in this file with the following code that removes the `JSONResponse` class and uses the `@api_view` decorator for the functions and the `rest_framework.response.Response` class. The modified lines are highlighted. The code file for the sample is included in the `restful_python_chapter_02_02` folder:

```python
from rest_framework.parsers import JSONParser
from rest_framework import status
from rest_framework.decorators import api_view
from rest_framework.response import Response
from games.models import Game
from games.serializers import GameSerializer


@api_view(['GET', 'POST'])
def game_list(request):
    if request.method == 'GET':
```

```
        games = Game.objects.all()
        games_serializer = GameSerializer(games, many=True)
        return Response(games_serializer.data)

    elif request.method == 'POST':
        game_serializer = GameSerializer(data=request.data)
        if game_serializer.is_valid():
            game_serializer.save()
            return Response(game_serializer.data,
status=status.HTTP_201_CREATED)
        return Response(game_serializer.errors,
status=status.HTTP_400_BAD_REQUEST)


@api_view(['GET', 'PUT', 'POST'])
def game_detail(request, pk):
    try:
        game = Game.objects.get(pk=pk)
    except Game.DoesNotExist:
        return Response(status=status.HTTP_404_NOT_FOUND)

    if request.method == 'GET':
        game_serializer = GameSerializer(game)
        return Response(game_serializer.data)

    elif request.method == 'PUT':
        game_serializer = GameSerializer(game, data=request.data)
        if game_serializer.is_valid():
            game_serializer.save()
            return Response(game_serializer.data)
        return Response(game_serializer.errors,
status=status.HTTP_400_BAD_REQUEST)

    elif request.method == 'DELETE':
        game.delete()
        return Response(status=status.HTTP_204_NO_CONTENT)
```

After you save the preceding changes, run the following command:

```
http OPTIONS :8000/games/
```

The following is the equivalent `curl` command:

```
curl -iX OPTIONS :8000/games/
```

The previous command will compose and send the following HTTP request: OPTIONS http://localhost:8000/games/. The request will match and run the views.game_list function, that is, the game_list function declared within the games/views.py file. We added the @api_view decorator to this function, and therefore, it is now capable of determining the supported HTTP verbs, parsing, and rendering capabilities. The following lines show the output:

```
HTTP/1.0 200 OK
Allow: GET, POST, OPTIONS
Content-Type: application/json
Date: Thu, 09 Jun 2016 20:24:31 GMT
Server: WSGIServer/0.2 CPython/3.5.1
Vary: Accept, Cookie
X-Frame-Options: SAMEORIGIN
{
    "description": "",
    "name": "Game List",
    "parses": [
        "application/json",
        "application/x-www-form-urlencoded",
        "multipart/form-data"
    ],
    "renders": [
        "application/json",
        "text/html"
    ]
}
```

The response header includes an Allow key with a comma-separated list of HTTP verbs supported by the resource collection as its value: GET, POST, OPTIONS. As our request didn't specify the allowed content type, the function rendered the response with the default application/json content type. The response body specifies the Content-type that the resource collection parses and the Content-type that it renders.

Run the following command to compose and send an HTTP request with the OPTIONS verb for a game resource. Don't forget to replace 3 with a primary key value of an existing game in your configuration.

```
http OPTIONS :8000/games/3/
```

The following is the equivalent curl command:

```
curl -iX OPTIONS :8000/games/3/
```

The preceding command will compose and send the following HTTP request: OPTIONS http://localhost:8000/games/3/. The request will match and run the views.game_detail function, that is, the game_detail function declared within the games/views.py file. We also added the @api_view decorator to this function, and therefore, it is capable of determining the supported HTTP verbs, parsing, and rendering capabilities. The following lines show the output:

```
HTTP/1.0 200 OK
Allow: GET, POST, OPTIONS, PUT
Content-Type: application/json
Date: Thu, 09 Jun 2016 21:35:58 GMT
Server: WSGIServer/0.2 CPython/3.5.1
Vary: Accept, Cookie
X-Frame-Options: SAMEORIGIN
{
    "description": "",
    "name": "Game Detail",
    "parses": [
        "application/json",
        "application/x-www-form-urlencoded",
        "multipart/form-data"
    ],
    "renders": [
        "application/json",
        "text/html"
    ]
}
```

The response header includes an Allow key with a comma-separated list of HTTP verbs supported by the resource as its value: GET, POST, OPTIONS, PUT. The response body specifies the content-type that the resource parses and the content-type that it renders, with the same contents received in the previous OPTIONS request applied to a resource collection, that is, to a games collection.

In Chapter 1, *Developing RESTful APIs with Django*, when we composed and sent POST and PUT commands, we had to use the use the -H "Content-Type: application/json" option to tell curl to send the data specified after the -d option as application/json instead of the default application/x-www-form-urlencoded. Now, in addition to application/json, our API is capable of parsing application/x-www-form-urlencoded and multipart/form-data data specified in the POST and PUT requests. Thus, we can compose and send a POST command that sends the data as application/x-www-form-urlencoded, with the changes made to our API.

We will compose and send an HTTP request to create a new game. In this case, we will use the -f option for HTTPie, that serializes data items from the command line as form fields and sets the `Content-Type` header key to the `application/x-www-form-urlencoded` value:

```
http -f POST :8000/games/ name='Toy Story 4' game_category='3D RPG'
played=false release_date='2016-05-18T03:02:00.776594Z'
```

The following is the equivalent curl command. Note that we don't use the -H option and curl will send the data in the default `application/x-www-form-urlencoded`:

```
curl -iX POST -d '{"name":"Toy Story 4", "game_category":"3D RPG",
"played":
    "false", "release_date": "2016-05-18T03:02:00.776594Z"}' :8000/games/
```

The previous commands will compose and send the following HTTP request: POST `http://localhost:8000/games/` with the `Content-Type` header key set to the `application/x-www-form-urlencoded` value and the following data:

```
name=Toy+Story+4&game_category=3D+RPG&played=false&release_date=2016-05-18T
03%3A02%3A00.776594Z
```

The request specifies /games/, and therefore, it will match '^games/$' and run the `views.game_list` function, that is, the updated `game_detail` function declared within the `games/views.py` file. As the HTTP verb for the request is POST, the `request.method` property is equal to 'POST', and therefore, the function will execute the code that creates a `GameSerializer` instance and passes `request.data` as the data argument for its creation. The `rest_framework.parsers.FormParser` class will parse the data received in the request, the code creates a new `Game` and, if the data is valid, it saves the new `Game`. If the new `Game` was successfully persisted in the database, the function returns an HTTP 201 Created status code and the recently persisted `Game` serialized to JSON in the response body. The following lines show an example response for the HTTP request, with the new `Game` object in the JSON response:

```
HTTP/1.0 201 Created
Allow: OPTIONS, POST, GET
Content-Type: application/json
Date: Fri, 10 Jun 2016 20:38:40 GMT
Server: WSGIServer/0.2 CPython/3.5.1
Vary: Accept, Cookie
X-Frame-Options: SAMEORIGIN
{
    "game_category": "3D RPG",
    "id": 20,
    "name": "Toy Story 4",
```

```
        "played": false,
        "release_date": "2016-05-18T03:02:00.776594Z"
}
```

We can run the following command after we make the changes in the code, to see what happens when we compose and send an HTTP request with an HTTP verb that is not supported:

```
http PUT :8000/games/
```

The following is the equivalent `curl` command:

```
curl -iX PUT :8000/games/
```

The previous command will compose and send the following HTTP request: PUT `http://localhost:8000/games/`. The request will match and try to run the `views.game_list` function, that is, the `game_list` function declared within the `games/views.py` file. The `@api_view` decorator we added to this function doesn't include `'PUT'` in the string list with the allowed HTTP verbs, and therefore, the default behavior returns a `405 Method Not Allowed` status code. The following lines show the output along with the response from the previous request. A JSON content provides a `detail` key with a string value, which indicates that the PUT method is not allowed:

```
HTTP/1.0 405 Method Not Allowed
Allow: GET, OPTIONS, POST
Content-Type: application/json
Date: Sat, 11 Jun 2016 00:49:30 GMT
Server: WSGIServer/0.2 CPython/3.5.1
Vary: Accept, Cookie
X-Frame-Options: SAMEORIGIN
{
    "detail": "Method "PUT" not allowed."
}
```

Browsing the API

With the recent edits, we made it possible for our API to use the default content renderers configured in Django REST Framework, and therefore, our API is capable of rendering the `text/html` content. We can take advantage of the browsable API, a feature included in Django REST Framework that generates human-friendly HTML output for each resource whenever the request specifies `text/html` as the value for the `Content-type` key in the request header.

Whenever we enter a URL for an API resource in a web browser, the browser will require an HTML response, and therefore, Django REST Framework will provide an HTML response built with Bootstrap (`http://getbootstrap.com`). This response will include a section that displays the resource content in JSON, buttons to perform different requests, and forms to submit data to the resources. As everything in Django REST Framework, we can customize the templates and themes used to generate the browsable API.

Open a web browser and enter `http://localhost:8000/games/`. The browsable API will compose and send a GET request to `/games/` and will display the results of its execution, that is, the headers and the JSON games list. The following screenshot shows the rendered web page after entering the URL in a web browser with the resource description-**Game List**:

If you decide to browse the API in a web browser running on another computer or device connected to the LAN, remember that you have to use the development computer's assigned IP address instead of `localhost`. For example, if the computer's assigned IPv4 IP address is `192.168.1.106`, instead of `http://localhost:8000/games/`, you should use `http://192.168.1.106:8000/games/`. Of course, you can also use the host name instead of the IP address.

The browsable API uses the information about the allowed methods for a resource to provide us with buttons to run these methods. At the right-hand side of the resource description, the browsable API shows an **OPTIONS** button and a **GET** drop-down button. The **OPTIONS** button allows us to make an `OPTIONS` request to `/games/`, that is, to the current resource. The **GET** drop-down button allows us to make a `GET` request to `/games/` again. If we click on or tap the down arrow, we can select the **json** option and the browsable API will display the raw JSON result of a `GET` request to `/games/` without the headers.

At the bottom of the rendered web page, the browsable API provides us some control to generate a `POST` request to `/games/`. The **Media type** dropdown allows us to select between the configured supported parsers for our API:

- `application/json`
- `application/x-www-form-urlencoded`
- `multipart/form-data`

The **Content** textbox allows us to specify the data to be sent to the `POST` request formatted as specified in the **Media type** dropdown. Select **application/json** in the **Media type** dropdown and enter the following JSON content in the **Content** textbox:

```
{
    "name": "Chuzzle 2",
    "release_date": "2016-05-18T03:02:00.776594Z",
    "game_category": "2D mobile",
    "played": false
}
```

Click or tap on `POST`. The browsable API will compose and send a `POST` request to `/games/` with the previously specified data as JSON, and we will see the results of the call in the web browser.

The following screenshot shows a web browser displaying the HTTP status code `201 Created` in the response and the previously explained dropdown and textbox with the `POST` button to allow us to continue composing and sending `POST` requests to `/games/`:

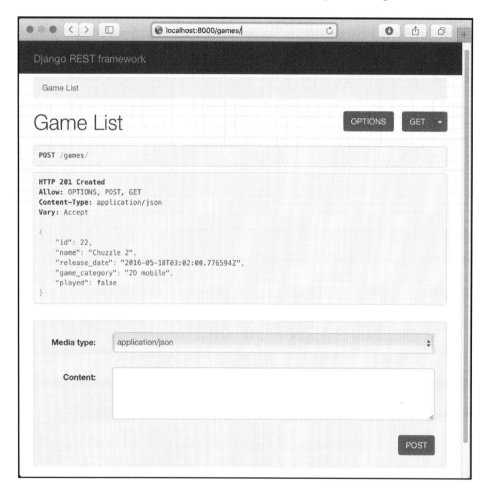

Now, enter the URL for an existing game resource, such as `http://localhost:8000/games/2/`. Make sure you replace 2 with the id or primary key of an existing game in the previously rendered **Games List**. The browsable API will compose and send a `GET` request to `/games/2/` and will display the results of its execution, that is, the headers and the JSON data for the game.

The following screenshot shows the rendered web page after entering the URL in a web browser with the resource description-**Game Detail:**

The browsable API feature allows us to easily check how the API works and to compose and send HTTP requests with different methods to any web browser that has access to our LAN. We will take advantage of the additional features included in the browsable API, such as HTML forms that allow us to easily create new resources, later, after we build a new RESTful API with Python and Django REST Framework.

Working with Class-Based Views and Hyperlinked APIs in Django

Designing a RESTful API to interact with a complex PostgreSQL database

So far, our RESTful API has performed CRUD operations on a single database table. Now, we want to create a more complex RESTful API with Django REST Framework to interact with a complex database model that has to allow us to register player scores for played games that are grouped into game categories. In our previous RESTful API, we used a string field to specify the game category for a game. In this case, we want to be able to easily retrieve all the games that belong to a specific game category, and therefore, we will have a relationship between a game and a game category.

We should be able to perform CRUD operations on different related resources and resource collections. The following list enumerates the resources and the model names that we will use to represent them in Django REST Framework:

- Game categories (GameCategory model)
- Games (Game model)
- Players (Player model)
- Player scores (PlayerScore model)

The game category (GameCategory) just requires a name, and we need the following data for a game (Game):

- A foreign key to a game category (GameCategory)
- A name
- A release date
- A bool value indicating whether the game was played at least once by a player or not
- A timestamp with the date and time in which the game was inserted in the database

We need the following data for a player (Player):

- A gender value
- A name
- A timestamp with the date and time in which the player was inserted in the database

We need the following data for the score achieved by a player (PlayerScore):

- A foreign key to a player (Player)
- A foreign key to a game (Game)
- A score value
- A date in which the score value was achieved by the player

 We will take advantage of all the resources and their relationships to analyze different options that Django REST Framework provides us when working with related resources. Instead of building an API that uses the same configuration to display related resources, we will use diverse configurations that will allow us to select the most appropriate options based on the particular requirements of the APIs that we are developing.

Understanding the tasks performed by each HTTP method

The following table shows the HTTP verbs, the scope, and the semantics for the methods that our new API must support. Each method is composed by an HTTP verb and a scope and all the methods have well-defined meanings for all the resources and collections.

HTTP verb	Scope	Semantics
GET	Collection of game categories	Retrieve all the stored game categories in the collection, sorted by their name in ascending order. Each game category must include a list of URLs for each game resource that belongs to the category.
GET	Game category	Retrieve a single game category. The game category must include a list of URLs for each game resource that belongs to the category.
POST	Collection of game categories	Create a new game category in the collection.
PUT	Game category	Update an existing game category.
PATCH	Game category	Update one or more fields of an existing game category.
DELETE	Game category	Delete an existing game category.

HTTP verb	Scope	Semantics
GET	Collection of games	Retrieve all the stored games in the collection, sorted by their name in ascending order. Each game must include its game category description.
GET	Game	Retrieve a single game. The game must include its game category description.
POST	Collection of games	Create a new game in the collection.
PUT	Game category	Update an existing game.
PATCH	Game category	Update one or more fields of an existing game.
DELETE	Game category	Delete an existing game.
GET	Collection of players	Retrieve all the stored players in the collection, sorted by their name in ascending order. Each player must include a list of the registered scores, sorted by score in descending order. The list must include all the details for the score achieved by the player and its related game.
GET	Player	Retrieve a single player. The player must include a list of the registered scores, sorted by score in descending order. The list must include all the details for the score achieved by the player and its related game.
POST	Collection of players	Create a new player in the collection.
PUT	Player	Update an existing player.
PATCH	Player	Update one or more fields of an existing player.
DELETE	Player	Delete an existing player.
GET	Collection of scores	Retrieve all the stored scores in the collection, sorted by score in descending order. Each score must include the player's name that achieved the score and the game's name.
GET	Score	Retrieve a single score. The score must include the player's name that achieved the score and the game's name.
POST	Collection of scores	Create a new score in the collection. The score must be related to an existing player and an existing game.
PUT	Score	Update an existing score.

HTTP verb	Scope	Semantics
PATCH	Score	Update one or more fields of an existing score.
DELETE	Score	Delete an existing score.

We want our API to be able to update a single field for an existing resource, and therefore, we will provide an implementation for the PATCH method. The PUT method is meant to replace an entire resource and the PATCH method is meant to apply a delta to an existing resource. In addition, our RESTful API must support the OPTIONS method for all the resources and collection of resources.

We don't want to spend time choosing and configuring the most appropriate ORM, as seen in our previous API; we just want to finish the RESTful API as soon as possible to start interacting with it. We will use all the features and reusable elements included in Django REST Framework to make it easy to build our API. We will work with a PostgreSQL database. However, in case you don't want to spend time installing PostgreSQL, you can skip the changes we make in Django REST Framework ORM configuration and continue working with the default SQLite database.

In the preceding table, we have a huge number of methods and scopes. The following list enumerates the URIs for each scope mentioned in the table, where {id} has to be replaced with the numeric id or the primary key of the resource:

- **Collection of game categories**: /game-categories/
- **Game category**: /game-category/{id}/
- **Collection of games**: /games/
- **Game**: /game/{id}/
- **Collection of players**: /players/
- **Player**: /player/{id}/
- **Collection of scores**: /player-scores/
- **Score**: /player-score/{id}/

Let's consider that http://localhost:8000/ is the URL for the API running on the Django development server. We have to compose and send an HTTP request with the following HTTP verb (GET) and request URL (http://localhost:8000/game-categories/) to retrieve all the stored game categories in the collection:

```
GET http://localhost:8000/game-categories/
```

Declaring relationships with the models

Make sure you quit the Django's development server. Remember that you just need to press *Ctrl + C* in the terminal or command-prompt window in which it is running. Now, we will create the models that we are going to use to represent and persist the game categories, games, players and scores, and their relationships. Open the `games/models.py` file and replace its contents with the following code. The lines that declare fields related to other models are highlighted in the code listing. The code file for the sample is included in the `restful_python_chapter_02_03` folder.

```python
from django.db import models


class GameCategory(models.Model):
    name = models.CharField(max_length=200)

    class Meta:
        ordering = ('name',)

    def __str__(self):
        return self.name


class Game(models.Model):
    created = models.DateTimeField(auto_now_add=True)
    name = models.CharField(max_length=200)
    game_category = models.ForeignKey(
        GameCategory,
        related_name='games',
        on_delete=models.CASCADE)
    release_date = models.DateTimeField()
    played = models.BooleanField(default=False)

    class Meta:
        ordering = ('name',)

    def __str__(self):
        return self.name


class Player(models.Model):
    MALE = 'M'
    FEMALE = 'F'
    GENDER_CHOICES = (
        (MALE, 'Male'),
        (FEMALE, 'Female'),
```

```
    )
    created = models.DateTimeField(auto_now_add=True)
    name = models.CharField(max_length=50, blank=False, default='')
    gender = models.CharField(
        max_length=2,
        choices=GENDER_CHOICES,
        default=MALE,
    )

    class Meta:
        ordering = ('name',)

    def __str__(self):
        return self.name


class PlayerScore(models.Model):
    player = models.ForeignKey(
        Player,
        related_name='scores',
        on_delete=models.CASCADE)
    game = models.ForeignKey(
        Game,
        on_delete=models.CASCADE)
    score = models.IntegerField()
    score_date = models.DateTimeField()

    class Meta:
        # Order by score descending
        ordering = ('-score',)
```

The preceding code declares the following four models, specifically four classes as subclasses of the django.db.models.Model class:

- GameCategory
- Game
- Player
- PlayerScore

Django automatically adds an auto-increment integer primary key column named id when it creates the database table related to each model. We specified the field types, maximum lengths, and defaults for many attributes. Each class declares a Meta inner class that declares an ordering attribute. The Meta inner class declared within the PlayerScore class specifies '-score' as the value of the ordering tuple, with a dash as a prefix of the field name and ordered by score in descending order, instead of the default ascending order.

The `GameCategory`, `Game`, and `Player` classes declare the __str__ method that returns the contents of the `name` attribute that provides the name or title for each of these models. So, Django will call this method whenever it has to provide a human-readable representation for the model.

The `Game` model declares the `game_category` field with the following line:

```
game_category = models.ForeignKey(
    GameCategory,
    related_name='games',
    on_delete=models.CASCADE)
```

The preceding line uses the django.db.models.ForeignKey class to provide a many-to-one relationship to the GameCategory model. The 'games' value specified for the related_name argument creates a backwards relation from the GameCategory model to the Game model. This value indicates the name to be used for the relation from the related GameCategory object back to a Game object. Now, we will be able to access all the games that belong to a specific game category. Whenever we delete a game category, we want all the games that belong to this category to be deleted too, and therefore, we specified the models.CASCADE value for the on_delete argument.

The `PlayerScore` model declares the `player` field with the following line:

```
player = models.ForeignKey(
    Player,
    related_name='scores',
    on_delete=models.CASCADE)
```

The preceding line uses the django.db.models.ForeignKey class to provide a many-to-one relationship to the Player model. The 'scores' value specified for the related_name argument creates a backwards relation from the Player model to the PlayerScore model. This value indicates the name to be used for the relation from the related Player object back to a PlayerScore object. Now, we will be able to access all the scores archive by a specific player. Whenever we delete a player, we want all the scores achieved by this player to be deleted too, and therefore, we specified the models.CASCADE value for the on_delete argument.

The `PlayerScore` model declares the `game` field with the following line:

```
game = models.ForeignKey(
    Game,
    on_delete=models.CASCADE)
```

The preceding line uses the django.db.models.ForeignKey class to provide a many-to-one relationship to the Game model. In this case, we don't create a backwards relation because we don't need it. Thus, we don't specify a value for the related_name argument. Whenever we delete a game, we want all the registered scores for this game to be deleted too, and therefore, we specified the models.CASCADE value for the on_delete argument.

In case you created a new virtual environment to work with this example or you downloaded the sample code for the book, you don't need to delete any existing database. However, in case you are making changes to the code for our previous API example, you have to delete the gamesapi/db.sqlite3 file and the games/migrations folder.

Then, it is necessary to create the initial migration for the new models we recently coded. We just need to run the following Python scripts and we will also synchronize the database for the first time. As we learned from our previous example API, by default, Django uses an SQLite database. In this example, we will be working with a PostgreSQL database. However, in case you want to use SQLite, you can skip the steps related to PostgreSQL, its configuration in Django, and jump to the migrations generation command.

You will have to download and install a PostgreSQL database in case you aren't already running it in your computer or in a development server. You can download and install this database management system from its web page-http://www.postgresql.org. In case you are working with macOS, Postgres.app provides an easy way to install and use PostgreSQL on this operating system-http://postgresapp.com.

You have to make sure that the PostgreSQL bin folder is included in the PATH environmental variable. You should be able to execute the psql command-line utility from your current terminal or command prompt. In case the folder isn't included in the PATH, you will receive an error indicating that the pg_config file cannot be found when trying to install the psycopg2 package. In addition, you will have to use the full path to each of the PostgreSQL command-line tools we will use in the subsequent steps.

We will use the PostgreSQL command-line tools to create a new database named games. In case you already have a PostgreSQL database with this name, make sure that you use another name in all the commands and configurations. You can perform the same task with any PostgreSQL GUI tool. In case you are developing on Linux, it is necessary to run the commands as the postgres user. Run the following command in macOS or Windows to create a new database named games. Note that the command won't produce any output:

```
createdb games
```

In Linux, run the following command to use the `postgres` user:

```
sudo -u postgres createdb games
```

Now, we will use the `psql` command-line tool to run some SQL statements to create a specific user that we will use in Django and assign the necessary roles for it. In macOS or Windows, run the following command to launch `psql`:

```
psql
```

In macOS, you might need to run the following command to launch psql with the `postgres` in case the previous command doesn't work, as it will depend on the way in which you installed PostgreSQL:

```
sudo -u postgres psql
```

In Linux, run the following command to use the `postgres` user.

```
sudo -u psql
```

Then, run the following SQL statements and finally enter \q to exit the psql command-line tool. Replace `user_name` with your desired user name to use in the new database and password with your chosen password. We will use the username and password in the Django configuration. You don't need to run the steps if you are already working with a specific user in PostgreSQL and you have already granted privileges to the database for the user:

```
CREATE ROLE user_name WITH LOGIN PASSWORD 'password';
GRANT ALL PRIVILEGES ON DATABASE games TO user_name;
ALTER USER user_name CREATEDB;
\q
```

The default SQLite database engine and the database file name are specified in the `gamesapi/settings.py` Python file. In case you decide to work with PostgreSQL instead of SQLite for this example, replace the declaration of the DATABASES dictionary with the following lines. The nested dictionary maps the database named `default` with the `django.db.backends.postgresql` database engine, the desired database name, and its settings. In this case, we will create a database named `games`. Make sure you specify the desired database name in the value for the `'NAME'` key and that you configure the user, password, host, and port based on your PostgreSQL configuration. In case you followed the previous steps, use the settings specified in these steps:

```
DATABASES = {
    'default': {
        'ENGINE': 'django.db.backends.postgresql',
```

```
# Replace games with your desired database name
'NAME': 'games',
# Replace username with your desired user name
'USER': 'user_name',
# Replace password with your desired password
'PASSWORD': 'password',
# Replace 127.0.0.1 with the PostgreSQL host
'HOST': '127.0.0.1',
# Replace 5432 with the PostgreSQL configured port
# in case you aren't using the default port
'PORT': '5432',
    }
}
```

In case you decided to use PostgreSQL, after making the preceding changes, it is necessary to install the Psycopg 2 package (psycopg2). This package is a Python-PostgreSQL Database Adapter and Django uses it to interact with a PostgreSQL database.

In macOS installations, we have to make sure that the PostgreSQL bin folder is included in the PATH environmental variable. For example, in case the path to the bin folder is /Applications/Postgres.app/Contents/Versions/latest/bin, we must execute the following command to add this folder to the PATH environmental variable:

```
export
PATH=$PATH:/Applications/Postgres.app/Contents/Versions/latest/bin
```

Once we have made sure that the PostgreSQL bin folder is included in the PATH environmental variable, we just need to run the following command to install this package:

```
pip install psycopg2
```

The last lines of the output will indicate that the psycopg2 package has been successfully installed:

```
Collecting psycopg2
Installing collected packages: psycopg2
Running setup.py install for psycopg2
Successfully installed psycopg2-2.6.2
```

Now, run the following Python script to generate the migrations that will allow us to synchronize the database for the first time:

```
python manage.py makemigrations games
```

The following lines show the output generated after running the previous command:

```
Migrations for 'games':
  0001_initial.py:
    - Create model Game
    - Create model GameCategory
    - Create model Player
    - Create model PlayerScore
    - Add field game_category to game
```

The output indicates that the gamesapi/games/migrations/0001_initial.py file includes the code to create the Game, GameCategory, Player, and PlayerScore models. The following lines show the code for this file that was automatically generated by Django. The code file for the sample is included in the restful_python_chapter_02_03 folder:

```
# -*- coding: utf-8 -*-
# Generated by Django 1.9.7 on 2016-06-17 20:39
from __future__ import unicode_literals

from django.db import migrations, models
import django.db.models.deletion


class Migration(migrations.Migration):

    initial = True

    dependencies = [
    ]

    operations = [
        migrations.CreateModel(
            name='Game',
            fields=[
                ('id', models.AutoField(auto_created=True,
primary_key=True, serialize=False, verbose_name='ID')),
                ('created', models.DateTimeField(auto_now_add=True)),
                ('name', models.CharField(max_length=200)),
                ('release_date', models.DateTimeField()),
                ('played', models.BooleanField(default=False)),
            ],
            options={
                'ordering': ('name',),
            },
        ),
        migrations.CreateModel(
            name='GameCategory',
            fields=[
```

```
                ('id', models.AutoField(auto_created=True,
primary_key=True, serialize=False, verbose_name='ID')),
                ('name', models.CharField(max_length=200)),
            ],
            options={
                'ordering': ('name',),
            },
        ),
        migrations.CreateModel(
            name='Player',
            fields=[
                ('id', models.AutoField(auto_created=True,
primary_key=True, serialize=False, verbose_name='ID')),
                ('created', models.DateTimeField(auto_now_add=True)),
                ('name', models.CharField(default='', max_length=50)),
                ('gender', models.CharField(choices=[('M', 'Male'), ('F',
'Female')], default='M', max_length=2)),
            ],
            options={
                'ordering': ('name',),
            },
        ),
        migrations.CreateModel(
            name='PlayerScore',
            fields=[
                ('id', models.AutoField(auto_created=True,
primary_key=True, serialize=False, verbose_name='ID')),
                ('score', models.IntegerField()),
                ('score_date', models.DateTimeField()),
                ('game',
models.ForeignKey(on_delete=django.db.models.deletion.CASCADE,
to='games.Game')),
                ('player',
models.ForeignKey(on_delete=django.db.models.deletion.CASCADE,
related_name='scores', to='games.Player')),
            ],
            options={
                'ordering': ('-score',),
            },
        ),
        migrations.AddField(
            model_name='game',
            name='game_category',
field=models.ForeignKey(on_delete=django.db.models.deletion.CASCADE,
related_name='games', to='games.GameCategory'),
        ),
    ]
```

The preceding code defines a subclass of the `django.db.migrations.Migration` class named `Migration` that defines an `operations` list with many `migrations.CreateModel`. Each `migrations.CreateModel` will create the table for each of the related models. Note that Django has automatically added an `id` field for each of the models. The `operations` are executed in the same order in which they appear in the list. The code creates `Game`, `GameCategory`, `Player`, `PlayerScore`, and finally adds the `game_category` field to `Game` with the foreign key to `GameCategory` because it created the `Game` model before the `GameCategory` model. The code creates the foreign keys for `PlayerScore` when it creates the model:

Now, run the following Python script to apply all the generated migrations.

```
python manage.py migrate
```

The following lines show the output generated after running the previous command:

```
Operations to perform:
  Apply all migrations: sessions, contenttypes, games, admin, auth
Running migrations:
  Rendering model states... DONE
  Applying contenttypes.0001_initial... OK
  Applying auth.0001_initial... OK
  Applying admin.0001_initial... OK
  Applying admin.0002_logentry_remove_auto_add... OK
  Applying contenttypes.0002_remove_content_type_name... OK
  Applying auth.0002_alter_permission_name_max_length... OK
  Applying auth.0003_alter_user_email_max_length... OK
  Applying auth.0004_alter_user_username_opts... OK
  Applying auth.0005_alter_user_last_login_null... OK
  Applying auth.0006_require_contenttypes_0002... OK
  Applying auth.0007_alter_validators_add_error_messages... OK
  Applying games.0001_initial... OK
  Applying sessions.0001_initial... OK
```

After we run the previous command, we can use the PostgreSQL command line or any other application that allows us to easily check the contents of the PostreSQL database to check the tables that Django generated. In case you are working with SQLite, we have already learned how to check the tables in Chapter 1, *Developing RESTful APIs with Django*.

Run the following command to list the generated tables:

```
psql --username=user_name --dbname=games --command="\dt"
```

The following lines show the output with all the generated table names:

```
                        List of relations
     Schema |              Name              | Type  |   Owner
    --------+------------------------------+-------+-----------
     public | auth_group                   | table | user_name
     public | auth_group_permissions       | table | user_name
     public | auth_permission              | table | user_name
     public | auth_user                    | table | user_name
     public | auth_user_groups             | table | user_name
     public | auth_user_user_permissions   | table | user_name
     public | django_admin_log             | table | user_name
     public | django_content_type          | table | user_name
     public | django_migrations            | table | user_name
     public | django_session               | table | user_name
     public | games_game                   | table | user_name
     public | games_gamecategory           | table | user_name
     public | games_player                 | table | user_name
     public | games_playerscore            | table | user_name
    (14 rows)
```

As seen in our previous example, Django uses the games_ prefix for the following four table names related to the games application. Django's integrated ORM generated these tables and the foreign keys, based on the information included in our models:

- games_game: Persists the Game model
- games_gamecategory: Persists the GameCategory model
- games_player: Persists the Player model
- games_playerscore: Persists the PlayerScore model

The following command will allow you to check the contents of the four tables after we compose and send HTTP requests to the RESTful API and make CRUD operations to the four tables. The commands assume that you are running PostgreSQL on the same computer in which you are running the command.

```
    psql --username=user_name --dbname=games --command="SELECT * FROM
games_gamecategory;"
    psql --username=user_name --dbname=games --command="SELECT * FROM
games_game;"
    psql --username=user_name --dbname=games --command="SELECT * FROM
games_player;"
    psql --username=user_name --dbname=games --command="SELECT * FROM
games_playerscore;"
```

Instead of working with the PostgreSQL command-line utility, you can use a GUI tool to check the contents of the PostgreSQL database. You can also use the database tools included in your favorite IDE to check the contents for the SQLite database.

Django generates additional tables that it requires to support the web framework and the authentication features that we will use later.

Managing serialization and deserialization with relationships and hyperlinks

Our new RESTful Web API has to be able to serialize and deserialize the `GameCategory`, `Game`, `Player`, and `PlayerScore` instances into JSON representations. In this case, we also have to pay special attention to the relationships between the different models when we create the serializer classes to manage serialization to JSON and deserialization from JSON.

In our last version of the previous API, we created a subclass of the `rest_framework.serializers.ModelSerializer` class to make it easier to generate a serializer and reduce boilerplate code. In this case, we will also declare a class that inherits from `ModelSerializer`, but the other classes will inherit from the `rest_framework.serializers.HyperlinkedModelSerializer` class.

The `HyperlinkedModelSerializer` is a type of `ModelSerializer` that uses hyperlinked relationships instead of primary key relationships, and therefore, it represents the realationships to other model instances with hyperlinks instead of primary key values. In addition, the `HyperlinkedModelSerializer` generated a field named `url` with the URL for the resource as its value. As seen in the case of `ModelSerializer`, the `HyperlinkedModelSerializer` class provides default implementations for the `create` and `update` methods.

Now, go to the `gamesapi/games` folder and open the `serializers.py` file. Replace the code in this file with the following code that declares the required imports and the `GameCategorySerializer` class. We will add more classes to this file later. The code file for the sample is included in the `restful_python_chapter_02_03` folder:

```
from rest_framework import serializers
from games.models import GameCategory
from games.models import Game
from games.models import Player
from games.models import PlayerScore
import games.views
```

```
class GameCategorySerializer(serializers.HyperlinkedModelSerializer):
    games = serializers.HyperlinkedRelatedField(
        many=True,
        read_only=True,
        view_name='game-detail')

    class Meta:
        model = GameCategory
        fields = (
            'url',
            'pk',
            'name',
            'games')
```

The GameCategorySerializer class is a subclass of the HyperlinkedModelSerializer class. The GameCategorySerializer class declares a games attribute as an instance of serializers.HyperlinkedRelatedField with many and read_only equal to True because it is a one-to-many relationship and it is read-only. We use the games name that we specified as the related_name string value when we created the game_category field as a models.ForeignKey instance in the Game model. This way, the games field will provide us with an array of hyperlinks to each game that belong to the game category. The view_name value is 'game-detail' because we want the browsable API feature to use the game detail view to render the hyperlink when the user clicks or taps on it.

The GameCategorySerializer class declares a Meta inner class that declares two attributes: model and fields. The model attribute specifies the model related to the serializer, that is, the GameCategory class. The fields attribute specifies a tuple of string whose values indicates the field names that we want to include in the serialization from the related model. We want to include both the primary key and the URL, and therefore, the code specified both 'pk' and 'url' as members of the tuple. There is no need to override either the create, or update method because the generic behavior will be enough in this case. The HyperlinkedModelSerializer superclass provides implementations for both methods.

Now, add the following code to the `serializers.py` file to declare the `GameSerializer` class. The code file for the sample is included in the `restful_python_chapter_02_03` folder:

```
class GameSerializer(serializers.HyperlinkedModelSerializer):
    # We want to display the game cagory's name instead of the id
    game_category =
serializers.SlugRelatedField(queryset=GameCategory.objects.all(),
slug_field='name')

    class Meta:
        model = Game
        fields = (
            'url',
            'game_category',
            'name',
            'release_date',
            'played')
```

The `GameSerializer` class is a subclass of the `HyperlinkedModelSerializer` class. The `GameSerializer` class declares a `game_category` attribute as an instance of `serializers.SlugRelatedField` with its `queryset` argument set to `GameCategory.objects.all()` and its `slug_field` argument set to `'name'`. A `SlugRelatedField` is a read-write field that represents the target of the relationship by a unique slug attribute, that is, the description. We created the `game_category` field as a `models.ForeignKey` instance in the `Game` model and we want to display the game category's name as the description (slug field) for the related `GameCategory`. Thus, we specified `'name'` as the `slug_field`. In case it is necessary to display the possible options for the related game category in a form in the browsable API, Django will use the expression specified in the `queryset` argument to retrieve all the possible instances and display their specified slug field.

The `GameCategorySerializer` class declares a `Meta` inner class that declares two attributes: `model` and `fields`. The `model` attribute specifies the model related to the serializer, that is, the `Game` class. The `fields` attribute specifies a tuple of string whose values indicate the field names that we want to include in the serialization from the related model. We just want to include the URL, and therefore, the code specified both `'url'` as a member of the tuple. The `game_category` field will specify the `name` field for the related `GameCategory`.

Now, add the following code to the `serializers.py` file to declare the `ScoreSerializer` class. The code file for the sample is included in the `restful_python_chapter_02_03` folder:

```
class ScoreSerializer(serializers.HyperlinkedModelSerializer):
    # We want to display all the details for the game
    game = GameSerializer()
    # We don't include the player because it will be nested in the player
    class Meta:
        model = PlayerScore
        fields = (
            'url',
            'pk',
            'score',
            'score_date',
            'game',
            )
```

The ScoreSerializer class is a subclass of the HyperlinkedModelSerializer class. We will use the ScoreSerializer class to serialize PlayerScore instances related to a Player, that is, to display all the scores for a specific player when we serialize a Player. We want to display all the details for the related Game but we don't include the related Player because the Player will use this ScoreSerializer serializer.

The ScoreSerializer class declares a game attribute as an instance of the previously coded GameSerializer class. We created the game field as a models.ForeignKey instance in the PlayerScore model and we want to serialize the same data for the game that we coded in the GameSerializer class.

The ScoreSerializer class declares a Meta inner class that declares two attributes: model and fields. The model attribute specifies the model related to the serializer, that is, the PlayerScore class. As previously explain, we don't include the 'player' field name in the fields tuple of string to avoid serializing the player again. We will use a PlayerSerializer as a master and the ScoreSerializer as the detail.

Now, add the following code to the serializers.py file to declare the PlayerSerializer class. The code file for the sample is included in the restful_python_chapter_02_03 folder:

```
class PlayerSerializer(serializers.HyperlinkedModelSerializer):
    scores = ScoreSerializer(many=True, read_only=True)
    gender = serializers.ChoiceField(
        choices=Player.GENDER_CHOICES)
    gender_description = serializers.CharField(
        source='get_gender_display',
        read_only=True)

    class Meta:
        model = Player
```

```
fields = (
    'url',
    'name',
    'gender',
    'gender_description',
    'scores',
)
```

The `PlayerSerializer` class is a subclass of the `HyperlinkedModelSerializer` class. We will use the `PlayerSerializer` class to serialize `Player` instances and we will use the previously declared `ScoreSerializer` class to serialize all the `PlayerScore` instances related to the `Player`.

The `PlayerSerializer` class declares a `scores` attribute as an instance of the previously coded `ScoreSerializer` class. The `many` argument is set to `True` because it is a one-to-many relationship. We use the `scores` name that we specified as the `related_name` string value when we created the `player` field as a `models.ForeignKey` instance in the `PlayerScore` model. This way, the `scores` field will render each `PlayerScore` that belongs to the `Player` using the previously declared `ScoreSerializer`.

The `Player` model declared `gender` as an instance of `models.CharField` with the `choices` attribute set to the `Player.GENDER_CHOICES` string tuple. The `ScoreSerializer` class declares a `gender` attribute as an instance of `serializers.ChoiceField` with the `choices` argument set to the `Player.GENDER_CHOICES` string tuple. In addition, the class declares a `gender_description` attribute with `read_only` set to `True` and the `source` argument set to `'get_gender_display'`. The `source` string is built with `get_` followed by the field name, `gender`, and `_display`. This way, the read-only `gender_description` attribute will render the description for the gender choices instead of the single char stored values.

The `ScoreSerializer` class declares a `Meta` inner class that declares two attributes: `model` and `fields`. The `model` attribute specifies the model related to the serializer, that is, the `PlayerScore` class. As previously explained, we don't include the `'player'` field name in the `fields` tuple of string to avoid serializing the player again. We will use a `PlayerSerializer` as a master and the `ScoreSerializer` as the detail.

Finally, add the following code to the `serializers.py` file to declare the `PlayerScoreSerializer` class. The code file for the sample is included in the `restful_python_chapter_02_03` folder:

```
class PlayerScoreSerializer(serializers.ModelSerializer):
    player = serializers.SlugRelatedField(queryset=Player.objects.all(),
slug_field='name')
```

```
    # We want to display the game's name instead of the id
    game = serializers.SlugRelatedField(queryset=Game.objects.all(),
slug_field='name')

    class Meta:
        model = PlayerScore
        fields = (
            'url',
            'pk',
            'score',
            'score_date',
            'player',
            'game',
        )
```

The PlayerScoreSerializer class is a subclass of the HyperlinkedModelSerializer class. We will use the PlayerScoreSerializer class to serialize PlayerScore instances. Previously, we created the ScoreSerializer class to serialize PlayerScore instances as the detail of a player. We will use the new PlayerScoreSerializer class when we want to display the related player's name and the related game's name. In the other serializer class, we didn't include any information related to the player and we included all the details for the game.

The PlayerScoreSerializer class declares a player attribute as an instance of serializers.SlugRelatedField with its queryset argument set to Player.objects.all() and its slug_field argument set to 'name'. We created the player field as a models.ForeignKey instance in the PlayerScore model and we want to display the player's name as the description (slug field) for the related Player. Thus, we specified 'name' as the slug_field. In case it is necessary to display the possible options for the related game category in a form in the browsable API, Django will use the expression specified in the queryset argument to retrieve all the possible players and display their specified slug field.

The PlayerScoreSerializer class declares a game attribute as an instance of serializers.SlugRelatedField with its queryset argument set to Game.objects.all() and its slug_field argument set to 'name'. We created the game field as a models.ForeignKey instance in the PlayerScore model and we want to display the game's name as the description (slug field) for the related Game.

Creating class-based views and using generic classes

This time, we will write our API views by declaring class-based views, instead of function-based views. We might code classes that inherit from the `rest_framework.views.APIView` class and declare methods with the same names than the HTTP verbs we want to process: `get`, `post`, `put`, `patch`, `delete`, and so on. These methods receive a `request` argument as happened with the functions that we created for the views. However, this approach would require us to write a lot of code. Instead, we can take advantage of a set of generic views that we can use as our base classes for our class-based views to reduce the required code to the minimum and take advantage of the behavior that has been generalized in Django REST Framework.

We will create subclasses of the two following generic class views declared in `rest_framework.generics`:

- `ListCreateAPIView`: Implements the `get` method that retrieves a listing of a queryset and the `post` method that creates a model instance.
- `RetrieveUpdateDestroyAPIView`: Implements the `get`, `put`, `patch`, and `delete` methods to retreive, completely update, partially update or delete a model instance.

Those two generic views are composed by combining reusable bits of behavior in Django REST Framework implemented as mixin classes declared in `rest_framework.mixins`. We can create a class that uses multiple inheritance and combine the features provided by many of these mixin classes. The following line shows the declaration of the `ListCreateAPIView` class as the composition of `ListModelMixin`, `CreateModelMixin` and `rest_framework.generics.GenericAPIView`:

```
class ListCreateAPIView(mixins.ListModelMixin,
                        mixins.CreateModelMixin,
                        GenericAPIView):
```

The following line shows the declaration of the `RetrieveUpdateDestroyAPIView` class as the composition of `RetrieveModelMixin`, `UpdateModelMixin`, `DestroyModelMixin` and `rest_framework.generics.GenericAPIView`:

```
class RetrieveUpdateDestroyAPIView(mixins.RetrieveModelMixin,
                                   mixins.UpdateModelMixin,
                                   mixins.DestroyModelMixin,
                                   GenericAPIView):
```

Now, we will create a Django class based views that will use the previously explained generic classes and the serializer classes to return JSON representations for each HTTP request that our API will handle. We will just have to specify a `queryset` that retrieves all the objects in the `queryset` attribute and the serializer class in the `serializer_class` attribute for each subclass that we declare. The generic classes will do the rest for us. In addition, we will declare a `name` attribute with the string name we will use to identify the view.

Taking advantage of generic class based views

Go to the `gamesapi/games` folder and open the `views.py` file. Replace the code in this file with the following code that declares the required imports and the class based views. We will add more classes to this file later. The code file for the sample is included in the `restful_python_chapter_02_03` folder:

```python
from games.models import GameCategory
from games.models import Game
from games.models import Player
from games.models import PlayerScore
from games.serializers import GameCategorySerializer
from games.serializers import GameSerializer
from games.serializers import PlayerSerializer
from games.serializers import PlayerScoreSerializer
from rest_framework import generics
from rest_framework.response import Response
from rest_framework.reverse import reverse


class GameCategoryList(generics.ListCreateAPIView):
    queryset = GameCategory.objects.all()
    serializer_class = GameCategorySerializer
    name = 'gamecategory-list'


class GameCategoryDetail(generics.RetrieveUpdateDestroyAPIView):
    queryset = GameCategory.objects.all()
    serializer_class = GameCategorySerializer
    name = 'gamecategory-detail'


class GameList(generics.ListCreateAPIView):
    queryset = Game.objects.all()
```

```
        serializer_class = GameSerializer
        name = 'game-list'


class GameDetail(generics.RetrieveUpdateDestroyAPIView):
        queryset = Game.objects.all()
        serializer_class = GameSerializer
        name = 'game-detail'


class PlayerList(generics.ListCreateAPIView):
        queryset = Player.objects.all()
        serializer_class = PlayerSerializer
        name = 'player-list'


class PlayerDetail(generics.RetrieveUpdateDestroyAPIView):
        queryset = Player.objects.all()
        serializer_class = PlayerSerializer
        name = 'player-detail'


class PlayerScoreList(generics.ListCreateAPIView):
        queryset = PlayerScore.objects.all()
        serializer_class = PlayerScoreSerializer
        name = 'playerscore-list'


class PlayerScoreDetail(generics.RetrieveUpdateDestroyAPIView):
        queryset = PlayerScore.objects.all()
        serializer_class = PlayerScoreSerializer
        name = 'playerscore-detail'
```

The following table summarizes the methods that each class-based view is going to process:

Scope	Class based view name	HTTP verbs that it will process
Collection of game categories-/game-categories/	GameCategoryList	GET and POST
Game category-/game-category/{id}/	GameCategoryDetail	GET, PUT, PATCH and DELETE
Collection of games-/games/	GameList	GET and POST
Game-/game/{id}/	GameDetail	GET, PUT, PATCH and DELETE

Scope	Class based view name	HTTP verbs that it will process
Collection of players-`/players/`	`PlayerList`	GET and POST
Player-`/player/{id}/`	`PlayerDetail`	GET, PUT, PATCH and DELETE
Collection of scores-`/player-scores/`	PlayerScoreList	GET and POST
Score-`/player-score/{id}/`	PlayerScoreDetail	GET, PUT, PATCH and DELETE

In addition, we will be able to execute the OPTIONS HTTP verb on any of the scopes.

Working with endpoints for the API

We want to create an endpoint for the root of our API to make it easier to browse the API with the browsable API feature and understand how everything works. Add the following code to the `views.py` file to declare the `ApiRoot` class. The code file for the sample is included in the `restful_python_chapter_02_03` folder.

```
class ApiRoot(generics.GenericAPIView):
    name = 'api-root'
    def get(self, request, *args, **kwargs):
        return Response({
            'players': reverse(PlayerList.name, request=request),
            'game-categories': reverse(GameCategoryList.name,
request=request),
            'games': reverse(GameList.name, request=request),
            'scores': reverse(PlayerScoreList.name, request=request)
            })
```

The `ApiRoot` class is a subclass of the `rest_framework.generics.GenericAPIView` class and declares the get method. The `GenericAPIView` class is the base class for all the other generic views. The `ApiRoot` class defines the `get` method that returns a `Response` object with key-value pairs of string that provide a descriptive name for the view and its URL, generated with the `rest_framework.reverse.reverse` function. This URL resolver function returns a fully qualified URL for the view.

Go to the `gamesapi/games` folder and open the `urls.py` file. Replace the code in this file with the following code. The following lines show the code for this file that defines the URL patterns that specifies the regular expressions that have to be matched in the request to run a specific method for a class-based view defined in the `views.py` file. Instead of specifying a function that represents a view we call the `as_view` method for the class-based view. We use the `as_view` method. The code file for the sample is included in the `restful_python_chapter_02_03` folder:

```python
from django.conf.urls import url
from games import views


urlpatterns = [
    url(r'^game-categories/$',
        views.GameCategoryList.as_view(),
        name=views.GameCategoryList.name),
    url(r'^game-categories/(?P<pk>[0-9]+)/$',
        views.GameCategoryDetail.as_view(),
        name=views.GameCategoryDetail.name),
    url(r'^games/$',
        views.GameList.as_view(),
        name=views.GameList.name),
    url(r'^games/(?P<pk>[0-9]+)/$',
        views.GameDetail.as_view(),
        name=views.GameDetail.name),
    url(r'^players/$',
        views.PlayerList.as_view(),
        name=views.PlayerList.name),
    url(r'^players/(?P<pk>[0-9]+)/$',
        views.PlayerDetail.as_view(),
        name=views.PlayerDetail.name),
    url(r'^player-scores/$',
        views.PlayerScoreList.as_view(),
        name=views.PlayerScoreList.name),
    url(r'^player-scores/(?P<pk>[0-9]+)/$',
        views.PlayerScoreDetail.as_view(),
        name=views.PlayerScoreDetail.name),
    url(r'^$',
        views.ApiRoot.as_view(),
        name=views.ApiRoot.name),
]
```

When we coded our previous version of the API, we replaced the code in the urls.py file in the gamesapi folder, specifically, the gamesapi/urls.py file. We made the necessary changes to define the root URL configuration and include the URL pattern declared in the previously coded games/urls.py file.

Now, we can launch Django's development server to compose and send HTTP requests to our still unsecure, yet much more complex Web API (we will definitely add security later). Execute any of the following two commands based on your needs to access the API in other devices or computers connected to your LAN. Remember that we analyzed the difference between them in Chapter 1, *Developing RESTful APIs with Django*:

```
python manage.py runserver
python manage.py runserver 0.0.0.0:8000
```

After we run any of the previous commands, the development server will start listening at port 8000.

Open a web browser and enter http://localhost:8000/ or the appropriate URL in case you are using another computer or device to access the browsable API. The browsable API will compose and send a GET request to / and will display the results of its execution, that is, the headers and the JSON response from the execution of the get method defined in the ApiRoot class within the views.py file. The following screenshot shows the rendered web page after entering the URL in a web browser with the resource description: **Api Root**.

The API Root provides us hyperlinks to see the list of game categories, games, players, and scores. This way, it becomes extremely easy to access the lists and perform operations on the different resources through the browsable API. In addition, when we visit the other URLs, the breadcrumb will allow us to go back to the **Api Root**.

In this new version of the API, we worked with the generic views that provide many featured under the hoods, and therefore, the browsable API will provide us additional features compared with the previous version. Click or tap on the URL on the right-hand side of **game-categories**. In case you are browsing in localhost, the URL will be http://localhost:8000/game-categories/. The browsable API will render the web page for the **Game Category List**.

At the bottom of the rendered web page, the browsable API provides us some controls to generate a POST request to /game-categories/. In this case, by default, the browsable API displays the HTML form tab with an automatically generated form that we can use to generate a POST request without having to deal with the raw data as we did in our previous version. The HTML forms make it easy to generate requests to test our API. The following screenshot shows the HTML form to create a new game category:

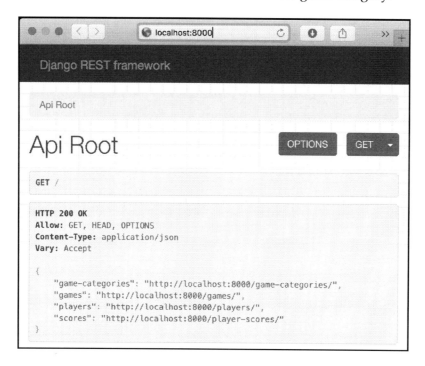

We just need to enter the desired name, **3D RPG**, in the **Name** textbox and click or tap on **POST** to create a new game category. The browsable API will compose and send a POST request to /game-categories/ with the previously specified data and we will see the results of the call in the web browser. The following screenshot shows a web browser displaying the HTTP status code 201 Created in the response and the previously explained HTML form with the **POST** button to allow us to continue composing and sending POST requests to /game-categories/:

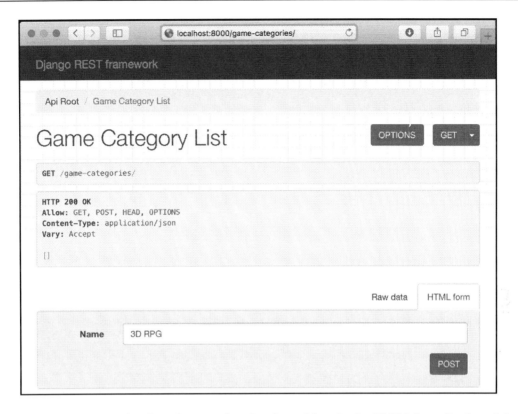

Now, click on the URL displayed as a value for the url key in the JSON data displayed for the game category, such as `http://localhost:8000/game-categories/3/`. Make sure you replace 2 with the id or primary key of an existing game category in the previously rendered **Games List**. The browsable API will compose and send a `GET` request to `/game-categories/3/` and will display the results of its execution, that is, the headers and the JSON data for the game category. The web page will display a **DELETE** button because we are working with the **Game Category Detail** view.

> We can use the breadcrumb to go back to the Api Root and start creating games related to a game category, players, and finally scores related to a game and a player. We can do all this with easy to use HTML forms and the browsable API feature.

Creating and retrieving related resources

Now, we will use the HTTPie command or its curl equivalents to compose and send HTTP requests to the API. We will use JSON for the requests that require additional data. Remember that you can perform the same tasks with your favorite GUI-based tool or with the browsable API.

First, we will compose and send an HTTP request to create a new game category. Remember that we used the browsable API to create a game category named '3D RPG'.

```
http POST :8000/game-categories/ name='2D mobile arcade'
```

The following is the equivalent `curl` command:

```
curl -iX POST -H "Content-Type: application/json" -d '{"name":"2D
mobile arcade"}' :8000/game-categories/
```

The preceding command will compose and send a POST HTTP request with the specified JSON key-value pair. The request specifies `/game-categories/`, and therefore, it will match `'^game-categories/$'` and run the `post` method for the `views.GameCategoryList` class-based view. Remember that the method is defined in the `ListCreateAPIView` superclass and it ends up calling the create method defined in `mixins.CreateModelMixin`. If the new `GameCategory` instance was successfully persisted in the database, the call to the method will return an `HTTP 201 Created` status code and the recently persisted `GameCategory` serialized to JSON in the response body. The following line shows a sample response for the HTTP request with the new `GameCategory` object in the JSON response. The response doesn't include the header. Note that the response includes both the primary key, `pk`, and the url, `url`, for the created category. The `games` array is empty because there aren't games related to the new category yet:

```
{
    "games": [],
    "name": "2D mobile arcade",
    "pk": 4,
    "url": "http://localhost:8000/game-categories/4/"
}
```

Now, we will compose and send HTTP requests to create two games that belong to the first category we recently created: 3D RPG. We will specify the game_category value with the name of the desired game category. However, the database table that persists the Game model will save the value of the primary key of the related GameCategory whose name value matches the one we provide:

```
    http POST :8000/games/ name='PvZ Garden Warfare 4' game_category='3D
RPG' played=false release_date='2016-06-21T03:02:00.776594Z'
    http POST :8000/games/ name='Superman vs Aquaman' game_category='3D
RPG' played=false release_date='2016-06-21T03:02:00.776594Z'
```

The following are the equivalent curl commands:

```
    curl -iX POST -H "Content-Type: application/json" -d '{"name":"PvZ
Garden Warfare 4", "game_category":"3D RPG", "played": "false",
"release_date": "2016-06-21T03:02:00.776594Z"}' :8000/games/
    curl -iX POST -H "Content-Type: application/json" -d '{"name":"
Superman vs Aquaman", "game_category":"3D RPG", "played": "false",
"release_date": "2016-06-21T03:02:00.776594Z"}' :8000/games/
```

The previous commands will compose and send two POST HTTP requests with the specified JSON key-value pairs. The request specifies /games/, and therefore, it will match '^games/$' and run the post method for the views.GameList class-based view. The following lines show sample responses for the two HTTP requests with the new Game objects in the JSON responses. The responses don't include the headers. Note that the response includes only the url, url, for the created games and doesn't include the primary key. The value for game_category is the name for the related GameCategory:

```
{
    "game_category": "3D RPG",
    "name": "PvZ Garden Warfare 4",
    "played": false,
    "release_date": "2016-06-21T03:02:00.776594Z",
    "url": "http://localhost:8000/games/2/"
}
{
    "game_category": "3D RPG",
    "name": "Superman vs Aquaman",
    "played": false,
    "release_date": "2016-06-21T03:02:00.776594Z",
    "url": "http://localhost:8000/games/3/"
}
```

We can run the previously explained commands to check the contents of the tables that Django created in the PostgreSQL database. We will notice that the game_category_id column for the games_game table saves the value of the primary key of the related row in the games_game_category table. The GameSerializer class uses the SlugRelatedField to display the name value for the related GameCategory. The following screenshot shows the contents of the games_game_category and the games_game table in a PostgreSQL database after running the HTTP requests:

Now, we will compose and send an HTTP request to retrieve the game category that is contains two games, that is the game category resource whose id or primary key is equal to 3. Don't forget to replace 3 with the primary key value of the game whose name is equal to '3D RPG' in your configuration:

```
http :8000/game-categories/3/
```

The following is the equivalent curl command:

```
curl -iX GET :8000/game-categories/3/
```

The previous commands will compose and send the following HTTP request: `GET http://localhost:8000/game-categories/3/`. The request has a number after `/game-categories/`, and therefore, it will match `'^game-categories/(?P<pk>[0-9]+)/$'` and run the `get` method for the `views.GameCategoryDetail` class based view. Remember that the method is defined in the `RetrieveUpdateDestroyAPIView` superclass and it ends up calling the `retrieve` method defined in `mixins.RetrieveModelMixin`. The following lines show a sample response for the HTTP request, with the `GameCategory` object and the hyperlinks of the related games in the JSON response:

```
HTTP/1.0 200 OK
Allow: GET, PUT, PATCH, DELETE, HEAD, OPTIONS
Content-Type: application/json
Date: Tue, 21 Jun 2016 23:32:04 GMT
Server: WSGIServer/0.2 CPython/3.5.1
Vary: Accept, Cookie
X-Frame-Options: SAMEORIGIN
{
    "games": [
        "http://localhost:8000/games/2/",
        "http://localhost:8000/games/3/"
    ],
    "name": "3D RPG",
    "pk": 3,
    "url": "http://localhost:8000/game-categories/3/"
}
```

The `GameCategorySerializer` class defined the `games` attribute as a `HyperlinkedRelatedField`, and therefore, the serializer renders the URL for each related `Game` instance in the value for the `games` array. If we view the results in a web browser through the browsable API, we will be able to click or tap on the hyperlink to see the details for each game.

Now, we will compose and send a `POST` HTTP request to create a game related to a game category name that doesn't exist: `'Virtual reality'`:

```
http POST :8000/games/ name='Captain America vs Thor'
game_category='Virtual reality' played=false
release_date='2016-06-21T03:02:00.776594Z'
```

The following is the equivalent curl command:

```
curl -iX POST -H "Content-Type: application/json" -d '{"name":"'Captain
America vs Thor", "game_category":"Virtual reality", "played": "false",
"release_date": "2016-06-21T03:02:00.776594Z"}' :8000/games/
```

Django won't be able to retrieve a `GameCategory` instance whose `name` is equal to the specified value, and therefore, we will receive a `400 Bad Request` status code in the response header and a message related to the value specified in for `game_category` in the JSON body. The following lines show a sample response:

```
HTTP/1.0 400 Bad Request
Allow: GET, POST, HEAD, OPTIONS
Content-Type: application/json
Date: Tue, 21 Jun 2016 23:51:19 GMT
Server: WSGIServer/0.2 CPython/3.5.1
Vary: Accept, Cookie
X-Frame-Options: SAMEORIGIN
{
    "game_category": [
        "Object with name=Virtual reality does not exist."
    ]
}
```

Now, we will compose and send HTTP requests to create two players:

```
http POST :8000/players/ name='Brandon' gender='M'
http POST :8000/players/ name='Kevin' gender='M'
```

The following are the equivalent `curl` commands:

```
curl -iX POST -H "Content-Type: application/json" -d
'{"name":"Brandon", "gender":"M"}' :8000/players/
curl -iX POST -H "Content-Type: application/json" -d '{"name":" Kevin",
"gender":"M"}' :8000/players/
```

The previous commands will compose and send two POST HTTP requests with the specified JSON key-value pairs. The request specifies /players/, and therefore, it will match '^players/$' and run the post method for the `views.PlayerList` class based view. The following lines show sample responses for the two HTTP requests with the new `Player` objects in the JSON responses. The responses don't include the headers. Notice that the response includes only the url, `url`, for the created players and doesn't include the primary key. The value for `gender_description` is the choice description for the `gender` char. The `scores` array is empty because there aren't scores related to each new player yet:

```
{
    "gender": "M",
    "name": "Brandon",
    "scores": [],
    "url": "http://localhost:8000/players/2/"
}
{
```

```
    "gender": "M",
    "name": "Kevin",
    "scores": [],
    "url": "http://localhost:8000/players/3/"
}
```

Now, we will compose and send HTTP requests to create four scores:

```
    http POST :8000/player-scores/ score=35000
score_date='2016-06-21T03:02:00.776594Z' player='Brandon' game='PvZ Garden
Warfare 4'
    http POST :8000/player-scores/ score=85125
score_date='2016-06-22T01:02:00.776594Z' player='Brandon' game='PvZ Garden
Warfare 4'
    http POST :8000/player-scores/ score=123200
score_date='2016-06-22T03:02:00.776594Z' player='Kevin' game='Superman vs
Aquaman'
    http POST :8000/player-scores/ score=11200
score_date='2016-06-22T05:02:00.776594Z' player='Kevin' game='PvZ Garden
Warfare 4'
```

The following are the equivalent curl commands:

```
    curl -iX POST -H "Content-Type: application/json" -d '{"score":"35000",
"score_date":"2016-06-21T03:02:00.776594Z", "player":"Brandon", "game":"PvZ
Garden Warfare 4"}' :8000/player-scores/
    curl -iX POST -H "Content-Type: application/json" -d '{"score":"85125",
"score_date":"2016-06-22T01:02:00.776594Z", "player":"Brandon", "game":"PvZ
Garden Warfare 4"}' :8000/player-scores/
    curl -iX POST -H "Content-Type: application/json" -d
'{"score":"123200", "score_date":"2016-06-22T03:02:00.776594Z",
"player":"Kevin", "game":"'Superman vs Aquaman"}' :8000/player-scores/
    curl -iX POST -H "Content-Type: application/json" -d '{"score":"11200",
"score_date":"2016-06-22T05:02:00.776594Z", "player":"Kevin", "game":"PvZ
Garden Warfare 4"}' :8000/player-scores/
```

The previous commands will compose and send four POST HTTP requests with the specified JSON key-value pairs. The request specifies /player-scores/, and therefore, it will match '^player-scores/$' and run the post method for the views.PlayerScoreList class based view. The following lines show sample responses for the four HTTP requests with the new Player objects in the JSON responses. The responses don't include the headers.

Django REST Framework uses the `PlayerScoreSerializer` class to generate the JSON response. Thus, the value for `game` is the name for the related `Game` instance and the value for `player` is the name for the related `Player` instance. The `PlayerScoreSerializer` class used `SlugRelatedField` for both fields:

```
{
    "game": "PvZ Garden Warfare 4",
    "pk": 3,
    "player": "Brandon",
    "score": 35000,
    "score_date": "2016-06-21T03:02:00.776594Z",
    "url": "http://localhost:8000/player-scores/3/"
}
{
    "game": "PvZ Garden Warfare 4",
    "pk": 4,
    "player": "Brandon",
    "score": 85125,
    "score_date": "2016-06-22T01:02:00.776594Z",
    "url": "http://localhost:8000/player-scores/4/"
}
{
    "game": "Superman vs Aquaman",
    "pk": 5,
    "player": "Kevin",
    "score": 123200,
    "score_date": "2016-06-22T03:02:00.776594Z",
    "url": "http://localhost:8000/player-scores/5/"
}
{
    "game": "PvZ Garden Warfare 4",
    "pk": 6,
    "player": "Kevin",
    "score": 11200,
    "score_date": "2016-06-22T05:02:00.776594Z",
    "url": "http://localhost:8000/player-scores/6/"
}
```

We can run the previously explained commands to check the contents of the tables that Django created in the PostgreSQL database. We will notice that the `game_id` column for the `games_playerscore` table saves the value of the primary key of the related row in the `games_game` table. In addition, the `player_id` column for the `games_playerscore` table saves the value of the primary key of the related row in the `games_player` table. The following screenshot shows the contents for the `games_game_category`, `games_game`, `games_player` and `games_playerscore` tables in a PostgreSQL database after running the HTTP requests:

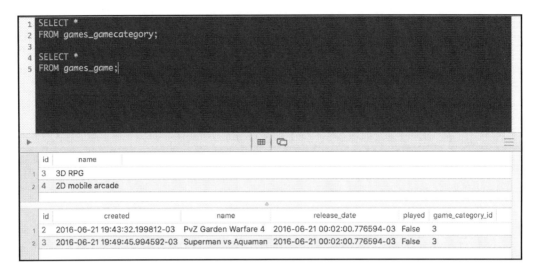

Now, we will compose and send an HTTP request to retrieve a specific player that contains two scores, which is the player resource whose id or primary key is equal to 3. Don't forget to replace 3 with the primary key value of the player whose name is equal to 'Kevin' in your configuration:

```
http :8000/players/3/
```

The following is the equivalent curl command:

```
curl -iX GET :8000/players/3/
```

The previous commands will compose and send the following HTTP request: GET http://localhost:8000/players/3/. The request has a number after /players/, and therefore, it will match '^players/(?P<pk>[0-9]+)/$' and run the get method for the views.PlayerDetail class based view. Remember that the method is defined in the RetrieveUpdateDestroyAPIView superclass and it ends up calling the retrieve method defined in mixins.RetrieveModelMixin. The following lines show a sample response for the HTTP request, with the Player object, the related PlayerScore objects and the Game object related to each PlayerScore object in the JSON response:

```
HTTP 200 OK
Allow: GET, PUT, PATCH, DELETE, HEAD, OPTIONS
Content-Type: application/json
Vary: Accept
{
    "url": "http://localhost:8000/players/3/",
    "name": "Kevin",
    "gender": "M",
```

```
    "gender_description": "Male",
    "scores": [
        {
            "url": "http://localhost:8000/player-scores/5/",
            "pk": 5,
            "score": 123200,
            "score_date": "2016-06-22T03:02:00.776594Z",
            "game": {
                "url": "http://localhost:8000/games/3/",
                "game_category": "3D RPG",
                "name": "Superman vs Aquaman",
                "release_date": "2016-06-21T03:02:00.776594Z",
                "played": false
            }
        },
        {
            "url": "http://localhost:8000/player-scores/6/",
            "pk": 6,
            "score": 11200,
            "score_date": "2016-06-22T05:02:00.776594Z",
            "game": {
                "url": "http://localhost:8000/games/2/",
                "game_category": "3D RPG",
                "name": "PvZ Garden Warfare 4",
                "release_date": "2016-06-21T03:02:00.776594Z",
                "played": false
            }
        }
    ]
}
```

The `PlayerSerializer` class defined the `scores` attribute as a `ScoreSerializer` with `many` equal to `True`, and therefore, this serializer renders each score related to the player. The `ScoreSerializer` class defined the `game` attribute as a `GameSerializer`, and therefore, this serializer renders each game related to the score. If we view the results in a web browser through the browsable API, we will be able to click or tap on the hyperlink of each of the related resources. However, in this case, we also see all their details without having to follow the hyperlink.

Test your knowledge

1. Under the hoods, the `@api_view` decorator is:
    1. A wrapper that converts a function-based view into a subclass of the `rest_framework.views.APIView` class.

2. A wrapper that converts a function-based view into a serializer.
3. A wrapper that converts a function-based view into a subclass of the `rest_framework.views.api_view` class.

2. The browsable API, a feature included in Django REST Framework that:
    1. Generates human-friendly JSON output for each resource whenever the request specifies `application/json` as the value for the `Content-type` key in the request header.
    2. Generates human-friendly HTML output for each resource whenever the request specifies `text/html` as the value for the `Content-type` key in the request header.
    3. Generates human-friendly HTML output for each resource whenever the request specifies `application/json` as the value for the `Content-type` key in the request header.

3. The `rest_framework.serializers.ModelSerializer` class:
    1. Automatically populates both a set of default constraints and a set of default parsers.
    2. populates both a set of default fields but doesn't automatically populate a set of default validators.

    Automatically populates both a set of default fields but doesn't automatically populate a set of default validators. Automatically populates both a set of default fields and a set of default validators.

4. The `rest_framework.serializers.ModelSerializer` class:
    1. Provides default implementations for the `get` and `patch` methods.
    2. Provides default implementations for the `get` and `put` methods.
    3. Provides default implementations for the `create` and `update` methods.

5. The `Serializer` and `ModelSerializer` classes in Django REST Framework are similar to the following two classes in Django Web Framework:
    1. `Form` and `ModelForm` classes.
    2. `View` and `ModelView` classes.
    3. `Controller` and `ModelController` classes.

Summary

In this chapter, we took advantage of the various features included in Django REST Framework that allowed us to eliminate duplicate code and build our API reusing generalized behaviors. We used model serializers, wrappers, default parsing, and rendering options, class based views, and generic classes.

We used the browsable API feature and we designed a RESTful API that interacted with a complex PostgreSQL database. We declared relationships with the models, managed serialization and deserialization with relationships, and hyperlinks. Finally, we created and retrieved related resources and we understood how things work under the hoods.

Now that we have built a complex API with Django REST Framework, we will use additional abstractions included in the framework to improve our API, we will add security and authentication, which is what we are going to discuss in the next chapter.

3

Improving and Adding Authentication to an API With Django

In this chapter, we will improve the RESTful API that we started in the previous chapter and also add authentication related security to it. We will:

- Add unique constraints to the models
- Update a single field for a resource with the PATCH method
- Take advantage of pagination
- Customize pagination classes
- Understand authentication, permissions and throttling
- Add security-related data to the models
- Create a customized permission class for object-level permissions
- Persist the user that makes a request
- Configure permission policies
- Set a default value for a new required field in migrations
- Compose requests with the necessary authentication
- Browse the API with authentication credentials

Adding unique constraints to the models

Our API has a few issues that we need to solve. Right now, it is possible to create many game categories with the same name. We shouldn't be able to do so, and therefore, we will make the necessary changes to the GameCategory model to add a unique constraint on the name field. We will also add a unique constraint on the name field for the Game and Player models. This way, we will learn the necessary steps to make changes to the constraints for many models and reflect the changes in the underlying database through migrations.

Make sure that you quit Django's development server. Remember that you just need to press *Ctrl + C* in the terminal or Command Prompt window in which it is running. Now, we will make changes to introduce unique constraints to the name field for the models that we use to represent and persist the game categories, games, and players. Open the games/models.py, file and replace the code that declares the GameCategory, Game and Player classes with the following code. The three lines that change are highlighted in the code listing. The code for the PlayerScore class remains the same. The code file for the sample is included in the restful_python_chapter_03_01 folder, as shown:

```python
class GameCategory(models.Model):
    name = models.CharField(max_length=200, unique=True)

    class Meta:
        ordering = ('name',)

    def __str__(self):
        return self.name


class Game(models.Model):
    created = models.DateTimeField(auto_now_add=True)
    name = models.CharField(max_length=200, unique=True)
    game_category = models.ForeignKey(
        GameCategory,
        related_name='games',
        on_delete=models.CASCADE)
    release_date = models.DateTimeField()
    played = models.BooleanField(default=False)

    class Meta:
        ordering = ('name',)

    def __str__(self):
        return self.name
```

```
class Player(models.Model):
    MALE = 'M'
    FEMALE = 'F'
    GENDER_CHOICES = (
        (MALE, 'Male'),
        (FEMALE, 'Female'),
    )
    created = models.DateTimeField(auto_now_add=True)
    name = models.CharField(max_length=50, blank=False, default='',
unique=True)
    gender = models.CharField(
        max_length=2,
        choices=GENDER_CHOICES,
        default=MALE,
    )

    class Meta:
        ordering = ('name',)

    def __str__(self):
        return self.name
```

We just needed to add `unique=True` as one of the named arguments for `models.CharField`. This way, we indicate that the field must be unique and Django will create the necessary unique constraints for the fields in the underlying database tables.

Now, run the following Python script to generate the migrations that will allow us to synchronize the database with the unique constraints we added for the fields in the models:

```
python manage.py makemigrations games
```

The following lines show the output generated after running the previous command:

```
Migrations for 'games':
  0002_auto_20160623_2131.py:
    - Alter field name on game
    - Alter field name on gamecategory
    - Alter field name on player
```

The output indicates that the
`gamesapi/games/migrations/0002_auto_20160623_2131.py` file includes the code to
alter the field named `name` on `game`, `gamecategory`, and `player`. Note that the generated
file name will be different in your configuration because it includes an encoded date and
time. The following lines show the code for this file, which was automatically generated by
Django. The code file for the sample is included in the `restful_python_chapter_03_01`
folder:

```
# -*- coding: utf-8 -*-
# Generated by Django 1.9.7 on 2016-06-23 21:31
from __future__ import unicode_literals

from django.db import migrations, models


class Migration(migrations.Migration):

    dependencies = [
        ('games', '0001_initial'),
    ]

    operations = [
        migrations.AlterField(
            model_name='game',
            name='name',
            field=models.CharField(max_length=200, unique=True),
        ),
        migrations.AlterField(
            model_name='gamecategory',
            name='name',
            field=models.CharField(max_length=200, unique=True),
        ),
        migrations.AlterField(
            model_name='player',
            name='name',
            field=models.CharField(default='', max_length=50, unique=True),
        ),
    ]
```

The code defines a subclass of the `django.db.migrations.Migration` class named
`Migration` that defines an `operations` list with many `migrations.AlterField`. Each
`migrations.AlterField` will alter the field in the the table for each of the related models.

Now, run the following Python script to apply all the generated migrations and execute the changes in the database tables:

```
python manage.py migrate
```

The following lines show the output generated after running the previous command. Note that the ordering for the migrations might be different in your configuration.

```
Operations to perform:
Operations to perform:
  Apply all migrations: admin, auth, contenttypes, games, sessions
Running migrations:
  Rendering model states... DONE
  Applying games.0002_auto_20160623_2131... OK
```

After we run the preceding command, we will have unique indexes on the name field for the `games_game`, `games_gamecategory`, and `games_player` tables in the PostgreSQL database. We can use the PostgreSQL command line or any other application that allows us to easily check the contents of the PostreSQL database to check the tables that Django updated. In case you decide to continue working with SQLite, use the commands or tools related to this database.

Now, we can launch Django's development server to compose and send HTTP requests. Execute any of the following two commands based on your needs to access the API in other devices or computers connected to your LAN. Remember that we analyzed the difference between them in `Chapter 1`, *Developing RESTful APIs with Django*:

```
python manage.py runserver
python manage.py runserver 0.0.0.0:8000
```

After we run any of the previous commands, the development server will start listening at port `8000`.

Now, we will compose and send an HTTP request to create a game category with a name that already exists: `'3D RPG'`:

```
http POST :8000/game-categories/ name='3D RPG'
```

The following is the equivalent `curl` command:

```
curl -iX POST -H "Content-Type: application/json" -d '{"name":"3D
RPG"}'
  :8000/game-categories/
```

Django won't be able to persist a `GameCategory` instance whose `name` is equal to the specified value because it would violate the unique constraint added to the `name` field. Thus, we will receive a `400 Bad Request` status code in the response header and a message related to the value specified for `name` in the JSON body. The following lines show a sample response:

```
HTTP/1.0 400 Bad Request
Allow: GET, POST, HEAD, OPTIONS
Content-Type: application/json
Date: Sun, 26 Jun 2016 03:37:05 GMT
Server: WSGIServer/0.2 CPython/3.5.1
Vary: Accept, Cookie
X-Frame-Options: SAMEORIGIN
{
    "name": [
        "GameCategory with this name already exists."
    ]
}
```

After we have made the changes, we won't be able to add duplicate values for the `name` field in game categories, games, or players. This way, we can be sure that whenever we specify the name of any of these resources, we are going to reference the same unique resource.

Updating a single field for a resource with the PATCH method

As we explained in `Chapter 2`, *Working with Class-Based Views and Hyperlinked APIs in Django*, our API can update a single field for an existing resource, and therefore, we provide an implementation for the `PATCH` method. For example, we can use the `PATCH` method to update an existing game and set the value for its `played` field to `true`. We don't want to use the `PUT` method because this method is meant to replace an entire game. The `PATCH` method is meant to apply a delta to an existing game, and therefore, it is the appropriate method to just change the value of the `played` field.

Now, we will compose and send an HTTP request to update an existing game, specifically, to update the value of the `played` field and set it to `true` because we just want to update a single field, we will use the `PATCH` method instead of `PUT`. Make sure you replace 2 with the id or primary key of an existing game in your configuration:

```
http PATCH :8000/games/2/ played=true
```

The following is the equivalent curl command:

```
curl -iX PATCH -H "Content-Type: application/json" -d
'{"played":"true"}'
    :8000/games/2/
```

The preceding command will compose and send a `PATCH` HTTP request with the specified JSON key-value pair. The request has a number after `/games/`, and therefore, it will match `'^games/(?P<pk>[0-9]+)/$'` and run the `patch` method for the `views.GameDetail` class-based view. Remember that the method is defined in the `RetrieveUpdateDestroyAPIView` superclass and it ends up calling the `update` method defined in `mixins.UpdateModelMixin`. If the `Game` instances with the updated value for the `played` field are valid and were successfully persisted in the database, the call to the method will return a `200 OK` status code and the recently updated `Game` serialized to JSON in the response body. The following lines show a sample response:

```
HTTP/1.0 200 OK
Allow: GET, PUT, PATCH, DELETE, HEAD, OPTIONS
Content-Type: application/json
Date: Sun, 26 Jun 2016 04:09:22 GMT
Server: WSGIServer/0.2 CPython/3.5.1
Vary: Accept, Cookie
X-Frame-Options: SAMEORIGIN
{
    "game_category": "3D RPG",
    "name": "PvZ Garden Warfare 4",
    "played": true,
    "release_date": "2016-06-21T03:02:00.776594Z",
    "url": "http://localhost:8000/games/2/"
}
```

Taking advantage of pagination

Our database has a few rows in each of the tables that persist the models we have defined. However, after we start working with our API in a real-life production environment, we will have thousands of player scores, players, games, and game categories, and therefore, we will have to deal with large result sets. We can take advantage of the pagination features available in Django REST Framework to make it easy to specify how we want large results sets to be split into individual pages of data.

First, we will compose and send HTTP requests to create 10 games that belong to one of the categories we have created: `2D mobile arcade`. This way, we will have a total of 12 games that persist in the database. We had 2 games and we will add 10 more:

```
    http POST :8000/games/ name='Tetris Reloaded' game_category='2D mobile
arcade' played=false release_date='2016-06-21T03:02:00.776594Z'
    http POST :8000/games/ name='Puzzle Craft' game_category='2D mobile
arcade' played=false release_date='2016-06-21T03:02:00.776594Z'
    http POST :8000/games/ name='Blek' game_category='2D mobile arcade'
played=false release_date='2016-06-21T03:02:00.776594Z'
    http POST :8000/games/ name='Scribblenauts Unlimited' game_category='2D
mobile arcade' played=false release_date='2016-06-21T03:02:00.776594Z'
    http POST :8000/games/ name='Cut the Rope: Magic' game_category='2D
mobile arcade' played=false release_date='2016-06-21T03:02:00.776594Z'
    http POST :8000/games/ name='Tiny Dice Dungeon' game_category='2D
mobile arcade' played=false release_date='2016-06-21T03:02:00.776594Z'
    http POST :8000/games/ name='A Dark Room' game_category='2D mobile
arcade' played=false release_date='2016-06-21T03:02:00.776594Z'
    http POST :8000/games/ name='Bastion' game_category='2D mobile arcade'
played=false release_date='2016-06-21T03:02:00.776594Z'
    http POST :8000/games/ name='Welcome to the Dungeon' game_category='2D
mobile arcade' played=false release_date='2016-06-21T03:02:00.776594Z'
    http POST :8000/games/ name='Dust: An Elysian Tail' game_category='2D
mobile arcade' played=false release_date='2016-06-21T03:02:00.776594Z'
```

The following are the equivalent `curl` commands:

```
    curl -iX POST -H "Content-Type: application/json" -d '{"name":"Tetris
Reloaded", "game_category":"2D mobile arcade", "played": "false",
"release_date": "2016-06-21T03:02:00.776594Z"}' :8000/games/
    curl -iX POST -H "Content-Type: application/json" -d '{"name":"Puzzle
Craft", "game_category":"2D mobile arcade", "played": "false",
"release_date": "2016-06-21T03:02:00.776594Z"}' :8000/games/
    curl -iX POST -H "Content-Type: application/json" -d '{"name":"Blek",
"game_category":"2D mobile arcade", "played": "false", "release_date":
"2016-06-21T03:02:00.776594Z"}' :8000/games/
    curl -iX POST -H "Content-Type: application/json" -d
```

```
'{"name":"Scribblenauts Unlimited", "game_category":"2D mobile arcade",
"played": "false", "release_date": "2016-06-21T03:02:00.776594Z"}'
:8000/games/
    curl -iX POST -H "Content-Type: application/json" -d '{"name":"Cut the
Rope: Magic", "game_category":"2D mobile arcade", "played": "false",
"release_date": "2016-06-21T03:02:00.776594Z"}' :8000/games/
    curl -iX POST -H "Content-Type: application/json" -d '{"name":"Tiny
Dice Dungeon", "game_category":"2D mobile arcade", "played": "false",
"release_date": "2016-06-21T03:02:00.776594Z"}' :8000/games/
    curl -iX POST -H "Content-Type: application/json" -d '{"name":"A Dark
Room", "game_category":"2D mobile arcade", "played": "false",
"release_date": "2016-06-21T03:02:00.776594Z"}' :8000/games/
    curl -iX POST -H "Content-Type: application/json" -d
'{"name":"Bastion", "game_category":"2D mobile arcade", "played": "false",
"release_date": "2016-06-21T03:02:00.776594Z"}' :8000/games/
    curl -iX POST -H "Content-Type: application/json" -d '{"name":"Welcome
to the Dungeon", "game_category":"2D mobile arcade", "played": "false",
"release_date": "2016-06-21T03:02:00.776594Z"}' :8000/games/
    curl -iX POST -H "Content-Type: application/json" -d '{"name":"Dust: An
Elysian Tail", "game_category":"2D mobile arcade", "played": "false",
"release_date": "2016-06-21T03:02:00.776594Z"}' :8000/games/
```

The preceding commands will compose and send ten POST HTTP requests with the specified JSON key-value pairs. The request specifies /games/, and therefore, it will match '^games/$' and run the post method for the views.GameList class-based view.

Now, we have 12 games in our database. However, we don't want to retrieve the 12 games when we compose and send a GET HTTP request to /games/. We will configure one of the customizable pagination styles included in Django REST Framework to include a maximum of five resources in each individual page of data.

 Our API uses the generic views that work with the mixin classes that can handle paginated responses, and therefore, they will automatically take into account the pagination settings we configure in Django REST Framework.

Open the gamesapi/settings.py file and add the following lines that declare a dictionary named REST_FRAMEWORK with key-value pairs that configure the global pagination settings. The code file for the sample is included in the restful_python_chapter_03_02 folder:

```
REST_FRAMEWORK = {
    'DEFAULT_PAGINATION_CLASS':
    'rest_framework.pagination.LimitOffsetPagination',
    'PAGE_SIZE': 5
}
```

The value for the `DEFAULT_PAGINATION_CLASS` settings key specifies a global setting with the default pagination class that the generic views will use to provide paginated responses. In this case, we will use the `rest_framework.pagination.LimitOffsetPagination` class, that provides a limit/offset-based style. This pagination style works with `limit` that indicates the maximum number of items to return and an `offset` that specifies the starting position of the query. The value for the `PAGE_SIZE` settings key specifies a global setting with the default value for the `limit`, also known as page size. We can specify a different limit when we perform the HTTP request by specifying the desired value in the `limit` query parameter. We can configure the class to have the maximum `limit` value in order to avoid the undesired huge result sets.

Now, we will compose and send an HTTP request to retrieve all the games, specifically the following HTTP `GET` method to `/games/`:

```
http GET :8000/games/
```

The following is the equivalent `curl` command:

```
curl -iX GET :8000/games/
```

The generic views will use the new settings that we added to enable the offset/limit pagination and the result will provide us the first 5 game resources (`results` key), the total number of games for the query (`count` key), and a link to the next (`next` key) and previous (`previous` key) pages. In this case, the resultset is the first page, and therefore, the link to the previous page (`previous` key) is `null`. We will receive a `200 OK` status code in the response header and the 5 games in the `results` array:

```
HTTP/1.0 200 OK
Allow: GET, POST, HEAD, OPTIONS
Content-Type: application/json
Date: Fri, 01 Jul 2016 00:57:55 GMT
Server: WSGIServer/0.2 CPython/3.5.1
Vary: Accept, Cookie
X-Frame-Options: SAMEORIGIN
{
    "count": 12,
    "next": "http://localhost:8000/games/?limit=5&offset=5",
    "previous": null,
    "results": [
        {
            "game_category": "2D mobile arcade",
            "name": "A Dark Room",
            "played": false,
            "release_date": "2016-06-21T03:02:00.776594Z",
            "url": "http://localhost:8000/games/10/"
```

```
            },
            {
                "game_category": "2D mobile arcade",
                "name": "Bastion",
                "played": false,
                "release_date": "2016-06-21T03:02:00.776594Z",
                "url": "http://localhost:8000/games/11/"
            },
            {

                "game_category": "2D mobile arcade",
                "name": "Blek",
                "played": false,
                "release_date": "2016-06-21T03:02:00.776594Z",
                "url": "http://localhost:8000/games/6/"
            },
            {

                "game_category": "2D mobile arcade",
                "name": "Cut the Rope: Magic",
                "played": false,
                "release_date": "2016-06-21T03:02:00.776594Z",
                "url": "http://localhost:8000/games/8/"
            },
            {

                "game_category": "2D mobile arcade",
                "name": "Dust: An Elysian Tail",
                "played": false,
                "release_date": "2016-06-21T03:02:00.776594Z",
                "url": "http://localhost:8000/games/13/"
            }
        ]
    }
```

In the preceding HTTP request, we didn't specify any value for either the limit or offset parameters. However, as we specified the default value of limit as 5 items in the global settings, the generic views use this configuration value and provide us with the first page. If we compose and send the following HTTP request to retrieve the first page of all the games by specifying 1 for the offset value, the API will provide the same results shown before:

```
http GET ':8000/games/?offset=0'
```

The following is the equivalent `curl` command:

```
curl -iX GET ':8000/games/?offset=0'
```

If we compose and send the following HTTP request to retrieve the first page of all the games by specifying 0 for the offset value and 5 for the limit, the API will also provide the same results as shown earlier:

```
http GET ':8000/games/?limit=5&offset=0'
```

The following is the equivalent curl command:

```
curl -iX GET ':8000/games/?limit=5&offset=0'
```

Now, we will compose and send an HTTP request to retrieve the next page, that is, the second page for the games, specifically an HTTP GET method to /games/ with the offset value set to 5. Remember that the value for the next key returned in the JSON body of the previous result provides us with the URL to the next page:

```
http GET ':8000/games/?limit=5&offset=5'
```

The following is the equivalent curl command:

```
curl -iX GET ':8000/games/?limit=5&offset=5'
```

The result will provide us the second set of the 5 game resource (results key), the total number of games for the query (count key), and a link to the next (next key) and previous (previous key) pages. In this case, the resultset is the second page, and therefore, the link to the previous page (previous key) is http://localhost:8000/games/?limit=5. We will receive a 200 OK status code in the response header and the 5 games in the results array:

```
HTTP/1.0 200 OK
Allow: GET, POST, HEAD, OPTIONS
Content-Type: application/json
Date: Fri, 01 Jul 2016 01:25:10 GMT
Server: WSGIServer/0.2 CPython/3.5.1
Vary: Accept, Cookie
X-Frame-Options: SAMEORIGIN
{
    "count": 12,
    "next": "http://localhost:8000/games/?limit=5&offset=10",
    "previous": "http://localhost:8000/games/?limit=5",
    "results": [
        {
            "game_category": "2D mobile arcade",
            "name": "Puzzle Craft",
            "played": false,
            "release_date": "2016-06-21T03:02:00.776594Z",
            "url": "http://localhost:8000/games/5/"
        },
```

```
{
        "game_category": "3D RPG",
        "name": "PvZ Garden Warfare 4",
        "played": true,
        "release_date": "2016-06-21T03:02:00.776594Z",
        "url": "http://localhost:8000/games/2/"
    },
    {
        "game_category": "2D mobile arcade",
        "name": "Scribblenauts Unlimited",
        "played": false,
        "release_date": "2016-06-21T03:02:00.776594Z",
        "url": "http://localhost:8000/games/7/"
    },
    {
        "game_category": "3D RPG",
        "name": "Superman vs Aquaman",
        "played": true,
        "release_date": "2016-06-21T03:02:00.776594Z",
        "url": "http://localhost:8000/games/3/"
    },
    {
        "game_category": "2D mobile arcade",
        "name": "Tetris Reloaded",
        "played": false,
        "release_date": "2016-06-21T03:02:00.776594Z",
        "url": "http://localhost:8000/games/4/"
    }
    ]
}
```

In the preceding HTTP request, we specified values for both the limit and offset parameters. However, as we specified the default value of limit in 5 items in the global settings, the following request will produce the same results than the previous request:

```
http GET ':8000/games/?offset=5'
```

The following is the equivalent curl command:

```
curl -iX GET ':8000/games/?offset=5'
```

Finally, we will compose and send an HTTP request to retrieve the last page, that is, the third page for the games, specifically an HTTP GET method to /games/ with the offset value set to 10. Remember that the value for the next key returned in the JSON body of the previous result provides us with the URL to the next page:

```
http GET ':8000/games/?limit=5&offset=10'
```

The following is the equivalent `curl` command:

```
curl -iX GET ':8000/games/?limit=5&offset=10'
```

The result will provide us the last set with 2 game resources (`results` key), the total number of games for the query (`count` key), and a link to the next (`next` key) and previous (`previous` key) pages. In this case, the resultset is the last page, and therefore, the link to the next page (`next` key) is `null`. We will receive a `200 OK` status code in the response header and the 2 games in the `results` array:

```
HTTP/1.0 200 OK
Allow: GET, POST, HEAD, OPTIONS
Content-Type: application/json
Date: Fri, 01 Jul 2016 01:28:13 GMT
Server: WSGIServer/0.2 CPython/3.5.1
Vary: Accept, Cookie
X-Frame-Options: SAMEORIGIN
{
    "count": 12,
    "next": null,
    "previous": "http://localhost:8000/games/?limit=5&offset=5",
    "results": [
        {
            "game_category": "2D mobile arcade",
            "name": "Tiny Dice Dungeon",
            "played": false,
            "release_date": "2016-06-21T03:02:00.776594Z",
            "url": "http://localhost:8000/games/9/"
        },
        {
            "game_category": "2D mobile arcade",
            "name": "Welcome to the Dungeon",
            "played": false,
            "release_date": "2016-06-21T03:02:00.776594Z",
            "url": "http://localhost:8000/games/12/"
        }
    ]
}
```

Customizing pagination classes

The `rest_framework.pagination.LimitOffsetPagination` class that we are using to provide paginated responses declares a `max_limit` class attribute that defaults to `None`. This attribute allows us to indicate the maximum allowable limit that can be specified using the `limit` query parameter. With the default setting, there is no limit and we will be able to process requests that specify a value for `1000000` for the limit query parameter. We definitely don't want our API to be able to generate a response with a million player scores or players with a single request. Unluckily, there is no setting that allows us to change the value that the class assigns to the `max_limit` class attribute. Thus, we will create our customized version of the limit/offset pagination style provided by Django REST Framework.

Create a new Python file named `pagination.py` within the `games` folder and enter the following code which declares the new `LimitOffsetPaginationWithMaxLimit` class. The code file for the sample is included in the `restful_python_chapter_03_03` folder:

```
from rest_framework.pagination import LimitOffsetPagination


class LimitOffsetPaginationWithMaxLimit(LimitOffsetPagination):
    max_limit = 10
```

The preceding lines declare the `LimitOffsetPaginationWithMaxLimit` class as a subclass of the `rest_framework.pagination.LimitOffsetPagination` class and overrides the value specified for the `max_limit` class attribute with `10`.

Open the `gamesapi/settings.py` file and replace the line that specified the value for the `DEFAULT_PAGINATION_CLASS` key in the dictionary named `REST_FRAMEWORK` with the highlighted line. The following lines show the new declaration of the dictionary named `REST_FRAMEWORK`. The code file for the sample is included in the `restful_python_chapter_03_03` folder:

```
REST_FRAMEWORK = {
    'DEFAULT_PAGINATION_CLASS':
    'games.pagination.LimitOffsetPaginationWithMaxLimit',
    'PAGE_SIZE': 5
}
```

Now, the generic views will use the recently declared
`games.pagination.LimitOffsetPaginationWithMaxLimit` class, that provides a
limit/offset based style with a maximum `limit` value equal to `10`. If a request specifies a
value for limit higher than `10`, the class will use the maximum limit value, that is, `10`, and
we will never return more than `10` items in a paginated response.

Now, we will compose and send an HTTP request to retrieve the first page for the games,
specifically an HTTP `GET` method to `/games/` with the `limit` value set to `10000`:

```
http GET ':8000/games/?limit=10000'
```

The following is the equivalent curl command:

```
curl -iX GET ':8000/games/?limit=10000'
```

The result will use a limit value equal to `10` instead of the indicated `10000` because we are
using our customized pagination class. The result will provide us the first set with 10 game
resources (`results` key), the total number of games for the query (`count` key), and a link to
the next (`next` key) and previous (`previous` key) pages. In this case, the resultset is the first
page, and therefore, the link to the next page (`next` key) is
`http://localhost:8000/games/?limit=10&offset=10`. We will receive a `200 OK`
status code in the response header and the first `10` games in the `results` array. The
following lines show the header and the first lines of the output:

```
HTTP/1.0 200 OK
Allow: GET, POST, HEAD, OPTIONS
Content-Type: application/json
Date: Fri, 01 Jul 2016 16:34:01 GMT
Server: WSGIServer/0.2 CPython/3.5.1
Vary: Accept, Cookie
X-Frame-Options: SAMEORIGIN
{
    "count": 12,
    "next": "http://localhost:8000/games/?limit=10&offset=10",
    "previous": null,
    "results": [
        {
```

It is a good practice to configure a maximum limit to avoid generating
huge responses.

Open a web browser and enter `http://localhost:8000/games/`. Replace localhost with the IP of the computer that is running the Django development server in case you use another computer or device to run the browser. The browsable API will compose and send a `GET` request to `/games/` and will display the results of its execution, that is, the headers and the JSON games list; since we have configured pagination, the rendered web page will include the default pagination template associated with the base pagination class we are using and will display the available page numbers at the upper-right corner of the web page. The following screenshot shows the rendered web page after entering the URL in a web browser with the resource description, **Game List**, and the three pages.

Understanding authentication, permissions and throttling

Our current version of the API processes all the incoming requests without requiring any kind of authentication. Django REST Framework allows us to easily use different authentication schemes to identify the user that originated the request or the token that signed the request. Then, we can use these credentials to apply the permission and throttling policies that will determine whether the request must be permitted or not.

Similar to other configurations, we can set the authentication schemes globally and then override them if necessary in a class-based view or a function view. A list of classes specifies the authentication schemes. Django REST framework will use all the specified classes in the list to authenticate a request before running the code for the view. The first class in the list that generates a successful authentication, in case we specify more than one class, will be responsible for setting the values for the following two properties:

- `request.user`: The user model instance. We will use an instance of the `django.contrib.auth.User` class, that is, a Django `User` instance, in our examples.
- `request.auth`: Additional authentication information, such as an authentication token.

After a successful authentication, we can use the `request.user` property in our class-based view methods that receive the `request` parameter to retrieve additional information about the user that generated the request.

Django REST Framework provides the following three authentication classes in the
`rest_framework.authentication` module. All of them are subclasses of the
`BaseAuthentication` class:

- `BasicAuthentication`: Provides an HTTP Basic authentication against
  username and password. If we use in production, we must make sure that the
  API is only available over HTTPS.
- `SessionAuthentication`: Works with Django's session framework for
  authentication.
- `TokenAuthentication`: Provides a simple token based authentication. The
  request must include the token generated for a user in the `Authorization` HTTP
  header with `"Token "` as a prefix for the token.

First, we will use a combination of `BasicAuthentication` and `SessionAuthentication`.
We could also take advantage of the `TokenAuthentication` class later. Make sure you
quit the Django's development server. Remember that you just need to press *Ctrl + C* in the
terminal or command-prompt window in which it is running.

Open the `gamesapi/settings.py` file and add the highlighted lines to the dictionary
named `REST_FRAMEWORK` with a key-value pair that configures the global default
authentication classes. The code file for the sample is included in the
`restful_python_chapter_03_04` folder, as shown:

```
REST_FRAMEWORK = {
    'DEFAULT_PAGINATION_CLASS':
    'games.pagination.LimitOffsetPaginationWithMaxLimit',
    'PAGE_SIZE': 5,
    'DEFAULT_AUTHENTICATION_CLASSES': (
        'rest_framework.authentication.BasicAuthentication',
        'rest_framework.authentication.SessionAuthentication',
        )
}
```

The value for the `DEFAULT_AUTHENTICATION_CLASSES` settings key specifies a global
setting with a tuple of string whose values indicate the classes that we want to use for
authentication.

Permissions use the authentication information included in the `request.user` and
`request.auth` properties to determine whether the request should be granted or denied
access. Permissions allow us to control which classes of users will be granted or denied
access to the different features or parts of our API.

For example, we will use the permissions features in Django REST framework to allow the authenticated users to create games. Unauthenticated users will only be allowed read-only access to games. Only the user that created the game will be able to make changes to this game, and therefore, we will make the necessary changes in our API to make a game have an owner user. We will use predefined permission classes and a customized permission class to define the explained permission policies.

Throttling also determines whether the request must be authorized. Throttles control the rate of requests that users can make to our API. For example, we want to limit unauthenticated users to a maximum of 5 requests per hour. We want to restrict authenticated users to a maximum of 20 requests to the games related views per day.

Adding security-related data to the models

We will associate a game with a creator or owner. Only the authenticated users will be able to create new games. Only the creator of a game will be able to update it or delete it. All the requests that aren't authenticated will only have read-only access to games.

Open the `games/models.py` file and replace the code that declares the `Game` class with the following code. The line that changes is highlighted in the code listing. The code file for the sample is included in the `restful_python_chapter_03_04` folder.

```python
class Game(models.Model):
    owner = models.ForeignKey(
        'auth.User',
        related_name='games',
        on_delete=models.CASCADE)
    created = models.DateTimeField(auto_now_add=True)
    name = models.CharField(max_length=200, unique=True)
    game_category = models.ForeignKey(
        GameCategory,
        related_name='games',
        on_delete=models.CASCADE)
    release_date = models.DateTimeField()
    played = models.BooleanField(default=False)

    class Meta:
        ordering = ('name',)

    def __str__(self):
        return self.name
```

The `Game` model declares a new `owner` field that uses the
`django.db.models.ForeignKey` class to provide a many-to-one relationship to the
`auth.User` model, specifically, to the `django.contrib.auth.User` model. This `User`
model represents the users within the Django authentication system. The `'games'` value
specified for the `related_name` argument creates a backwards relation from the `User`
model to the `Game` model. This value indicates the name to be used for the relation from the
related `User` object back to a `Game` object. This way, we will be able to access all the games
owned by a specific user. Whenever we delete a user, we want all the games owned by this
user to be deleted too, and therefore, we specified the `models.CASCADE` value for the
`on_delete` argument.

Now, we will run the `createsuperuser` subcommand for `manage.py` to create the
`superuser` for Django that we will use to easily authenticate our requests. We will create
more users later:

```
python manage.py createsuperuser
```

The command will ask you for the `username` you want to use for the `superuser`. Enter the
desired user name and press **Enter**. We will use `superuser` as the user name for this
example. You will see a line similar to the following one:

```
Username (leave blank to use 'gaston'):
```

Then, the command will ask you for the e-mail address. Enter an e-mail address and press
Enter:

```
Email address:
```

Finally, the command will ask you for the password for the new superuser. Enter your
desired password and press *Enter*.

```
Password:
```

The command will ask you to enter the password again. Enter it and press *Enter*. If both
entered passwords match, the superuser will be created:

```
Password (again):
Superuser created successfully.
```

Now, go to the `gamesapi/games` folder and open the `serializers.py` file. Add the following code after the last line that declares the imports, before the declaration of the `GameCategorySerializer` class. The code file for the sample is included in the `restful_python_chapter_03_04` folder:

```
from django.contrib.auth.models import User


class UserGameSerializer(serializers.HyperlinkedModelSerializer):
    class Meta:
        model = Game
        fields = (
            'url',
            'name')


class UserSerializer(serializers.HyperlinkedModelSerializer):
    games = UserGameSerializer(many=True, read_only=True)

    class Meta:
        model = User
        fields = (
            'url',
            'pk',
            'username',
            'games')
```

The `UserGameSerializer` class is a subclass of the `HyperlinkedModelSerializer` class. We use this new serializer class to serialize the games related to a user. This class declares a `Meta` inner class that declares two attributes: `model` and `fields`. The `model` attribute specifies the model related to the serializer, that is, the `Game` class. The `fields` attribute specifies a tuple of string whose values indicate the field names that we want to include in the serialization from the related model. We just want to include the URL and the game's name, and therefore, the code specified `'url'` and `'name'` as members of the tuple. We don't want to use the `GameSerializer` serializer class for the games related to a user because we want to serialize fewer fields, and therefore, we created the `UserGameSerializer` class.

The `UserSerializer` class is a subclass of the `HyperlinkedModelSerializer` class. This class declares a `Meta` inner class that declares two attributes-`model` and `fields`. The `model` attribute specifies the model related to the serializer, that is, the `django.contrib.auth.models.User` class.

The `UserSerializer` class declares a `games` attribute as an instance of the previously explained `UserGameSerializer` with `many` and `read_only` equal to `True` because it is a one-to-many relationship and it is read-only. We use the `games` name that we specified as the `related_name` string value when we added the `owner` field as a `models.ForeignKey` instance in the `Game` model. This way, the `games` field will provide us with an array of URLs and names for each game that belongs to the user.

We will make more changes to the `serializers.py` file in the `gamesapi/games` folder. We will add an `owner` field to the existing `GameSerializer` class. The following lines show the new code for the `GameSerializer` class. The new lines are highlighted. The code file for the sample is included in the `restful_python_chapter_03_04` folder:

```
class GameSerializer(serializers.HyperlinkedModelSerializer):
    # We just want to display the owner username (read-only)
    owner = serializers.ReadOnlyField(source='owner.username')
    # We want to display the game cagory's name instead of the id
    game_category =
serializers.SlugRelatedField(queryset=GameCategory.objects.all(),
slug_field='name')

    class Meta:
        model = Game
        depth = 4
        fields = (
                'url',
                'owner',
                'game_category',
                'name',
                'release_date',
                'played')
```

Now, the `GameSerializer` class declares an `owner` attribute as an instance of `serializers.ReadOnlyField` with `source` equal to `'owner.username'`. This way, we will serialize the value for the `username` field of the related `django.contrib.auth.User` hold in the `owner` field. We use the `ReadOnlyField` because the owner is automatically populated when an authenticated user creates a game, and therefore, it won't be possible to change the owner after a game has been created. This way, the `owner` field will provide us with the user name that created the game. In addition, we added `'owner'` to the field's string tuple.

Creating a customized permission class for object-level permissions

Create a new Python file named `permissions.py` within the `games` folder and enter the following code that, declares the new `IsOwnerOrReadOnly` class. The code file for the sample is included in the `restful_python_chapter_03_04` folder:

```
from rest_framework import permissions


class IsOwnerOrReadOnly(permissions.BasePermission):
    def has_object_permission(self, request, view, obj):
        if request.method in permissions.SAFE_METHODS:
            return True
        else:
            return obj.owner == request.user
```

The `rest_framework.permissions.BasePermission` class is the base class from which all permission classes should inherit. The previous lines declare the `IsOwnerOrReadOnly` class as a subclass of the `BasePermission` class and overrides the `has_object_permission` method defined in the superclass that returns a `bool` value indicating whether the permission should be granted or not. If the HTTP verb specified in the request (`request.method`) is any of the three safe methods specified in `permission.SAFE_METHODS` (GET, HEAD , or OPTIONS), the `has_object_permission` method returns `True` and grants permission to the request. These HTTP verbs do not make changes to the related resources, and therefore, they are included in the `permissions.SAFE_METHODS` tuple of string.

If the HTTP verb specified in the request (`request.method`) is not any of the three safe methods, the code returns `True` and grants permission only when the `owner` attribute of the received `obj` (`obj.owner`) matches the user that created the request (`request.user`). This way, only the owner of the related resource will be granted permission to requests that include HTTP verbs that aren't safe.

We will use the new `IsOwnerOrReadOnly` permission class to make sure that only the game owners can make changes to an existing game. We will combine this permission class with the `rest_framework.permissions.IsAuthenticatedOrReadOnly` permission class that only allows read-only access to resources when the request is not authenticated as a user.

Persisting the user that makes a request

We want to be able to list all the users and retrieve the details for a single user. We will create subclasses of the two following generic class views declared in `rest_framework.generics`:

- `ListAPIView`: Implements the `get` method that retrieves a listing of a queryset
- `RetrieveAPIView`: Implements the `get` method to retrieve a model instance

Go to the `gamesapi/games` folder and open the `views.py` file. Add the following code after the last line that declares the imports, before the declaration of the `GameCategoryList` class. The code file for the sample is included in the `restful_python_chapter_03_04` folder:

```python
from django.contrib.auth.models import User
from games.serializers import UserSerializer
from rest_framework import permissions
from games.permissions import IsOwnerOrReadOnly


class UserList(generics.ListAPIView):
    queryset = User.objects.all()
    serializer_class = UserSerializer
    name = 'user-list'


class UserDetail(generics.RetrieveAPIView):
    queryset = User.objects.all()
    serializer_class = UserSerializer
    name = 'user-detail'
```

Add the following highlighted lines to the ApiRoot class declared in the `views.py` file. Now, we will be able to navigate to the user-related views throughout the browsable API. The code file for the sample is included in the `restful_python_chapter_03_04` folder.

```python
class ApiRoot(generics.GenericAPIView):
    name = 'api-root'
    def get(self, request, *args, **kwargs):
        return Response({
            'players': reverse(PlayerList.name, request=request),
            'game-categories': reverse(GameCategoryList.name,
request=request),
            'games': reverse(GameList.name, request=request),
            'scores': reverse(PlayerScoreList.name, request=request),
            'users': reverse(UserList.name, request=request),
```

```
})
```

Go to the `gamesapi/games` folder and open the `urls.py` file. Add the following elements to the `urlpatterns` string list. The new strings define the URL patterns that specify the regular expressions that have to be matched in the request to run a specific method for the previously created class based-views in the `views.py` file: `UserList` and `UserDetail`. The code file for the sample is included in the `restful_python_chapter_03_04` folder:

```
url(r'^users/$',
    views.UserList.as_view(),
    name=views.UserList.name),
url(r'^users/(?P<pk>[0-9]+)/$',
    views.UserDetail.as_view(),
    name=views.UserDetail.name),
```

We have to add a line in the `urls.py` file in the `gamesapi` folder, specifically, the `gamesapi/urls.py` file. The file defines the root URL configurations and we want to include the URL patterns to allow the browsable API to display the login and logout views. The following lines show the new code for the `gamesapi/urls.py` file. The new line is highlighted. The code file for the sample is included in the `restful_python_chapter_03_04` folder:

```
from django.conf.urls import url, include

urlpatterns = [
    url(r'^', include('games.urls')),
    url(r'^api-auth/', include('rest_framework.urls'))
]
```

We have to make changes to the `GameList` class-based view. We will override the `perform_create` method to populate the `owner` before a new `Game` instance is persisted in the database. The following lines show the new code for the `GameList` class in the `views.py` file. The new lines are highlighted. The code file for the sample is included in the `restful_python_chapter_03_04` folder:

```
class GameList(generics.ListCreateAPIView):
    queryset = Game.objects.all()
    serializer_class = GameSerializer
    name = 'game-list'
    def perform_create(self, serializer):
        # Pass an additional owner field to the create method
        # To Set the owner to the user received in the request
        serializer.save(owner=self.request.user)
```

The `GameList` class inherits the `perform_create` method from the `rest_framework.mixins.CreateModelMixin` class. Remember that the `generics.ListCreateAPIView` class inherits from `CreateModelMixin` class and other classes. The code for the overridden `perform_create` method passes an additional `owner` field to the create method by setting a value for the `owner` argument for the call to the `serializer.save` method. The code sets the owner attribute to the value of `self.request.user`, that is, to the user associated to the request. This way, whenever a new game is persisted, it will save the user associated to the request as its owner.

Configuring permission policies

Now, we will configure permission policies for the class-based views related to games. We will override the value for the `permission_classes` class attribute for the `GameList` and `GameDetail` classes.

The following lines show the new code for the `GameList` class in the `views.py` file. The new lines are highlighted. Don't remove the code we added for the `perform_create` method for this class. The code file for the sample is included in the `restful_python_chapter_03_04` folder:

```
class GameList(generics.ListCreateAPIView):
    queryset = Game.objects.all()
    serializer_class = GameSerializer
    name = 'game-list'
    permission_classes = (
        permissions.IsAuthenticatedOrReadOnly,
        IsOwnerOrReadOnly,
        )
```

The following lines show the new code for the `GameDetail` class in the `views.py` file. The new lines are highlighted. Don't remove the code we added for the `perform_create` method for this class. The code file for the sample is included in the `restful_python_chapter_03_04` folder:

```
class GameDetail(generics.RetrieveUpdateDestroyAPIView):
    queryset = Game.objects.all()
    serializer_class = GameSerializer
    name = 'game-detail'
    permission_classes = (
        permissions.IsAuthenticatedOrReadOnly,
        IsOwnerOrReadOnly)
```

We added the same lines in the two classes. We have included the
`IsAuthenticatedOrReadOnly` class and our previously created `IsOwnerOrReadOnly`
permission class in the `permission_classes` tuple.

Setting a default value for a new required field in migrations

We have persisted many games in our database and added a new `owner` field for the games
that is a required field. We don't want to delete all the existing games, and therefore, we
will take advantage of some features in Django that make it easy for us to make the changes
in the underlying database without losing the existing data.

Now, we need to retrieve the `id` for the `superuser` we have created to use it as the default
owner for the existing games. Django will allow us to easily update the existing games to
set the owner user for them.

Run the following commands to retrieve the `id` from the `auth_user` table for the row that
whose username is equal to `'superuser'`. Replace `superuser` with the user name you
selected for the previously created superuser. In addition, replace `user_name` in the
command with the user name you used to create the PostgreSQL database and `password`
with your chosen password for this database user. The command assumes that you are
running PostgreSQL on the same computer in which you are running the command. In case
you are working with a SQLite database, you can run the equivalent command in the
PostgreSQL command line or a GUI-based tool to execute the same query.

```
psql --username=user_name --dbname=games --command="SELECT id FROM
auth_user WHERE username = 'superuser';"
```

The following lines show the output with the value for `id`: 1

```
id
----
  1
(1 row)
```

Now, run the following Python script to generate the migrations that will allow us to
synchronize the database with the new field we added to the Game model:

```
python manage.py makemigrations games
```

Django will display the following question:

```
    You are trying to add a non-nullable field 'owner' to game without a
default; we can't do that (the database needs something to populate
existing rows).
    Please select a fix:
    1) Provide a one-off default now (will be set on all existing rows)
    2) Quit, and let me add a default in models.py
    Select an option:
```

We want to provide the one-off default that will be set on all existing rows, and therefore, enter 1 to select the first option and press *Enter*.

Django will display the following text asking us to enter the default value:

```
    Please enter the default value now, as valid Python
    The datetime and django.utils.timezone modules are available, so you
can do e.g. timezone.now()
    >>>
```

Enter the value for the previously retrieved id, 1 in our example, and press Enter. The following lines show the output generated after running the preceding command:

```
    Migrations for 'games':
      0003_game_owner.py:
        - Add field owner to game
```

The output indicates that the `gamesapi/games/migrations/0003_game_owner.py` file includes the code to add the field named `owner` to `game`. The following lines show the code for this file that was automatically generated by Django. The code file for the sample is included in the `restful_python_chapter_03_04` folder:

```python
# -*- coding: utf-8 -*-
# Generated by Django 1.9.7 on 2016-07-01 21:06
from __future__ import unicode_literals
from django.conf import settings
from django.db import migrations, models
import django.db.models.deletion
class Migration(migrations.Migration):
    dependencies = [
        migrations.swappable_dependency(settings.AUTH_USER_MODEL),
        ('games', '0002_auto_20160623_2131'),
    ]
    operations = [
        migrations.AddField(
            model_name='game',
            name='owner',
```

```
              field=models.ForeignKey(default=1,
      on_delete=django.db.models.deletion.CASCADE, related_name='games',
      to=settings.AUTH_USER_MODEL),
              preserve_default=False,
          ),
      ]
```

The code declares a subclass of the `django.db.migrations.Migration` class named `Migration` that defines an `operations` list with a `migrations.AddField` that will add the the owner field to the table related to the `game` model.

Now, run the following python script to apply all the generated migrations and execute the changes in the database tables:

```
python manage.py migrate
```

The following lines show the output generated after running the previous command. Note that the ordering for the migrations might be different in your configuration:

```
Operations to perform:
  Apply all migrations: admin, auth, contenttypes, games, sessions
Running migrations:
  Rendering model states... DONE
  Applying games.0003_game_owner... OK
```

After we run the previous command, we will have a new `owner_id` field added to the `games_game` table in the PostgreSQL database. The existing rows in the `games_game` table will use the default value we indicated Django to use for the new `owner_id` field. We can use the PostgreSQL command line or any other application that allows us to easily check the contents of the PostreSQL database to check the `games_game` table that Django updated. In case you decide to continue working with SQLite, use the commands or tools related to this database.

Run the following command to launch the interactive shell. Make sure you are within the `gamesapi` folder in the Terminal or Command Prompt:

```
python manage.py shell
```

You will notice that a line that says (**InteractiveConsole**) is displayed after the usual lines that introduce your default Python interactive shell. Enter the following code in the Python interactive to create another user that is not a superuser. We will use this user and the superuser to test our changes in the permissions policies. The code file for the sample is included in the `restful_python_chapter_03_04` folder, in the `users_test_01.py` file.

You can replace `kevin` with your desired user name, `kevin@eaxmple.com` with the e-mail and `kevinpassword` with the password you want to use for this user. However, take into account that we will be using these credentials in the following sections. Make sure you always replace the credentials with your own credentials:

```
from django.contrib.auth.models import User
user = User.objects.create_user('kevin', 'kevin@example.com',
'kevinpassword')
user.save()
```

Finally, quit the interactive console by entering the following command:

```
quit()
```

Now, we can launch Django's development server to compose and send HTTP requests. Execute any of the following two commands based on your needs to access the API in other devices or computers connected to your LAN. Remember that we analyzed the difference between them in Chapter 1, *Developing RESTful APIs with Django*:

```
python manage.py runserver
python manage.py runserver 0.0.0.0:8000
```

After we run any of the preceding commands, the development server will start listening at port `8000`.

Composing requests with the necessary authentication

Now, we will compose and send an HTTP request to create a new game without authentication credentials:

```
http POST :8000/games/ name='The Last of Us' game_category='3D RPG'
played=false release_date='2016-06-21T03:02:00.776594Z'
```

The following is the equivalent curl command:

```
curl -iX POST -H "Content-Type: application/json" -d '{"name":"The Last
of Us", "game_category":"3D RPG", "played": "false", "release_date":
"2016-06-21T03:02:00.776594Z"}' :8000/games/
```

We will receive a `401 Unauthorized` status code in the response header and a detail message indicating that we didn't provide authentication credentials in the JSON body. The following lines show a sample response:

```
HTTP/1.0 401 Unauthorized
Allow: GET, POST, HEAD, OPTIONS
Content-Type: application/json
Date: Sun, 03 Jul 2016 22:23:07 GMT
Server: WSGIServer/0.2 CPython/3.5.1
Vary: Accept, Cookie
WWW-Authenticate: Basic realm="api"
X-Frame-Options: SAMEORIGIN
{
    "detail": "Authentication credentials were not provided."
}
```

If we want to create a new game, that is, to make a `POST` request to `/games/`, we need to provide authentication credentials using HTTP authentication. Now, we will compose and send an HTTP request to create a new game with authentication credentials, that is, with the `superuser` name and his password. Remember to replace `superuser` with the name you used for the `superuser` and `password` with the password you configured for this user:

```
http -a superuser:'password' POST :8000/games/ name='The Last of Us'
game_category='3D RPG' played=false
release_date='2016-06-21T03:02:00.776594Z'
```

The following is the equivalent `curl` command:

```
curl --user superuser:'password' -iX POST -H "Content-Type:
application/json" -d '{"name":"The Last of Us", "game_category":"3D RPG",
"played": "false", "release_date": "2016-06-21T03:02:00.776594Z"}'
:8000/games/
```

If the new `Game` with the superuser user as its owner was successfully persisted in the database, the function returns an `HTTP 201 Created` status code and the recently persisted `Game` serialized to JSON in the response body. The following lines show an example response for the HTTP request, with the new `Game` object in the JSON response:

```
HTTP/1.0 201 Created
Allow: GET, POST, HEAD, OPTIONS
Content-Type: application/json
Date: Mon, 04 Jul 2016 02:45:36 GMT
Location: http://localhost:8000/games/16/
Server: WSGIServer/0.2 CPython/3.5.1
Vary: Accept
X-Frame-Options: SAMEORIGIN
```

```
{
    "game_category": "3D RPG",
    "name": "The Last of Us",
    "owner": "superuser",
    "played": false,
    "release_date": "2016-06-21T03:02:00.776594Z",
    "url": "http://localhost:8000/games/16/"
}
```

Now, we will compose and send an HTTP request to update the `played` field value for the previously created game with authentication credentials. However, in this case, we will use the other user we created in Django to authenticate the request. Remember to replace `kevin` with the name you used for the user and `kevinpassword` with the password you configured for this user. In addition, replace `16` with the id generated for the previously created game in your configuration. We will use the `PATCH` method.

```
http -a kevin:'kevinpassword' PATCH :8000/games/16/ played=true
```

The following is the equivalent `curl` command:

```
curl --user kevin:'kevinpassword' -iX PATCH -H "Content-Type:
application/json" -d '{"played": "true"}' :8000/games/16/
```

We will receive a `403 Forbidden` status code in the response header and a detail message indicating that we do not have permission to perform the action in the JSON body. The owner for the game we want to update is `superuser` and the authentication credentials for this request use a different user. Thus, the operation is rejected by the `has_object_permission` method in the `IsOwnerOrReadOnly` class. The following lines show a sample response:

```
HTTP/1.0 403 Forbidden
Allow: GET, PUT, PATCH, DELETE, HEAD, OPTIONS
Content-Type: application/json
Date: Mon, 04 Jul 2016 02:59:15 GMT
Server: WSGIServer/0.2 CPython/3.5.1
Vary: Accept
X-Frame-Options: SAMEORIGIN
{
    "detail": "You do not have permission to perform this action."
}
```

If we compose and send an HTTP request with the same authentication credentials for the same resource with the GET method, we will be able to retrieve the game that the specified user doesn't own. It will work because GET is one of the safe methods and a user that is not the owner is allowed to read the resource. Remember to replace kevin with the name you used for the user and kevinpassword with the password you configured for this user. In addition, replace 16 with the id generated for the previously created game in your configuration:

```
http -a kevin:'kevinpassword' GET :8000/games/16/
```

The following is the equivalent curl command:

```
curl --user kevin:'kevinpassword' -iX GET :8000/games/16/
```

Browsing the API with authentication credentials

Open a web browser and enter http://localhost:8000/. Replace localhost by the IP of the computer that is running the Django development server in case you use another computer or device to run the browser. The browsable API will compose and send a GET request to / and will display the results of its execution, that is, the Api Root. You will notice that there is a **Log in** hyperlink in the upper-right corner.

Click Log in and the browser will display the Django REST Framework login page. Enter kevin in username, kevinpassword in password, and click **Log In**. Remember to replace kevin with the name you used for the user and kevinpassword with the password you configured for this user. Now, you will be logged in as kevin and all the requests you compose and send through the browsable API will use this user. You will be redirected again to the **Api Root** and you will notice the **Log In** hyperlink is replaced with the username (**kevin**) and a drop-down menu that allows you to Log Out. The following screenshot shows the Api Root after we are logged in as kevin.

Click or tap on the URL on the right-hand side of **users**. In case you are browsing in localhost, the URL will be http://localhost:8000/users/. The Browsable API will render the web page for the **Users List**. The following lines show the JSON body with the first lines and the last lines with the results for the GET request to localhost:8000/users/.

The games array includes the URL and the name for each game that the user owns because the UserGameSerializer class is serializing the content for each game:

```
HTTP 200 OK
Allow: GET, HEAD, OPTIONS
Content-Type: application/json
Vary: Accept
{
    "count": 2,
    "next": null,
    "previous": null,
    "results": [
        {
            "url": "http://localhost:8000/users/1/",
            "pk": 1,
            "username": "superuser",
            "games": [
                {
                    "url": "http://localhost:8000/games/10/",
                    "name": "A Dark Room"
                },
                {
                    "url": "http://localhost:8000/games/11/",
                    "name": "Bastion"
                },
                ...
            ]
        },
        {
            "url": "http://localhost:8000/users/3/",
            "pk": 3,
            "username": "kevin",
            "games": []
        }
    ]
}
```

Click or tap on one of the URLs for the games listed as owned by the superuser user. The Browsable API will render the web page for the **Game Detail**. Click or tap on **OPTIONS** and the **DELETE** button will appear. Click or tap on **DELETE**. The web browser will display a confirmation dialog box. Click or tap on **DELETE**. We will receive a 403 Forbidden status code in the response header and a detail message indicating that we do not have permission to perform the action in the JSON body.

The owner for the game we want to delete is `superuser` and the authentication credentials for this request use a different user, specifically, `kevin`. Thus, the operation is rejected by the `has_object_permission` method in the `IsOwnerOrReadOnly` class. The following screenshot shows a sample response:

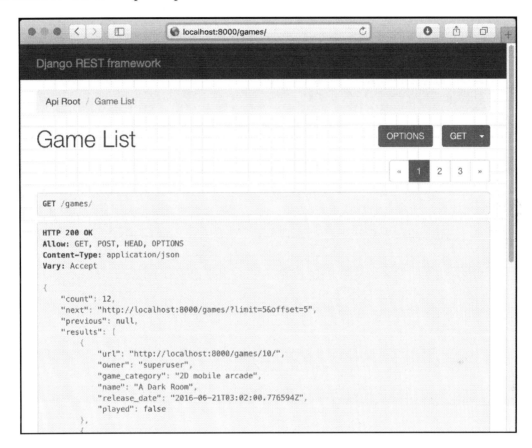

We can also take advantage of other authentication plugins that Django REST Framework provides us. You can read more about all the possibilities that the framework provides us for authentication at `http ://www.django-rest-framework.org/api-guide/authentication/`

Test your knowledge

1. Which is the most appropriate HTTP method to update a single field for an existing resource:
   1. PUT
   2. POST
   3. PATCH

2. Which of the following pagination classes provides a limit/offset based style in Django REST Framework:
   1. rest_framework.pagination.LimitOffsetPagination
   2. rest_framework.pagination.LimitOffsetPaging
   3. rest_framework.styles.LimitOffsetPagination

3. The rest_framework.authentication.BasicAuthentication class:
   1. Works with Django's session framework for authentication.
   2. Provides an HTTP Basic authentication against username and password.
   3. Provides a simple token based authentication.

4. The rest_framework.authentication.SessionAuthentication class:
   1. Works with Django's session framework for authentication.
   2. Provides an HTTP Basic authentication against username and password.
   3. Provides a simple token based authentication.

5. The value of which of the following settings keys specify a global setting with a tuple of string whose values indicate the classes that we want to use for authentication:
   1. DEFAULT_AUTH_CLASSES
   2. AUTHENTICATION_CLASSES
   3. DEFAULT_AUTHENTICATION_CLASSES

Summary

In this chapter, we improved the REST API in many ways. We added unique constraints to the model and updated the database, we made it easy to update single fields with the PATCH method and we took advantage of pagination.

Then, we started working with authentication, permissions, and throttling. We added security-related data to the models and we updated the database. We made numerous changes in the different pieces of code to achieve a specific security goal and we took advantage of Django REST Framework authentication and permissions features.

Now that we have built an improved and complex API that takes into account authentication and uses permission policies, we will use additional abstractions included in the framework, we will add throttling and tests, which is what we are going to discuss in the next chapter.

4

Throttling, Filtering, Testing, and Deploying an API with Django

In this chapter, we will use the additional features included in Django and Django REST Framework to improve our RESTful API. We will also write and execute unit tests and learn a few things related to deployment. We will cover the following topics in this chapter:

- Understanding throttling classes
- Configuring throttling policies
- Testing throttle policies
- Understanding filtering, searching and ordering classes
- Configuring filtering, searching, and ordering for views
- Testing filtering, searching and ordering features
- Filter, search, and order in the browsable API
- Writing a first round of unit tests
- Running unit tests and checking testing coverage
- Improving testing coverage
- Understanding strategies for deployments and scalability

Understanding throttling classes

So far, we haven't established any limits on the usage of our API, and therefore, both authenticated and unauthenticated users can compose and send as many requests as they want to. We only took advantage of the pagination features available in Django REST Framework to specify how we wanted large results sets to be split into individual pages of data. However, any user can compose and send thousands of requests to be processed without any kind of limitation.

We will use throttling to configure the following limitations of the usage of our API:

- **Unauthenticated users**: A maximum of five requests per hour.

- **Authenticated users**: A maximum of 20 requests per hour.

In addition, we want to configure a maximum of 100 requests per hour to the game categories related views, no matter whether the user is authenticated or not.

Django REST Framework provides the following three throttling classes in the `rest_framework.throttling` module. All of them are subclasses of the `SimpleRateThrottle` class, which is a subclass of the `BaseThrottle` class. The classes allow us to set the maximum number of requests per period that are computed based on different mechanisms to determine the previous request information used to specify the scope. The previous request information for throttling is stored in the cache and the classes override the `get_cache_key` method that determines the scope.

- `AnonRateThrottle`: This class limits the rate of request that an anonymous user can make. The IP address of the request is the unique cache key, and therefore, all the requests coming from the same IP address will accumulate the total number of requests.
- `UserRateThrottle`: This class limits the rate at which a specific user can make requests. For authenticated users, the authenticated user ID is the unique cache key. For anonymous users, the IP address of the request is the unique cache key.
- `ScopedRateThrottle`: This class limits the rate of request for specific parts of the API identified with the value assigned to the `throttle_scope` property. The class is useful when we want to restrict access to specific parts of the API with different rates.

Configuring throttling policies

We will use a combination of the three throttling classes, discussed earlier, to achieve our previously explained goals. Make sure you quit Django's development server. Remember that you just need to press *Ctrl + C* in the Terminal or Command Prompt window in which it is running.

Open the `gamesapi/settings.py` file and add the highlighted lines to the dictionary named `REST_FRAMEWORK` with two key-value pairs that configure the global default throttling classes and their rates. The code file for the sample is included in the `restful_python_chapter_04_01` folder:

```
REST_FRAMEWORK = {
    'DEFAULT_PAGINATION_CLASS':
    'games.pagination.LimitOffsetPaginationWithMaxLimit',
    'PAGE_SIZE': 5,
    'DEFAULT_AUTHENTICATION_CLASSES': (
        'rest_framework.authentication.BasicAuthentication',
        'rest_framework.authentication.SessionAuthentication',
        ),
    'DEFAULT_THROTTLE_CLASSES': (
        'rest_framework.throttling.AnonRateThrottle',
        'rest_framework.throttling.UserRateThrottle',
    ),
    'DEFAULT_THROTTLE_RATES': {
        'anon': '5/hour',
        'user': '20/hour',
        'game-categories': '30/hour',
    }
}
```

The value for the `DEFAULT_THROTTLE_CLASSES` settings key specifies a global setting with a tuple of string whose values indicate the default classes that we want to use for throttling-`AnonRateThrottle` and `UserRateThrottle`. The `DEFAULT_THROTTLE_RATES` settings key specifies a dictionary with default throttle rates. The value specified for the `'anon'` key indicates that we want a maximum of five requests per hour for anonymous users. The value specified for the `'user'` key indicates that we want a maximum of 20 requests per hour for authenticated users. The value specified for the `'game-categories'` key indicates that we want a maximum of 30 requests per hour for the scope with that name.

The maximum rate is a string that specifies the number of requests per period with the following format: `'number_of_requests/period'`, where period can be any of the following:

- `s`: second
- `sec`: second
- `m`: minute
- `min`: minute
- `h`: hour
- `hour`: hour
- `d`: day
- `day`: day

Now, we will configure throttling policies for the class-based views related to game categories. We will override the value for the `throttle_scope` and `throttle_classes` class attributes for the `GameCategoryList` and `GameCategoryDetail` classes. First, we have to add the following `import` statement after the last import in the `views.py` file. The code file for the sample is included in the `restful_python_chapter_04_01` folder:

```
from rest_framework.throttling import ScopedRateThrottle
```

The following lines show the new code for the `GameCategoryList` class in the `views.py` file. The new lines are highlighted. The code file for the sample is included in the `restful_python_chapter_04_01` folder:

```
class GameCategoryList(generics.ListCreateAPIView):
    queryset = GameCategory.objects.all()
    serializer_class = GameCategorySerializer
    name = 'gamecategory-list'
    throttle_scope = 'game-categories'
    throttle_classes = (ScopedRateThrottle,)
```

The following lines show the new code for the `GameCategoryDetail` class in the `views.py` file. The new lines are highlighted in the following code. The code file for the sample is included in the `restful_python_chapter_04_01` folder:

```
class GameCategoryDetail(generics.RetrieveUpdateDestroyAPIView):
    queryset = GameCategory.objects.all()
    serializer_class = GameCategorySerializer
    name = 'gamecategory-detail'
    throttle_scope = 'game-categories'
    throttle_classes = (ScopedRateThrottle,)
```

We added the same lines in the two classes. We set `'game-categories'` as the value for the `throttle_scope` class attribute and we included `ScopedRateThrottle` in the tuple that defines the value for `throttle_classes`. This way, the two class-based views will use the settings specified for the `'game-categories'` scope and the `ScopeRateThrottle` class for throttling. These views will be able to serve 30 requests per hour and won't take into account the global settings that apply to the default classes that we use for throttling: `AnonRateThrottle` and `UserRateThrottle`.

Before Django runs the main body of a view, it performs the checks for each throttle class specified in the throttle classes. In the views related to the game categories, we wrote code that overrides the default settings. If a single throttle check fails, the code will raise a `Throttled` exception and Django won't execute the main body of the view. The cache is responsible of storing previous requests' information for throttling checking.

Testing throttling policies

Now, we can launch Django's development server to compose and send HTTP requests. Execute any of the following two commands based on your needs to access the API in other devices or computers connected to your LAN. Remember that we analyzed the difference between them in Chapter 1, *Developing RESTful APIs with Django*.

```
python manage.py runserver
python manage.py runserver 0.0.0.0:8000
```

After we run any of the previous commands, the development server will start listening at port 8000.

Now, we will compose and send an HTTP request to retrieve all the player's scores without authentication credentials six times:

```
http :8000/player-scores/
```

We can also use the features of the shell in macOS or Linux to run the previous command six times with just a single line. We can also run the command in a Cygwin terminal in Windows. We can execute the next line in a bash shell. However, we will see all the results one after the other and you will have to scroll to understand what happened with each execution:

```
for i in {1..6}; do http :8000/player-scores/; done;
```

The following is the equivalent curl command that we must execute six times:

```
curl -iX GET :8000/player-scores/
```

The following is the equivalent curl command that is executed six times with a single line in a bash shell in macOS or Linux, or a Cygwin terminal in Windows:

```
for i in {1..6}; do curl -iX GET :8000/player-scores/; done;
```

Django won't process the sixth request because `AnonRateThrottle` is configured as one of the default throttle classes and its throttle settings specify five requests per hour. Thus, we will receive a `429 Too many requests` status code in the response header and a message indicating that the request was throttled and the time in which the server will be able to process an additional request. The `Retry-After` key in the response header provides the number of seconds that it is necessary to wait until the next request: `3189`. The following lines show a sample response:

```
HTTP/1.0 429 Too Many Requests
Allow: GET, POST, HEAD, OPTIONS
Content-Type: application/json
Date: Tue, 05 Jul 2016 03:37:50 GMT
Retry-After: 3189
Server: WSGIServer/0.2 CPython/3.5.1
Vary: Accept, Cookie
X-Frame-Options: SAMEORIGIN
{
    "detail": "Request was throttled. Expected available in 3189
seconds."
}
```

Now, we will compose and send an HTTP request to retrieve the player's scores with authentication credentials, that is, with the `superuser` name and his password. We will execute the same request six times. Remember to replace `superuser` with the name you used for the `superuser` and `password` with the password you configured for this user in `Chapter 3`, *Improving and Adding Authentication to an API with Django*:

```
http -a superuser:'password' :8000/player-scores/
```

We can also run the previous command six times with just a single line:

```
for i in {1..6}; do http -a superuser:'password' :8000/player-scores/;
done;
```

The following is the equivalent curl command that we must execute six times:

```
curl --user superuser:'password' -iX GET :8000/player-scores/
```

The following is the equivalent `curl` command that is executed six times with a single line:

```
for i in {1..6}; do curl --user superuser:'password' -iX GET
:8000/player-scores/; done;
```

Django will process the sixth request because we have composed and sent six authenticated requests with the same user, `UserRateThrottle` is configured as one of the default throttle classes and its throttle settings specify 20 requests per hour.

If we run the previous commands 15 times more, we will accumulate 21 requests and we will will receive a `429 Too many requests` status code in the response header and a message indicating that the request was throttled and the time in which the server will be able to process an additional request after the last execution.

Now, we will compose and send an HTTP request to retrieve all the game categories thirty times without the authentication credentials:

```
http :8000/game-categories/
```

We can also run the previous command thirty times with just a single line:

```
for i in {1..30}; do http :8000/game-categories/; done;
```

The following is the equivalent `curl` command that we must execute thirty times:

```
curl -iX GET :8000/game-categories/
```

The following is the equivalent `curl` command that is executed thirty times with a single line:

```
for i in {1..30}; do curl -iX GET :8000/game-categories/; done;
```

Django will process the thirty requests because we have composed and sent 30 unauthenticated requests to a URL that is identified with the `'game-categories'` throttle scope and uses the `ScopedRateThrottle` class for throttle permission control. The throttle settings for the throttle scope identified with `'game-categories'` are configured with 30 requests per hour.

If we run the previous command once again, we will accumulate 31 requests and we will receive a `429 Too many requests` status code in the response header and a message indicating that the request was throttled and the time in which the server will be able to process an additional request after the last execution.

Understanding filtering, searching, and ordering classes

We took advantage of the pagination features available in Django REST Framework to specify how we wanted large results sets to be split into individual pages of data. However, we have always been working with the entire queryset as the result set. Django REST Framework makes it easy to customize filtering, searching, and sorting capabilities to the views we have already coded.

First, we will install the `django-filter` package in our virtual environment. This way, we will be able to use field filtering features that we can easily customize in Django REST Framework. Make sure that you quit the Django's development server. Remember that you just need to press *Ctrl + C* in the terminal or Command Prompt window in which it is running. Then, we just need to run the following command to install the `django-filter` package:

```
pip install django-filter
```

The last lines for the output will indicate that the `django-filter` package has been successfully installed.

```
Collecting django-filter
  Downloading django_filter-0.13.0-py2.py3-none-any.whl
Installing collected packages: django-filter
Successfully installed django-filter-0.13.0
```

In addition, we will install the `django-cripsy-forms` package in our virtual environment. This package enhances how the browsable API renders the different filters. Run the following command to install the `django-cripsy-forms` package: We just need to run the following command to install this package:

```
pip install django-crispy-forms
```

The last lines for the output will indicate that the `django-crispy-forms` package has been successfully installed:

```
Collecting django-crispy-forms
Installing collected packages: django-crispy-forms
  Running setup.py install for django-crispy-forms
Successfully installed django-crispy-forms-1.6.0
```

Open the `gamesapi/settings.py` file and add the highlighted lines to the
`REST_FRAMEWORK` dictionary. The code file for the sample is included in the
`restful_python_chapter_04_02` folder:

```
REST_FRAMEWORK = {
    'DEFAULT_PAGINATION_CLASS':
    'games.pagination.LimitOffsetPaginationWithMaxLimit',
    'PAGE_SIZE': 5,
    'DEFAULT_FILTER_BACKENDS': (
        'rest_framework.filters.DjangoFilterBackend',
        'rest_framework.filters.SearchFilter',
        'rest_framework.filters.OrderingFilter',
        ),
    'DEFAULT_AUTHENTICATION_CLASSES': (
        'rest_framework.authentication.BasicAuthentication',
        'rest_framework.authentication.SessionAuthentication',
        ),
    'DEFAULT_THROTTLE_CLASSES': (
        'rest_framework.throttling.AnonRateThrottle',
        'rest_framework.throttling.UserRateThrottle',
    ),
    'DEFAULT_THROTTLE_RATES': {
        'anon': '5/hour',
        'user': '20/hour',
        'game-categories': '30/hour',
    }
}
```

The value for the `'DEFAULT_FILTER_BACKENDS` settings key specifies a global setting with
a tuple of string whose values indicate the default classes that we want to use for filter
backends. We will use the following three classes:

- `rest_framework.filters.DjangoFilterBackend`: This class provides field
  filtering capabilities. It uses the previously installed `django-filter` package.
  We can specify the set of fields we want to be able to filter against or create a
  `rest_framework.filters.FilterSet` class with more customized settings
  and associate it with the view.
- `rest_framework.filters.SearchFilter`: This class provides single query
  parameter-based searching capabilities and it is based on Django admin's search
  function. We can specify the set of fields we want to include for the search and
  the client will be able to filter items by making queries that search these fields
  with a single query. It is useful when we want to make it possible for a request to
  search multiple fields with a single query.

- `rest_framework.filters.OrderingFilter`: This class allows the client to control how the results are ordered with a single-query parameter. We can also specify the fields that can be ordered against.

> We can also configure the filter backends by including any of the previously enumerated classes in a tuple and assign it to the `filter_backends` class attribute for the generic view classes. However, in this case, we will use the default configuration for all our class-based views.

Add `'crispy_forms'` to the installed apps in the `settings.py` file, specifically, to the `INSTALLED_APPS` string list. The following code shows the lines we must add as the highlighted code. The code file for the sample is included in the `restful_python_chapter_04_02` folder:

```
INSTALLED_APPS = [
    'django.contrib.admin',
    'django.contrib.auth',
    'django.contrib.contenttypes',
    'django.contrib.sessions',
    'django.contrib.messages',
    'django.contrib.staticfiles',
    # Django REST Framework
    'rest_framework',
    # Games application
    'games.apps.GamesConfig',
    # Crispy forms
    'crispy_forms',
]
```

> We have to be careful with the fields we configure to be available in the filtering, searching, and ordering features. The configuration will have an impact on the queries executed on the database, and therefore, we must ensure that we have the appropriate database optimizations considering the queries that will be executed.

Configuring filtering, searching, and ordering for views

Go to the `gamesapi/games` folder and open the `views.py` file. Add the following code after the last line that declares the imports but before the declaration of the `UserList` class. The code file for the sample is included in the `restful_python_chapter_04_02` folder:

```
from rest_framework import filters
from django_filters import NumberFilter, DateTimeFilter, AllValuesFilter
```

Add the following highlighted lines to the `GameCategoryList` class declared in the `views.py` file. The code file for the sample is included in the `restful_python_chapter_04_02` folder:

```
class GameCategoryList(generics.ListCreateAPIView):
    queryset = GameCategory.objects.all()
    serializer_class = GameCategorySerializer
    name = 'gamecategory-list'
    throttle_scope = 'game-categories'
    throttle_classes = (ScopedRateThrottle,)
    filter_fields = ('name',)
    search_fields = ('^name',)
    ordering_fields = ('name',)
```

The `filter_fields` attribute specifies a tuple of string whose values indicate the field names that we want to be able to filter against. Under the hoods, Django REST Framework will automatically create a `rest_framework.filters.FilterSet` class and associate it to the `GameCategoryList` view. This way, we will be able to filter against the `name` field.

The `search_fields` attribute specifies a tuple of string whose values indicate the text-type field names that we want to include in the search feature. In this case, we want to search only against the name field and perform a starts-with match. The `'^'` included as a prefix of the field name indicates that we want to restrict the search behavior to a starts-with match.

The `ordering_fields` attribute specifies a tuple of string whose values indicate the field names that the client can specify to sort the results. In case the client doesn't specify a field for ordering, the response will use the default ordering fields indicated in the model related to the view.

Add the following highlighted lines to the `GameList` class declared in the `views.py` file. The new lines specify the fields to be used in the filter, search, and ordering features. The code file for the sample is included in the `restful_python_chapter_04_02` folder:

```
class GameList(generics.ListCreateAPIView):
    queryset = Game.objects.all()
    serializer_class = GameSerializer
    name = 'game-list'
    permission_classes = (
        permissions.IsAuthenticatedOrReadOnly,
        IsOwnerOrReadOnly,
        )
    filter_fields = (
        'name',
        'game_category',
        'release_date',
        'played',
        'owner',
        )
    search_fields = (
        '^name',
        )
    ordering_fields = (
        'name',
        'release_date',
        )

    def perform_create(self, serializer):
        serializer.save(owner=self.request.user)
```

In this case, we specified many field names in the `filter_fields` attribute. We included `'game_category'` and `'owner'` in the string tuple, and therefore, the client will be able to include the id values for any of these two fields in the filter. We will take advantage of other options for related models, which will later allow us to filter the related models by field. This way, we will understand the different customizations available.

The `ordering_fields` attribute specifies two field names for the tuple of string, and therefore, the client will be able to order the results by either `name` or `release_date`.

Add the following highlighted lines to the `PlayerList` class declared in the `views.py` file. The new lines specify the fields to be used in the filter, search, and ordering features. The code file for the sample is included in the `restful_python_chapter_04_02` folder:

```
class PlayerList(generics.ListCreateAPIView):
    queryset = Player.objects.all()
    serializer_class = PlayerSerializer
```

```
name = 'player-list'
filter_fields = (
    'name',
    'gender',
    )
search_fields = (
    '^name',
    )
ordering_fields = (
    'name',
    )
```

Add the following lines to create the new `PlayerScoreFilter` class in the `views.py` file but before the declaration of the `PlayerScoreList` class. The code file for the sample is included in the `restful_python_chapter_04_02` folder:

```python
class PlayerScoreFilter(filters.FilterSet):
    min_score = NumberFilter(
        name='score', lookup_expr='gte')
    max_score = NumberFilter(
        name='score', lookup_expr='lte')
    from_score_date = DateTimeFilter(
        name='score_date', lookup_expr='gte')
    to_score_date = DateTimeFilter(
        name='score_date', lookup_expr='lte')
    player_name = AllValuesFilter(
        name='player__name')
    game_name = AllValuesFilter(
        name='game__name')

    class Meta:
        model = PlayerScore
        fields = (
            'score',
            'from_score_date',
            'to_score_date',
            'min_score',
            'max_score',
            #player__name will be accessed as player_name
            'player_name',
            #game__name will be accessed as game_name
            'game_name',
            )
```

The `PlayerScoreFilter` is a subclass of the `rest_framework.filters.FilterSet` class. We want to customize settings for the fields that we will use for filtering in the `PlayerScoreList` class-based view, and therefore, we created the new `PlayerScoreFilter` class. The class declares the following six class attributes:

- `min_score`: It is a `django_filters.NumberFilter` instance that allows the client to filter the player scores whose `score` numeric value is greater than or equal to the specified number. The value for `name` indicates the field to which the numeric filter is applied, `'score'`, and the `lookup_expr` value indicates the lookup expression, `'gte'`, which means greater than or equal to.

- `max_score`: It is a `django_filters.NumberFilter` instance that allows the client to filter the player scores whose `score` numeric value is less than or equal to the specified number. The value for `name` indicates the field to which the numeric filter is applied, `'score'`, and the `lookup_expr` value indicates the lookup expression, `'lte'`, which means less than or equal to.

- `from_score_date`: It is a `django_filters.DateTimeFilter` instance that allows the client to filter the player scores whose `score_datedatetime` value is greater than or equal to the specified `datetime` value. The value for `name` indicates the field to which the datetime filter is applied, `'score_date'`, and the `lookup_expr` value indicates the lookup expression, `'gte'`.

- `to_score_date`: It is a `django_filters.DateTimeFilter` instance that allows the client to filter the player scores whose `score_datedatetime` value is less than or equal to the specified `datetime` value. The value for `name` indicates the field to which the `datetime` filter is applied, `'score_date'`,and the `lookup_expr` value indicates the lookup expression, `'lte'`.

- `player_name`: It is a `django_filters.AllValuesFilter`: It is an instance that allows the client to filter the player scores whose player's name matches the specified string value. The value for `name` indicates the field to which the filter is applied, `'player__name'`. Note that the value has a double underscore (__) and you can read it as the `name` field for the `player` model or simply replace the double underscore with a dot and read `player.name`. The name uses Django's double underscore syntax. However, we don't want the client to use `player__name` to specify the filter for the player's name. Thus, the instance is stored in the class attribute named `player_name`, with just a single underscore between player and name. The browsable API will display a dropdown with all the possible values for the player's name to use as a filter. The dropdown will only include the players' names that have registered scores because we used the `AllValuesFilter` class.

- `game_name`: This is a `django_filters.AllValuesFilter` instance that allows the client to filter the player scores whose game's name matches the specified string value. The value for `name` indicates the field on which the filter is applied, `'game__name'`. The name uses the previously explained Django's double underscore syntax. As happened with `player_name`, we don't want the client to use `game__name` to specify the filter for the game's name, and therefore, we stored the instance in the class attribute named `game_name`, with just a single underscore between game and name. The browsable API will display a dropdown with all the possible values for the game's name to use as a filter. The dropdown will only include the game's names that have registered scores because we used the `AllValuesFilter` class.

In addition, the `PlayerScoreFilter` class declares a `Meta` inner class that declares two attributes: `model` and `fields`. The `model` attribute specifies the model related to the filter set, that is, the `PlayerScore` class. The `fields` attribute specifies a tuple of string whose values indicate the field names and filter names that we want to include in the filters for the related model. We included `'scores'` and the names for all the previously declared filters. The string `'scores'` refers to the `score` field name and we want to apply the default numeric filter that will be built under the hoods to allow the client to filter by an exact match on the `score` field.

Finally, add the following highlighted lines to the `PlayerScoreList` class declared in the `views.py` file. The code file for the sample is included in the `restful_python_chapter_04_02` folder:

```
class PlayerScoreList(generics.ListCreateAPIView):
    queryset = PlayerScore.objects.all()
    serializer_class = PlayerScoreSerializer
    name = 'playerscore-list'
    filter_class = PlayerScoreFilter
    ordering_fields = (
        'score',
        'score_date',
        )
```

The `filter_class` attribute specifies the `FilterSet` subclass that we want to use for this class-based view: `PlayerScoreFilter`. In addition, we specified the two field names that the client will be able to use for ordering in the `ordering_fields` tuple of string.

Testing filtering, searching, and ordering

Now, we can launch Django's development server to compose and send HTTP requests. Execute any of the following two commands based on your needs to access the API in other devices or computers connected to your LAN. Remember that we analyzed the difference between them in `Chapter 1`, *Developing RESTful APIs with Django*.

```
python manage.py runserver
python manage.py runserver 0.0.0.0:8000
```

After we run any of the previous commands, the development server will start listening at port `8000`:

Now, we will compose and send an HTTP request to retrieve all the game categories whose name matches `3D RPG`:

```
http :8000/game-categories/?name=3D+RPG
```

The following is the equivalent `curl` command:

```
curl -iX GET :8000/game-categories/?name=3D+RPG
```

The following lines show a sample response with the single game category whose name matches the specified name in the filter. The following lines only show the JSON body without the headers:

```
{
    "count": 1,
    "next": null,
    "previous": null,
    "results": [
        {
            "games": [
                "http://localhost:8000/games/2/",
                "http://localhost:8000/games/15/",
                "http://localhost:8000/games/3/",
                "http://localhost:8000/games/16/"
            ],
            "name": "3D RPG",
            "pk": 3,
            "url": "http://localhost:8000/game-categories/3/"
        }
    ]
}
```

We will compose and send an HTTP request to retrieve all the games whose related category id is equal to 3 and the value for the played field is equal to `True`. We want to sort the results by `release_date` in descending order, and therefore, we specify – `release_date` in the value for `ordering`. The hyphen (–) before the field name specifies the ordering feature to use descending order instead of the default ascending order. Make sure you replace 3 with the pk value of the previously retrieved game category named 3D RPG. The played field is a `bool` field, and therefore, we have to use Python-valid `bool` values (`True` and `False`) when specifying the desired values for the `bool` field in the filter:

```
http ':8000/games/?game_category=3&played=True&ordering=-release_date'
```

The following is the equivalent `curl` command:

```
curl -iX GET ':8000/games/?game_category=3&played=True&ordering=-
release_date'
```

The following lines show a sample response with the two games that match the specified criteria in the filter. The following lines only show the JSON body without the headers:

```
{
    "count": 2,
    "next": null,
    "previous": null,
    "results": [
        {
            "game_category": "3D RPG",
            "name": "PvZ Garden Warfare 4",
            "owner": "superuser",
            "played": true,
            "release_date": "2016-06-21T03:02:00.776594Z",
            "url": "http://localhost:8000/games/2/"
        },
        {
            "game_category": "3D RPG",
            "name": "Superman vs Aquaman",
            "owner": "superuser",
            "played": true,
            "release_date": "2016-06-21T03:02:00.776594Z",
            "url": "http://localhost:8000/games/3/"
        }
    ]
}
```

In the `GameList` class, we specified `'game_category'` as one of the strings in the `filter_fields` tuple of string. Thus, we had to use the game category id in the filter. Now, we will use a filter on the game's name related to a registered score. The `PlayerScoreFilter` class provides us a filter to the name of the related game in `game_name`. We will combine the filter with another filter on the player's name related to a registered score. The `PlayerScoreFilter` class provides us a filter to the name of the related player in `player_name`. Both conditions specified in the criteria must be met, and therefore, the filters are combined with the AND operator:

```
http ':8000/player-
scores/?player_name=Kevin&game_name=Superman+vs+Aquaman'
```

The following is the equivalent `curl` command:

```
curl -iX GET ':8000/player-
scores/?player_name=Kevin&game_name=Superman+vs+Aquaman'
```

The following lines show a sample response with the score that matches the specified criteria in the filters. The following lines only show the JSON body without the headers:

```
{
    "count": 1,
    "next": null,
    "previous": null,
    "results": [
        {
            "game": "Superman vs Aquaman",
            "pk": 5,
            "player": "Kevin",
            "score": 123200,
            "score_date": "2016-06-22T03:02:00.776594Z",
            "url": "http://localhost:8000/player-scores/5/"
        }
    ]
}
```

We will compose and send an HTTP request to retrieve all the scores that match the following criteria. The results will be ordered by `score_date` in descending order.

- The `score` value is between 30,000 and 150,000
- The `score_date` is between 2016-06-21 and 2016-06-22

```
http ':8000/player-
scores/?score=&from_score_date=2016-06-01&to_score_date=2016-06-28&min_scor
e=30000&max_score=150000&ordering=-score_date'
```

The following is the equivalent `curl` command:

```
curl -iX GET ':8000/player-
scores/?score=&from_score_date=2016-06-01&to_score_date=2016-06-28&min_scor
e=30000&max_score=150000&ordering=-score_date'
```

The following lines show a sample response with the three games that match the specified criteria in the filters. We overrode the default ordering specified in the model with the specified ordering in the request. The following lines only show the JSON body without the headers:

```json
{
    "count": 3,
    "next": null,
    "previous": null,
    "results": [
        {
            "game": "Superman vs Aquaman",
            "pk": 5,
            "player": "Kevin",
            "score": 123200,
            "score_date": "2016-06-22T03:02:00.776594Z",
            "url": "http://localhost:8000/player-scores/5/"
        },
        {
            "game": "PvZ Garden Warfare 4",
            "pk": 4,
            "player": "Brandon",
            "score": 85125,
            "score_date": "2016-06-22T01:02:00.776594Z",
            "url": "http://localhost:8000/player-scores/4/"
        },
        {
            "game": "PvZ Garden Warfare 4",
            "pk": 3,
            "player": "Brandon",
            "score": 35000,
            "score_date": "2016-06-21T03:02:00.776594Z",
            "url": "http://localhost:8000/player-scores/3/"
        }
    ]
}
```

In the preceding requests, all the responses didn't have more than one page. In case the response requires more than one page, the values for the `previous` and `next` keys will display the URLs that include the combination of the filters, search, ordering and pagination.

We will compose and send an HTTP request to retrieve all the games whose name starts with 'S'. We will use the search feature that we configured to restrict the search behavior to a starts-with match on the name field:

```
http ':8000/games/?search=S'
```

The following is the equivalent curl command:

```
curl -iX GET ':8000/games/?search=S'
```

The following lines show a sample response with the two games that match the specified search criteria, that is, those games whose name starts with 'S'. The following lines only show the JSON body without the headers:

```
{
    "count": 2,
    "next": null,
    "previous": null,
    "results": [
        {
            "game_category": "2D mobile arcade",
            "name": "Scribblenauts Unlimited",
            "owner": "superuser",
            "played": false,
            "release_date": "2016-06-21T03:02:00.776594Z",
            "url": "http://localhost:8000/games/7/"
        },
        {
            "game_category": "3D RPG",
            "name": "Superman vs Aquaman",
            "owner": "superuser",
            "played": true,
            "release_date": "2016-06-21T03:02:00.776594Z",
            "url": "http://localhost:8000/games/3/"
        }
    ]
}
```

We can change the search and ordering parameter's default names: 'search' and 'ordering'. We just need to specify the desired names in the SEARCH_PARAM and the ORDERING_PARAM settings.

Filtering, searching, and ordering in the Browsable API

We can take advantage of the browsable API to easily test filter, search, and order features through a web browser. Open a web browser and enter `http://localhost:8000/player-scores/`. In case you use another computer or device to run the browser, replace `localhost` with the IP of the computer that is running the Django development server. The browsable API will compose and send a GET request to `/player-scores/` and will display the results of its execution, that is, the headers and the JSON player scores list. You will notice that there is a new **Filters** button located on the left-hand side of the **OPTIONS** button.

Click on **Filters** and the browsable API will display the **Filters** dialog box with the appropriate controls for each filter that you can apply below **Field Filters** and the different ordering options below **Ordering**. The following screenshot shows the **Filters** dialog box:

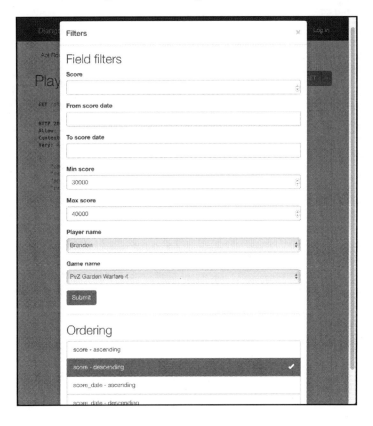

Both the **Player name** and **Game name** dropdowns will only include the related player's and game's names that have registered scores because we used the `AllValuesFilter` class for both filters. After we enter all the values for the filters, we can select the desired ordering option or click **Submit**. The browsable API will compose and send the appropriate HTTP request and will render a web page with the results of its execution. The results will include the HTTP request that was made to the Django server. The following screenshot shows an example of the result of executing the next request, that is, the request we built using the browsable API:

```
GET /player-
scores/?score=&from_score_date=&to_score_date=&min_score=30000&max_score=40
000&player_name=Brandon&game_name=PvZ+Garden+Warfare+4
```

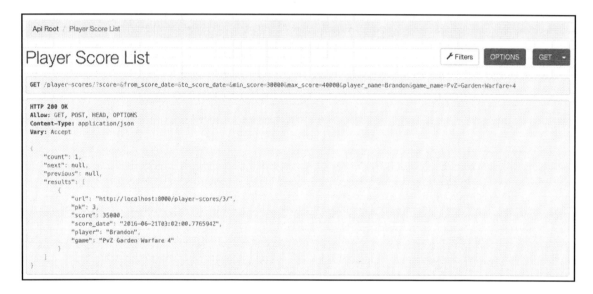

Setting up unit tests

First, we will install the `coverage` and `django-nose` packages in our virtual environment. We will make the necessary configurations to use the `django_nose.NoseTestRunner` class to run all the tests we code and we will use the necessary configurations to improve the accuracy of the test coverage measurements.

Make sure that you quit Django's development server. Remember that you just need to press Ctrl + C in the terminal or the Command Prompt window in which it is running. We just need to run the following command to install the coverage package:

```
pip install coverage
```

The last few lines of the output indicate that the django-nose package has been successfully installed:

```
Collecting coverage
  Downloading coverage-4.1.tar.gz
Installing collected packages: coverage
  Running setup.py install for coverage
Successfully installed coverage-4.1
```

We just need to run the following command to install the django-nose package:

```
pip install django-nose
```

The last few lines of the output indicate that the django-nose package has been successfully installed.

```
Collecting django-nose
  Downloading django_nose-1.4.4-py2.py3-none-any.whl
Collecting nose>=1.2.1 (from django-nose)
  Downloading nose-1.3.7-py3-none-any.whl
Installing collected packages: nose, django-nose
Successfully installed django-nose-1.4.4 nose-1.3.7
```

Add 'django_nose' to the installed apps in the settings.py file, specifically, to the INSTALLED_APPS string list. The following code shows the lines we need to add as highlighted code. The code file for the sample is included in the restful_python_chapter_04_03 folder:

```
INSTALLED_APPS = [
    'django.contrib.admin',
    'django.contrib.auth',
    'django.contrib.contenttypes',
    'django.contrib.sessions',
    'django.contrib.messages',
    'django.contrib.staticfiles',
    # Django REST Framework
    'rest_framework',
    # Games application
    'games.apps.GamesConfig',
    # Crispy forms
    'crispy_forms',
```

```
      # Django nose
      'django_nose',
]
```

Open the `gamesapi/settings.py` file and add the following lines to configure the `django_nose.NoseTestRunner` class as our test runner and specify the default command-line options that we will use when we run our tests. The code file for the sample is included in the `restful_python_chapter_04_03` folder:

```
# We want to use nose to run all the tests
TEST_RUNNER = 'django_nose.NoseTestSuiteRunner'

# We want nose to measure coverage on the games app
NOSE_ARGS = [
    '--with-coverage',
    '--cover-erase',
    '--cover-inclusive',
    '--cover-package=games',
]
```

The `NOSE_ARGS` settings specify the following command-line options for the nose test suite runner and for coverage:

- `--with-coverage`: This option specifies that we always want to generate a test coverage report.
- `--cover-erase`: This option makes sure the the test runner deletes the coverage test results from the previous run.
- `--cover-inclusive`: This option includes all the Python files under the working directory in the coverage report. This way, we make sure that we discover holes in test coverage when we don't import all the files in our test suite. We will create a test suite that won't import all the files, and therefore, this option is very important to have an accurate test coverage report.
- `--cover-package=games`: This option indicates the module that we want to cover: `games`.

Finally, create a new text file named `.coveragerc` within the `gamesapi` root folder with the following content:

```
[run]
omit = *migrations*
```

This way, the `coverage` utility won't take into account many things related to the generated migrations when providing us with the test coverage report. We will have a more accurate test coverage report with this settings file.

Writing a first round of unit tests

Now, we will write the first round of unit tests. Specifically, we will write unit tests related to the game category class-based views: `GameCategoryList` and `GameCategoryDetail`. Open the existing `games/test.py` file and replace the existing code with the following lines that declare many `import` statements and the `GameCategoryTests` class. The code file for the sample is included in the `restful_python_chapter_04_04` folder, as shown:

```
from django.test import TestCase
from django.core.urlresolvers import reverse
from django.utils.http import urlencode
from rest_framework import status
from rest_framework.test import APITestCase
from games.models import GameCategory


class GameCategoryTests(APITestCase):
    def create_game_category(self, name):
        url = reverse('gamecategory-list')
        data = {'name': name}
        response = self.client.post(url, data, format='json')
        return response

    def test_create_and_retrieve_game_category(self):
        """
        Ensure we can create a new GameCategory and then retrieve it
        """
        new_game_category_name = 'New Game Category'
        response = self.create_game_category(new_game_category_name)
        self.assertEqual(response.status_code, status.HTTP_201_CREATED)
        self.assertEqual(GameCategory.objects.count(), 1)
        self.assertEqual(
            GameCategory.objects.get().name,
            new_game_category_name)
        print("PK {0}".format(GameCategory.objects.get().pk))
```

The GameCategoryTests class is a subclass of rest_framework.test.APITestCase. The class declares the create_game_category method that receives the desired name for the new game category as an argument. The method builds the URL and the data dictionary to compose and send an HTTP POST method to the view associated with the gamecategory-list view name and returns the response generated by this request. The code uses self.client to access the APIClient instance that allows us to easily compose and send HTTP requests for testing. In this case, the code calls the post method with the built url, the data dictionary, and the desired format for the data-'json'. Many test methods will call the create_game_category method to create a game category and then compose and send other HTTP requests to the API.

The test_create_and_retrieve_game_category method tests whether we can create a new GameCategory and then retrieve it. The method calls the create_game_category method explained earlier and then uses assertEqual to check for the following expected results:

- The status_code for the response is HTTP 201 Created (status.HTTP_201_CREATED)
- The total number of GameCategory objects retrieved from the database is 1

Add the following methods to the GameCategoryTests class we created in the games/test.py file. The code file for the sample is included in the restful_python_chapter_04_04 folder:

```python
def test_create_duplicated_game_category(self):
    """
    Ensure we can create a new GameCategory.
    """
    url = reverse('gamecategory-list')
    new_game_category_name = 'New Game Category'
    data = {'name': new_game_category_name}
    response1 = self.create_game_category(new_game_category_name)
    self.assertEqual(
        response1.status_code,
        status.HTTP_201_CREATED)
    response2 = self.create_game_category(new_game_category_name)
    self.assertEqual(
        response2.status_code,
        status.HTTP_400_BAD_REQUEST)

def test_retrieve_game_categories_list(self):
    """
    Ensure can retrieve a game cagory
    """
```

```python
new_game_category_name = 'New Game Category'
self.create_game_category(new_game_category_name)
url = reverse('gamecategory-list')
response = self.client.get(url, format='json')
self.assertEqual(
    response.status_code,
    status.HTTP_200_OK)
self.assertEqual(
    response.data['count'],
    1)
self.assertEqual(
    response.data['results'][0]['name'],
    new_game_category_name)

def test_update_game_category(self):
    """
    Ensure we can update a single field for a game category
    """
    new_game_category_name = 'Initial Name'
    response = self.create_game_category(new_game_category_name)
    url = reverse(
        'gamecategory-detail',
        None,
        {response.data['pk']})
    updated_game_category_name = 'Updated Game Category Name'
    data = {'name': updated_game_category_name}
    patch_response = self.client.patch(url, data, format='json')
    self.assertEqual(
        patch_response.status_code,
        status.HTTP_200_OK)
    self.assertEqual(
        patch_response.data['name'],
        updated_game_category_name)

def test_filter_game_category_by_name(self):
    """
    Ensure we can filter a game category by name
    """
    game_category_name1 = 'First game category name'
    self.create_game_category(game_category_name1)
    game_caregory_name2 = 'Second game category name'
    self.create_game_category(game_caregory_name2)
    filter_by_name = { 'name' : game_category_name1 }
    url = '{0}?{1}'.format(
        reverse('gamecategory-list'),
        urlencode(filter_by_name))
    response = self.client.get(url, format='json')
    self.assertEqual(
```

```
            response.status_code,
            status.HTTP_200_OK)
        self.assertEqual(
            response.data['count'],
            1)
        self.assertEqual(
            response.data['results'][0]['name'],
            game_category_name1)
```

We added the following methods that start whose name start with the `test_` prefix:

- `test_create_duplicated_game_category`: Tests whether the unique constraints don't make it possible for us to create two game categories with the same name. The second time we compose and send an HTTP POST request with a duplicate category name, we must receive an HTTP 400 Bad Request status code (`status.HTTP_400_BAD_REQUEST`)
- `test_retrieve_game_categories_list`: Tests whether we can retrieve a specific game category by its primary key or id
- `test_update_game_category`: Tests whether we can update a single field for a game category
- `test_filter_game_category_by_name`: Tests whether we can filter a game category by name

> Note that each test that requires a specific condition in the database must execute all the necessary code for the database to be in this specific condition. For example, in order to update an existing game category, first we must create a new game category and then we can update it. Each test method will be executed without data from the previously executed test methods in the database, that is, each test will run with a database cleaned of data from previous tests.

The last three methods in the preceding list check the data included in the response JSON body by inspecting the `data` attribute for the response. For example, the first line checks whether the value for `count` is equal to 1 and the next lines check whether the `name` key for the first element in the `results` array is equal to the value hold in the `new_game_category_name` variable:

```
self.assertEqual(response.data['count'], 1)
self.assertEqual(
    response.data['results'][0]['name'],
    new_game_category_name)
```

The `test_filter_game_category_by_name` method calls the `django.utils.http.urlencode` function to generate an encoded URL from the `filter_by_name` dictionary that specifies the field name and the value we want to use to filter the retrieved data. The following lines show the code that generates the URL and saves it in the `url` variable. If `game_cagory_name1` is `'First game category name'`, the result of the call to the `urlencode` function will be `'name=First+game+category+name'`.

```
filter_by_name = { 'name' : game_category_name1 }
url = '{0}?{1}'.format(
    reverse('gamecategory-list'),
    urlencode(filter_by_name))
```

Running unit tests and checking testing coverage

Now, run the following command to create a test database, run all the migrations and use the Django nose test running to execute all the tests we created. The test runner will execute all the methods for our `GameCategoryTests` class that start with the `test_` prefix and will display the results.

 The tests won't make changes to the database we have been using when working on the API.

Remember that we configured many default command-line options that will be used without the need to enter them in our command-line. Run the following command within the same virtual environment we have been using. We will use the `-v 2` option to use the verbosity level 2 because we want to check all the things that the test runner is doing:

```
python manage.py test -v 2
```

The following lines show the sample output:

```
nosetests --with-coverage --cover-package=games --cover-erase --cover-
inclusive -v --verbosity=2
Creating test database for alias 'default' ('test_games')...
Operations to perform:
  Synchronize unmigrated apps: django_nose, staticfiles, crispy_forms,
messages, rest_framework
  Apply all migrations: games, admin, auth, contenttypes, sessions
```

```
Synchronizing apps without migrations:
  Creating tables...
    Running deferred SQL...
Running migrations:
  Rendering model states... DONE
  Applying contenttypes.0001_initial... OK
  Applying auth.0001_initial... OK
  Applying admin.0001_initial... OK
  Applying admin.0002_logentry_remove_auto_add... OK
  Applying contenttypes.0002_remove_content_type_name... OK
  Applying auth.0002_alter_permission_name_max_length... OK
  Applying auth.0003_alter_user_email_max_length... OK
  Applying auth.0004_alter_user_username_opts... OK
  Applying auth.0005_alter_user_last_login_null... OK
  Applying auth.0006_require_contenttypes_0002... OK
  Applying auth.0007_alter_validators_add_error_messages... OK
  Applying games.0001_initial... OK
  Applying games.0002_auto_20160623_2131... OK
  Applying games.0003_game_owner... OK
  Applying sessions.0001_initial... OK
Ensure we can create a new GameCategory and then retrieve it ... ok
Ensure we can create a new GameCategory. ... ok
Ensure we can filter a game category by name ... ok
Ensure we can retrieve a game cagory ... ok
Ensure we can update a single field for a game category ... ok
Name                    Stmts   Miss   Cover
---------------------------------------------
games.py                   0      0    100%
games/admin.py             1      1      0%
games/apps.py              3      3      0%
games/models.py           36     35      3%
games/pagination.py        3      0    100%
games/permissions.py       6      3     50%
games/serializers.py      45      0    100%
games/urls.py              3      0    100%
games/views.py            91      2     98%
---------------------------------------------
TOTAL                    188     44     77%
---------------------------------------------
Ran 5 tests in 0.143s
OK
Destroying test database for alias 'default' ('test_games')...
```

The output provides the details indicating that the test runner executed 5 tests and all of them passed. After the details about the migrations are executed, the output displays the comments we included for each method in the `GameCategoryTests` class that started with the `test_` prefix and represented a test to be executed. The following list shows the description included in the comments and the method that they represent:

- Ensures we can create a new GameCategory and then retrieve it: `test_create_and_retrieve_game_category`.
- Ensures we can create a new GameCategory: `test_create_duplicated_game_category`.
- Ensures we can filter a game category by name: `test_retrieve_game_categories_list`.
- Ensures we can retrieve a game cagory: `test_update_game_category`.
- Ensures we can update a single field for a game category: `test_filter_game_category_by_name`.

The test code coverage measurement report provided by the `coverage` package uses the code analysis tools and the tracing hooks included in the Python standard library to determine which lines of code are executable and which of these lines have been executed. The report provides a table with the following columns:

- `Name`: The Python module name.
- `Stmts`: The count of executable statements for the Python module.
- `Miss`: The number of executable statements missed, that is, the ones that weren't executed.
- `Cover`: The coverage of executable statements, expressed as a percentage.

We definitely have a very low coverage for `models.py` based on the measurements shown in the report. In fact, we just wrote a few tests related to the `GameCategory` model, and therefore, it makes sense that the coverage is really low for the models:

We can run the `coverage` command with the `-m` command-line option to display the line numbers of the missing statements in a new `Missing` column.

```
coverage report -m
```

The command will use the information from the last execution and will display the missing statements. The next lines show a sample output that correspond to the previous execution of the unit tests:

Name	Stmts	Miss	Cover	Missing
games/__init__.py	0	0	100%	
games/admin.py	1	1	0%	1
games/apps.py	3	3	0%	1-5
games/models.py	36	35	3%	1-10, 14-70
games/pagination.py	3	0	100%	
games/permissions.py	6	3	50%	6-9
games/serializers.py	45	0	100%	
games/tests.py	55	0	100%	
games/urls.py	3	0	100%	
games/views.py	91	2	98%	83, 177
TOTAL	243	44	82%	

Now, run the following command to get annotated HTML listings detailing missed lines:

```
coverage html
```

Open the `index.html` HTML file generated in the `htmlcov` folder with your web browser. The following picture shows an example report that coverage generated in HTML format.

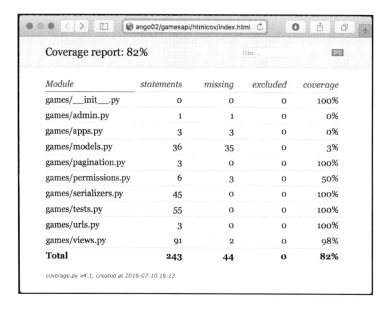

Click or tap on `games/models.py` and the web browser will render a web page that displays the statements that were run, the missing ones and the excluded, with different colors. We can click or tap on the **run**, **missing,** and **excluded** buttons to show or hide the background color that represents the status for each line of code. By default, the missing lines of code will be displayed with a pink background. Thus, we must write unit tests that target these lines of code to improve our tests coverage:

Coverage for **games/models.py** : 3%

36 statements   1 run   35 missing   0 excluded

```python
1   from django.db import models
2
3
4   class GameCategory(models.Model):
5       name = models.CharField(max_length=200, unique=True)
6
7       class Meta:
8           ordering = ('name',)
9
10      def __str__(self):
11          return self.name
12
13
14  class Game(models.Model):
15      owner = models.ForeignKey(
16          'auth.User',
17          related_name='games',
18          on_delete=models.CASCADE)
19      created = models.DateTimeField(auto_now_add=True)
20      name = models.CharField(max_length=200, unique=True)
21      game_category = models.ForeignKey(
22          GameCategory,
23          related_name='games',
24          on_delete=models.CASCADE)
25      release_date = models.DateTimeField()
26      played = models.BooleanField(default=False)
27
28      class Meta:
29          ordering = ('name',)
30
31      def __str__(self):
32          return self.name
33
34
35  class Player(models.Model):
36      MALE = 'M'
37      FEMALE = 'F'
38      GENDER_CHOICES = (
39          (MALE, 'Male'),
40          (FEMALE, 'Female'),
41      )
```

Improving testing coverage

Now, we will write additional unit tests to improve the testing coverage. Specifically, we will write unit tests related to the player class based views: `PlayerList` and `PlayerDetail`. Open the existing `games/test.py` file and insert the following lines after the last line that declares imports. We need a new `import` statement and we will declare the new `PlayerTests` class. The code file for the sample is included in the `restful_python_chapter_04_05` folder:

```
from games.models import Player

class PlayerTests(APITestCase):
    def create_player(self, name, gender):
        url = reverse('player-list')
        data = {'name': name, 'gender': gender}
        response = self.client.post(url, data, format='json')
        return response

    def test_create_and_retrieve_player(self):
        """
        Ensure we can create a new Player and then retrieve it
        """
        new_player_name = 'New Player'
        new_player_gender = Player.MALE
        response = self.create_player(new_player_name, new_player_gender)
        self.assertEqual(response.status_code, status.HTTP_201_CREATED)
        self.assertEqual(Player.objects.count(), 1)
        self.assertEqual(
            Player.objects.get().name,
            new_player_name)

    def test_create_duplicated_player(self):
        """
        Ensure we can create a new Player and we cannot create a duplicate.
        """
        url = reverse('player-list')
        new_player_name = 'New Female Player'
        new_player_gender = Player.FEMALE
        response1 = self.create_player(new_player_name, new_player_gender)
        self.assertEqual(
            response1.status_code,
            status.HTTP_201_CREATED)
        response2 = self.create_player(new_player_name, new_player_gender)
        self.assertEqual(
            response2.status_code,
            status.HTTP_400_BAD_REQUEST)
```

```python
def test_retrieve_players_list(self):
    """
    Ensure we can retrieve a player
    """
    new_player_name = 'New Female Player'
    new_player_gender = Player.FEMALE
    self.create_player(new_player_name, new_player_gender)
    url = reverse('player-list')
    response = self.client.get(url, format='json')
    self.assertEqual(
        response.status_code,
        status.HTTP_200_OK)
    self.assertEqual(
        response.data['count'],
        1)
    self.assertEqual(
        response.data['results'][0]['name'],
        new_player_name)
    self.assertEqual(
        response.data['results'][0]['gender'],
        new_player_gender)
```

The `PlayerTests` class is a subclass of `rest_framework.test.APITestCase`. The class declares the `create_player` method that receives the desired `name` and `gender` for the new player as arguments. The method builds the url and the data dictionary to compose and send an HTTP `POST` method to the view associated with the `player-list` view name and returns the response generated by this request. Many test methods will call the `create_player` method to create a player and then compose and send other HTTP requests to the API.

The class declares the following methods that start whose name start with the `test_` prefix:

- `test_create_and_retrieve_player`: Tests whether we can create a new `Player` and then retrieve it.
- `test_create_duplicated_player`: Tests whether the unique constraints don't make it possible for us to create two players with the same name. The second time we compose and send an HTTP POST request with a duplicate player name, we must receive an HTTP 400 Bad Request status code (`status.HTTP_400_BAD_REQUEST`).
- `test_retrieve_player_list`: Tests whether we can retrieve a specific game category by its primary key or id.

We just coded a few tests related to players to improve test coverage and notice the impact on the test coverage report.

Now, run the following command within the same virtual environment we have been using. We will use the -v 2 option to use the verbosity level 2 because we want to check all the things that the test runner is doing:

```
python manage.py test -v 2
```

The following lines show the last lines of the sample output:

```
Ensure we can create a new GameCategory and then retrieve it ... ok
Ensure we can create a new GameCategory. ... ok
Ensure we can filter a game category by name ... ok
Ensure we can retrieve a game cagory ... ok
Ensure we can update a single field for a game category ... ok
Ensure we can create a new Player and then retrieve it ... ok
Ensure we can create a new Player and we cannot create a duplicate. ...
ok
Ensure we can retrieve a player ... ok
Name                       Stmts   Miss  Cover
------------------------------------------------
games.py                       0      0   100%
games/admin.py                 1      1     0%
games/apps.py                  3      3     0%
games/models.py               36     34     6%
games/pagination.py            3      0   100%
games/permissions.py           6      3    50%
games/serializers.py          45      0   100%
games/urls.py                  3      0   100%
games/views.py                91      2    98%
------------------------------------------------
TOTAL                        188     43    77%
--------------------------------------------------------------------
Ran 8 tests in 0.168s
OK
Destroying test database for alias 'default' ('test_games')...
```

The output provides details that indicate that the test runner executed 8 tests and all of them passed. The test code coverage measurement report provided by the coverage package increased the Cover percentage from 3% in the previous run to 6%. The additional tests we wrote execute code for the Player model, and therefore, there is an impact in the coverage report.

We just created a few unit tests to understand how we can code them. However, of course, it would be necessary to write more tests to provide an appropriate coverage of all the featured and execution scenarios included in the API.

Understanding strategies for deployments and scalability

One of the biggest drawbacks related to Django and Django REST Framework is that each HTTP request is blocking. Thus, whenever the Django server receives an HTTP request, it doesn't start working on any other HTTP requests in the incoming queue until the server sends the response for the first HTTP request it received.

However, one of the greatest advantages of RESTful Web Services is that they are stateless, that is, they shouldn't keep a client state on any server. Our API is a good example of a stateless RESTful Web Service. Thus, we can make the API run on as many servers as necessary to achieve our scalability goals. Obviously, we must take into account that we can easily transform the database server in our scalability bottleneck.

Nowadays, we have a huge number of cloud-based alternatives to deploy a RESTful web service that uses Django and Django REST Framework and make it extremely scalable. Just to mention a few examples, we have Heroku, PythonAnywhere, Google App Engine, OpenShift, AWS Elastic Beanstalk, and Windows Azure.

Each platform includes detailed instructions to deploy our application. All of them will require us to generate the `requirements.txt` file that lists the application dependencies together with their versions. This way, the platforms will be able to install all the necessary dependencies listed in the file.

Run the following `pip freeze`, to generate the `requirements.txt` file:

```
pip freeze > requirements.txt
```

The following lines show the contents of a sample generated `requirements.txt` file. However, bear in mind that many packages increase their version number quickly and you might see different versions in your configuration:

```
coverage==4.1
Django==1.9.7
django-braces==1.9.0
```

```
django-crispy-forms==1.6.0
django-filter==0.13.0
django-nose==1.4.4
django-oauth-toolkit==0.10.0
djangorestframework==3.3.3
nose==1.3.7
oauthlib==1.0.3
psycopg2==2.6.2
six==1.10.0
```

We always have to make sure that we profile the API and the database before we deploy our first version of the RESTful Web Service. It is very important to make sure that the generated queries run properly on the underlying database and that the most popular queries do not end up in sequential scans. It is usually necessary to add the appropriate indexes to the tables in the database.

We have been using basic HTTP authentication. In case we decide to use this authentication or other mechanisms, we must make sure that the API runs under HTTPS in production environments. In addition, we must make sure that we change the following line in the `settings.py` file:

```
DEBUG = True
```

We must always turn off the debug mode in production, and therefore, we must replace the previous line with the following one:

```
DEBUG = False
```

Test your knowledge

1. The `ScopedRateThrottle` class:
    1. Limits the rate of requests that a specific user can make.
    2. Limits the rate of requests for specific parts of the API identified with the value assigned to the `throttle_scope` property.
    3. Limits the rate of requests that an anonymous user can make.
2. The `UserRateThrottle` class:
    1. Limits the rate of requests that a specific user can make.
    2. Limits the rate of requests for specific parts of the API identified with the value assigned to the `throttle_scope` property.
    3. Limits the rate of requests that an anonymous user can make.

3. The `DjangoFilterBackend` class:
    1. Provides single query parameter based searching capabilities and it is based on the Django admin's search function.
    2. Allows the client to control how the results are ordered with a single query parameter.
    3. Provides field filtering capabilities.
4. The `SearchFilter` class:
    1. Provides single query parameter based searching capabilities and it is based on the Django admin's search function.
    2. Allows the client to control how the results are ordered with a single query parameter.
    3. Provides field filtering capabilities.
5. In a subclass of `APITestCase`, `self.client` is:
    1. The `APIClient` instance that allows us to easily compose and send HTTP requests for testing.
    2. The `APITestClient` instance that allows us to easily compose and send HTTP requests for testing.
    3. The `APITestCase` instance that allows us to easily compose and send HTTP requests for testing.

Summary

In this chapter, we took advantage of the features included in Django REST Framework to define throttling policies. We used filtering, searching, and ordering classes to make it easy to configure filters, search queries, and desired order for the results in HTTP requests. We used the browsable API feature to test these new features included in our API.

We wrote the first round of unit tests, measured test coverage, and then we wrote additional unit tests to improve test coverage. Finally, we understood many considerations for deployment and scalability.

Now that we built a complex API with Django REST Framework and tested it, we will move to another popular Python web framework, Flask, which is what we are going to discuss in the next chapter.

5
Developing RESTful APIs with Flask

In this chapter, we will start working with Flask and its Flask-RESTful extension; we will also create a RESTful Web API that performs CRUD operations on a simple list. We will:

- Design a RESTful API that performs CRUD operations in Flask with the Flask-RESTful extension
- Understand the tasks performed by each HTTP method
- Set up the virtual environment with Flask and its Flask-RESTful extension
- Declare status codes for the responses
- Create the model to represent a resource
- Use a dictionary as a repository
- Configure output fields for serialized responses
- Work with resourceful routing on top of Flask pluggable views
- Configure resource routing and endpoints
- Make HTTP requests to the Flask API
- Work with command-line tools to interact with the Flask API
- Work with GUI tools to interact with the Flask API

Designing a RESTful API to interact with a simple data source

Imagine that we have to configure the messages to be displayed in an OLED display wired to an **IoT** (**Internet of Things**) device, the IoT device is capable of running Python 3.5, Flask, and other Python packages. There is a team that is writing code that retrieves string messages from a dictionary and displays them in the OLED display wired to the IoT device. We have to start working on a mobile app and a website that has to interact with a RESTful API to perform CRUD operations with string messages.

We don't need an ORM because we won't persist the string messages on a database. We will just work with an in-memory dictionary as our data source. It is one of the requirements for this RESTful API. In this case, the RESTful web service will be running on the IoT device, that is, we will run the Flask development server on the IoT device.

 We will definitely lose scalability for our RESTful API because we have the in-memory data source in the server, and therefore, we cannot run the RESTful API in another IoT device. However, we will work with another example related to a more complex data source that will be able to scale in the RESTful way later. The first example is going to allow us to understand how Flask and Flask-RESTful work together with a very simple in-memory data source.

We have chosen Flask because it is more lightweight than Django, we don't need to configure an ORM and we want to start running the RESTful API on the IoT device, as soon as possible, to allow all the teams to interact with it. We will code the website with Flask too, and therefore, we want to use the same web micro-framework to power the website and the RESTful web service.

There are many extensions available for Flask that makes it easier to perform specific tasks with the Flask micro-framework. We will take advantage of Flask-RESTful, an extension that will allow us to encourage best practices while building our RESTful API. In this case, we will work with a Python dictionary as the data source. As previously explained, we will work with more complex data sources in the forthcoming examples.

First, we must specify the requirements for our main resource: a message. We need the following attributes or fields for a message:

- An integer identifier
- A string message
- A duration in seconds that indicates the time the message has to be printed on the OLED display
- A creation date and time-the timestamp will be added automatically when adding a new message to the collection
- A message category description, such as "Warning" and "Information"
- An integer counter that indicates the times the message has been printed in the OLED display
- A `bool` value indicating whether the message was printed at least once on the OLED display

The following table shows the HTTP verbs, the scope, and the semantics for the methods that our first version of the API must support. Each method is composed by an HTTP verb and a scope and all the methods have a well-defined meaning for all the messages and collections. In our API, each message has its own unique URL.

HTTP verb	Scope	Semantics
GET	Collection of messages	Retrieve all the stored messages in the collection, sorted by their name in ascending order
GET	Message	Retrieve a single message
POST	Collection of messages	Create a new message in the collection
PATCH	Message	Update a field for an existing message
DELETE	Message	Delete an existing message

Understanding the tasks performed by each HTTP method

Let's consider that `http://localhost:5000/api/messages/` is the URL for the collection of messages. If we add a number to the preceding URL, we identify a specific message whose id is equal to the specified numeric value. For example, `http://localhost:5000/api/messsages/6` identifies the message whose id is equal to 6.

We want our API to be able to differentiate collections from a single resource of the collection in the URLs. When we refer a collection, we will use a slash (/) as the last character for the URL, as in `http://localhost:5000/api/messages/`. When we refer to a single resource of the collection we won't use a slash (/) as the last character for the URL, as in `http://localhost:5000/api/messages/6`.

We have to compose and send an HTTP request with the POST HTTP verb and the `http://localhost:5000/api/messages/` request URL to create a new message. In addition, we have to provide the JSON key-value pairs with the field names and the values to create the new message. As a result of the request, the server will validate the provided values for the fields, make sure that it is a valid message, and persist it in the messages dictionary.

The server will return a 201 Created status code and a JSON body with the recently added message serialized to JSON, including the assigned id that was automatically generated by the server to the message object:

```
POST http://localhost:5000/api/messages/
```

We have to compose and send an HTTP request with the GET HTTP verb and the `http://localhost:5000/api/messages/{id}` request URL to retrieve the message whose id matches the specified numeric value in the place where {id} is written. For example, if we use the request URL `http://localhost:5000/api/messages/82`, the server will retrieve the game whose id matches 82. As a result of the request, the server will retrieve a message with the specified id from the dictionary.

If a message is found, the server will serialize the message object into JSON and return a 200 OK status code and a JSON body with the serialized message object. If no message matches the specified id or primary key, the server will return a 404 Not Found status:

```
GET http://localhost:5000/api/messages/{id}
```

We have to compose and send an HTTP request with the PATCH HTTP verb and the `http://localhost:5000/api/messages/{id}` request URL to update one or more fields for the message whose id matches the specified numeric value in the place where {id} is written. In addition, we have to provide the JSON key-value pairs with the field names to be updated and their new values. As a result of the request, the server will validate the provided values for the fields, update these fields on the message that matches the specified id, and update the message in the dictionary, if it is a valid message.

The server will return a 200 OK status code and a JSON body with the recently updated game serialized to JSON. If we provide invalid data for the fields to be updated, the server will return a 400 Bad Request status code. If the server doesn't find a message with the specified id, the server will return just a 404 Not Found status:

```
PATCH http://localhost:5000/api/messages/{id}
```

 The PATCH method will allow us to easily update two fields for a message: the integer counter, that indicates the times the message has been printed and the bool value, that specifies whether the message was printed at least once.

We have to compose and send an HTTP request with the DELETE HTTP verb and the http://localhost:5000/api/messages/{id} request URL to remove the message whose id matches the specified numeric value in the place where {id} is written. For example, if we use the request URL http://localhost:5000/api/messages/15, the server will delete the message whose id matches 15. As a result of the request, the server will retrieve a message with the specified id from the dictionary. If a message is found, the server will request the dictionary to delete the entry associated with this message object and return a 204 No Content status code. If no message matches the specified id, the server will return a 404 Not Found status:

```
DELETE http://localhost:5000/api/messages/{id}
```

Setting up a virtual environment with Flask and Flask-RESTful

In Chapter 1, *Developing RESTful APIs with Django*, we learned that, throughout this book, we were going to work with the lightweight virtual environments introduced in Python 3.4 and improved in Python 3.4. Now, we will follow the steps to create a new lightweight virtual environment to work with Flask and Flask-RESTful. It is highly recommended to read Chapter 1, *Developing RESTful APIs with Django*, in case you don't have experience with lightweight virtual environments in Python. The chapter includes all the detailed explanations of the effects of the steps we are going to follow.

First, we have to select the target folder or directory for our virtual environment. We will use the following path in the example for macOS and Linux. The target folder for the virtual environment will be the `PythonREST/Flask01` folder within our home directory. For example, if our home directory in macOS or Linux is `/Users/gaston`, the virtual environment will be created within `/Users/gaston/PythonREST/Flask01`. You can replace the specified path with your desired path in each command, as shown:

```
~/PythonREST/Flask01
```

We will use the following path in the example for Windows. The target folder for the virtual environment will be the `PythonREST\Flask01` folder within our user profile folder. For example, if our user profile folder is `C:\Users\Gaston`, the virtual environment will be created within `C:\Users\gaston\PythonREST\Flask01`. You can replace the specified path with your desired path in each command, as shown:

```
%USERPROFILE%\PythonREST\Flask01
```

Open a Terminal in macOS or Linux and execute the following command to create a virtual environment:

`python3 -m venv ~/PythonREST/Flask01`

In Windows, execute the following command to create a virtual environment:

`python -m venv %USERPROFILE%\PythonREST\Flask01`

The preceding command doesn't produce any output. Now that we have created a virtual environment, we will run a platform-specific script to activate it. After we activate the virtual environment, we will install packages that will only be available in this virtual environment.

If your Terminal is configured to use the `bash` shell in macOS or Linux, run the following command to activate the virtual environment. The command also works for the `zsh` shell:

`source ~/PythonREST/Flask01/bin/activate`

If your Terminal is configured to use either the `csh` or `tcsh` shell, run the following command to activate the virtual environment:

`source ~/PythonREST/Flask01/bin/activate.csh`

If your Terminal is configured to use either the `fish` shell, run the following command to activate the virtual environment:

```
source ~/PythonREST/Flask01/bin/activate.fish
```

In Windows, you can run either a batch file in the Command Prompt or a Windows PowerShell script to activate the virtual environment. If you prefer the Command Prompt, run the following command in the Windows command line to activate the virtual environment:

```
%USERPROFILE%\PythonREST\Flask01\Scripts\activate.bat
```

If you prefer the Windows PowerShell, launch it and run the following commands to activate the virtual environment. However, note that you should have the scripts execution enabled in Windows PowerShell to be able to run the script:

```
cd $env:USERPROFILE
PythonREST\Flask01\Scripts\Activate.ps1
```

After you activate the virtual environment, the Command Prompt will display the virtual environment root folder name, enclosed in parenthesis, as a prefix for the default prompt, to remind us that we are working in the virtual environment. In this case, we will see (`Flask01`) as a prefix for the Command Prompt because the root folder for the activated virtual environment is `Flask01`.

We have created and activated a virtual environment. Now it is time to run the commands that will be the same for macOS, Linux, or Windows; we must run the following command to install Flask-RESTful with pip. Flask is a dependency for Flask-RESTful, and therefore, pip will install it automatically, too:

```
pip install flask-restful
```

The last lines for the output will indicate all the packages that have been successfully installed, including `flask-restful` and `Flask`:

```
    Installing collected packages: six, pytz, click, itsdangerous,
  MarkupSafe, Jinja2, Werkzeug, Flask, python-dateutil, aniso8601, flask-
  restful
      Running setup.py install for click
      Running setup.py install for itsdangerous
      Running setup.py install for MarkupSafe
      Running setup.py install for aniso8601
    Successfully installed Flask-0.11.1 Jinja2-2.8 MarkupSafe-0.23
  Werkzeug-0.11.10 aniso8601-1.1.0 click-6.6 flask-restful-0.3.5
  itsdangerous-0.24 python-dateutil-2.5.3 pytz-2016.4 six-1.10.0
```

Declaring status codes for the responses

Neither Flask nor Flask-RESTful includes the declaration of variables for the different HTTP status codes. We don't want to return numbers as status codes. We want our code to be easy to read and understand, and therefore, we will use descriptive HTTP status codes. We will borrow the code that declares useful functions and variables related to HTTP status codes from the `status.py` file included in Django REST Framework, that is, the framework we have been using in the preceding chapters.

First, create a folder named `api` within the root folder for the recently created virtual environment, and then create a new `status.py` file within the `api` folder. The following lines show the code that declares functions and variables with descriptive HTTP status codes in the `api/models.py` file borrowed from the `rest_framework.status` module. We don't want to reinvent the wheel, and the module provides everything we need to work with HTTP status codes in our Flask-based API. The code file for the sample is included in the `restful_python_chapter_05_01` folder:

```
def is_informational(code):
    return code >= 100 and code <= 199


def is_success(code):
    return code >= 200 and code <= 299


def is_redirect(code):
    return code >= 300 and code <= 399


def is_client_error(code):
    return code >= 400 and code <= 499


def is_server_error(code):
    return code >= 500 and code <= 599


HTTP_100_CONTINUE = 100
HTTP_101_SWITCHING_PROTOCOLS = 101
HTTP_200_OK = 200
HTTP_201_CREATED = 201
HTTP_202_ACCEPTED = 202
HTTP_203_NON_AUTHORITATIVE_INFORMATION = 203
HTTP_204_NO_CONTENT = 204
HTTP_205_RESET_CONTENT = 205
```

```
HTTP_206_PARTIAL_CONTENT = 206
HTTP_300_MULTIPLE_CHOICES = 300
HTTP_301_MOVED_PERMANENTLY = 301
HTTP_302_FOUND = 302
HTTP_303_SEE_OTHER = 303
HTTP_304_NOT_MODIFIED = 304
HTTP_305_USE_PROXY = 305
HTTP_306_RESERVED = 306
HTTP_307_TEMPORARY_REDIRECT = 307
HTTP_400_BAD_REQUEST = 400
HTTP_401_UNAUTHORIZED = 401
HTTP_402_PAYMENT_REQUIRED = 402
HTTP_403_FORBIDDEN = 403
HTTP_404_NOT_FOUND = 404
HTTP_405_METHOD_NOT_ALLOWED = 405
HTTP_406_NOT_ACCEPTABLE = 406
HTTP_407_PROXY_AUTHENTICATION_REQUIRED = 407
HTTP_408_REQUEST_TIMEOUT = 408
HTTP_409_CONFLICT = 409
HTTP_410_GONE = 410
HTTP_411_LENGTH_REQUIRED = 411
HTTP_412_PRECONDITION_FAILED = 412
HTTP_413_REQUEST_ENTITY_TOO_LARGE = 413
HTTP_414_REQUEST_URI_TOO_LONG = 414
HTTP_415_UNSUPPORTED_MEDIA_TYPE = 415
HTTP_416_REQUESTED_RANGE_NOT_SATISFIABLE = 416
HTTP_417_EXPECTATION_FAILED = 417
HTTP_428_PRECONDITION_REQUIRED = 428
HTTP_429_TOO_MANY_REQUESTS = 429
HTTP_431_REQUEST_HEADER_FIELDS_TOO_LARGE = 431
HTTP_451_UNAVAILABLE_FOR_LEGAL_REASONS = 451
HTTP_500_INTERNAL_SERVER_ERROR = 500
HTTP_501_NOT_IMPLEMENTED = 501
HTTP_502_BAD_GATEWAY = 502
HTTP_503_SERVICE_UNAVAILABLE = 503
HTTP_504_GATEWAY_TIMEOUT = 504
HTTP_505_HTTP_VERSION_NOT_SUPPORTED = 505
HTTP_511_NETWORK_AUTHENTICATION_REQUIRED = 511
```

The code declares five functions that receive the HTTP status code in the code argument and determine which of the following categories the status code belongs to: informational, success, redirect, client error, or server error categories. We will use the previous variables when we have to return a specific status code. For example, in case we have to return a 404 Not Found status code, we will return status.HTTP_404_NOT_FOUND, instead of just 404.

Creating the model

Now, we will create a simple `MessageModel` class that we will use to represent messages. Remember that we won't be persisting the model in the database, and therefore, in this case, our class will just provide the required attributes and no mapping information. Create a new `models.py` file in the `api` folder. The following lines show the code that creates a `MessageModel` class in the `api/models.py` file. The code file for the sample is included in the `restful_python_chapter_05_01` folder:

```
class MessageModel:
    def __init__(self, message, duration, creation_date, message_category):
        # We will automatically generate the new id
        self.id = 0
        self.message = message
        self.duration = duration
        self.creation_date = creation_date
        self.message_category = message_category
        self.printed_times = 0
        self.printed_once = False
```

The `MessageModel` class just declares a constructor, that is, the `__init__` method. This method receives many arguments and then uses them to initialize the attributes with the same names: `message`, `duration`, `creation_date`, and `message_category`. The `id` attribute is set to 0, `printed_times` is set to 0, and `printed_once` is set to `False`. We will automatically increment the identifier for each new message generated with API calls.

Using a dictionary as a repository

Now, we will create a `MessageManager` class that we will use to persist the `MessageModel` instances in an in-memory dictionary. Our API methods will call methods for the `MessageManager` class to retrieve, insert, update, and delete `MessageModel` instances. Create a new `api.py` file in the `api` folder. The following lines show the code that creates a `MessageManager` class in the `api/api.py` file. In addition, the following lines declare all the `imports` we will need for all the code we will write in this file. The code file for the sample is included in the `restful_python_chapter_05_01` folder.

```
from flask import Flask
from flask_restful import abort, Api, fields, marshal_with, reqparse,
Resource
from datetime import datetime
from models import MessageModel
import status
```

```
from pytz import utc


class MessageManager():
    last_id = 0
    def __init__(self):
        self.messages = {}

    def insert_message(self, message):
        self.__class__.last_id += 1
        message.id = self.__class__.last_id
        self.messages[self.__class__.last_id] = message

    def get_message(self, id):
        return self.messages[id]

    def delete_message(self, id):
         del self.messages[id]
```

The MessageManager class declares a last_id class attribute and initializes it to 0. This class attribute stores the last id that has been generated and assigned to a MessageModel instance stored in a dictionary. The constructor, that is, the __init__ method, creates and initializes the messages attribute as an empty dictionary.

The code declares the following three methods for the class:

- insert_message: This method receives a recently created MessageModel instance in the message argument. The code increases the value for the last_id class attribute and then assigns the resulting value to the id for the received message. The code uses self.__class__ to reference the type of the current instance. Finally, the code adds the message as a value to the key identified with the generated id, last_id, in the self.messages dictionary.
- get_message: This method receives the id of the message that has to be retrieved from the self.messages dictionary. The code returns the value related to the key that matches the received id in the self.messages dictionary that we are using as our data source.
- delete_message: This method receives the id of the message that has to be removed from the self.messages dictionary. The code deletes the key-value pair whose key matches the received id in the self.messages dictionary that we are using as our data source.

We don't need a method to update a message because we will just make changes to the attributes of the `MessageModel` instance that is already stored in the `self.messages` dictionary. The value stored in the dictionary is a reference to the `MessageModel` instance that we are updating, and therefore, we don't need to call a specific method to update the instance in the dictionary. However, in case we were working with a database, we would need to call an update method for our ORM or data repository.

Configuring output fields

Now, we will create a `message_fields` dictionary that we will use to control the data that we want Flask-RESTful to render in our response, when we return `MessageModel` instances. Open the previously created `api/api.py` file and add the following lines. The code file for the sample is included in the `restful_python_chapter_05_01` folder.

```
message_fields = {
    'id': fields.Integer,
    'uri': fields.Url('message_endpoint'),
    'message': fields.String,
    'duration': fields.Integer,
    'creation_date': fields.DateTime,
    'message_category': fields.String,
    'printed_times': fields.Integer,
    'printed_once': fields.Boolean
}


message_manager = MessageManager()
```

We declared the `message_fields` dictionary (`dict`) with key-value pairs of strings and classes declared in the `flask_restful.fields` module. The keys are the names of the attributes we want to render from the `MessageModel` class and the values are the classes that format and return the value for the field. In the previous code, we worked with the following classes, that format and return the value for the specified field in the key:

- `field.Integer`: Outputs an integer value.
- `fields.Url`: Generates a string representation of a URL. By default, this class generates a relative URI for the resource that is being requested. The code specifies `'message_endpoint'` for the `endpoint` argument. This way, the class will use the specified endpoint name. We will declare this endpoint later in the `api.py` file. We don't want to include the hostname in the generated URI, and therefore, we use the default value for the `absolute` bool attribute, which is `False`.

- `fields.DateTime`: Outputs a formatted `datetime` string in UTC, in the default RFC 822 format.
- `fields.Boolean`: Generates a string representation of a bool value.

The `'uri'` field uses `fields.Url` and it is related to the specified endpoint instead of being associated to an attribute of the `MessageModel` class. It is the only case in which the specified field name doesn't have an attribute in the `MessageModel` class. The other strings specified as keys indicate all the attributes we want to be rendered in the output when we use the `message_fields` dictionary to make up the final serialized response output.

After we declared the `message_fields` dictionary, the next line of code creates an instance of the previously created `MessageManager` class named `message_manager`. We will use this instance to create, retrieve, and delete `MessageModel` instances.

Working with resourceful routing on top of Flask pluggable views

Flask-RESTful uses resources built on top of Flask pluggable views as the main building block for a RESTful API. We just need to create a subclass of the `flask_restful.Resource` class and declare the methods for each supported HTTP verb. A subclass of `flask_restful.Resource` represents a RESTful resource and therefore, we will have to declare one class to represent the collection of messages and another one to represent the message resource.

First, we will create a `Message` class that we will use to represent the message resource. Open the previously created `api/api.py` file and add the following lines. The code file for the sample is included in the `restful_python_chapter_05_01` folder, as shown:

```
class Message(Resource):
    def abort_if_message_doesnt_exist(self, id):
        if id not in message_manager.messages:
            abort(
                status.HTTP_404_NOT_FOUND,
                message="Message {0} doesn't exist".format(id))

    @marshal_with(message_fields)
    def get(self, id):
        self.abort_if_message_doesnt_exist(id)
        return message_manager.get_message(id)

    def delete(self, id):
```

```
    self.abort_if_message_doesnt_exist(id)
    message_manager.delete_message(id)
    return '', status.HTTP_204_NO_CONTENT

@marshal_with(message_fields)
def patch(self, id):
    self.abort_if_message_doesnt_exist(id)
    message = message_manager.get_message(id)
    parser = reqparse.RequestParser()
    parser.add_argument('message', type=str)
    parser.add_argument('duration', type=int)
    parser.add_argument('printed_times', type=int)
    parser.add_argument('printed_once', type=bool)
    args = parser.parse_args()
    if 'message' in args:
        message.message = args['message']
    if 'duration' in args:
        message.duration = args['duration']
    if 'printed_times' in args:
        message.printed_times = args['printed_times']
    if 'printed_once' in args:
        message.printed_once = args['printed_once']
    return message
```

The `Message` class is a subclass of `flask_restful.Resource` and declares the following three methods, that will be called when the HTTP method with the same name arrives as a request on the represented resource:

- `get`: This method receives the id of the message that has to be retrieved in the `id` argument. The code calls the `self.abort_if_message_doesnt_exist` method to abort in case there is no message with the requested id. In case the message exists, the code returns the `MessageModel` instance whose `id` that matches the specified `id` returned by the `message_manager.get_message` method. The `get` method uses the `@marshal_with` decorator with `message_fields` as an argument. The decorator will take the `MessageModel` instance and apply the field filtering and output formatting specified in `message_fields`.

- `delete`: This method receives the id of the message that has to be deleted in the `id` argument. The code calls the `self.abort_if_message_doesnt_exist` method to abort, in case there is no message with the requested id. In case the ```message exists, the code calls the `message_manager.delete_message` method with the received id as an argument to remove the `MessageModel` instance from our data repository. Then, the code returns an empty response body and a `204 No Content` status code.

- `patch`: This method receives the id of the message that has to be updated or patched in the `id` argument. The code calls the `self.abort_if_message_doesnt_exist` method to abort in case there is no message with the requested id. In case the message exists, the code saves the `MessageModel` instance whose `id` that matches the specified `id` returned by the `message_manager.get_message` method in the `message` variable. The next line creates a `flask_restful.reqparse.RequestParser` instance named `parser`. The `RequestParser` instance allows us to add arguments with their names and types and then easily parse the arguments received with the request. The code makes four calls to the `parser.add_argument` with the argument name and the type of the four arguments we want to parse. Then, the code calls the `parser.parse_args` method to parse all the arguments from the request and saves the returned dictionary (`dict`) in the `args` variable. The code updates all the attributes that have new values in the `args` dictionary in the `MessageModel` instance: `message`. In case the request didn't include values for certain fields, the code won't make changes to the realted attributes. The request doesn't require to include the four fields that can be updated with values. The code returns the updated `message`. The `patch` method uses the `@marshal_with` decorator with `message_fields` as an argument. The decorator will take the `MessageModel` instance, `message`, and apply the field filtering and output formatting specified in `message_fields`.

We used multiple return values to set the response code.

As previously explained, the three methods call the internal `abort_if_message_doesnt_exist` method that receives the id for an existing `MessageModel` instance in the `id` argument. If the received `id` is not present in the keys of the `message_manager.messages` dictionary, the method calls the `flask_restful.abort` function with `status.HTTP_404_NOT_FOUND` as the `http_status_code` argument and a message indicating that the message with the specified id doesn't exists. The `abort` function raises an `HTTPException` for the received `http_status_code` and attaches the additional keyword arguments to the exception for later processing. In this case, we generate an HTTP `404 Not Found` status code.

Both the `get` and `patch` methods use the `@marshal_with` decorator that takes a single data object or a list of data objects and applies the field filtering and output formatting specifies as an argument. The marshalling can also work with dictionaries (dicts). In both methods, we specified `message_fields` as an argument, and therefore, the code renders the following fields: `id`, `uri`, `message`, `duration`, `creation_date`, `message_category`, `printed_times` and `printed_once`. When we use the `@marshal_with` decorator, we are automatically returning an HTTP 200 OK status code.

The following `return` statement with the `@marshal_with(message_fields)` decorator returns an `HTTP 200 OK` status code because we didn't specify any status code after the returned object (`message`):

```
return message
```

The next line is the line of code that is really executed with the `@marshal_with(message_fields)` decorator, and we can use it instead of working with the decorator:

```
return marshal(message, resource_fields), status.HTTP_200_OK
```

For example, we can call the `marshal` function as shown in the previous line instead of using the `@marshal_with` decorator and the code will produce the same result.

Now, we will create a `MessageList` class that we will use to represent the collection of messages. Open the previously created `api/api.py` file and add the following lines. The code file for the sample is included in the `restful_python_chapter_05_01` folder:

```
class MessageList(Resource):
    @marshal_with(message_fields)
    def get(self):
        return [v for v in message_manager.messages.values()]

    @marshal_with(message_fields)
    def post(self):
        parser = reqparse.RequestParser()
        parser.add_argument('message', type=str, required=True,
help='Message cannot be blank!')
        parser.add_argument('duration', type=int, required=True,
help='Duration cannot be blank!')
        parser.add_argument('message_category', type=str, required=True,
help='Message category cannot be blank!')
        args = parser.parse_args()
        message = MessageModel(
            message=args['message'],
            duration=args['duration'],
```

```
        creation_date=datetime.now(utc),
        message_category=args['message_category']
        )
    message_manager.insert_message(message)
    return message, status.HTTP_201_CREATED
```

The `MessageList` class is a subclass of `flask_restful.Resource` and declares the following two methods that will be called when the HTTP method with the same name arrives as a request on the represented resource:

- `get`: This method returns a list with all the `MessageModel` instances saved in the `message_manager.messages` dictionary. The `get` method uses the `@marshal_with` decorator with `message_fields` as an argument. The decorator will take each `MessageModel` instance in the returned list and apply the field filtering and output formatting specified in `message_fields`.
- `post`: This method creates a `flask_restful.reqparse.RequestParser` instance named `parser`. The `RequestParser` instance allows us to add arguments with their names and types and then easily parse the arguments received with the POST request to create a new `MessageModel` instance. The code makes three calls to the `parser.add_argument` with the argument name and the type of the three arguments we want to parse. Then, the code calls the `parser.parse_args` method to parse all the arguments from the request and saves the returned dictionary (`dict`) in the `args` variable. The code uses the parsed arguments in the dictionary to specify the values for the `message`, `duration` and `message_category` attributes to create a new `MessageModel` instance and save it in the `message` variable. The value for the `creation_date` argument is set to the current `datetime` with time zone info, and therefore, it isn't parsed from the request. Then, the code calls the `message_manager.insert_message` method with the new `MessageModel` instance (`message`) to add this new instance to the dictionary. The `post` method uses the `@marshal_with` decorator with `message_fields` as an argument. The decorator will take the recently created and stored `MessageModel` instance, `message`, and apply the field filtering and output formatting specified in `message_fields`. The code returns an HTTP 201 Created status code.

The following table shows the method of our previously created classes that we want to be executed for each combination of HTTP verb and scope:

HTTP verb	Scope	Class and method
GET	Collection of messages	MessageList.get
GET	Message	Message.get
POST	Collection of messages	MessageList.post
PATCH	Message	Message.patch
DELETE	Message	Message.delete

If the request results in the invocation of a resource with an unsupported HTTP method, Flask-RESTful will return a response with the HTTP 405 Method Not Allowed status code.

Configuring resource routing and endpoints

We must make the necessary resource routing configurations to call the appropriate methods and pass them all the necessary arguments by defining URL rules. The following lines create the main entry point for the application, initialize it with a Flask application and configure the resource routing for the api. Open the previously created api/api.py file and add the following lines. The code file for the sample is included in the restful_python_chapter_05_01 folder:

```
app = Flask(__name__)
api = Api(app)
api.add_resource(MessageList, '/api/messages/')
api.add_resource(Message, '/api/messages/<int:id>',
endpoint='message_endpoint')


if __name__ == '__main__':
    app.run(debug=True)
```

The code creates an instance of the `flask_restful.Api` class and saves it in the `api` variable. Each call to the `api.add_resource` method routes a URL to a resource, specifically to one of the previously declared subclasses of the `flask_restful.Resource` class. When there is a request to the API and the URL matches one of the URLs specified in the `api.add_resource` method, Flask will call the method that matches the HTTP verb in the request for the specified class. The method follows standard Flask routing rules.

For example, the following line will make an HTTP GET request to `/api/messages/` without any additional parameters to call the `MessageList.get` method:

```
api.add_resource(MessageList, '/api/messages/')
```

Flask will pass the URL variables to the called method as arguments. For example, the following line will make an HTTP GET request to `/api/messages/12` to call the `Message.get` method with `12` passed as the value for the `id` argument:

```
api.add_resource(Message, '/api/messages/<int:id>',
endpoint='message_endpoint')
```

In addition, we can specify a string value for the endpoint argument to make it easy to reference the specified route in `fields.Url` fields. We pass the same endpoint name, `'message_endpoint'` as an argument in the `uri` field declared as `fields.Url` in the `message_fields` dictionary that we use to render each `MessageModel` instance. This way, `fields.Url` will generate a URI considering this route.

We just required a few lines of code to configure resource routing and endpoints. The last line just calls the `app.run` method to start the Flask application with the `debug` argument set to `True` to enable debugging. In this case, we start the application by calling the `run` method to immediately launch a local server. We could also achieve the same goal by using the `flask` command-line script. However, this option would require us to configure environment variables and the instructions are different for the platforms that we are covering in this book-macOS, Windows and Linux.

As with any other Web framework, you should never enable debugging in a production environment.

Making HTTP requests to the Flask API

Now, we can run the `api/api.py` script that launches Flask's development server to compose and send HTTP requests to our unsecure and simple Web API (we will definitely add security later). Execute the following command.

```
python api/api.py
```

The following lines show the output after we execute the previous command. The development server is listening at port `5000`.

```
* Running on http://127.0.0.1:5000/ (Press CTRL+C to quit)
* Restarting with stat
* Debugger is active!
* Debugger pin code: 294-714-594
```

With the previous command, we will start Flask development server and we will only be able to access it in our development computer. The previous command starts the development server in the default IP address, that is, `127.0.0.1` (`localhost`). It is not possible to access this IP address from other computers or devices connected on our LAN. Thus, if we want to make HTTP requests to our API from other computers or devices connected to our LAN, we should use the development computer IP address, `0.0.0.0` (for IPv4 configurations) or `::` (for IPv6 configurations), as the desired IP address for our development server.

If we specify `0.0.0.0` as the desired IP address for IPv4 configurations, the development server will listen on every interface on port 5000. In addition, it is necessary to open the default port `5000` in our firewalls (software and/or hardware) and configure port-forwarding to the computer that is running the development server.

We just need to specify `'0.0.0.0'` as the value for the host argument in the call to the `app.run` method, specifically, the last line in the `api/api.py` file. The following line shows the new call to `app.run` that launches Flask's development server in an IPv4 configuration and allows requests to be made from other computers and devices connected to our LAN. The line generates an externally visible server. The code file for the sample is included in the `restful_python_chapter_05_02` folder:

```
if __name__ == '__main__':
    app.run(host='0.0.0.0', debug=True)
```

If you decide to compose and send HTTP requests from other computers or devices connected to the LAN, remember that you have to use the development computer's assigned IP address instead of `localhost`. For example, if the computer's assigned IPv4 IP address is `192.168.1.103`, instead of `localhost:5000`, you should use `192.168.1.103:5000`. Of course, you can also use the host name instead of the IP address. The previously explained configurations are very important because mobile devices might be the consumers of our RESTful APIs and we will always want to test the apps that make use of our APIs in our development environments. In addition, we can work with useful tools such as ngrok that allow us to generate secure tunnels to localhost. You can read more information about ngrok at `http://www.ngrok.com`.

The Flask development server is running on localhost (`127.0.0.1`), listening on port `5000`, and waiting for our HTTP requests. Now, we will compose and send HTTP requests locally in our development computer or from other computer or devices connected to our LAN.

Working with command-line tools – curl and httpie

We will start composing and sending HTTP requests with the command-line tools we have introduced in `Chapter 1`, *Developing RESTful APIs with Django*, curl and HTTPie. In case you haven't installed HTTPie, make sure you activate the virtual environment and then run the following command in the terminal or command prompt to install the HTTPie package.

```
pip install --upgrade httpie
```

In case you don't remember how to activate the virtual environment that we created for this example, read the following section in this chapter- *Setting up the virtual environment with Django REST framework.*

Open a Cygwin Terminal in Windows or a Terminal in macOS or Linux, and run the following command. It is very important that you enter the ending slash (/) when specified /api/messages won't match any of the configured URL routes. Thus, we must enter `/api/messages/`, including the ending slash (/). We will compose and send an HTTP request to create a new message:

```
http POST :5000/api/messages/ message='Welcome to IoT' duration=10
message_category='Information'
```

The following is the equivalent curl command. It is very important to use the -H
"Content-Type: application/json" option to indicate curl to send the data specified
after the -d option as application/json instead of the default application/x-www-
form-urlencoded:

```
curl -iX POST -H "Content-Type: application/json" -d
'{"message":"Welcome to IoT", "duration":10, "message_category":
"Information"}' :5000/api/messages/
```

The previous commands will compose and send the following HTTP request: POST
http://localhost:5000/api/messages/ with the following JSON key-value pairs:

```
{
    "message": "Welcome to IoT",
    "duration": 10,
    "message_category": "Information"
}
```

The request specifies /api/messages/, and therefore, it will match '/api/messages/'
and run the MessageList.post method. The method doesn't receive arguments because
the URL route doesn't include any parameters. As the HTTP verb for the request is POST,
Flask calls the post method. If the new MessageModel was successfully persisted in the
dictionary, the function returns an HTTP 201 Created status code and the recently
persisted MessageModel serialized serialized to JSON in the response body. The following
lines show an example response for the HTTP request, with the new MessageModel object
in the JSON response:

```
HTTP/1.0 201 CREATED
Content-Length: 245
Content-Type: application/json
Date: Wed, 20 Jul 2016 04:43:24 GMT
Server: Werkzeug/0.11.10 Python/3.5.1
{
    "creation_date": "Wed, 20 Jul 2016 04:43:24 -0000",
    "duration": 10,
    "id": 1,
    "message": "Welcome to IoT",
    "message_category": "Information",
    "printed_once": false,
    "printed_times": 0,
    "uri": "/api/messages/1"
}
```

We will compose and send an HTTP request to create another message. Go back to the Cygwin terminal in Windows or the Terminal in macOS or Linux, and run the following command:

```
http POST :5000/api/messages/ message='Measuring ambient temperature'
duration=5 message_category='Information'
```

The following is the equivalent `curl` command:

```
curl -iX POST -H "Content-Type: application/json" -d
'{"message":"Measuring ambient temperature", "duration":5,
"message_category": "Information"}' :5000/api/messages/
```

The previous commands will compose and send the following HTTP request, POST `http://localhost:5000/api/messages/`, with the following JSON key-value pairs:

```
{
    "message": "Measuring ambient temperature",
    "duration": 5,
    "message_category": "Information"
}
```

The following lines show an example response for the HTTP request, with the new `MessageModel` object in the JSON response:

```
HTTP/1.0 201 CREATED
Content-Length: 259
Content-Type: application/json
Date: Wed, 20 Jul 2016 18:27:05 GMT
Server: Werkzeug/0.11.10 Python/3.5.1
{
    "creation_date": "Wed, 20 Jul 2016 18:27:05 -0000",
    "duration": 5,
    "id": 2,
    "message": "Measuring ambient temperature",
    "message_category": "Information",
    "printed_once": false,
    "printed_times": 0,
    "uri": "/api/messages/2"
}
```

We will compose and send an HTTP request to retrieve all the messages. Go back to the Cygwin terminal in Windows or the Terminal in macOS or Linux, and run the following command:

```
http :5000/api/messages/
```

The following is the equivalent curl command:

```
curl -iX GET -H :5000/api/messages/
```

The previous commands will compose and send the following HTTP request: GET
http://localhost:5000/api/messages/. The request specifies /api/messages/, and
therefore, it will match '/api/messages/' and run the MessageList.get method. The
method doesn't receive arguments because the URL route doesn't include any parameters.
As the HTTP verb for the request is GET, Flask calls the get method. The method retrieves
all the MessageModel objects and generates a JSON response with all of these
MessageModel objects serialized.

The following lines show an example response for the HTTP request. The first lines show
the HTTP response headers, including the status (200 OK) and the Content-type
(application/json). After the HTTP response headers, we can see the details for the two
MessageModel objects in the JSON response:

```
HTTP/1.0 200 OK
Content-Length: 589
Content-Type: application/json
Date: Wed, 20 Jul 2016 05:32:28 GMT
Server: Werkzeug/0.11.10 Python/3.5.1
[
    {
        "creation_date": "Wed, 20 Jul 2016 05:32:06 -0000",
        "duration": 10,
        "id": 1,
        "message": "Welcome to IoT",
        "message_category": "Information",
        "printed_once": false,
        "printed_times": 0,
        "uri": "/api/messages/1"
    },
    {
        "creation_date": "Wed, 20 Jul 2016 05:32:18 -0000",
        "duration": 5,
        "id": 2,
        "message": "Measuring ambient temperature",
        "message_category": "Information",
        "printed_once": false,
        "printed_times": 0,
        "uri": "/api/messages/2"
    }
]
```

After we run the three requests, we will see the following lines in the window that is running the Flask development server. The output indicates that the server received three HTTP requests, specifically two POST requests and one GET request with /api/messages/ as the URI. The server processed the three HTTP requests, returned status code 201 for the first two requests and 200 for the last request:

```
127.0.0.1 - - [20/Jul/2016 02:32:06] "POST /api/messages/ HTTP/1.1" 201 -

127.0.0.1 - - [20/Jul/2016 02:32:18] "POST /api/messages/ HTTP/1.1" 201 -

127.0.0.1 - - [20/Jul/2016 02:32:28] "GET /api/messages/ HTTP/1.1" 200 -
```

The following image shows two Terminal windows side-by-side on macOS. The Terminal window at the left-hand side is running the Flask development server and displays the received and processed HTTP requests. The Terminal window at the right-hand side is running http commands to generate the HTTP requests. It is a good idea to use a similar configuration to check the output while we compose and send the HTTP requests:

Now, we will compose and send an HTTP request to retrieve a message that doesn't exist. For example, in the previous list, there is no message with an `id` value equal to `800`. Run the following command to try to retrieve this message. Make sure you use an `id` value that doesn't exist. We must make sure that the utilities display the headers as part of the response to see the returned status code:

```
http :5000/api/messages/800
```

The following is the equivalent `curl` command:

```
curl -iX GET :5000/api/messages/800
```

The previous commands will compose and send the following HTTP request: `GET http://localhost:5000/api/messages/800`. The request is the same than the previous one we have analyzed, with a different number for the `id` parameter. The server will run the `Message.get` method with `800` as the value for the `id` argument. The method will execute the code that retrieves the `MessageModel` object whose id matches the `id` value received as an argument. However, the first line in the `MessageList.get` method calls the `abort_if_message_doesnt_exist` method that won't find the id in the dictionary keys and it will call the `flask_restful.abort` function because there is no message with the specified `id` value. Thus, the code will return an HTTP `404 Not Found` status code. The following lines show an example header response for the HTTP request and the message included in the body. In this case, we just leave the default message. Of course, we can customize it based on our specific needs:

```
HTTP/1.0 404 NOT FOUND
Content-Length: 138
Content-Type: application/json
Date: Wed, 20 Jul 2016 18:08:04 GMT
Server: Werkzeug/0.11.10 Python/3.5.1
{
    "message": "Message 800 doesn't exist. You have requested this URI
[/api/messages/800] but did you mean /api/messages/<int:id> ?"
}
```

Our API is able to update a single field for an existing resource, and therefore, we provide an implementation for the `PATCH` method. For example, we can use the `PATCH` method to update two fields for an existing message and set the value for its `printed_once` field to `true` and `printed_times` to `1`. We don't want to use the `PUT` method because this method is meant to replace an entire message. The `PATCH` method is meant to apply a delta to an existing message, and therefore, it is the appropriate method to just change the value of the `printed_once` and `printed_times` fields.

Now, we will compose and send an HTTP request to update an existing message, specifically, to update the value of two fields. Make sure you replace 2 with the id of an existing message in your configuration:

```
http PATCH :5000/api/messages/2 printed_once=true printed_times=1
```

The following is the equivalent `curl` command:

```
curl -iX PATCH -H "Content-Type: application/json" -d
'{"printed_once":"true", "printed_times":1}' :5000/api/messages/2
```

The previous command will compose and send a PATCH HTTP request with the specified JSON key-value pairs. The request has a number after `/api/messages/`, and therefore, it will match '`/api/messages/<int:id>`' and run the `Message.patch` method, that is, the `patch` method for the `Message` class. If a `MessageModel` instance with the specified id exists and it was successfully updated, the call to the method will return an HTTP 200 OK status code and the recently updated `MessageModel` instance serialized to JSON in the response body. The following lines show a sample response:

```
HTTP/1.0 200 OK
Content-Length: 231
Content-Type: application/json
Date: Wed, 20 Jul 2016 18:28:01 GMT
Server: Werkzeug/0.11.10 Python/3.5.1
{
"creation_date": "Wed, 20 Jul 2016 18:27:05 -0000",
"duration": 0,
"id": 2,
"message": "Measuring ambient temperature",
"message_category": "Information",
"printed_once": true,
"printed_times": 1,
"uri": "/api/messages/2"
    }
```

The IoT device will make the previously explained HTTP request when it displays the message for the first time. Then, it will make additional PATCH requests to update the value for the `printed_times` field.

Now, we will compose and send an HTTP request to delete an existing message, specifically, the last message we added. As happened in our last HTTP requests, we have to check the value assigned to `id` in the previous response and replace 2 in the command with the returned value:

```
http DELETE :5000/api/messages/2
```

The following is the equivalent `curl` command:

```
curl -iX DELETE :5000/api/messages/2
```

The previous commands will compose and send the following HTTP request: `DELETE http://localhost:5000/api/messages/2`. The request has a number after `/api/messages/`, and therefore, it will match `'/api/messages/<int:id>'` and run the `Message.delete` method, that is, the `delete` method for the `Message` class. If a `MessageModel` instance with the specified id exists and it was successfully deleted, the call to the method will return an HTTP `204 No Content` status code. The following lines show a sample response:

```
HTTP/1.0 204 NO CONTENT
Content-Length: 0
Content-Type: application/json
Date: Wed, 20 Jul 2016 18:50:12 GMT
Server: Werkzeug/0.11.10 Python/3.5.1
```

Working with GUI tools – Postman and others

So far, we have been working with two terminal-based or command-line tools to compose and send HTTP requests to our Flask development server-cURL and HTTPie. Now, we will work with one of the GUI tools we used when composing and sending HTTP requests to the Django development server-Postman.

Now, we will use the **Builder** tab in Postman to easily compose and send HTTP requests to `localhost:5000` and test the RESTful API with this GUI tool. Remember that Postman doesn't support curl-like shorthands for localhost, and therefore, we cannot use the same shorthands we have been using when composing requests with curl and HTTPie.

Select **GET** in the dropdown menu at the left-hand side of the **Enter request URL** textbox, and enter `localhost:5000/api/messages/` in this textbox at the right-hand side of the dropdown. Then, click **Send** and Postman will display the Status (**200 OK**), the time it took for the request to be processed and the response body with all the games formatted as JSON with syntax highlighting (**Pretty** view). The following screenshot shows the JSON response body in Postman for the HTTP GET request.

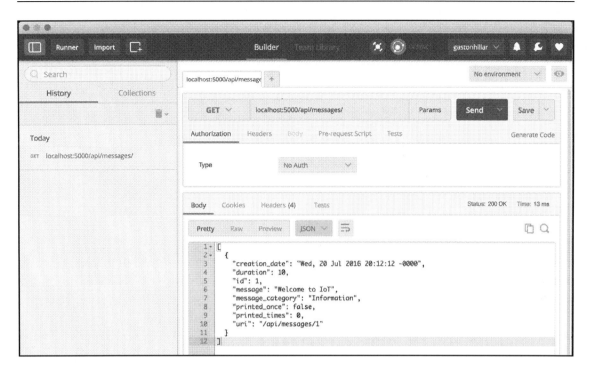

Click on **Headers** at the right-hand side of **Body** and **Cookies** to read the response headers. The following screenshot shows the layout for the response headers that Postman displays for the previous response. Notice that Postman displays the **Status** at the right-hand side of the response and doesn't include it as the first line of the Headers, as happened when we worked with both the cURL and HTTPie utilities:

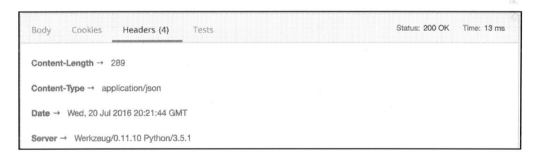

Now, we will use the **Builder** tab in Postman to compose and send an HTTP request to create a new message, specifically, a POST request. Follow the next steps:

1. Select **POST** in the drop-down menu at the left-hand side of the **Enter request URL** textbox, and enter `localhost:5000/api/messages/` in this textbox at the right-hand side of the dropdown.

2. Click **Body** at the right-hand side of **Authorization** and **Headers**, within the panel that composes the request.

3. Activate the **raw** radio button and select **JSON (application/json)** in the dropdown at the right-hand side of the **binary** radio button. Postman will automatically add a **Content-type = application/json** header, and therefore, you will notice the **Headers** tab will be renamed to **Headers (1)**, indicating us that there is one key-value pair specified for the request headers.

4. Enter the following lines in the textbox below the radio buttons, within the **Body** tab:

```
{
    "message": "Measuring distance",
    "duration": 5,
    "message_category": "Information"
}
```

The following screenshot shows the request body in Postman:

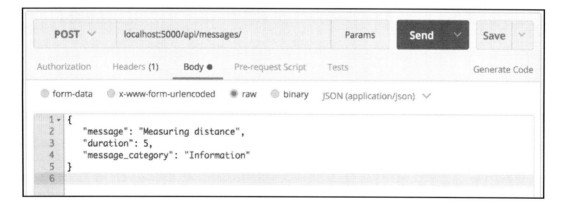

We followed the necessary steps to create an HTTP POST request with a JSON body that specifies the necessary key-value pairs to create a new game. Click **Send** and Postman will display the Status (**201 Created**), the time it took for the request to be processed and the response body with the recently added game formatted as JSON with syntax highlighting (**Pretty** view). The following screenshot shows the JSON response body in Postman for the HTTP POST request:

```
Body    Cookies    Headers (4)    Tests                    Status: 201 CREATED    Time: 17 ms

Pretty    Raw    Preview    JSON ∨  ⇉                                              ⧉  Q

 1 ▾ {
 2       "creation_date": "Wed, 20 Jul 2016 20:35:06 -0000",
 3       "duration": 5,
 4       "id": 2,
 5       "message": "Measuring distance",
 6       "message_category": "Information",
 7       "printed_once": false,
 8       "printed_times": 0,
 9       "uri": "/api/messages/2"
10   }
```

> If we want to compose and send an HTTP PATCH request for our API with Postman, it is necessary to follow the previously explained steps to provide JSON data within the request body.

Click or tap on the value for the url field in the JSON response body-`/api/messages/2`. You will notice that the value will be underlined when you hover the mouse pointer over it. Postman will automatically generate a `GET` request to `localhost:5000/api/messages/2`. Click **Send** to run it and retrieve the recently added message. The field is useful to browse the API with a tool such as Postman.

Because we made the necessary changes to generate an externally visible Flask development server, we can also use apps that can compose and send HTTP requests from mobile devices to work with the RESTful API. For example, we can work with the iCurlHTTP App on iOS devices such as iPad Pro and iPhone. In Android devices, we can work with the previously introduced HTTP Request App.

The following screenshot shows the results of composing and sending the following HTTP request with the iCurlHTTP App: GET `http://192.168.2.3:5000/api/messages/`. Remember that you have to perform the previously explained configurations in your LAN and router to be able to access the Flask development server from other devices connected to your LAN. In this case, the IP assigned to the computer running the Flask Web server is `192.168.2.3`, and therefore, you must replace this IP with the IP assigned to your development computer.

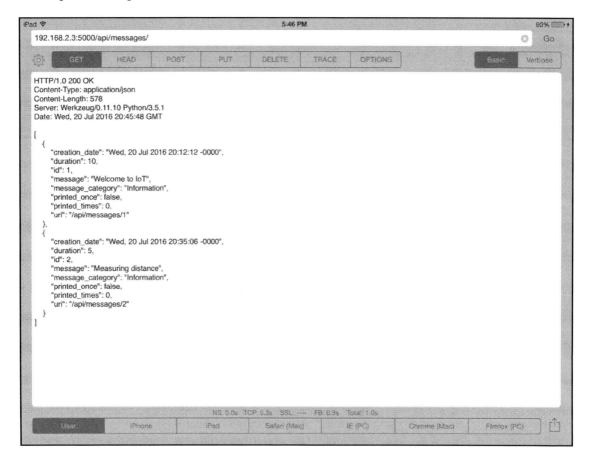

Test your knowledge

1. Flask-RESTful uses which of the following as the main building block for a RESTful API?
    1. Resources built on top of Flask pluggable views
    2. Statuses built on top of Flask resource views.
    3. Resources built on top of Flask pluggable controllers.

2. In order to be able to process an HTTP POST request on a resource, we must declare a method with the following name in a subclass of `flask_restful.Resource`.
    1. `post_restful`
    2. `post_method`
    3. `post`

3. In order to be able to process an HTTP GET request on a resource, we must declare a method with the following name in a subclass of `flask_restful.Resource`.
    1. `get_restful`
    2. `get_method`
    3. `get`

4. A subclass of `flask_restful.Resource` represents:
    1. `A controller resource.`
    2. `A RESTful resource.`
    3. `A single RESTful HTTP verb.`

5. If we use the `@marshal_with` decorator with `message_fields` as an argument, the decorator will:
    1. Apply the field filtering and output formatting specified in `message_fields` to the appropriate instance.
    2. Apply the field filtering specified in `message_fields` to the appropriate instance, without considering output formatting.
    3. Apply the output formatting specified in `message_fields` to the appropriate instance, without considering field filtering.

Summary

In this chapter, we designed a RESTful API to interact with a simple dictionary that acted as a data repository and perform CRUD operations with messages. We defined the requirements for our API and we understood the tasks performed by each HTTP method. We set up a virtual environment with Flask and Flask-RESTful.

We created a model to represent and persist messages. We learned to configure serialization of messages into JSON representations with the features included in Flask-RESTful. We wrote classes that represent resources and process the different HTTP requests and we configured the URL patterns to route URLs to classes.

Finally, we started Flask development server and we used command-line tools to compose and send HTTP requests to our RESTful API and analyzed how each HTTP request was processed in our code. We also worked with GUI tools to compose and send HTTP requests.

Now that we understand the basics of the combination of Flask and Flask-RESTful to create RESTful APIs, we will expand the capabilities of the RESTful Web API by taking advantage of advanced features included in Flask-RESTful and related ORMs, which is what we are going to discuss in the next chapter.

6
Working with Models, SQLAlchemy, and Hyperlinked APIs in Flask

In this chapter, we will expand the capabilities of the RESTful API that we started in the previous chapter. We will use SQLAlchemy as our ORM to work with a PostgreSQL database and we will take advantage of advanced features included in Flask and Flask-RESTful that will allow us to easily organize code for complex APIs, such as models and blueprints. In this chapter, we will:

- Design a RESTful API to interact with a PostgreSQL database
- Understand the tasks performed by each HTTP method
- Install packages to simplify our common tasks
- Create and configure the database
- Write code for the models with their relationships
- Use schemas to validate, serialize, and deserialize models
- Combine blueprints with resourceful routing
- Register the blueprint and run migrations
- Create and retrieve related resources

Designing a RESTful API to interact with a PostgreSQL database

So far, our RESTful API has performed CRUD operations on a simple dictionary that acted as a data repository. Now, we want to create a more complex RESTful API with Flask RESTful to interact with a database model that has to allow us to work with messages that are grouped into message categories. In our previous RESTful API, we used a string attribute to specify the message category for a message. In this case, we want to be able to easily retrieve all the messages that belong to a specific message category, and therefore, we will have a relationship between a message and a message category.

We must be able to perform CRUD operations on different related resources and resource collections. The following list enumerates the resources and the class name that we will create to represent the model:

- Message categories (`Category` model)
- Messages (`Message` model)

The message category (`Category`) just requires an integer name, and we need the following data for a message (`Message`):

- An integer identifier
- A foreign key to a message category (`Category`)
- A string message

- The duration in seconds that will indicate the time the message has to be printed on the OLED display

- The creation date and time. The timestamp will be added automatically when adding a new message to the collection

- An integer counter that indicates the times the message has been printed in the OLED display

- A `bool` value indicating whether the message was printed at least once on the OLED display

 We will take advantage of the many packages related to Flask RESTful and SQLAlchemy that make it easier to serialize and deserialize data, perform validations, and integrate SQLAlchemy with Flask and Flask RESTful.

Understanding the tasks performed by each HTTP method

The following table shows the HTTP verbs, the scope, and the semantics for the methods that our new API must support. Each method is composed of an HTTP verb, a scope, and all the methods have well-defined meanings for all the resources and collections:

HTTP verb	Scope	Semantics
GET	Collection of message categories	Retrieve all the stored message categories in the collection and return them sorted by their name in ascending order. Each category must include the full URL for the resource. Each category must include a list with all the details for the messages that belong to the category. The messages don't have to include the category in order to avoid repeating data.
GET	Message category	Retrieve a single message category. The category must include the same information explained for each category when we retrieve a collection of message category.
POST	Collection of message categories	Create a new message category in the collection.
PATCH	Message category	Update the name of an existing message category.
DELETE	Message category	Delete an existing message category.
GET	Collection of messages	Retrieve all the stored messages in the collection, sorted by their message in ascending order. Each message must include its message category details, including the full URL to access the related resource. The message category details don't have to include the messages that belong to the category. The message must include the full URL to access the resource.
GET	Message	Retrieve a single message. The message must include the same information explained for each message when we retrieve a collection of messages.
POST	Collection of messages	Create a new message in the collection.

HTTP verb	Scope	Semantics
PATCH	Message	Update any of the following fields of an existing message: message, duration, printed_times, and printed_once.
DELETE	Message	Delete an existing message.

In addition, our RESTful API must support the OPTIONS method for all the resources and collection of resources. We will use SQLAlchemy as our ORM and we will work with a PostgreSQL database. However, in case you don't want to spend time installing PostgreSQL, you can use any other database supported by SQLAlchemy, such as MySQL. In case you want the simplest database, you can work with SQLite.

In the preceding table, there are many methods and scopes. The following list enumerates the URIs for each scope mentioned in the preceding table, where {id} has to be replaced with the numeric id or primary key of the resource. As happened in the previous example, we want our API to differentiate collections from a single resource of the collection in the URLs. When we refer to a collection, we will use a slash (/) as the last character for the URL and when we refer to a single resource of the collection, we won't use a slash (/) as the last character for the URL:

- **Collection of message categories**: /categories/
- **Message category**: /category/{id}
- **Collection of messages**: /messages/
- **Message**: /message/{id}

Let's consider that http://localhost:5000/api/ is the URL for the API running on the Flask development server. We have to compose and send an HTTP request with the following HTTP verb (GET) and request URL (http://localhost:5000/api/categories/) to retrieve all the stored message categories in the collection. Each category will include a list with all the messages that belong to the category.

```
GET http://localhost:5000/api/categories/
```

Installing packages to simplify our common tasks

Make sure you quit Flask's development server. Remember that you just need to press *Ctrl + C* in the Terminal or Command Prompt window in which it is running. Now, we will install many additional packages. Make sure you have activated the virtual environment we have created in the previous chapter and we named `Flask01`. In case you created a new virtual environment to work with this example or you downloaded the sample code for the book, make sure you install the packages we used in the previous example.

After you activate the virtual environment, it is time to run commands that will be the same for either macOS, Linux, or Windows. We can install all the necessary packages with pip with a single command. However, we will run independent commands to make it easier to detect any problems in case a specific installation fails.

Now, we must run the following command to install Flask-SQLAlchemy with pip. Flask-SQLAlchemy adds support for the SQLAlchemy ORM to Flask applications. This extension simplifies executing common SQLAlchemy tasks within a Flask application. SQLAlchemy is a dependency for Flask-SQLAlchemy, and therefore, pip will install it automatically, too:

```
pip install Flask-SQLAlchemy
```

The last lines of the output will indicate all the packages that have been successfully installed, including `SQLAlchemy` and `Flask-SQLAlchemy`:

```
Installing collected packages: SQLAlchemy, Flask-SQLAlchemy
  Running setup.py install for SQLAlchemy
  Running setup.py install for Flask-SQLAlchemy
Successfully installed Flask-SQLAlchemy-2.1 SQLAlchemy-1.0.14
```

Run the following command to install Flask-Migrate with pip. Flask-Migrate uses the Alembic package to handle SQLAlchemy database migrations for Flask applications. We will use Flask-Migrate to set up our PostgreSQL database. Flask-Script is one of the dependencies for Flask-Migrate, and therefore, pip will install it automatically. Flask-Script adds support for writing external scripts in Flask, including scripts to set up a database.

```
pip install Flask-Migrate
```

The last lines for the output will indicate all the packages that have been successfully installed, including `Flask-Migrate` and `Flask-Script`. The other installed packages are additional dependencies:

```
Installing collected packages: Mako, python-editor, alembic, Flask-
Script, Flask-Migrate
    Running setup.py install for Mako
    Running setup.py install for python-editor
    Running setup.py install for alembic
    Running setup.py install for Flask-Script
    Running setup.py install for Flask-Migrate
  Successfully installed Flask-Migrate-2.0.0 Flask-Script-2.0.5
Mako-1.0.4 alembic-0.8.7 python-editor-1.0.1
```

Run the following command to install marshmallow with pip. Marshmallow is a lightweight library for converting complex datatypes to and from native Python datatypes. Marshmallow provides schemas that we can use to validate input data, deserialize input data to app-level objects, and serialize app-level objects to Python primitive types:

```
pip install marshmallow
```

The last lines for the output will indicate `marshmallow` has been successfully installed:

```
Installing collected packages: marshmallow
Successfully installed marshmallow-2.9.1
```

Run the following command to install Marshmallow-sqlalchemy with pip. Marshmallow-sqlalchemy provides SQLAlchemy integration with the previously installed marshmallow validation, serialization, and deserialization lightweight library:

```
pip install marshmallow-sqlalchemy
```

The last lines for the output will indicate `marshmallow-sqlalchemy` has been successfully installed:

```
Installing collected packages: marshmallow-sqlalchemy
Successfully installed marshmallow-sqlalchemy-0.10.0
```

Finally, run the following command to install Flask-Marshmallow with pip. Flask-Marshmallow integrates the previously installed `marshmallow` library with Flask applications and makes it easy to generate a URL and Hyperlink fields:

```
pip install Flask-Marshmallow
```

The last lines for the output will indicate `Flask-Marshmallow` has been successfully installed:

```
Installing collected packages: Flask-Marshmallow
Successfully installed Flask-Marshmallow-0.7.0
```

Creating and configuring the database

Now, we will create the PostgreSQL database that we will use as a repository for our API. You will have to download and install a PostgreSQL database in case you aren't already running it in your computer or in a development server. You can download and install this database management system from its web page: `http://www.postgresql.org`. In case you are working with macOS, `Postgres.app` provides a really easy way to install and use PostgreSQL on this operating system: `http://postgresapp.com`:

 You have to make sure that the PostgreSQL bin folder is included in the PATH environmental variable. You should be able to execute the `psql` command-line utility from your current Terminal or Command Prompt. In case the folder isn't included in the PATH, you will receive an error indicating that the `pg_config` file cannot be found when trying to install the `psycopg2` package. In addition, you will have to use the full path to each of the PostgreSQL command-line tools we will use in the next steps.

We will use the PostgreSQL command-line tools to create a new database named `messages`. In case you already have a PostgreSQL database with this name, make sure that you use another name in all the commands and configurations. You can perform the same task with any PostgreSQL GUI tool. In case you are developing on Linux, it is necessary to run the commands as the `postgres` user. Run the following command in macOS or Windows to create a new database named `messages`. Note that the command won't produce any output:

```
createdb messages
```

In Linux, run the following command to use the `postgres` user:

```
sudo -u postgres createdb messages
```

Now, we will use the `psql` command-line tool to run some SQL statements to create a specific user that we will use in Flask and assign the necessary roles for it. In macOS or Windows, run the following command to launch psql:

```
psql
```

In Linux, run the following command to use the postgres user:

```
sudo -u psql
```

Then, run the following SQL statements and finally enter \q to exit the psql command-line tool. Replace user_name with your desired user name to use in the new database and password with your chosen password. We will use the user name and password in the Flask configuration. You don't need to run the steps in case you are already working with a specific user in PostgreSQL and you have already granted privileges to the database for the user. You will see the output indicating that the permission was granted.

```
CREATE ROLE user_name WITH LOGIN PASSWORD 'password';
GRANT ALL PRIVILEGES ON DATABASE messages TO user_name;
ALTER USER user_name CREATEDB;
\q
```

It is necessary to install the Psycopg 2 package (psycopg2). This package is a Python-PostgreSQL Database Adapter and SQLAlchemy will use it to interact with our recently created PostgreSQL database.

Once we made sure that the PostgreSQL bin folder is included in the PATH environmental variable, we just need to run the following command to install this package:

```
pip install psycopg2
```

The last lines of the output will indicate that the psycopg2 package has been successfully installed:

```
Collecting psycopg2
Installing collected packages: psycopg2
   Running setup.py install for psycopg2
Successfully installed psycopg2-2.6.2
```

In case you are using the same virtual environment that we created for the previous example, the api folder already exists. If you create a new virtual environment, create a folder named api within the root folder for the created virtual environment.

Create a new config.py file within the api folder. The following lines show the code that declares variables that determine the configuration for Flask and SQLAlchemy. The SQL_ALCHEMY_DATABASE_URI variable generates an SQLAlchemy URI for the PostgreSQL database.

Make sure you specify the desired database name in the value for DB_NAME and that you configure the user, password, host, and port based on your PostgreSQL configuration. In case you followed the previous steps, use the settings specified in these steps. The code file for the sample is included in the restful_python_chapter_06_01 folder:

```
import os


basedir = os.path.abspath(os.path.dirname(__file__))
DEBUG = True
PORT = 5000
HOST = "127.0.0.1"
SQLALCHEMY_ECHO = False
SQLALCHEMY_TRACK_MODIFICATIONS = True
SQLALCHEMY_DATABASE_URI =
"postgresql://{DB_USER}:{DB_PASS}@{DB_ADDR}/{DB_NAME}".format(DB_USER="user
_name", DB_PASS="password", DB_ADDR="127.0.0.1", DB_NAME="messages")
SQLALCHEMY_MIGRATE_REPO = os.path.join(basedir, 'db_repository')
```

We will specify the module created earlier as an argument to a function that will create a *Flask* app. This way, we have one module that specifies all the values for the different configuration variables and another module that creates a *Flask* app. We will create the Flask app factory as our final step towards our new API.

Creating models with their relationships

Now, we will create the models that we can use to represent and persist the message categories, messages, and their relationships. Open the api/models.py file and replace its contents with the following code. The lines that declare fields related to other models are highlighted in the code listing. In case you created a new virtual environment, create a new models.py file within the api folder. The code file for the sample is included in the restful_python_chapter_06_01 folder:

```
from marshmallow import Schema, fields, pre_load
from marshmallow import validate
from flask_sqlalchemy import SQLAlchemy
from flask_marshmallow import Marshmallow


db = SQLAlchemy()
ma = Marshmallow()


class AddUpdateDelete():
```

```
    def add(self, resource):
        db.session.add(resource)
        return db.session.commit()

    def update(self):
        return db.session.commit()

    def delete(self, resource):
        db.session.delete(resource)
        return db.session.commit()


class Message(db.Model, AddUpdateDelete):
    id = db.Column(db.Integer, primary_key=True)
    message = db.Column(db.String(250), unique=True, nullable=False)
    duration = db.Column(db.Integer, nullable=False)
    creation_date = db.Column(db.TIMESTAMP,
server_default=db.func.current_timestamp(), nullable=False)
    category_id = db.Column(db.Integer, db.ForeignKey('category.id',
ondelete='CASCADE'), nullable=False)
    category = db.relationship('Category', backref=db.backref('messages',
lazy='dynamic' , order_by='Message.message'))
    printed_times = db.Column(db.Integer, nullable=False,
server_default='0')
    printed_once = db.Column(db.Boolean, nullable=False,
server_default='false')

    def __init__(self, message, duration, category):
        self.message = message
        self.duration = duration
        self.category = category


class Category(db.Model, AddUpdateDelete):
    id = db.Column(db.Integer, primary_key=True)
    name = db.Column(db.String(150), unique=True, nullable=False)

    def __init__(self, name):
        self.name = name
```

First, the code creates an instance of the `flask_sqlalchemy.SQLAlchemy` class named `db`. This instance will allow us to control the SQLAlchemy integration for our Flask application. In addition, the instance will provide access to all the SQLAlchemy functions and classes.

Then, the code creates an instance of the flask_marshmallow.Marshmallow class named ma. It is very important to create the flask_sqlalchemy.SQLAlchemy instance before the Marshmallow instance, and therefore, order matters in this case. Marshmallow is a wrapper class that integrates Mashmallow with a *Flask* application. The instance named ma will provide access to the Schema class, the fields defined in marshmallow.fields, and the Flask-specific fields declared in flask_marshmallow.fields. We will use them later when we declare the schemas related to our models.

The code creates the AddUpdateDelete class that declares the following three methods to add, update, and delete a resource through SQLAlchemy sessions:

- add: This method receives the object to be added in the resource argument and calls the db.session.add method with the received resource as an argument to create the object in the underlying database. Finally, the code commits the session.
- update: This method just commits the session to persist the changes made to the objects in the underlying database.
- delete: This method receives the object to be deleted in the resource argument and calls the db.session.delete method with the received resource as an argument to remove the object in the underlying database. Finally, the code commits the session.

The code declares the following two models, specifically, two classes, as a subclass of both the db.Model, and the AddUpdateDelete classes:

- Message
- Category

We specified the field types, maximum lengths, and defaults for many attributes. The attributes that represent fields without any relationship are instances of the db.Column class. Both models declare an id attribute and specify the True value for the primary_key argument to indicate it is the primary key. SQLAlchemy will use the data to generate the necessary tables in the PostgreSQL database.

The Message model declares the category field with the following line:

```
category = db.relationship('Category', backref=db.backref('messages',
lazy='dynamic', order_by='Message.message'))
```

The previous line uses the db.relationship function to provide a many-to-one relationship to the Category model. The backref argument specifies a call to the db.backref function with 'messages' as the first value that indicates the name to use for the relation from the related Category object back to a Message object. The order_by argument specifies 'Message.message' because we want the messages for each category to be sorted by the value of the message field in ascending order.

Both models declare a constructor, that is, the __init__ method. This constructor for the Message model receives many arguments and uses them to initialize the attributes with the same names: message, duration, and category. The constructor for the Category model receives a name argument and uses it to initialize the attribute with the same name.

Creating schemas to validate, serialize, and deserialize models

Now, we will create the Flask-Marshmallow schemas that we will use to validate, serialize, and deserialize the previously declared Category and Message models and their relationships. Open the api/models.py file and add the following code after the existing lines. The lines that declare the fields related to the other schemas are highlighted in the code listing. The code file for the sample is included in the restful_python_chapter_06_01 folder:

```
class CategorySchema(ma.Schema):
    id = fields.Integer(dump_only=True)
    name = fields.String(required=True, validate=validate.Length(3))
    url = ma.URLFor('api.categoryresource', id='<id>', _external=True)
    messages = fields.Nested('MessageSchema', many=True,
exclude=('category',))

 class MessageSchema(ma.Schema):
    id = fields.Integer(dump_only=True)
    message = fields.String(required=True, validate=validate.Length(1))
    duration = fields.Integer()
    creation_date = fields.DateTime()
    category = fields.Nested(CategorySchema, only=['id', 'url', 'name'],
required=True)
    printed_times = fields.Integer()
    printed_once = fields.Boolean()
    url = ma.URLFor('api.messageresource', id='<id>', _external=True)

    @pre_load
    def process_category(self, data):
```

```
                category = data.get('category')
                if category:
                    if isinstance(category, dict):
                        category_name = category.get('name')
                    else:
                        category_name = category
                    category_dict = dict(name=category_name)
                else:
                    category_dict = {}
                data['category'] = category_dict
                return data
```

The code declares the following two schemas, specifically, two subclasses of the `ma.Schema` class:

- `CategorySchema`
- `MessageSchema`

We don't use the Flask-Marshmallow features that allow us to automatically determine the appropriate type for each attribute based on the fields declared in a model because we want to use specific options for each field. We declare the attributes that represent fields as instances of the appropriate class declared in the `marshmallow.fields` module. Whenever we specify the `True` value for the `dump_only` argument, it means that we want the field to be read-only. For example, we won't be able to provide a value for the `id` field in any of the schemas. The value for this field will be automatically generated by the auto-increment primary key in the database.

The `CategorySchema` class declares the `name` attribute as an instance of `fields.String`. The `required` argument is set to `True` to specify that the field cannot be an empty string. The `validate` argument is set to `validate.Length(3)` to specify that the field must have a minimum length of 3 characters.

The class declares the `url` field with the following line:

```
url = ma.URLFor('api.categoryresource', id='<id>', _external=True)
```

The `url` attribute is an instance of the `ma.URLFor` class, and this field will output the full URL of the resource, that is, of the message category resource. The first argument is the Flask endpoint name-`'api.categoryresource'`. We will create a `CategoryResource` class later and the `URLFor` class will use it to generate the URL. The `id` argument specifies `'<id>'` because we want the `id` to be pulled from the object to be serialized. The `id` string enclosed within less than (<) and greater than (>) symbols specifies that we want the field to be pulled from the object that has to be serialized. The `_external` attribute is set to `True` because we want to generate the full URL for the resource. This way, each time we serialize a `Category`, it will include the full URL for the resource in the `url` key.

> In this case, we are using our insecure API behind HTTP. In case our API is configured with HTTPS, we should set the `_scheme` argument to `'https'` when we create the `ma.URLFor` instance.

The class declares the `messages` field with the following line:

```
messages = fields.Nested('MessageSchema', many=True,
exclude=('category',)0029
```

The `messages` attribute is an instance of the `marshmallow.fields.Nested` class, and this field will nest a collection of `Schema`, and therefore, we specify `True` for the `many` argument. The first argument specifies the name for the nested `Schema` class as a string. We declare the `MessageSchema` class after we defined the `CategorySchema` class. Thus, we specify the `Schema` class name as a string instead of using the type that we haven't defined yet.

In fact, we will end up with two objects that nest to each other, that is, we will create a two-way nesting between categories and messages. We use the `exclude` parameter with a tuple of string to indicate that we want the `category` field to be excluded from the fields that are serialized for each message. This way, we can avoid infinite recursion because the inclusion of the category field would serialize all the messages related to the category.

When we declared the `Message` model, we used the `db.relationship` function to provide a many-to-one relationship to the `Category` model. The `backref` argument specified a call to the `db.backref` function with `'messages'` as the first value that indicates the name to use for the relation from the related `Category` object back to a `Message` object. With the previously explained line, we created the messages fields that uses the same name we indicated for the `db.backref` function.

The `MessageSchema` class declares the `message` attribute as an instance of `fields.String`. The `required` argument is set to `True` to specify that the field cannot be an empty string. The `validate` argument is set to `validate.Length(1)` to specify that the field must have a minimum length of 1 character. The class declares the `duration`, `creation_date`, `printed_times` and `printed_once` fields with the corresponding classes based on the types we used in the `Message` model.

The class declares the `category` field with the following line:

```
category = fields.Nested(CategorySchema, only=['id', 'url', 'name'],
required=True)
```

The `category` attribute is an instance of the `marshmallow.fields.Nested` class and this field will nest a single `CategorySchema`. We specify `True` for the `required` argument because a message must belong to a category. The first argument specifies the name for the nested `Schema` class. We already declared the `CategorySchema` class, and therefore, we specify `CategorySchema` as the value for the first argument. We use the only parameter with a list of string to indicate the field names that we want to be included when the nested `CategorySchema` is serialized. We want the `id`, `url`, and `name` fields to be included. We don't specify the `messages` field because we don't want the category to serialize the list of messages that belong to it.

The class declares the `url` field with the following line:

```
url = ma.URLFor('api.messageresource', id='<id>', _external=True)
```

The `url` attribute is an instance of the `ma.URLFor` class and this field will output the full URL of the resource, that is, of the message resource. The first argument is the Flask endpoint name: `'api.messageresource'`. We will create a `MessageResource` class later and the `URLFor` class will use it to generate the URL. The `id` argument specifies `'<id>'` because we want the `id` to be pulled from the object to be serialized. The `_external` attribute is set to `True` because we want to generate the full URL for the resource. This way, each time we serialize a `Message`, it will include the full URL for the resource in the `url` key.

The `MessageSchema` class declares a `process_category` method that uses the `@pre_load` decorator, specifically, `marshmallow.pre_load`. This decorator registers a method to invoke before deserializing an object. This way, before Marshmallow deserializes a message, the `process_category` method will be executed.

The method receives the data to be deserialized in the `data` argument and it returns the processed data. When we receive a request to `POST` a new message, the category name can be specified in a key named `'category'`. If a category with the specified name exists, we will use the existing category as the one that is related to the new message. If a category with the specified name doesn't exist, we will create a new category and then we will use this new category as the one that is related to the new message. This way, we make it easy for the user to create new messages.

The `data` argument might have a category name specified as a string for the `'category'` key. However, in other cases, the `'category'` key will include the key-value pairs with the field name and field values for an existing category. The code in the `process_category` method checks the value for the `'category'` key and returns a dictionary with the appropriate data to make it sure that we are able to deserialize a category with the appropriate key-value pairs, no matter the differences of the incoming data. Finally, the methods returned the processed dictionary. We will dive deep on the work done by the `process_category` method later when we start composing and sending HTTP requests to the API.

Combining blueprints with resourceful routing

Now, we will create the resources that compose our main building blocks for the RESTful API. First, we will create a few instances that we will use in the different resources. Then, we will create a `MessageResource` class, that we will use to represent the message resource. Create a new `views.py` file within the `api` folder and add the following lines. The code file for the sample is included in the `restful_python_chapter_06_01` folder, as shown:

```
from flask import Blueprint, request, jsonify, make_response
from flask_restful import Api, Resource
from models import db, Category, CategorySchema, Message, MessageSchema
from sqlalchemy.exc import SQLAlchemyError
import status


api_bp = Blueprint('api', __name__)
category_schema = CategorySchema()
message_schema = MessageSchema()
api = Api(api_bp)
```

```
class MessageResource(Resource):
    def get(self, id):
        message = Message.query.get_or_404(id)
        result = message_schema.dump(message).data
        return result

    def patch(self, id):
        message = Message.query.get_or_404(id)
        message_dict = request.get_json(force=True)
        if 'message' in message_dict:
            message.message = message_dict['message']
        if 'duration' in message_dict:
            message.duration = message_dict['duration']
        if 'printed_times' in message_dict:
            message.printed_times = message_dict['printed_times']
        if 'printed_once' in message_dict:
            message.printed_once = message_dict['printed_once']
        dumped_message, dump_errors = message_schema.dump(message)
        if dump_errors:
            return dump_errors, status.HTTP_400_BAD_REQUEST
        validate_errors = message_schema.validate(dumped_message)
        #errors = message_schema.validate(data)
        if validate_errors:
            return validate_errors, status.HTTP_400_BAD_REQUEST
        try:
            message.update()
            return self.get(id)
        except SQLAlchemyError as e:
                db.session.rollback()
                resp = jsonify({"error": str(e)})
                return resp, status.HTTP_400_BAD_REQUEST
    def delete(self, id):
        message = Message.query.get_or_404(id)
        try:
            delete = message.delete(message)
            response = make_response()
            return response, status.HTTP_204_NO_CONTENT
        except SQLAlchemyError as e:
                db.session.rollback()
                resp = jsonify({"error": str(e)})
                return resp, status.HTTP_401_UNAUTHORIZED
```

The first lines declare the imports and create the following instances that we will use in the different classes:

- `api_bp`: It is an instance of the `flask.Blueprint` class that will allow us to factor the Flask application into this blueprint. The first argument specifies the URL prefix on which we want to register the blueprint: `'api'`.
- `category_schema`: It is an instance of the `CategorySchema` class we declared in the `models.py` module. We will use `category_schema` to validate, serialize, and deserialize categories.
- `message_schema`: It is an instance of the `MessageSchema` class we declared in the `models.py` module. We will use `message_schema` to validate, serialize and, deserialize categories.
- `api`: It is an instance of the `flask_restful.Api` class that represents the main entry point for the application. We pass the previously created `flask.Blueprint` instance named `api_bp` as an argument to link the `Api` to the `Blueprint`.

The `MessageResource` class is a subclass of `flask_restful.Resource` and declares the following three methods that will be called when the HTTP method with the same name arrives as a request on the represented resource:

- `get`: This method receives the id of the message that has to be retrieved in the `id` argument. The code calls the `Message.query.get_or_404` method to return an HTTP `404 Not Found` status in case there is no message with the requested id in the underlying database. In case the message exists, the code calls the `message_schema.dump` method with the retrieved message as an argument to use the `MessageSchema` instance to serialize the `Message` instance whose `id` matches the specified `id`. The `dump` method takes the `Message` instance and applies the field filtering and output formatting specified in the `MessageSchema` class. The code returns the `data` attribute of the result returned by the `dump` method, that is, the serialized message in JSON format as the body, with the default HTTP `200 OK` status code.

- `delete`: This method receives the id of the message that has to be deleted in the `id` argument. The code calls the `Message.query.get_or_404` method to return an HTTP `404 Not Found` status in case there is no message with the requested id in the underlying database. In case the message exists, the code calls the `message.delete` method with the retrieved message as an argument to use the `Message` instance to erase itself from the database. Then, the code returns an empty response body and a `204 No Content` status code.

- `patch`: This method receives the id of the message that has to be updated or patched in the `id` argument. The code calls the `Message.query.get_or_404` method to return an HTTP `404 Not Found` status in case there is no message with the requested id in the underlying database. In case the message exists, the code calls the `request.get_json` method to retrieve the key-value pairs received as arguments with the request. The code updates specific attributes in case they have new values in the `message_dict` dictionary in the `Message` instance: `message`. Then, the code calls the `message_schema.dump` method to retrieve any errors generated when serializing the updated message. In case there were errors, the code returns the errors and an HTTP `400 Bad Request` status. If the serialization didn't generate errors, the code calls the `message_schema.validate` method to retrieve any errors generated while validating the updated message. In case there were validation errors, the code returns the validation errors and an HTTP `400 Bad Request` status. If the validation is successful, the code calls the update method for the Message instance to persist the changes in the database and returns the results of calling the previously explained `self.get` method with the id of the updated message as an argument. This way, the method returns the serialized updated message in JSON format as the body, with the default HTTP `200 OK` status code.

Now, we will create a `MessageListResource` class that we will use to represent the collection of messages. Open the previously created `api/views.py` file and add the following lines. The code file for the sample is included in the `restful_python_chapter_06_01` folder:

```
class MessageListResource(Resource):
    def get(self):
        messages = Message.query.all()
        result = message_schema.dump(messages, many=True).data
        return result

    def post(self):
        request_dict = request.get_json()
        if not request_dict:
```

```
        response = {'message': 'No input data provided'}
        return response, status.HTTP_400_BAD_REQUEST
    errors = message_schema.validate(request_dict)
    if errors:
        return errors, status.HTTP_400_BAD_REQUEST
    try:
        category_name = request_dict['category']['name']
        category = Category.query.filter_by(name=category_name).first()
        if category is None:
            # Create a new Category
            category = Category(name=category_name)
            db.session.add(category)
        # Now that we are sure we have a category
        # create a new Message
        message = Message(
            message=request_dict['message'],
            duration=request_dict['duration'],
            category=category)
        message.add(message)
        query = Message.query.get(message.id)
        result = message_schema.dump(query).data
        return result, status.HTTP_201_CREATED
    except SQLAlchemyError as e:
        db.session.rollback()
        resp = jsonify({"error": str(e)})
        return resp, status.HTTP_400_BAD_REQUEST
```

The `MessageListResource` class is a subclass of `flask_restful.Resource` and declares the following two methods that will be called when the HTTP method with the same name arrives as a request on the represented resource:

- `get`: This method returns a list with all the `Message` instances saved in the database. First, the code calls the `Message.query.all` method to retrieve all the `Message` instances persisted in the database. Then, the code calls the `message_schema.dump` method with the retrieved messages and the `many` argument set to `True` to serialize the iterable collection of objects. The `dump` method will take each `Message` instance retrieved from the database and apply the field filtering and output formatting specified the `MessageSchema` class. The code returns the `data` attribute of the result returned by the dump method, that is, the serialized messages in JSON format as the body with the default HTTP 200 OK status code.

- `post`: This method retrieves the key-value pairs received in the JSON body, creates a new `Message` instance and persists it in the database. In case the specified category name exists, it uses the existing category. Otherwise, the method creates a new `Category` instance and associates the new message to this new category. First, the code calls the `request.get_json` method to retrieve the key-value pairs received as arguments with the request. Then, the code calls the `message_schema.validate` method to validate the new message built with the retrieved key-value pairs. Remember that the `MessageSchema` class will execute the previously explained `process_category` method before we call the validate method, and therefore, the data will be processed before the validation takes place. In case there were validation errors, the code returns the validation errors and an HTTP `400 Bad Request` status. If the validation is successful, the code retrieves the category name received in the JSON body, specifically in the value for the `'name'` key of the `'category'` key. Then, the code calls the `Category.query.filter_by` method to retrieve a category that matches the retrieved category name. If no match is found, the code creates a new `Category` with the retrieved name and persists in the database. Then, the code creates a new message with the `message`, `duration`, and the appropriate `Category` instance, and persists it in the database. Finally, the code returns the serialized saved message in JSON format as the body, with the HTTP `201 Created` status code.

Now, we will create a `CategoryResource` class that we will use to represent a category resource. Open the previously created `api/views.py` file and add the following lines. The code file for the sample is included in the `restful_python_chapter_06_01` folder:

```python
class CategoryResource(Resource):
    def get(self, id):
        category = Category.query.get_or_404(id)
        result = category_schema.dump(category).data
        return result

    def patch(self, id):
        category = Category.query.get_or_404(id)
        category_dict = request.get_json()
        if not category_dict:
            resp = {'message': 'No input data provided'}
            return resp, status.HTTP_400_BAD_REQUEST
        errors = category_schema.validate(category_dict)
        if errors:
            return errors, status.HTTP_400_BAD_REQUEST
        try:
            if 'name' in category_dict:
```

```
                category.name = category_dict['name']
            category.update()
            return self.get(id)
        except SQLAlchemyError as e:
            db.session.rollback()
            resp = jsonify({"error": str(e)})
            return resp, status.HTTP_400_BAD_REQUEST
    def delete(self, id):
        category = Category.query.get_or_404(id)
        try:
            category.delete(category)
            response = make_response()
            return response, status.HTTP_204_NO_CONTENT
        except SQLAlchemyError as e:
            db.session.rollback()
            resp = jsonify({"error": str(e)})
            return resp, status.HTTP_401_UNAUTHORIZED
```

The CategoryResource class is a subclass of flask_restful.Resource and declares the following three methods that will be called when the HTTP method with the same name arrives as a request on the represented resource:

- get: This method receives the id of the category that has to be retrieved in the id argument. The code calls the Category.query.get_or_404 method to return an HTTP 404 Not Found status in case there is no category with the requested id in the underlying database. In case the message exists, the code calls the category_schema.dump method with the retrieved category as an argument to use the CategorySchema instance to serialize the Category instance whose id matches the specified id. The dump method takes the Category instance and applies the field filtering and output formatting specified in the CategorySchema class. The code returns the data attribute of the result returned by the dump method, that is, the serialized message in JSON format as the body, with the default HTTP 200 OK status code.

- `patch`: This method receives the id of the category that has to be updated or patched in the `id` argument. The code calls the `Category.query.get_or_404` method to return an HTTP `404 Not Found` status in case there is no category with the requested id in the underlying database. In case the category exists, the code calls the `request.get_json` method to retrieve the key-value pairs received as arguments with the request. The code updates just the name attribute in case it has a new value in the `category_dict` dictionary in the `Category` instance: `category`. Then, the code calls the `category_schema.validate` method to retrieve any errors generated when validating the updated category. In case there were validation errors, the code returns the validation errors and an HTTP `400 Bad Request` status. If the validation is successful, the code calls the update method for the `Category` instance to persist the changes in the database and returns the results of calling the previously explained `self.get` method with the id of the updated category as an argument. This way, the method returns the serialized updated message in JSON format as the body, with the default HTTP `200 OK` status code.
- `delete`: This method receives the id of the category that has to be deleted in the `id` argument. The code calls the `Category.query.get_or_404` method to return an HTTP `404 Not Found` status in case there is no category with the requested id in the underlying database. In case the category exists, the code calls the `category.delete` method with the retrieved category as an argument to use the `Category` instance to erase itself from the database. Then, the code returns an empty response body and a `204 No Content` status code.

Now, we will create a `CategoryListResource` class that we will use to represent the collection of categories. Open the previously created `api/views.py` file and add the following lines. The code file for the sample is included in the `restful_python_chapter_06_01` folder:

```
class CategoryListResource(Resource):
    def get(self):
        categories = Category.query.all()
        results = category_schema.dump(categories, many=True).data
        return results

    def post(self):
        request_dict = request.get_json()
        if not request_dict:
            resp = {'message': 'No input data provided'}
            return resp, status.HTTP_400_BAD_REQUEST
        errors = category_schema.validate(request_dict)
        if errors:
```

```
        return errors, status.HTTP_400_BAD_REQUEST
    try:
        category = Category(request_dict['name'])
        category.add(category)
        query = Category.query.get(category.id)
        result = category_schema.dump(query).data
        return result, status.HTTP_201_CREATED
    except SQLAlchemyError as e:
        db.session.rollback()
        resp = jsonify({"error": str(e)})
        return resp, status.HTTP_400_BAD_REQUEST
```

The `CategoryListResource` class is a subclass of `flask_restful.Resource` and declares the following two methods that will be called when the HTTP method with the same name arrives as a request on the represented resource:

- `get`: This method returns a list with all the `Category` instances saved in the database. First, the code calls the `Category.query.all` method to retrieve all the `Category` instances persisted in the database. Then, the code calls the `category_schema.dump` method with the retrieved messages and the `many` argument set to `True` to serialize the iterable collection of objects. The `dump` method will take each `Category` instance retrieved from the database and apply the field filtering and output formatting specified the `CategorySchema` class. The code returns the `data` attribute of the result returned by the dump method, that is, the serialized messages in JSON format as the body, with the default HTTP `200 OK` status code.

- `post`: This method retrieves the key-value pairs received in the JSON body, creates a new `Category` instance and persists it in the database. First, the code calls the `request.get_json` method to retrieve the key-value pairs received as arguments with the request. Then, the code calls the `category_schema.validate` method to validate the new category built with the retrieved key-value pairs. In case there were validation errors, the code returns the validation errors and an HTTP `400 Bad Request` status. If the validation is successful, the code creates a new category with the specified `name`, and persists it in the database. Finally, the code returns the serialized saved category in JSON format as the body, with the HTTP `201 Created` status code.

The following table shows the method of our previously created classes that we want to be executed for each combination of HTTP verb and scope:

HTTP verb	Scope	Class and method
GET	Collection of messages	MessageListResource.get
GET	Message	MessageResource.get
POST	Collection of messages	MessageListResource.post
PATCH	Message	MessageResource.patch
DELETE	Message	MessageResource.delete
GET	Collection of categories	CategoryListResource.get
GET	Message	CategoryResource.get
POST	Collection of messages	CategoryListResource.post
PATCH	Message	CategoryResource.patch
DELETE	Message	CategoryResource.delete

If the request results in the invocation of a resource with an unsupported HTTP method, Flask-RESTful will return a response with the HTTP 405 Method Not Allowed status code.

We must make the necessary resource routing configurations to call the appropriate methods and pass them all the necessary arguments by defining URL rules. The following lines configure the resource routing for the api. Open the api/views.py file created earlier and add the following lines. The code file for the sample is included in the restful_python_chapter_06_01 folder:

```
api.add_resource(CategoryListResource, '/categories/')
api.add_resource(CategoryResource, '/categories/<int:id>')
api.add_resource(MessageListResource, '/messages/')
api.add_resource(MessageResource, '/messages/<int:id>')
```

Each call to the api.add_resource method routes a URL to a resource, specifically to one of the previously declared subclasses of the flask_restful.Resource class. When there is a request to the API and the URL matches one of the URLs specified in the api.add_resource method, Flask will call the method that matches the HTTP verb in the request for the specified class.

Registering the blueprint and running migrations

Create a new `app.py` file within the `api` folder. The following lines show the code that creates a Flask application. The code file for the sample is included in the `restful_python_chapter_06_01` folder.

```
from flask import Flask


def create_app(config_filename):
    app = Flask(__name__)
    app.config.from_object(config_filename)

    from models import db
    db.init_app(app)

    from views import api_bp
    app.register_blueprint(api_bp, url_prefix='/api')

    return app
```

The code in the `api/app.py` file declares a `create_app` function that receives the configuration file name in the `config_filename` argument, set ups a *Flask* app with this configuration file, and returns the `app` object. First, the function creates the main entry point for the Flask application named `app`. Then, the code calls the `app.config.from_object` method with the `config_filename` received as an argument. This way, the Flask app uses the values that are specified in the variables defined in the Python module received as an argument to set up the settings for the *Flask* app.

The next line calls the `init_app` method for the `flask_sqlalchemy.SQLAlchemy` instance created in the `models` module named `db`. The code passes app as an argument to link the created Flask app with the SQLAlchemy instance.

The next line calls the `app.register_blueprint` method to register the blueprint created in the `views` module, named `api_bp`. The url_prefix argument is set to `'/api'` because we want the resources to be available with `/api` as a prefix. Now `http://localhost:5000/api/` is going to be the URL for the API running on the Flask development server. Finally, the function returns the `app` object.

Create a new `run.py` file within the `api` folder. The following lines show the code that uses the previously defined create_app function to create a Flask application and run it. The code file for the sample is included in the `restful_python_chapter_06_01` folder.

```
from app import create_app


app = create_app('config')


if __name__ == '__main__':
    app.run(host=app.config['HOST'],
            port=app.config['PORT'],
            debug=app.config['DEBUG'])
```

The code in the `api/run.py` file calls the `create_app` function, declared in the `app` module, with `'config'` as an argument. The function will set up a *Flask* app with this module as the configuration file.

The last line just calls the `app.run` method to start the Flask application with the host, port and debug values read from the `config` module. The code starts the application by calling the `run` method to immediately launch a local server. Remember that we could also achieve the same goal using the `flask` command-line script.

Create a new `migrate.py` file within the `api` folder. The following lines show the code that use `flask_script` and `flask_migrate` to run migrations. The code file for the sample is included in the `restful_python_chapter_06_01` folder:

```
from flask_script import Manager
from flask_migrate import Migrate, MigrateCommand
from models import db
from run import app


migrate = Migrate(app, db)
manager = Manager(app)
manager.add_command('db', MigrateCommand)


if __name__ == '__main__':
    manager.run()
```

The code creates an instance of `flask_migrate.Migrate` with the *Flask* app created in the previously explained `run` module, app, and the `flask_sqlalchemy.SQLAlchemy` instance created in the models module, db. Then, the code creates a `flask_script.Manager` class with the Flask app as an argument and saves its reference in the `manager` variable. The next line calls the `add_command` method with `'db'` and `MigrateCommand` as arguments. The main function calls the run method for the `Manager` instance.

This way, after the extension initializes, the code adds a db group to the command-line options. The db group has many sub-commands that we will use through the `migrate.py` script.

Now, we will run the scripts to run migrations and generate the necessary tables in the PostgreSQL database. Make sure you run the scripts in the terminal or Command Prompt window in which you have activated the virtual environment and that you are located in the `api` folder.

Run the first script, that initializes migration support for the application.

```
python migrate.py db init
```

The following lines show the sample output generated after running the previous script. Your output will be different according to the base folder in which you have created the virtual environment:

```
    Creating directory /Users/gaston/PythonREST/Flask02/api/migrations ...
done
    Creating directory
/Users/gaston/PythonREST/Flask02/api/migrations/versions ... done
    Generating /Users/gaston/PythonREST/Flask02/api/migrations/alembic.ini
... done
    Generating /Users/gaston/PythonREST/Flask02/api/migrations/env.py ...
done
    Generating /Users/gaston/PythonREST/Flask02/api/migrations/README ...
done
    Generating
/Users/gaston/PythonREST/Flask02/api/migrations/script.py.mako ... done
    Please edit configuration/connection/logging settings in
    '/Users/gaston/PythonREST/Flask02/api/migrations/alembic.ini' before
proceeding.
```

The script generated a new `migrations` sub-folder within the `api` folder with a versions sub-folder and many other files.

Run the second script that populates the migration script with the detected changes in the models. In this case, it is the first time we populate the migration script, and therefore, the migration script will generate the tables that will persist our two models: `Category` and `Message`:

```
python migrate.py db migrate
```

The following lines show the sample output generated after running the previous script. Your output will be different according to the base folder in which you have created the virtual environment:

```
INFO   [alembic.runtime.migration] Context impl PostgresqlImpl.
INFO   [alembic.runtime.migration] Will assume transactional DDL.
INFO   [alembic.autogenerate.compare] Detected added table 'category'
INFO   [alembic.autogenerate.compare] Detected added table 'message'
    Generating
/Users/gaston/PythonREST/Flask02/api/migrations/versions/417543056ac3_.py
... done
```

The output indicates that the `api/migrations/versions/417543056ac3_.py` file includes the code to create the `category` and `message` tables. The following lines show the code for this file that was automatically generated based on the models. Note that the filename will be different in your configuration. The code file for the sample is included in the `restful_python_chapter_06_01` folder:

```
"""empty message

Revision ID: 417543056ac3
Revises: None
Create Date: 2016-08-08 01:05:31.134631

"""

# revision identifiers, used by Alembic.
revision = '417543056ac3'
down_revision = None

from alembic import op
import sqlalchemy as sa


def upgrade():
    ### commands auto generated by Alembic - please adjust! ###
    op.create_table('category',
    sa.Column('id', sa.Integer(), nullable=False),
    sa.Column('name', sa.String(length=150), nullable=False),
    sa.PrimaryKeyConstraint('id'),
```

```
    sa.UniqueConstraint('name')
    )
    op.create_table('message',
    sa.Column('id', sa.Integer(), nullable=False),
    sa.Column('message', sa.String(length=250), nullable=False),
    sa.Column('duration', sa.Integer(), nullable=False),
    sa.Column('creation_date', sa.TIMESTAMP(),
server_default=sa.text('CURRENT_TIMESTAMP'), nullable=False),
    sa.Column('category_id', sa.Integer(), nullable=False),
    sa.Column('printed_times', sa.Integer(), server_default='0',
nullable=False),
    sa.Column('printed_once', sa.Boolean(), server_default='false',
nullable=False),
    sa.ForeignKeyConstraint(['category_id'], ['category.id'],
ondelete='CASCADE'),
    sa.PrimaryKeyConstraint('id'),
    sa.UniqueConstraint('message')
    )
    ### end Alembic commands ###


def downgrade():
    ### commands auto generated by Alembic - please adjust! ###
    op.drop_table('message')
    op.drop_table('category')
    ### end Alembic commands ###
```

The code defines two functions: upgrade and downgrade. The upgrade function runs the necessary code to create the category and message tables by making calls to alembic.op.create_table. The downgrade function runs the necessary code to go back to the previous version.

Run the third script to upgrade the database:

```
python migrate.py db upgrade
```

The following lines show the sample output generated after running the previous script:

```
    INFO  [alembic.runtime.migration] Context impl PostgresqlImpl.
    INFO  [alembic.runtime.migration] Will assume transactional DDL.
    INFO  [alembic.runtime.migration] Running upgrade  -> 417543056ac3,
empty message
```

The previous script called the upgrade function defined in the automatically generated api/migrations/versions/417543056ac3_.py script. Don't forget that the file name will be different in your configuration.

After we run the previous scripts, we can use the PostgreSQL command line or any other application that allows us to easily verify the contents of the PostreSQL database to check the tables that the migration generated.

Run the following command to list the generated tables. In case the database name you are using is not named `messages`, make sure you use the appropriate database name.

```
psql --username=user_name --dbname=messages --command="\dt"
```

The following lines show the output with all the generated table names:

```
                        List of relations
     Schema |      Name          | Type  |   Owner
    --------+--------------------+-------+-----------
     public | alembic_version    | table | user_name
     public | category           | table | user_name
     public | message            | table | user_name
    (3 rows)
```

SQLAlchemy generated the tables, the unique constraints, and the foreign keys based on the information included in our models.

- `category`: Persists the `Category` model.
- `message`: Persists the `Message` model.

The following command will allow you to check the contents of the four tables after we compose and send HTTP requests to the RESTful API and make CRUD operations to the two tables. The commands assume that you are running PostgreSQL on the same computer in which you are running the command:

```
psql --username=user_name --dbname=messages --command="SELECT * FROM category;"
psql --username=user_name --dbname=messages --command="SELECT * FROM message;"
```

> Instead of working with the PostgreSQL command-line utility, you can use a GUI tool to check the contents of the PostgreSQL database. You also use also the database tools included in your favorite IDE to check the contents for the SQLite database.

Alembic generated an additional table named `alembic_version` that saves the version number for the database in the `version_num` column. This table makes is possible for the migration scripts to retrieve the current version of the database and upgrade or downgrade it based on our needs.

Creating and retrieving related resources

Now, we can run the `api/run.py` script that launches Flask's development. Execute the following command in the api folder.

```
python run.py
```

The following lines show the output after we execute the preceding command. The development server is listening at port 5000.

```
* Running on http://127.0.0.1:5000/ (Press CTRL+C to quit)
* Restarting with stat
* Debugger is active!
* Debugger pin code: 198-040-402
```

Now, we will use the HTTPie command or its curl equivalents to compose and send HTTP requests to the API. We will use JSON for the requests that require additional data. Remember that you can perform the same tasks with your favorite GUI-based tool.

First, we will compose and send HTTP requests to create two message categories:

```
http POST :5000/api/categories/ name='Information'
http POST :5000/api/categories/ name='Warning'
```

The following are the equivalent `curl` commands:

```
    curl -iX POST -H "Content-Type: application/json" -d
'{"name":"Information"}' :5000/api/categories/
    curl -iX POST -H "Content-Type: application/json" -d
'{"name":"Warning"}' :5000/api/categories/
```

The preceding commands will compose and send two POST HTTP requests with the specified JSON key-value pair. The requests specify `/api/categories/`, and therefore, they will match the `'/api'url_prefix` for the `api_bp` blueprint. Then, the request will match the `'/categories/'` URL route for the `CategoryList` resource and run the `CategoryList.post` method. The method doesn't receive arguments because the URL route doesn't include any parameters. As the HTTP verb for the request is POST, Flask calls the `post` method. If the two new `Category` instances were successfully persisted in the database, the two calls will return an `HTTP 201 Created` status code and the recently persisted `Category` serialized to JSON in the response body. The following lines show an example response for the two HTTP requests, with the new `Category` objects in the JSON responses.

Note that the responses include the URL, `url`, for the created categories. The `messages` array is empty in both cases because there aren't messages related to each new category yet:

```
HTTP/1.0 201 CREATED
Content-Length: 116
Content-Type: application/json
Date: Mon, 08 Aug 2016 05:26:58 GMT
Server: Werkzeug/0.11.10 Python/3.5.1
{
    "id": 1,
    "messages": [],
    "name": "Information",
    "url": "http://localhost:5000/api/categories/1"
}
HTTP/1.0 201 CREATED
Content-Length: 112
Content-Type: application/json
Date: Mon, 08 Aug 2016 05:27:05 GMT
Server: Werkzeug/0.11.10 Python/3.5.1
{
    "id": 2,
    "messages": [],
    "name": "Warning",
    "url": "http://localhost:5000/api/categories/2"
}
```

Now, we will compose and send HTTP requests to create two messages that belong to the first message category we recently created: `Information`. We will specify the `category` key with the name of the desired message category. The database table that persists the `Message` model will save the value of the primary key of the related `Category` whose name value matches the one we provide:

```
http POST :5000/api/messages/ message='Checking temperature sensor'
duration=5 category="Information"
http POST :5000/api/messages/ message='Checking light sensor'
duration=8 category="Information"
```

The following are the equivalent `curl` commands:

```
curl -iX POST -H "Content-Type: application/json" -d '{"message":"
Checking temperature sensor", "category":"Information"}'
:5000/api/messages/
curl -iX POST -H "Content-Type: application/json" -d '{"message":"
Checking light sensor", "category":"Information"}' :5000/api/messages/
```

The first command will compose and send the following HTTP request: POST
`http://localhost:5000/api/messages/` with the following JSON key-value pairs:

```
{
    "message": "Checking temperature sensor",
    "category": "Information"
}
```

The second command will compose and send the same HTTP request with the following
JSON key-value pairs:

```
{
    "message": "Checking light sensor",
    "category": "Information"
}
```

The requests specify `/api/categories/`, and therefore, they will match the
`'/api'url_prefix` for the `api_bp` blueprint. Then, the request will match the
`'/messages/'` URL route for the `MessageList` resource and run the `MessageList.post`
method. The method doesn't receive arguments because the URL route doesn't include any
parameters. As the HTTP verb for the request is POST, Flask calls the `post` method. The the
`MessageSchema.process_category` method will process the data for the category and
the `MessageListResource.post` method will retrieve the `Category` that matches the
specified category name from the database, to use it as the related category for the new
message. If the two new `Message` instances were successfully persisted in the database, the
two calls will return an HTTP 201 Created status code and the recently persisted `Message`
serialized to JSON in the response body. The following lines show an example response for
the two HTTP requests, with the new `Message` objects in the JSON responses. Note that the
responses include the URL, `url`, for the created messages. In addition, the response
includes the id, name, and `url` for the related category.

```
HTTP/1.0 201 CREATED
Content-Length: 369
Content-Type: application/json
Date: Mon, 08 Aug 2016 15:18:43 GMT
Server: Werkzeug/0.11.10 Python/3.5.1
{
    "category": {
        "id": 1,
        "name": "Information",
        "url": "http://localhost:5000/api/categories/1"
    },
    "creation_date": "2016-08-08T12:18:43.260474+00:00",
    "duration": 5,
    "id": 1,
```

```
    "message": "Checking temperature sensor",
    "printed_once": false,
    "printed_times": 0,
    "url": "http://localhost:5000/api/messages/1"
}
HTTP/1.0 201 CREATED
Content-Length: 363
Content-Type: application/json
Date: Mon, 08 Aug 2016 15:27:30 GMT
Server: Werkzeug/0.11.10 Python/3.5.1
{
    "category": {
        "id": 1,
        "name": "Information",
        "url": "http://localhost:5000/api/categories/1"
    },
    "creation_date": "2016-08-08T12:27:30.124511+00:00",
    "duration": 8,
    "id": 2,
    "message": "Checking light sensor",
    "printed_once": false,
    "printed_times": 0,
    "url": "http://localhost:5000/api/messages/2"
}
```

We can run the preceding commands to check the contents of the tables that the migrations created in the PostgreSQL database. We will notice that the category_id column for the message table saves the value of the primary key of the related row in the category table. The MessageSchema class uses a fields.Nested instance to render the id, url and name fields for the related Category. The following screenshot shows the contents for the category and the message table in a PostgreSQL database after running the HTTP requests:

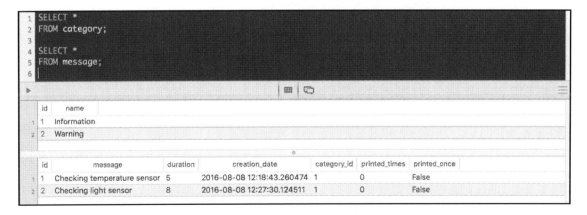

Now, we will compose and send an HTTP request to retrieve the category that contains two messages, that is the category resource whose id or primary key is equal to 1. Don't forget to replace 1 with the primary key value of the category whose name is equal to 'Information' in your configuration:

```
http :5000/api/categories/1
```

The following is the equivalent curl command:

```
curl -iX GET :5000/api/categories/1
```

The preceding command will compose and send a GET HTTP request. The request has a number after /api/categories/, and therefore, it will match '/categories/<int:id>' and run the CategoryResource.get method, that is, the get method for the CategoryResource class. If a Category instance with the specified id exists in the database, the call to the method will will return an HTTP 200 OK status code and the Category instance serialized to JSON in the response body. The CategorySchema class uses a fields.Nested instance to render all the fields for all the messages related to the category excepting the category field. The following lines show a sample response:

```
HTTP/1.0 200 OK
Content-Length: 1078
Content-Type: application/json
Date: Mon, 08 Aug 2016 16:09:10 GMT
Server: Werkzeug/0.11.10 Python/3.5.1
{
    "id": 1,
    "messages": [
        {
            "category": {
                "id": 1,
                "name": "Information",
                "url": "http://localhost:5000/api/categories/1"
            },
            "creation_date": "2016-08-08T12:27:30.124511+00:00",
            "duration": 8,
            "id": 2,
            "message": "Checking light sensor",
            "printed_once": false,
            "printed_times": 0,
            "url": "http://localhost:5000/api/messages/2"
        },
        {
            "category": {
                "id": 1,
                "name": "Information",
```

```
                    "url": "http://localhost:5000/api/categories/1"
                },
                "creation_date": "2016-08-08T12:18:43.260474+00:00",
                "duration": 5,
                "id": 1,
                "message": "Checking temperature sensor",
                "printed_once": false,
                "printed_times": 0,
                "url": "http://localhost:5000/api/messages/1"
            }
        ],
        "name": "Information",
        "url": "http://localhost:5000/api/categories/1"
    }
```

Now, we will compose and send a POST HTTP request to create a message related to a category name that doesn't exist: 'Error':

```
http POST :5000/api/messages/ message='Temperature sensor error'
duration=10 category="Error"
```

The following are the equivalent curl commands:

```
curl -iX POST -H "Content-Type: application/json" -d '{"message":"
Temperature sensor error", "category":"Error"}' :5000/api/messages/
```

The CategoryListResource.post method won't be able to retrieve a Category instance whose name is equal to the specified value, and therefore, the method will create a new Category, save it and use it as the related category for the new message. The following lines show an example response for the HTTP request, with the new Message object in the JSON responses and the details for the new Category object related to the message:

```
HTTP/1.0 201 CREATED
Content-Length: 361
Content-Type: application/json
Date: Mon, 08 Aug 2016 17:20:22 GMT
Server: Werkzeug/0.11.10 Python/3.5.1
{
    "category": {
        "id": 3,
        "name": "Error",
        "url": "http://localhost:5000/api/categories/3"
    },
    "creation_date": "2016-08-08T14:20:22.103752+00:00",
    "duration": 10,
    "id": 3,
    "message": "Temperature sensor error",
```

```
    "printed_once": false,
    "printed_times": 0,
    "url": "http://localhost:5000/api/messages/3"
}
```

We can run the commands explained earlier to check the contents of the tables that the migrations created in the PostgreSQL database. We will notice that we have a new row in the category table with the recently added category when we created a new message. The following screenshot shows the contents for the `category` and `message` tables in a PostgreSQL database after running the HTTP requests:

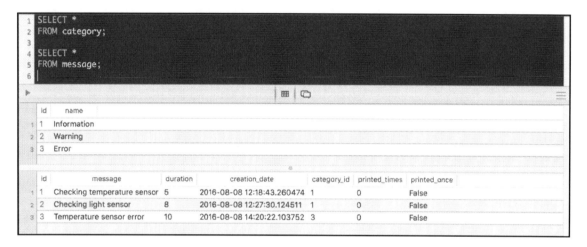

Test your knowledge

1. Marshmallow is:
    1. A lightweight library for converting complex datatypes to and from native Python datatypes.
    2. An ORM .
    3. A lightweight web framework that replaces Flask.

2. SQLAlchemy is:
    1. A lightweight library for converting complex datatypes to and from native Python datatypes.
    2. An ORM .
    3. A lightweight web framework that replaces Flask.

3. The `marshmallow.pre_load` decorator:
   1. Registers a method to run after any instance of the `MessageSchema` class is created.
   2. Registers a method to invoke after serializing an object.
   3. Registers a method to invoke before deserializing an object.

4. The `dump` method for any instance of a Schema subclass:
   1. Routes URLs to Python primitives.
   2. Persists the instance or collection of instances passed as an argument to the database.
   3. Takes the instance or collection of instances passed as an argument and applies the field filtering and output formatting specified in the Schema subclass to the instance or collection of instances.

5. When we declare an attribute as an instance of the `marshmallow.fields.Nested` class:
   1. The field will nest a single `Schema` or a collection of `Schema` based on the value for the `many` argument.
   2. The field will nest a single `Schema`. If we want to nest a collection of `Schema`, we have to use an instance of the `marshmallow.fields.NestedCollection` class.
   3. The field will nest a collection of `Schema`. If we want to nest a single `Schema`, we have to use an instance of the `marshmallow.fields.NestedSingle` class.

Summary

In this chapter, we expanded the capabilities of the previous version of the RESTful API that we created in the previous chapter. We used SQLAlchemy as our ORM to work with a PostgreSQL database. We installed many packages to simplify many common tasks, wrote code for the models and their relationships, and worked with schemas to validate, serialize, and deserialize these models.

We combined blueprints with resourceful routing and were able to generate the database from the models. We composed and sent many HTTP requests to our RESTful API and analyzed how each HTTP request was processed in our code and how the models persisted in the database tables.

Now that we built a complex API with Flask, Flask-RESTful, and SQLAlchemy, we will use additional features and add security and authentication, which is what we are going to discuss in the next chapter.

7
Improving and Adding Authentication to an API with Flask

In this chapter, we will improve the RESTful API that we started in the previous chapter and we will add authentication related security to it. We will:

- Improve unique constraints in the models
- Update fields for a resource with the PATCH method
- Code a generic pagination class
- Add pagination features to the API
- Understand the steps to add authentication and permissions
- Add a user model
- Create a schema to validate, serialize and deserialize users
- Add authentication to resources
- Create resource classes to handle users
- Run migrations to generate the user table
- Compose requests with the necessary authentication

Improving unique constraints in the models

When we created the `Category` model, we specified the `True` value for the unique argument when we created the `db.Column` instance named `name`. As a result, the migrations generated the necessary unique constraint to make sure that the `name` field has unique values in the `category` table. This way, the database won't allow us to insert duplicate values for `category.name`. However, the error message generated when we try to do so is not clear.

Run the following command to create a category with a duplicate name. There is already an existing category with the name equal to `'Information'`:

```
http POST :5000/api/categories/ name='Information'
```

The following is the equivalent `curl` command:

```
curl -iX POST -H "Content-Type: application/json" -d
'{"name":"Information"}'
   :5000/api/categories/
```

The previous command will compose and send a POST HTTP request with the specified JSON key-value pair. The unique constraint in the `category.name` field won't allow the database table to persist the new category. Thus, the request will return an HTTP `400 Bad Request` status code with an integrity error message. The following lines show a sample response:

```
HTTP/1.0 400 BAD REQUEST
Content-Length: 282
Content-Type: application/json
Date: Mon, 15 Aug 2016 03:53:27 GMT
Server: Werkzeug/0.11.10 Python/3.5.1
{
    "error": "(psycopg2.IntegrityError) duplicate key value violates
unique
        constraint "category_name_key"\nDETAIL:  Key (name)=(Information)
        already exists.\n [SQL: 'INSERT INTO category (name) VALUES
(%(name)s)
        RETURNING category.id'] [parameters: {'name': 'Information'}]"
}
```

Obviously, the error message is extremely technical and provides too many details about the database and the query that failed. We might parse the error message to automatically generate a more user friendly error message. However, instead of doing so, we want to avoid trying to insert a row that we know will fail. We will add code to make sure that a category is unique before we try to persist it. Of course, there is still a chance to receive the previously shown error if somebody inserts a category with the same name between the time we run our code, indicating that a category name is unique, and persist the changes in the database. However, the chances are lower and we can reduce the changes of the previously shown error message to be shown.

 In a production-ready REST API we should never return the error messages returned by SQLAlchemy or any other database-related data, as it might include sensitive data that we don't want the users of our API to be able to retrieve. In this case, we are returning all the errors for debugging purposes and to be able to improve our API.

Now, we will add a new class method to the Category class to allow us to determine whether a name is unique or not. Open the api/models.py file and add the following lines within the declaration of the Category class. The code file for the sample is included in the restful_python_chapter_07_01 folder:

```
@classmethod
def is_unique(cls, id, name):
    existing_category = cls.query.filter_by(name=name).first()
    if existing_category is None:
        return True
    else:
        if existing_category.id == id:
            return True
        else:
            return False
```

The new Category.is_unique class method receives the id and the name for the category that we want to make sure that has a unique name. If the category is a new one that hasn't been saved yet, we will receive a 0 for the id value. Otherwise, we will receive the category id in the argument.

The method calls the query.filter_by method for the current class to retrieve a category whose name matches the other category name. In case there is a category that matches the criteria, the method will return True only if the id is the same one than the one received in the argument. In case no category matches the criteria, the method will return True.

We will use the previously created class method to check whether a category is unique or not before creating and persisting it in the `CategoryListResource.post` method. Open the `api/views.py` file and replace the existing `post` method declared in the `CategoryListResource` class with the following lines. The lines that have been added or modified are highlighted. The code file for the sample is included in the `restful_python_chapter_07_01` folder:

```
def post(self):
    request_dict = request.get_json()
    if not request_dict:
        resp = {'message': 'No input data provided'}
        return resp, status.HTTP_400_BAD_REQUEST
    errors = category_schema.validate(request_dict)
    if errors:
        return errors, status.HTTP_400_BAD_REQUEST
    category_name = request_dict['name']
    if not Category.is_unique(id=0, name=category_name):
        response = {'error': 'A category with the same name already
exists'}
        return response, status.HTTP_400_BAD_REQUEST
    try:
        category = Category(category_name)
        category.add(category)
        query = Category.query.get(category.id)
        result = category_schema.dump(query).data
        return result, status.HTTP_201_CREATED
    except SQLAlchemyError as e:
        db.session.rollback()
        resp = {"error": str(e)}
        return resp, status.HTTP_400_BAD_REQUEST
```

Now, we will perform the same validation in the `CategoryResource.patch` method. Open the `api/views.py` file and replace the existing `patch` method declared in the `CategoryResource` class with the following lines. The lines that have been added or modified are highlighted. The code file for the sample is included in the `restful_python_chapter_07_01` folder:

```
def patch(self, id):
    category = Category.query.get_or_404(id)
    category_dict = request.get_json()
    if not category_dict:
        resp = {'message': 'No input data provided'}
        return resp, status.HTTP_400_BAD_REQUEST
    errors = category_schema.validate(category_dict)
    if errors:
        return errors, status.HTTP_400_BAD_REQUEST
```

```
        try:
            if 'name' in category_dict:
                category_name = category_dict['name']
                if Category.is_unique(id=id, name=category_name):
                    category.name = category_name
                else:
                    response = {'error': 'A category with the same name
already
                       exists'}
                    return response, status.HTTP_400_BAD_REQUEST
            category.update()
            return self.get(id)
                except SQLAlchemyError as e:
                db.session.rollback()
                resp = {"error": str(e)}
                return resp, status.HTTP_400_BAD_REQUEST
```

Run the following command to again create a category with a duplicate name:

```
http POST :5000/api/categories/ name='Information'
```

The following is the equivalent `curl` command:

```
curl -iX POST -H "Content-Type: application/json" -d
'{"name":"Information"}'
   :5000/api/categories/
```

The previous command will compose and send a POST HTTP request with the specified JSON key-value pair. The changes we made will generate a response with a user friendly error message and will avoid trying to persist the changes. The request will return an HTTP `400 Bad Request` status code with the error message in the JSON body. The following lines show a sample response:

```
HTTP/1.0 400 BAD REQUEST
Content-Length: 64
Content-Type: application/json
Date: Mon, 15 Aug 2016 04:38:43 GMT
Server: Werkzeug/0.11.10 Python/3.5.1
{
    "error": "A category with the same name already exists"
}
```

Now, we will add a new `class` method to the `Message` class to allow us to determine whether a message is unique or not. Open the `api/models.py` file and add the following lines within the declaration of the `Message` class. The code file for the sample is included in the `restful_python_chapter_07_01` folder:

```
@classmethod
def is_unique(cls, id, message):
    existing_message = cls.query.filter_by(message=message).first()
    if existing_message is None:
        return True
    else:
        if existing_message.id == id:
            return True
        else:
            return False
```

The new `Message.is_unique` class method receives the `id` and the `message` for the message that we want to make sure that has a unique value for the message field. If the message is a new one that hasn't been saved yet, we will receive a `0` for the `id` value. Otherwise, we will receive the message id in the argument.

The method calls the `query.filter_by` method for the current class to retrieve a message whose message field matches the other message's message. In case there is a message that matches the criteria, the method will return `True` only if the id is the same one than the one received in the argument. In case no message matches the criteria, the method will return `True`.

We will use the previously created class method to check whether a message is unique or not before creating and persisting it in the `MessageListResource.post` method. Open the `api/views.py` file and replace the existing `post` method declared in the `MessageListResource` class with the following lines. The lines that have been added or modified are highlighted. The code file for the sample is included in the `restful_python_chapter_07_01` folder:

```
def post(self):
    request_dict = request.get_json()
    if not request_dict:
        response = {'message': 'No input data provided'}
        return response, status.HTTP_400_BAD_REQUEST
    errors = message_schema.validate(request_dict)
    if errors:
        return errors, status.HTTP_400_BAD_REQUEST
    message_message = request_dict['message']
    if not Message.is_unique(id=0, message=message_message):
        response = {'error': 'A message with the same message already
```

```
        exists'}
        return response, status.HTTP_400_BAD_REQUEST
try:
    category_name = request_dict['category']['name']
    category = Category.query.filter_by(name=category_name).first()
    if category is None:
        # Create a new Category
        category = Category(name=category_name)
        db.session.add(category)
    # Now that we are sure we have a category
    # create a new Message
    message = Message(
        message=message_message,
        duration=request_dict['duration'],
        category=category)
    message.add(message)
    query = Message.query.get(message.id)
    result = message_schema.dump(query).data
    return result, status.HTTP_201_CREATED
except SQLAlchemyError as e:
    db.session.rollback()
    resp = {"error": str(e)}
    return resp, status.HTTP_400_BAD_REQUEST
```

Now, we will perform the same validation in the `MessageResource.patch` method. Open the `api/views.py` file and replace the existing `patch` method declared in the `MessageResource` class with the following lines. The lines that have been added or modified are highlighted. The code file for the sample is included in the `restful_python_chapter_07_01` folder:

```
def patch(self, id):
    message = Message.query.get_or_404(id)
    message_dict = request.get_json(force=True)
    if 'message' in message_dict:
        message_message = message_dict['message']
        if Message.is_unique(id=id, message=message_message):
            message.message = message_message
        else:
            response = {'error': 'A message with the same message
already
            exists'}
            return response, status.HTTP_400_BAD_REQUEST
    if 'duration' in message_dict:
        message.duration = message_dict['duration']
    if 'printed_times' in message_dict:
        message.printed_times = message_dict['printed_times']
    if 'printed_once' in message_dict:
```

```
        message.printed_once = message_dict['printed_once']
    dumped_message, dump_errors = message_schema.dump(message)
    if dump_errors:
        return dump_errors, status.HTTP_400_BAD_REQUEST
    validate_errors = message_schema.validate(dumped_message)
    if validate_errors:
        return validate_errors, status.HTTP_400_BAD_REQUEST
    try:
        message.update()
        return self.get(id)
    except SQLAlchemyError as e:
            db.session.rollback()
            resp = {"error": str(e)}
            return resp, status.HTTP_400_BAD_REQUEST
```

Run the following command to create a message with a duplicate value for the message field:

```
http POST :5000/api/messages/ message='Checking temperature sensor'
duration=25 category="Information"
```

The following is the equivalent `curl` command:

```
curl -iX POST -H "Content-Type: application/json" -d
'{"message":"Checking temperature sensor", "duration":25, "category":
"Information"}' :5000/api/messages/
```

The previous command will compose and send a POST HTTP request with the specified JSON key-value pair. The changes we made will generate a response with a user friendly error message and will avoid trying to persist the changes in the message. The request will return an HTTP 400 Bad Request status code with the error message in the JSON body. The following lines show a sample response:

```
HTTP/1.0 400 BAD REQUEST
Content-Length: 66
Content-Type: application/json
Date: Mon, 15 Aug 2016 04:55:46 GMT
Server: Werkzeug/0.11.10 Python/3.5.1
{
    "error": "A message with the same message already exists"
}
```

Updating fields for a resource with the PATCH method

As we explained in Chapter 6, *Working with Models, SQLAlchemy, and Hyperlinked APIs in Flask*, our API is able to update a single field for an existing resource, and therefore, we provide an implementation for the PATCH method. For example, we can use the PATCH method to update an existing message and set the value for its printed_once and printed_times fields to true and 1. We don't want to use the PUT method because this method is meant to replace an entire message. The PATCH method is meant to apply a delta to an existing message, and therefore, it is the appropriate method to just change the value of those two fields.

Now, we will compose and send an HTTP request to update an existing message, specifically, to update the value of the printed_once and printed_times fields. Because we just want to update two fields, we will use the PATCH method instead of PUT. Make sure you replace 1 with the id or primary key of an existing message in your configuration:

```
http PATCH :5000/api/messages/1 printed_once=true printed_times=1
```

The following is the equivalent curl command:

```
curl -iX PATCH -H "Content-Type: application/json" -d
'{"printed_once":"true", "printed_times":1}' :5000/api/messages/1
```

The previous command will compose and send a PATCH HTTP request with the following specified JSON key-value pairs:

```
{
    "printed_once": true,
    "printed_times": 1
}
```

The request has a number after /api/messages/, and therefore, it will match '/messages/<int:id>' and run the MessageResource.patch method, that is, the patch method for the MessageResource class. If a Message instance with the specified id exists, the code will retrieve the values for the printed_times and printed_once keys in the request dictionary update the Message instance and validate it.

If the updated `Message` instance is valid, the code will persist the changes in the database and the call to the method will return an HTTP `200 OK` status code and the recently updated `Message` instance serialized to JSON in the response body. The following lines show a sample response:

```
HTTP/1.0 200 OK
Content-Length: 368
Content-Type: application/json
Date: Tue, 09 Aug 2016 22:38:39 GMT
Server: Werkzeug/0.11.10 Python/3.5.1
{
    "category": {
        "id": 1,
        "name": "Information",
        "url": "http://localhost:5000/api/categories/1"
    },
    "creation_date": "2016-08-08T12:18:43.260474+00:00",
    "duration": 5,
    "id": 1,
    "message": "Checking temperature sensor",
    "printed_once": true,
    "printed_times": 1,
    "url": "http://localhost:5000/api/messages/1"
}
```

We can run the commands explained in Chapter 6, *Working with Models, SQLAlchemy, and Hyperlinked APIs in Flask*, to check the contents of the tables that the migrations created in the PostgreSQL database. We will notice that the `printed_times` and `printed_once` values have been updated for the row in the message table. The following screenshot shows the contents for the updated row of the `message` table in a PostgreSQL database after running the HTTP request. The screenshot shows the results of executing the following SQL query: `SELECT * FROM message WHERE id = 1`:

Coding a generic pagination class

Our database has a few rows for each of the tables that persist the models we have defined. However, after we start working with our API in a real-life production environment, we will have hundreds of messages, and therefore, we will have to deal with large result sets. Thus, we will create a generic pagination class and we will use it to easily specify how we want large results sets to be split into individual pages of data.

First, we will compose and send HTTP requests to create 9 messages that belong to one of the categories we have created: `Information`. This way, we will have a total of 12 messages persisted in the database. We had 3 messages and we add 9 more.

```
    http POST :5000/api/messages/ message='Initializing light controller'
duration=25 category="Information"
    http POST :5000/api/messages/ message='Initializing light sensor'
duration=20 category="Information"
    http POST :5000/api/messages/ message='Checking pressure sensor'
duration=18 category="Information"
    http POST :5000/api/messages/ message='Checking gas sensor' duration=14
category="Information"
    http POST :5000/api/messages/ message='Setting ADC resolution'
duration=22 category="Information"
    http POST :5000/api/messages/ message='Setting sample rate' duration=15
category="Information"
    http POST :5000/api/messages/ message='Initializing pressure sensor'
duration=18 category="Information"
    http POST :5000/api/messages/ message='Initializing gas sensor'
duration=16 category="Information"
    http POST :5000/api/messages/ message='Initializing proximity sensor'
duration=5 category="Information"
```

The following are the equivalent `curl` commands:

```
curl -iX POST -H "Content-Type: application/json" -d '{"message":"
Initializing light controller", "duration":25, "category": "Information"}'
:5000/api/messages/
curl -iX POST -H "Content-Type: application/json" -d
'{"message":"Initializing light sensor", "duration":20, "category":
"Information"}' :5000/api/messages/
curl -iX POST -H "Content-Type: application/json" -d '{"message":"Checking
pressure sensor", "duration":18, "category": "Information"}'
:5000/api/messages/
curl -iX POST -H "Content-Type: application/json" -d '{"message":"Checking
gas sensor", "duration":14, "category": "Information"}' :5000/api/messages/
curl -iX POST -H "Content-Type: application/json" -d '{"message":"Setting
ADC resolution", "duration":22, "category": "Information"}'
:5000/api/messages/
```

```
curl -iX POST -H "Content-Type: application/json" -d '{"message":"Setting
sample rate", "duration":15, "category": "Information"}'
:5000/api/messages/
curl -iX POST -H "Content-Type: application/json" -d
'{"message":"Initializing pressure sensor", "duration":18, "category":
"Information"}' :5000/api/messages/
curl -iX POST -H "Content-Type: application/json" -d
'{"message":"Initializing gas sensor", "duration":16, "category":
"Information"}' :5000/api/messages/
curl -iX POST -H "Content-Type: application/json" -d
'{"message":"Initializing proximity sensor", "duration":5, "category":
"Information"}' :5000/api/messages/
```

The previous commands will compose and send nine POST HTTP requests with the specified JSON key-value pairs. The request specifies /api/messages/, and therefore, it will match '/messages/' and run the MessageListResource.post method, that is, the post method for the MessageListResource class.

Now, we have 12 messages in our database. However, we don't want to retrieve the 12 messages when we compose and send a GET HTTP request to /api/messages/. We will create a customizable generic pagination class to include a maximum of 5 resources in each individual page of data.

Open the api/config.py file and add the following lines that declare two variables that configure the global pagination settings. The code file for the sample is included in the restful_python_chapter_07_01 folder:

```
PAGINATION_PAGE_SIZE = 5
PAGINATION_PAGE_ARGUMENT_NAME = 'page'
```

The value for the PAGINATION_PAGE_SIZE variable specifies a global setting with the default value for the page size, also known as limit. The value for the PAGINATION_PAGE_ARGUMENT_NAME specifies a global setting with the default value for the argument name that we will use in our requests to specify the page number we want to retrieve.

Create a new helpers.py file within the api folder. The following lines show the code that creates a new PaginationHelper class. The code file for the sample is included in the restful_python_chapter_07_01 folder:

```
from flask import url_for
from flask import current_app


class PaginationHelper():
```

```
    def __init__(self, request, query, resource_for_url, key_name, schema):
        self.request = request
        self.query = query
        self.resource_for_url = resource_for_url
        self.key_name = key_name
        self.schema = schema
        self.results_per_page = current_app.config['PAGINATION_PAGE_SIZE']
        self.page_argument_name =
        current_app.config['PAGINATION_PAGE_ARGUMENT_NAME']

    def paginate_query(self):
        # If no page number is specified, we assume the request wants page
#1
        page_number = self.request.args.get(self.page_argument_name, 1,
type=int)
        paginated_objects = self.query.paginate(
            page_number,
            per_page=self.results_per_page,
            error_out=False)
        objects = paginated_objects.items
        if paginated_objects.has_prev:
            previous_page_url = url_for(
                self.resource_for_url,
                page=page_number-1,
                _external=True)
        else:
            previous_page_url = None
        if paginated_objects.has_next:
            next_page_url = url_for(
                self.resource_for_url,
                page=page_number+1,
                _external=True)
        else:
            next_page_url = None
        dumped_objects = self.schema.dump(objects, many=True).data
        return ({
            self.key_name: dumped_objects,
            'previous': previous_page_url,
            'next': next_page_url,
            'count': paginated_objects.total
        })
```

The `PaginationHelper` class declares a constructor, that is, the __init__ method that received many arguments and uses them to initialize the attributes with the same names:

- `request`: The Flask request object that will allow the `paginate_query` method to retrieve the page number value specified with the HTTP request.
- `query`: The SQLAlchemy query that the `paginate_query` method has to paginate.
- `resource_for_url`: A string with the resource name that the `paginate_query` method will use to generate the full URLs for the previous page and the next page.
- `key_name`: A string with the key name that the `paginate_query` method will use to return the serialized objects.
- `schema`: The Flask-Marshmallow `Schema` subclass that the `paginate_query` method must use to serialize the objects.

In addition, the constructor reads and saves the values for the configuration variables we added to the `config.py` file in the `results_per_page` and `page_argument_name` attributes.

The class declares the `paginate_query` method. First, the code retrieves the page number specified in the request and saves it in the `page_number` variable. In case no page number is specified, the code assumes that request requires the first page. Then, the code calls the `self.query.paginate` method to retrieve the page number specified by `page_number` of the paginated result of objects from the database, with a number of results per page indicated by the value of the `self.results_per_page` attribute. The next line saves the paginated items from the `paginated_object.items` attribute in the `objects` variable.

If the value for the `paginated_objects.has_prev` attribute is `True`, it means that there is a previous page available. In this case, the code calls the `flask.url_for` function to generate the full URL for the previous page with the value of the `self.resource_for_url` attribute. The `_external` argument is set to `True` because we want to provide the full URL.

If the value for the `paginated_objects.has_next` attribute is `True`, it means that there is a next page available. In this case, the code calls the `flask.url_for` function to generate the full URL for the next page with the value of the `self.resource_for_url` attribute.

Then, the code calls the `self.schema.dump` method to serialize the partial results previously saved in the `object` variable, with the `many` argument set to `True`. The `dumped_objects` variable saves the reference to the `data` attribute of the results returned by the call to the `dump` method.

Finally, the method returns a dictionary with the following key-value pairs:

- `self.key_name`: The serialized partial results saved in the `dumped_objects` variable.
- `'previous'`: The full URL for the previous page saved in the `previous_page_url` variable.
- `'previous'`: The full URL for the next page saved in the `next_page_url` variable.
- `'count'`: The total number of objects available in the complete resultset retrieved from the `paginated_objects.total` attribute.

Adding pagination features

Open the `api/views.py` file and replace the code for the `MessageListResource.get` method with the highlighted lines in the next listing. In addition, make sure that you add the import statement. The code file for the sample is included in the `restful_python_chapter_07_01` folder:

```
from helpers import PaginationHelper


class MessageListResource(Resource):
    def get(self):
        pagination_helper = PaginationHelper(
            request,
            query=Message.query,
            resource_for_url='api.messagelistresource',
            key_name='results',
            schema=message_schema)
        result = pagination_helper.paginate_query()
        return result
```

The new code for the `get` method creates an instance of the previously explained `PaginationHelper` class named `pagination_helper` with the `request` object as the first argument. The named arguments specify the `query`, `resource_for_url`, `key_name`, and `schema` that the `PaginationHelper` instance has to use to provide a paginated query result.

The next line calls the `pagination_helper.paginate_query` method that will return the results of the paginated query with the page number specified in the request. Finally, the method returns the results of the call to this method that include the previously explained dictionary. In this case, the paginated resultset with the messages will be rendered as a value of the `'results'` key, specified in the `key_name` argument.

Now, we will compose and send an HTTP request to retrieve all the messages, specifically an HTTP GET method to `/api/messages/`.

```
http :5000/api/messages/
```

The following is the equivalent curl command:

```
curl -iX GET :5000/api/messages/
```

The new code for the `MessageListResource.get` method will work with pagination and the result will provide us the first 5 messages (`results` key), the total number of messages for the query (`count` key) and a link to the next (`next` key) and previous (`previous` key) pages. In this case, the resultset is the first page, and therefore, the link to the previous page (`previous` key) is `null`. We will receive a `200 OK` status code in the response header and the 5 messages in the `results` array:

```
HTTP/1.0 200 OK
Content-Length: 2521
Content-Type: application/json
Date: Wed, 10 Aug 2016 18:26:44 GMT
Server: Werkzeug/0.11.10 Python/3.5.1
{
    "count": 12,
    "results": [
        {
            "category": {
                "id": 1,
                "name": "Information",
                "url": "http://localhost:5000/api/categories/1"
            },
            "creation_date": "2016-08-08T12:27:30.124511+00:00",
            "duration": 8,
            "id": 2,
```

```
            "message": "Checking light sensor",
            "printed_once": false,
            "printed_times": 0,
            "url": "http://localhost:5000/api/messages/2"
    },
    {
            "category": {
                "id": 3,
                "name": "Error",
                "url": "http://localhost:5000/api/categories/3"
            },
            "creation_date": "2016-08-08T14:20:22.103752+00:00",
            "duration": 10,
            "id": 3,
            "message": "Temperature sensor error",
            "printed_once": false,
            "printed_times": 0,
            "url": "http://localhost:5000/api/messages/3"
    },
    {
            "category": {
                "id": 1,
                "name": "Information",
                "url": "http://localhost:5000/api/categories/1"
            },
            "creation_date": "2016-08-08T12:18:43.260474+00:00",
            "duration": 5,
            "id": 1,
            "message": "Checking temperature sensor",
            "printed_once": true,
            "printed_times": 1,
            "url": "http://localhost:5000/api/messages/1"
    },
    {
            "category": {
                "id": 1,
                "name": "Information",
                "url": "http://localhost:5000/api/categories/1"
            },
            "creation_date": "2016-08-09T20:18:26.648071+00:00",
            "duration": 25,
            "id": 4,
            "message": "Initializing light controller",
            "printed_once": false,
            "printed_times": 0,
            "url": "http://localhost:5000/api/messages/4"
    },
    {
```

```
        "category": {
            "id": 1,
            "name": "Information",
            "url": "http://localhost:5000/api/categories/1"
        },
        "creation_date": "2016-08-09T20:19:16.174807+00:00",
        "duration": 20,
        "id": 5,
        "message": "Initializing light sensor",
        "printed_once": false,
        "printed_times": 0,
        "url": "http://localhost:5000/api/messages/5"
    }
  ],
  "next": "http://localhost:5000/api/messages/?page=2",
  "previous": null
}
```

In the previous HTTP request, we didn't specify any value for the `page` parameter, and therefore the `paginate_query` method in the `PaginationHelper` class requests the first page to the paginated query. If we compose and send the following HTTP request to retrieve the first page of all the messages by specifying 1 for the `page` value, the API will provide the same results shown before:

```
http ':5000/api/messages/?page=1'
```

The following is the equivalent curl command:

```
curl -iX GET ':5000/api/messages/?page=1'
```

 The code in the `PaginationHelper` class considers that first page is page number 1. Thus, we don't work with zero-based numbering for pages.

Now, we will compose and send an HTTP request to retrieve the next page, that is, the second page for the messages, specifically an HTTP GET method to `/api/messages/` with the `page` value set to 2. Remember that the value for the `next` key returned in the JSON body of the previous result provides us with the full URL to the next page:

```
http ':5000/api/messages/?page=2'
```

The following is the equivalent `curl` command:

```
curl -iX GET ':5000/api/messages/?page=2'
```

The result will provide us the second set of the five message resource (`results` key), the total number of messages for the query (`count` key), a link to the next (`next` key), and previous (`previous` key) pages. In this case, the resultset is the second page, and therefore, the link to the previous page (previous `key`) is

`http://localhost:5000/api/messages/?page=1`. We will receive a `200 OK` status code in the response header and the 5 messages in the `results` array.

```
HTTP/1.0 200 OK
Content-Length: 2557
Content-Type: application/json
Date: Wed, 10 Aug 2016 19:51:50 GMT
Server: Werkzeug/0.11.10 Python/3.5.1
{
    "count": 12,
    "next": "http://localhost:5000/api/messages/?page=3",
    "previous": "http://localhost:5000/api/messages/?page=1",
    "results": [
        {
            "category": {
                "id": 1,
                "name": "Information",
                "url": "http://localhost:5000/api/categories/1"
            },
            "creation_date": "2016-08-09T20:19:22.335600+00:00",
            "duration": 18,
            "id": 6,
            "message": "Checking pressure sensor",
            "printed_once": false,
            "printed_times": 0,
            "url": "http://localhost:5000/api/messages/6"
        },
        {
            "category": {
                "id": 1,
                "name": "Information",
                "url": "http://localhost:5000/api/categories/1"
            },
            "creation_date": "2016-08-09T20:19:26.189009+00:00",
            "duration": 14,
            "id": 7,
            "message": "Checking gas sensor",
            "printed_once": false,
            "printed_times": 0,
            "url": "http://localhost:5000/api/messages/7"
        },
        {
            "category": {
```

```
                "id": 1,
                "name": "Information",
                "url": "http://localhost:5000/api/categories/1"
            },
            "creation_date": "2016-08-09T20:19:29.854576+00:00",
            "duration": 22,
            "id": 8,
            "message": "Setting ADC resolution",
            "printed_once": false,
            "printed_times": 0,
            "url": "http://localhost:5000/api/messages/8"
        },
        {
            "category": {
                "id": 1,
                "name": "Information",
                "url": "http://localhost:5000/api/categories/1"
            },
            "creation_date": "2016-08-09T20:19:33.838977+00:00",
            "duration": 15,
            "id": 9,
            "message": "Setting sample rate",
            "printed_once": false,
            "printed_times": 0,
            "url": "http://localhost:5000/api/messages/9"
        },
        {
            "category": {
                "id": 1,
                "name": "Information",
                "url": "http://localhost:5000/api/categories/1"
            },
            "creation_date": "2016-08-09T20:19:37.830843+00:00",
            "duration": 18,
            "id": 10,
            "message": "Initializing pressure sensor",
            "printed_once": false,
            "printed_times": 0,
            "url": "http://localhost:5000/api/messages/10"
        }
    ]
}
```

Finally, we will compose and send an HTTP request to retrieve the last page, that is, the third page for the messages, specifically an HTTP GET method to /api/messages/ with the page value set to 3. Remember that the value for the next key returned in the JSON body of the previous result provides us with the URL to the next page:

```
http ':5000/api/messages/?page=3'
```

The following is the equivalent curl command:

```
curl -iX GET ':5000/api/messages/?page=3'
```

The result will provide us the last set with two message resources (results key), the total number of messages for the query (count key), a link to the next (next key), and previous (previous key) pages. In this case, the resultset is the last page, and therefore, the link to the next page (next key) is null. We will receive a 200 OK status code in the response header and the 2 messages in the results array:

```
HTTP/1.0 200 OK
Content-Length: 1090
Content-Type: application/json
Date: Wed, 10 Aug 2016 20:02:00 GMT
Server: Werkzeug/0.11.10 Python/3.5.1
{
    "count": 12,
    "next": null,
    "previous": "http://localhost:5000/api/messages/?page=2",
    "results": [
        {
            "category": {
                "id": 1,
                "name": "Information",
                "url": "http://localhost:5000/api/categories/1"
            },
            "creation_date": "2016-08-09T20:19:41.645628+00:00",
            "duration": 16,
            "id": 11,
            "message": "Initializing gas sensor",
            "printed_once": false,
            "printed_times": 0,
            "url": "http://localhost:5000/api/messages/11"
        },
        {
            "category": {
                "id": 1,
                "name": "Information",
                "url": "http://localhost:5000/api/categories/1"
            },
```

```
            "creation_date": "2016-08-09T20:19:45.304391+00:00",
            "duration": 5,
            "id": 12,
            "message": "Initializing proximity sensor",
            "printed_once": false,
            "printed_times": 0,
            "url": "http://localhost:5000/api/messages/12"
        }
    ]
}
```

Understanding the steps to add authentication and permissions

Our current version of the API processes all the incoming requests without requiring any kind of authentication. We will use a Flask extension and other packages to use an HTTP authentication scheme to identify the user that originated the request or the token that signed the request. Then, we will use these credentials to apply the permissions that will determine whether the request must be permitted or not. Unluckily, neither Flask nor Flask-RESTful provides an authentication framework that we can easily plug and configure. Thus, we will have to write code to perform many tasks related to authentication and permissions.

We want to be able to create a new user without any authentication. However, all the other API calls are only going to be available for authenticated users.

First, we will install a Flask extension to make it easier for us to work with HTTP authentication, `Flask-HTTPAuth`, and a package to allow us to hash a password and check whether a provided password is valid or not, `passlib`.

We will create a new `User` model that will represent a user. The model will provide methods to allow us to hash a password and verify whether a password provided for a user is valid or not. We will create a `UserSchema` class to specify how we want to serialize and deserialize a user.

Then, we will configure the Flask extension to work with our `User` model to verify passwords and set the authenticated user associated with a request. We will make changes to the existing resources to require authentication and we will new resources to allow us to retrieve existing users and create a new one. Finally, we will configure the routes for the resources related to users.

Once we have completed the previously mentioned tasks, we will run migrations to generate the new table that persists the users in the database. Then, we will compose and send HTTP requests to understand how the authentication and permissions work with our new version of the API.

Make sure you quit the Flask development server. Remember that you just need to press *Ctrl* + *C* in the terminal or a Command Prompt window in which it is running. It is time to run many commands that will be the same for either macOS, Linux, or Windows. We can install all the necessary packages with pip with a single command. However, we will run two independent commands to make it easier to detect any problems in case a specific installation fails.

Now, we must run the following command to install Flask-HTTPAuth with pip. This package makes it easy to add basic HTTP authentication to any Flask application:

```
pip install Flask-HTTPAuth
```

The last lines for the output will indicate the `Flask-HTTPAuth` package has been successfully installed:

```
Installing collected packages: Flask-HTTPAuth
   Running setup.py install for Flask-HTTPAuth
Successfully installed Flask-HTTPAuth-3.2.1
```

Run the following command to install passlib with pip. This package is a popular one that provides a comprehensive password hashing framework that supports more than 30 schemes. We definitely don't want to write our own error-prone and probably highly insecure password hashing code, and therefore, we will take advantage of a library that provides these services:

```
pip install passlib
```

The last lines for the output will indicate the `passlib` package has been successfully installed:

```
Installing collected packages: passlib
Successfully installed passlib-1.6.5
```

Adding a user model

Now, we will create the model that we will use to represent and persist the user. Open the `api/models.py` file and add the following lines after the declaration of the `AddUpdateDelete` class. Make sure that you add the import statements. The code file for the sample is included in the `restful_python_chapter_07_02` folder:

```python
from passlib.apps import custom_app_context as password_context
import re


class User(db.Model, AddUpdateDelete):
    id = db.Column(db.Integer, primary_key=True)
    name = db.Column(db.String(50), unique=True, nullable=False)
    # I save the hashed password
    hashed_password = db.Column(db.String(120), nullable=False)
    creation_date = db.Column(db.TIMESTAMP,
server_default=db.func.current_timestamp(), nullable=False)

    def verify_password(self, password):
        return password_context.verify(password, self.hashed_password)

    def check_password_strength_and_hash_if_ok(self, password):
        if len(password) < 8:
            return 'The password is too short', False
        if len(password) > 32:
            return 'The password is too long', False
        if re.search(r'[A-Z]', password) is None:
            return 'The password must include at least one uppercase
letter',
            False
        if re.search(r'[a-z]', password) is None:
            return 'The password must include at least one lowercase
letter',
            False
        if re.search(r'\d', password) is None:
            return 'The password must include at least one number', False
        if re.search(r"[ !#$%&'()*+,-./[\\\]^_`{|}~"+r'"]', password) is
None:
            return 'The password must include at least one symbol', False
        self.hashed_password = password_context.encrypt(password)
        return '', True

    def __init__(self, name):
        self.name = name
```

The code declares the `User` model, specifically a subclasses of both the `db.Model` and the `AddUpdateDelete` classes. We specified the field types, maximum lengths and defaults for the following three attributes-`id`, `name`, `hashed_password` and `creation_date`. These attributes represent fields without any relationship, and therefore, they are instances of the `db.Column` class. The model declares an `id` attribute and specifies the `True` value for the `primary_key` argument to indicate it is the primary key. SQLAlchemy will use the data to generate the necessary table in the PostgreSQL database.

The `User` class declares the following methods:

- `check_password_strength_and_hash_if_ok`: This method uses the `re` module that provides regular expression matching operations to check whether the `password` received as an argument fulfils many qualitative requirements. The code requires the password to be longer than eight characters, with a maximum of 32 characters. The password must include at least one uppercase letter, one lowercase letter, one number, and one symbol. The code checks the results of many calls to the `re.search` method to determine whether the received password fulfils each requirement. In case any of the requirements isn't fulfilled, the code returns a tuple with an error message and `False`. Otherwise, the code calls the `encrypt` method for the `passlib.apps.custom_app_context` instance imported as `password_context`, with the received `password` as an argument. The `encrypt` method chooses a reasonably strong scheme based on the platform, with the default settings for rounds selection and the code saves the hashed password in the `hash_password` attribute. Finally, the code returns a tuple with an empty string and `True`, indicating that the password fulfilled the qualitative requirements and it was hashed.

  By default, the `passlib` library will use the SHA-512 scheme for 64-bit platforms and SHA-256 for 32-bit platforms. In addition, the minimum number of rounds will be set to 535,000. We will use the default configuration values for this example. However, you must take into account that these values might require too much processing time for each request that has to validate the password. You should definitely select the most appropriate algorithm and number of rounds based on your security requirements.

- **verify_password**: This method calls the `verify` method for the `passlib.apps.custom_app_context` instance imported as `password_context`, with the received `password` and the stored hashed password for the user, `self.hashed_password`, as the arguments. The `verify` method hashes the received password and returns `True` only if the hashed received password matches the stored hashed password. We never restore the saved password to its original state. We just compare hashed values.

The model declares a constructor, that is, the `__init__` method. This constructor receives the user name in the `name` argument and saves it in an attribute with the same name.

Creating a schemas to validate, serialize, and deserialize users

Now, we will create the Flask-Marshmallow schema that we will use to validate, serialize and deserialize the previously declared `User` model. Open the `api/models.py` file and add the following code after the existing lines. The code file for the sample is included in the `restful_python_chapter_07_02` folder:

```
class UserSchema(ma.Schema):
    id = fields.Integer(dump_only=True)
    name = fields.String(required=True, validate=validate.Length(3))
    url = ma.URLFor('api.userresource', id='<id>', _external=True)
```

The code declares the `UserSchema` schema, specifically a subclass of the `ma.Schema` class. Remember that the previous code we wrote for the `api/models.py` file created a `flask_marshmallow.Mashmallow` instance named `ma`.

We declare the attributes that represent fields as instances of the appropriate class declared in the `marshmallow.fields` module. The `UserSchema` class declares the `name` attribute as an instance of `fields.String`. The `required` argument is set to `True` to specify that the field cannot be an empty string. The `validate` argument is set to `validate.Length(3)` to specify that the field must have a minimum length of 3 characters.

The validation for the password isn't included in the schema. We will use the `check_password_strength_and_hash_if_ok` method defined in the `User` class to validate the password.

Adding authentication to resources

We will configure the Flask-HTTPAuth extension to work with our User model to verify passwords and set the authenticated user associated with a request. We will declare a custom function that this extension will use as a callback to verify a password. We will create a new base class for our resources that will require authentication. Open the api/views.py file and add the following code after the last line that uses the import statement and before the lines that declares the Blueprint instance . The code file for the sample is included in the restful_python_chapter_07_02 folder:

```python
from flask_httpauth import HTTPBasicAuth
from flask import g
from models import User, UserSchema


auth = HTTPBasicAuth()


@auth.verify_password
def verify_user_password(name, password):
    user = User.query.filter_by(name=name).first()
    if not user or not user.verify_password(password):
        return False
    g.user = user
    return True


class AuthRequiredResource(Resource):
    method_decorators = [auth.login_required]
```

First, we create an instance of the flask_httpauth.HTTPBasicAuth class named auth. Then, we declare the verify_user_password function that receives a name and a password as arguments. The function uses the @auth.verify_password decorator to make this function become the callback that Flask-HTTPAuth will use to verify the password for a specific user. The function retrieves the user whose name matches the name specified in the argument and saves its reference in the user variable. If a user is found, the code checks the results of the user.verify_password method with the received password as an argument.

If either a user isn't found or the call to `user.verify_password` returns `False`, the function returns `False` and the authentication will fail. If the call to `user.verify_password` returns `True`, the function stores the authenticated `User` instance in the user attribute for the `flask.g` object.

> The `flask.g` object is a proxy that allows us to store on this whatever we want to share for one request only. The `user` attribute we added to the `flask.g` object will be only valid for the active request and it will return different values for each different request. This way, it is possible to use `flask.g.user` in another function or method called during a request to access details about the authenticated user for the request.

Finally, we declared the `AuthRequiredResource` class as a subclass of `flask_restful.Resource`. We just specified `auth.login_required` as one of the members of the list that we assign to the `method_decorators` property inherited from the base class. This way, all the methods declared in a resource that uses the new `AuthRequiredResource` class as its superclass will have the `auth.login_required` decorator applied to them, and therefore, any method that is called to the resource will require authentication.

Now, we will replace the base class for the existing resource classes to make them inherit from `AuthRequiredResource` instead of `Resource`. We want any of the requests that retrieve or modify categories and messages to be authenticated.

The following lines show the declarations for the four resource classes:

```
class MessageResource(Resource):
class MessageListResource(Resource):
class CategoryResource(Resource):
class CategoryListResource(Resource):
```

Open the `api/views.py` file and replace `Resource` by `AuthRequiredResource` in the previously shown four lines that declare the resource classes. The following lines show the new code for each resource class declaration:

```
class MessageResource(AuthRequiredResource):
class MessageListResource(AuthRequiredResource):
class CategoryResource(AuthRequiredResource):
class CategoryListResource(AuthRequiredResource):
```

Creating resource classes to handle users

We just want to be able to create users and use them to authenticate requests. Thus, we will just focus on creating resource classes with just a few methods. We won't create a complete user management system.

We will create the resource classes that represent the user and the collection of users. First, we will create a `UserResource` class that we will use to represent a user resource. Open the `api/views.py` file and add the following lines after the line that creates the `Api` instance. The code file for the sample is included in the `restful_python_chapter_07_02` folder:

```
class UserResource(AuthRequiredResource):
    def get(self, id):
        user = User.query.get_or_404(id)
        result = user_schema.dump(user).data
        return result
```

The `UserResource` class is a subclass of the previously coded `AuthRequiredResource` and declares a `get` methods that will be called when the `HTTP` method with the same name arrives as a request on the represented resource. The method receives the id of the user that has to be retrieved in the `id` argument. The code calls the `User.query.get_or_404` method to return an HTTP `404 Not Found` status in case there is no user with the requested id in the underlying database. In case the user exists, the code calls the `user_schema.dump` method with the retrieved user as an argument to use the `UserSchema` instance to serialize the `User` instance whose `id` matches the specified `id`. The `dump` method takes the `User` instance and applies the field filtering and output formatting specified in the `UserSchema` class. The field filtering specifies that we don't want the hashed password to be serialized. The code returns the `data` attribute of the result returned by the `dump` method, that is, the serialized message in JSON format as the body, with the default HTTP `200 OK` status code.

Now, we will create a `UserListResource` class that we will use to represent the collection of users. Open the `api/views.py` file and add the following lines after the code that creates the `UserResource` class. The code file for the sample is included in the `restful_python_chapter_07_02` folder:

```
class UserListResource(Resource):
    @auth.login_required
    def get(self):
        pagination_helper = PaginationHelper(
            request,
            query=User.query,
            resource_for_url='api.userlistresource',
```

```
                key_name='results',
                schema=user_schema)
        result = pagination_helper.paginate_query()
        return result

    def post(self):
        request_dict = request.get_json()
        if not request_dict:
            response = {'user': 'No input data provided'}
            return response, status.HTTP_400_BAD_REQUEST
        errors = user_schema.validate(request_dict)
        if errors:
            return errors, status.HTTP_400_BAD_REQUEST
        name = request_dict['name']
        existing_user = User.query.filter_by(name=name).first()
        if existing_user is not None:
            response = {'user': 'An user with the same name already
exists'}
            return response, status.HTTP_400_BAD_REQUEST
        try:
            user = User(name=name)
            error_message, password_ok = \
user.check_password_strength_and_hash_if_ok(request_dict['password'])
            if password_ok:
                user.add(user)
                query = User.query.get(user.id)
                result = user_schema.dump(query).data
                return result, status.HTTP_201_CREATED
            else:
                return {"error": error_message},
status.HTTP_400_BAD_REQUEST
        except SQLAlchemyError as e:
            db.session.rollback()
            resp = {"error": str(e)}
            return resp, status.HTTP_400_BAD_REQUEST
```

The UserListResource class is a subclass of flask_restful.Resource because we don't want all the methods to require authentication. We want to be able to create a new user without being authenticated, and therefore, we apply the @auth.login_required decorator only for the get method. The post method doesn't require authentication. The class declares the following two methods that will be called when the HTTP method with the same name arrives as a request on the represented resource:

- `get`: This method returns a list with all the `User` instances saved in the database. First, the code calls the `User.query.all` method to retrieve all the `User` instances persisted in the database. Then, the code calls the `user_schema.dump` method with the retrieved messages and the `many` argument set to `True` to serialize the iterable collection of objects. The `dump` method will take each `User` instance retrieved from the database and apply the field filtering and output formatting specified the `CategorySchema` class. The code returns the `data` attribute of the result returned by the dump method, that is, the serialized messages in JSON format as the body, with the default HTTP `200 OK` status code.
- `post`: This method retrieves the key-value pairs received in the JSON body, creates a new `User` instance and persists it in the database. First, the code calls the `request.get_json` method to retrieve the key-value pairs received as arguments with the request. Then, the code calls the `user_schema.validate` method to validate the new user built with the retrieved key-value pairs. In this case, the call to this method will just validate the `name` field for the user. In case there were validation errors, the code returns the validation errors and an HTTP `400 Bad Request` status. If the validation is successful, the code checks whether an user with the same name already exists in the database or not to return an appropriate error for the field that must be unique. If the user name is unique, the code creates a new user with the specified `name` and calls its `check_password_strength_and_hash_if_ok` method. If the provided password fulfils all the quality requirements, the code persists the user with its hashed password in the database. Finally, the code returns the serialized saved user in JSON format as the body, with the HTTP `201 Created` status code:

The following table shows the method of our previously created classes related to usres that we want to be executed for each combination of `HTTP` verb and scope.

HTTP verb	Scope	Class and method	Requires authentication
GET	Collection of users	UserListResource.get	Yes
GET	User	UserResource.get	Yes
POST	Collection of users	UserListResource.post	No

We must make the necessary resource routing configurations to call the appropriate methods and pass them all the necessary arguments by defining URL rules. The following lines configure the resource routing for the user related resources to the api. Open the `api/views.py` file and add the following lines at the end of the code. The code file for the sample is included in the `restful_python_chapter_07_02` folder:

```
api.add_resource(UserListResource, '/users/')
api.add_resource(UserResource, '/users/<int:id>')
```

Each call to the `api.add_resource` method routes a URL to one of the previously coded user related resources. When there is a request to the API and the URL matches one of the URLs specified in the `api.add_resource` method, Flask will call the method that matches the `HTTP` verb in the request for the specified class.

Running migrations to generate the user table

Now, we will run many scripts to run migrations and generate the necessary table in the PostgreSQL database. Make sure you run the scripts in the terminal or the Command Prompt window in which you have activated the virtual environment and that you are located in the `api` folder.

Run the first script that populates the migration script with the detected changes in the models. In this case, it is the second time we populate the migration script, and therefore, the migration script will generate the new table that will persist our new `User` model: model:

```
python migrate.py db migrate
```

The following lines show the sample output generated after running the previous script. Your output will be different according to the base folder in which you have created the virtual environment.

```
INFO [alembic.runtime.migration] Context impl PostgresqlImpl.
INFO [alembic.runtime.migration] Will assume transactional DDL.
INFO [alembic.autogenerate.compare] Detected added table 'user'
INFO [alembic.ddl.postgresql] Detected sequence named 'message_id_seq' as
owned by integer column 'message(id)', assuming SERIAL and omitting
Generating
  /Users/gaston/PythonREST/Flask02/api/migrations/versions/c8c45e615f6d_.py
... done
```

The output indicates that the `api/migrations/versions/c8c45e615f6d_.py` file includes the code to create the `user` tables. The following lines show the code for this file that was automatically generated based on the models. Notice that the file name will be different in your configuration. The code file for the sample is included in the `restful_python_chapter_06_01` folder:

```
"""empty message

Revision ID: c8c45e615f6d
Revises: 417543056ac3
Create Date: 2016-08-11 17:31:44.989313

"""

# revision identifiers, used by Alembic.
revision = 'c8c45e615f6d'
down_revision = '417543056ac3'

from alembic import op
import sqlalchemy as sa


def upgrade():
    ### commands auto generated by Alembic - please adjust! ###
    op.create_table('user',
    sa.Column('id', sa.Integer(), nullable=False),
    sa.Column('name', sa.String(length=50), nullable=False),
    sa.Column('hashed_password', sa.String(length=120), nullable=False),
    sa.Column('creation_date', sa.TIMESTAMP(),
server_default=sa.text('CURRENT_TIMESTAMP'), nullable=False),
    sa.PrimaryKeyConstraint('id'),
    sa.UniqueConstraint('name')
    )
    ### end Alembic commands ###


def downgrade():
    ### commands auto generated by Alembic - please adjust! ###
    op.drop_table('user')
    ### end Alembic commands ###
```

The code defines two functions: `upgrade` and `downgrade`. The `upgrade` function runs the necessary code to create the `user` table by making calls to `alembic.op.create_table`. The `downgrade` function runs the necessary code to go back to the previous version.

Run the second script to upgrade the database:

```
python migrate.py db upgrade
```

The following lines show the sample output generated after running the previous script:

```
INFO  [alembic.runtime.migration] Context impl PostgresqlImpl.
INFO  [alembic.runtime.migration] Will assume transactional DDL.
INFO  [alembic.runtime.migration] Running upgrade 417543056ac3 ->
c8c45e615f6d, empty message
```

The previous script called the `upgrade` function defined in the automatically generated `api/migrations/versions/c8c45e615f6d_.py` script. Don't forget that the file name will be different in your configuration.

After we run the previous scripts, we can use the PostgreSQL command line or any other application that allows us to easily verify the contents of the PostreSQL database to check the new table that the migration generated. Run the following command to list the generated tables. In case the database name you are using is not named `messages`, make sure you use the appropriate database name:

```
psql --username=user_name --dbname=messages --command="\dt"
```

The following lines show the output with all the generated table names. The migrations upgrade generate a new table named `user`.

```
                     List of relations
     Schema |      Name        |  Type  |   Owner
    --------+------------------+--------+------------
     public | alembic_version  | table  | user_name
     public | category         | table  | user_name
     public | message          | table  | user_name
     public | user             | table  | user_name
    (4 rows)
```

SQLAlchemy generated the user table with its primary key, its unique constraint on the name field and the password field based on the information included in our `User` model.

The following command will allow you to check the contents of the user table after we compose and send HTTP requests to the RESTful API and create new users. The commands assume that you are running PostgreSQL on the same computer in which you are running the command:

```
psql --username=user_name --dbname=messages --command="SELECT * FROM
public.user;"
```

Now, we can run the `api/run.py` script that launches Flask's development. Execute the following command in the `api` folder:

```
python run.py
```

After we execute the previous command, the development server will start listening at port `5000`.

Composing requests with the necessary authentication

Now, we will compose and send an HTTP request to retrieve the first page of the messages without authentication credentials:

```
http POST ':5000/api/messages/?page=1'
```

The following is the equivalent `curl` command:

```
curl -iX GET ':5000/api/messages/?page=1'
```

We will receive a `401 Unauthorized` status code in the response header. The following lines show a sample response:

```
HTTP/1.0 401 UNAUTHORIZED
Content-Length: 19
Content-Type: text/html; charset=utf-8
Date: Mon, 15 Aug 2016 01:16:36 GMT
Server: Werkzeug/0.11.10 Python/3.5.1
WWW-Authenticate: Basic realm="Authentication Required"
```

If we want to retrieve messages, that is, to make a `GET` request to `/api/messages/`, we need to provide authentication credentials using HTTP authentication. However, before we can do this, it is necessary to create a new user. We will use the new user to test our new resource classes related to users and our changes in the permissions policies.

```
http POST :5000/api/users/ name='brandon' password='brandonpassword'
```

The following is the equivalent `curl` command:

```
curl -iX POST -H "Content-Type: application/json" -d '{"name":
"brandon",
    "password": "brandonpassword"}' :5000/api/users/
```

Of course, the creation of a user and the execution of the methods that require authentication should only be possible under HTTPS. This way, the username and the password would be encrypted.

The previous command will compose and send a POST HTTP request with the specified JSON key-value pairs. The requests specify /api/user/, and therefore, it will match the '/users/' URL route for the UserList resource and run the UserList.post method that doesn't require authentication. The method doesn't receive arguments because the URL route doesn't include any parameters. As the HTTP verb for the request is POST, Flask calls the post method.

The previously specified password only includes lowercase letters, and therefore, it doesn't fulfil all the qualitative requirements we have specified for the passwords in the User.check_password_strength_and_hash_if_ok method. Thus, We will receive a 400 Bad Request status code in the response header and the error message indicating the requirement that the password didn't fulfil in the JSON body. The following lines show a sample response:

```
HTTP/1.0 400 BAD REQUEST
Content-Length: 75
Content-Type: application/json
Date: Mon, 15 Aug 2016 01:29:55 GMT
Server: Werkzeug/0.11.10 Python/3.5.1

{
    "error": "The password must include at least one uppercase letter"
}
```

The following command will create a user with a valid password:

```
http POST :5000/api/users/ name='brandon' password='iA4!V3riS#c^R9'
```

The following is the equivalent curl command:

```
curl -iX POST -H "Content-Type: application/json" -d '{"name":
"brandon", "password": "iA4!V3riS#c^R9"}' :5000/api/users/
```

If the new User instance is successfully persisted in the database, the call will return an HTTP 201 Created status code and the recently persisted User serialized to JSON in the response body. The following lines show an example response for the HTTP requests, with the new User object in the JSON responses. Note that the response includes the URL, url, for the created user and doesn't include any information related to the password.

```
HTTP/1.0 201 CREATED
Content-Length: 87
Content-Type: application/json
Date: Mon, 15 Aug 2016 01:33:23 GMT
Server: Werkzeug/0.11.10 Python/3.5.1
{
    "id": 1,
    "name": "brandon",
    "url": "http://localhost:5000/api/users/1"
}
```

We can run the previously explained command to check the contents of the `user` table that the migrations created in the PostgreSQL database. We will notice that the `hashed_password` field contents are hashed for the new row in the `user` table. The following screenshot shows the contents for the new row of the `user` table in a PostgreSQL database after running the HTTP request:

If we want to retrieve the first page of messages, that is, to make a `GET` request to `/api/messages/`, we need to provide authentication credentials using HTTP authentication. Now, we will compose and send an HTTP request to retrieve the first page of messages with authentication credentials, that is, with the user name and the password we have recently created:

```
http -a 'brandon':'iA4!V3riS#c^R9' ':5000/api/messages/?page=1'
```

The following is the equivalent `curl` command:

```
curl --user 'brandon':'iA4!V3riS#c^R9' -iX GET
':5000/api/messages/?page=1'
```

The user will be successfully authenticated and we will be able to process the request to retrieve the first page of messages. With all the changes we have made to our API, unauthenticated requests can only create a new user.

Test your knowledge

1. The `flask.g` object is:
    1. A proxy that provides access to the current request.
    2. An instance of the `flask_httpauth.HTTPBasicAuth` class.
    3. A proxy that allows us to store on this whatever we want to share for one request only.

2. The `passlib` package provides:
    1. A password hashing framework that supports more than 30 schemes.
    2. An authentication framework that automatically adds models for users and permissios to a Flask application.
    3. A lightweight web framework that replaces Flask.

3. The `auth.verify_password` decorator applied to a function:
    1. Makes this function become the callback that `Flask-HTTPAuth` will use to hash the password for a specific user.
    2. Makes this function become the callback that `SQLAlchmey` will use to verify the password for a specific user.
    3. Makes this function become the callback that `Flask-HTTPAuth` will use to verify the password for a specific user.

4. When you assign a list that includes `auth.login_required` to the `method_decorators` property of any subclass of `flask_restful.Resource`, considering that auth is an instance of the `flask_httpauth.HTTPBasicAuth()`:
    1. All the methods declared in the resource will have the `auth.login_required` decorator applied to them.
    2. The `post` method declared in the resource will have `auth.login_required` decorator applied to it.
    3. Any of the following methods declared in the resource will have `auth.login_required` decorator applied to them: `delete`, `patch`, `post` and `put`.

5. Which of the following lines retrieves the integer value for the `'page'` argument from the request object, considering that the code would be running within a method defined in a subclass of `flask_restful.Resource` class?
    1. `page_number = request.get_argument('page', 1, type=int)`
    2. `page_number = request.args.get('page', 1, type=int)`
    3. `page_number = request.arguments.get('page', 1, type=int)`

Summary

In this chapter, we improved the RESTful API in many ways. We added user friendly error messages when resources aren't unique. We tested how to update single or multiple fields with the `PATCH` method and we created our own generic pagination class.

Then, we started working with authentication and permissions. We added a user model and we updated the database. We made many changes in the different pieces of code to achieve a specific security goal and we took advantage of Flask-HTTPAuth and passlib to use HTTP authentication in our API.

Now that we have built an improved a complex API that uses pagination and authentication, we will use additional abstractions included in the framework and we will code, execute, and improve unit test, which is what we are going to discuss in the next chapter.

8
Testing and Deploying an API with Flask

In this chapter, we will configure, write, and execute unit tests and learn a few things related to deployment. We will:

- Set up unit tests
- Create a database for testing
- Write a first round of unit tests
- Run unit tests and check testing coverage
- Improve testing coverage
- Understand strategies for deployments and scalability

Setting up unit tests

We will use nose2 to make it easier to discover and run unit tests. We will measure test coverage, and therefore, we will install the necessary package to allow us to run coverage with nose2. First, we will install the nose2 and cov-core packages in our virtual environment. The cov-core package will allow us to measure test coverage with nose2. Then, we will create a new PostgreSQL database that we will use for testing. Finally, we will create the configuration file for the testing environment.

Make sure you quit the Flask's development server. Remember that you just need to press *Ctrl + C* in the terminal or the Command Prompt window in which it is running. We just need to run the following command to install the nose2 package:

```
pip install nose2
```

The last lines of the output will indicate that the `django-nose` package has been successfully installed.

```
Collecting nose2
Collecting six>=1.1 (from nose2)
  Downloading six-1.10.0-py2.py3-none-any.whl
Installing collected packages: six, nose2
Successfully installed nose2-0.6.5 six-1.10.0
```

We just need to run the following command to install the `cov-core` package that will also install the `coverage` dependency:

```
pip install cov-core
```

The last lines for the output will indicate that the `django-nose` package has been successfully installed:

```
Collecting cov-core
Collecting coverage>=3.6 (from cov-core)
Installing collected packages: coverage, cov-core
Successfully installed cov-core-1.15.0 coverage-4.2
```

Now, we will create the PostgreSQL database that we will use as a repository for our testing environment. You will have to download and install a PostgreSQL database, in case you aren't already running it on the testing environment on your computer or in a testing server.

> Remember to make sure that the PostgreSQL bin folder is included in the PATH environmental variable. You should be able to execute the `psql` command-line utility from your current Terminal or Command Prompt.

We will use the PostgreSQL command-line tools to create a new database named `test_messages`. In case you already have a PostgreSQL database with this name, make sure that you use another name in all the commands and configurations. You can perform the same task with any PostgreSQL GUI tool. In case you are developing on Linux, it is necessary to run the commands as the `postgres` user. Run the following command in macOS or Windows to create a new database named `test_messages`. Note that the command won't generate any output:

```
createdb test_messages
```

In Linux, run the following command to use the `postgres` user:

```
sudo -u postgres createdb test_messages
```

Now, we will use the `psql` command-line tool to run some SQL statements to grant privileges on the database to a user. In case you are using a different server than the development server, you will have to create the user before granting privileges. In macOS or Windows, run the following command to launch psql:

```
psql
```

In Linux, run the following command to use the postgres user

```
sudo -u psql
```

Then, run the following SQL statements and finally enter \q to exit the psql command-line tool. Replace user_name with your desired user name to use in the new database and password with your chosen password. We will use the user name and password in the Flask testing configuration. You don't need to run the steps in case you are already working with a specific user in PostgreSQL and you have already granted privileges to the database for the user:

```
GRANT ALL PRIVILEGES ON DATABASE test_messages TO user_name;
\q
```

Create a new `test_config.py` file within the `api` folder. The following lines show the code that declares variables that determine the configuration for Flask and SQLAlchemy for our testing environment. The `SQL_ALCHEMY_DATABASE_URI` variable generates a SQLAlchemy URI for the PostgreSQL database that we will use to run all the migrations before starting tests and we will drop all the elements after executing all the tests. Make sure you specify the desired test database name in the value for `DB_NAME` and that you configure the user, password, host, and port based on your PostgreSQL configuration for the testing environment. In case you followed the previous steps, use the settings specified in these steps. The code file for the sample is included in the `restful_python_chapter_08_01` folder.

```python
import os


basedir = os.path.abspath(os.path.dirname(__file__))
DEBUG = True
PORT = 5000
HOST = "127.0.0.1"
SQLALCHEMY_ECHO = False
SQLALCHEMY_TRACK_MODIFICATIONS = True
SQLALCHEMY_DATABASE_URI =
"postgresql://{DB_USER}:{DB_PASS}@{DB_ADDR}/{DB_NAME}".format(DB_USER="user
_name", DB_PASS="password", DB_ADDR="127.0.0.1", DB_NAME="test_messages")
SQLALCHEMY_MIGRATE_REPO = os.path.join(basedir, 'db_repository')
```

```
TESTING = True
SERVER_NAME = '127.0.0.1:5000'
PAGINATION_PAGE_SIZE = 5
PAGINATION_PAGE_ARGUMENT_NAME = 'page'
#Disable CSRF protection in the testing configuration
WTF_CSRF_ENABLED = False
```

As we did with the similar test file we created for our development environment, we will specify the previously created module as an argument to a function that will create a Flask app that we will use for testing. This way, we have one module that specifies all the values for the different configuration variables for our testing environment and another module that creates a *Flask* app for our testing environment. It is also possible to create a class hierarchy with one class for each environment we want to use. However, in our sample case, it is easier to create a new configuration file for our testing environment.

Writing a first round of unit tests

Now, we will write a first round of unit tests. Specifically, we will write unit tests related to the user and message category resources: `UserResource`, `UserListResource`, `CategoryResource`, and `CategoryListResource`. Create a new `tests` sub-folder within the `api` folder. Then, create a new `test_views.py` file within the new `api/tests` sub-folder. Add the following lines, that declare many `import` statements and the first methods for the `InitialTests` class. The code file for the sample is included in the `restful_python_chapter_08_01` folder:

```python
from app import create_app
from base64 import b64encode
from flask import current_app, json, url_for
from models import db, Category, Message, User
import status
from unittest import TestCase


class InitialTests(TestCase):
    def setUp(self):
        self.app = create_app('test_config')
        self.test_client = self.app.test_client()
        self.app_context = self.app.app_context()
        self.app_context.push()
        self.test_user_name = 'testuser'
        self.test_user_password = 'T3s!p4s5w0RDd12#'
        db.create_all()

    def tearDown(self):
```

```
            db.session.remove()
            db.drop_all()
            self.app_context.pop()

    def get_accept_content_type_headers(self):
            return {
                'Accept': 'application/json',
                'Content-Type': 'application/json'
            }

    def get_authentication_headers(self, username, password):
            authentication_headers = self.get_accept_content_type_headers()
            authentication_headers['Authorization'] = \
                'Basic ' + b64encode((username + ':' + password).encode('utf-
                8')).decode('utf-8')
            return authentication_headers
```

The `InitialTests` class is a subclass of `unittest.TestCase`. The class overrides the `setUp` method that will be executed before each test method runs. The method calls the `create_app` function, declared in the `app` module, with `'test_config'` as an argument. The function will set up a Flask app with this module as the configuration file, and therefore, the app will use the previously created configuration file that specifies the desired values for our testing database and environment. Then, the code sets the testing attribute for the recently created `app` to `True` in order for the exception to propagate to the test client.

The next line calls the `self.app.test_client` method to create a test client for the previously created Flask application and saves the test client in the `test_client` attribute. We will use the test client in our test methods to easily compose and send requests to our API. Then, the code saves and pushes the application context and creates two attributes with the user name and password we will use for our tests. Finally, the method calls the `db.create_all` method to create all the necessary tables in our test database configured in the `test_config.py` file.

The `InitialTests` class overrides the `tearDown` method that will be executed after each test method runs. The code removes the SQLAlchemy session, drops all the tables that we created in the test database before starting the execution of the tests, and pops the application context. This way, after each test finishes its execution, the test database will be empty again.

The `get_accept_content_type_headers` method builds and returns a dictionary (`dict`) with the values of the `Accept` and `Content-Type` header keys set to `'application/json'`. We will call this method in our tests whenever we have to build a header to compose our requests without authentication.

The `get_authentication_headers` method calls the previously explained `get_accept_content_type_headers` method to generate the header key-value pairs without authentication. Then, the code adds the necessary value to the `Authorization` key with the appropriate encoding to provide the user name and password received in the `username` and `password` arguments. The last line returns the generated dictionary that includes authentication information. We will call this method in our tests whenever we have to build a header to compose our requests with authentication. We will use the user name and password we stored in attributes the `setUp` method.

Open the previously created `test_views.py` file within the new `api/tests` sub-folder. Add the following lines that declare many methods for the `InitialTests` class. The code file for the sample is included in the `restful_python_chapter_08_01` folder.

```python
    def test_request_without_authentication(self):
        """
        Ensure we cannot access a resource that requirest authentication
    without an appropriate authentication header
        """
        response = self.test_client.get(
            url_for('api.messagelistresource', _external=True),
            headers=self.get_accept_content_type_headers())
        self.assertTrue(response.status_code ==
status.HTTP_401_UNAUTHORIZED)

    def create_user(self, name, password):
        url = url_for('api.userlistresource', _external=True)
        data = {'name': name, 'password': password}
        response = self.test_client.post(
            url,
            headers=self.get_accept_content_type_headers(),
            data=json.dumps(data))
        return response

    def create_category(self, name):
        url = url_for('api.categorylistresource', _external=True)
        data = {'name': name}
        response = self.test_client.post(
            url,
            headers=self.get_authentication_headers(self.test_user_name,
            self.test_user_password),
            data=json.dumps(data))
        return response

    def test_create_and_retrieve_category(self):
        """
        Ensure we can create a new Category and then retrieve it
```

```
            """
            create_user_response = self.create_user(self.test_user_name,
            self.test_user_password)
            self.assertEqual(create_user_response.status_code,
            status.HTTP_201_CREATED)
            new_category_name = 'New Information'
            post_response = self.create_category(new_category_name)
            self.assertEqual(post_response.status_code,
    status.HTTP_201_CREATED)
            self.assertEqual(Category.query.count(), 1)
            post_response_data =
    json.loads(post_response.get_data(as_text=True))
            self.assertEqual(post_response_data['name'], new_category_name)
            new_category_url = post_response_data['url']
            get_response = self.test_client.get(
                new_category_url,
                headers=self.get_authentication_headers(self.test_user_name,
                self.test_user_password))
            get_response_data = json.loads(get_response.get_data(as_text=True))
            self.assertEqual(get_response.status_code, status.HTTP_200_OK)
            self.assertEqual(get_response_data['name'], new_category_name)
```

The `test_request_without_authentication` method tests whether we have been rejected access to a resource that requires authentication when we don't provide an appropriate authentication header with the request. The method uses the test client to compose and send an HTTP GET request to the URL generated for the `'api.messagelistresource'` resource to retrieve the list of messages. We need an authenticated request to retrieve the list of messages. However, the code calls the `get_authentication_headers` method to set the value for the headers argument in the call to `self.test_client.get`, and therefore, the code generates a request without authentication. Finally, the method uses `assertTrue` to check that the `status_code` for the response is HTTP 401 Unauthorized (`status.HTTP_401_UNAUTHORIZED`).

The `create_user` method uses the test client to compose and send an HTTP POST request to the URL generated for the `'api.userlistresource'` resource to create a new user with the name and password received as arguments. We don't need an authenticated request to create a new user, and therefore, the code calls the previously explained `get_accept_content_type_headers` method to set the value for the headers argument in the call to `self.test_client.post`. Finally, the code returns the response from the POST request. Whenever we have to create an authenticated request, we will call the `create_user` method to create a new user.

The `create_category` method uses the test client to compose and send an HTTP POST request to the URL generated for the `'api.categorylistresource'` resource to create a new `Category` with the name received as an argument. We need an authenticated request to create a new `Category`, and therefore, the code calls the previously explained `get_authentication_headers` method to set the value for the headers argument in the call to `self.test_client.post`. The user name and password are set to `self.test_user_name` and `self.test_user_password`. Finally, the code returns the response from the POST request. Whenever we have to create a category, we will call the `create_category` method after the appropriate user that authenticates the request has been created.

The `test_create_and_retrieve_category` method tests whether we can create a new `Category` and then retrieve it. The method calls the previously explained `create_user` method to create a new user and then use it to authenticate the HTTP POST request generated in the `create_game_category` method. Then, the code composes and sends an HTTP GET method to retrieve the recently created Category with the URL received in the response of the previous HTTP POST request. The method uses `assertEqual` to check for the following expected results:

- The `status_code` for the HTTP POST response is HTTP 201 Created (`status.HTTP_201_CREATED`)
- The total number of `Category` objects retrieved from the database is 1
- The `status_code` for the HTTP GET response is HTTP 200 OK (`status.HTTP_200_OK`)
- The value for the `name` key in the HTTP GET response is equal to the name specified for the new category

Open the previously created `test_views.py` file within the new `api/tests` sub-folder. Add the following lines that declare many methods for the `InitialTests` class. The code file for the sample is included in the `restful_python_chapter_08_01` folder.

```python
def test_create_duplicated_category(self):
    """
    Ensure we cannot create a duplicated Category
    """
    create_user_response = self.create_user(self.test_user_name,
    self.test_user_password)
    self.assertEqual(create_user_response.status_code,
    status.HTTP_201_CREATED)
    new_category_name = 'New Information'
    post_response = self.create_category(new_category_name)
    self.assertEqual(post_response.status_code,
```

```
status.HTTP_201_CREATED)
        self.assertEqual(Category.query.count(), 1)
        post_response_data =
json.loads(post_response.get_data(as_text=True))
        self.assertEqual(post_response_data['name'], new_category_name)
        second_post_response = self.create_category(new_category_name)
        self.assertEqual(second_post_response.status_code,
        status.HTTP_400_BAD_REQUEST)
        self.assertEqual(Category.query.count(), 1)


    def test_retrieve_categories_list(self):
        """
        Ensure we can retrieve the categories list
        """
        create_user_response = self.create_user(self.test_user_name,
        self.test_user_password)
        self.assertEqual(create_user_response.status_code,
        status.HTTP_201_CREATED)
        new_category_name_1 = 'Error'
        post_response_1 = self.create_category(new_category_name_1)
        self.assertEqual(post_response_1.status_code,
status.HTTP_201_CREATED)
        new_category_name_2 = 'Warning'
        post_response_2 = self.create_category(new_category_name_2)
        self.assertEqual(post_response_2.status_code,
status.HTTP_201_CREATED)
        url = url_for('api.categorylistresource', _external=True)
        get_response = self.test_client.get(
            url,
            headers=self.get_authentication_headers(self.test_user_name,
            self.test_user_password))
        get_response_data = json.loads(get_response.get_data(as_text=True))
        self.assertEqual(get_response.status_code, status.HTTP_200_OK)
        self.assertEqual(len(get_response_data), 2)
        self.assertEqual(get_response_data[0]['name'], new_category_name_1)
        self.assertEqual(get_response_data[1]['name'], new_category_name_2)


        """
        Ensure we can update the name for an existing category
        """
        create_user_response = self.create_user(self.test_user_name,
        self.test_user_password)
        self.assertEqual(create_user_response.status_code,
        status.HTTP_201_CREATED)
        new_category_name_1 = 'Error 1'
        post_response_1 = self.create_category(new_category_name_1)
        self.assertEqual(post_response_1.status_code,
status.HTTP_201_CREATED)
```

```
        post_response_data_1 =
json.loads(post_response_1.get_data(as_text=True))
        new_category_url = post_response_data_1['url']
        new_category_name_2 = 'Error 2'
        data = {'name': new_category_name_2}
        patch_response = self.test_client.patch(
            new_category_url,
            headers=self.get_authentication_headers(self.test_user_name,
            self.test_user_password),
            data=json.dumps(data))
        self.assertEqual(patch_response.status_code, status.HTTP_200_OK)
        get_response = self.test_client.get(
            new_category_url,
            headers=self.get_authentication_headers(self.test_user_name,
            self.test_user_password))
        get_response_data = json.loads(get_response.get_data(as_text=True))
        self.assertEqual(get_response.status_code, status.HTTP_200_OK)
        self.assertEqual(get_response_data['name'], new_category_name_2)
```

The class declares the following methods whose name start with the `test_` prefix:

- `test_create_duplicated_ category`: Tests whether the unique constraints don't make it possible for us to create two categories with the same name or not. The second time we compose and send an HTTP POST request with a duplicate category name, we must receive an HTTP 400 Bad Request status code (`status.HTTP_400_BAD_REQUEST`) and the total number of `Category` objects retrieved from the database must be 1.

- `test_retrieve_categories_list`: Tests whether we can retrieve the categories list or not. First, the method creates two categories and then it makes sure that the retrieved list includes the two created categories.

- `test_update_game_category`: Tests whether we can update a single field for a category, specifically, its name field. The code makes sure that the name has been updated.

Note that each test that requires a specific condition in the database must execute all the necessary code for the database to be in this specific condition. For example, in order to update an existing category, first we must create a new category and then we can update it. Each test method will be executed without data from the previously executed test methods in the database, that is, each test will run with a database cleaned of data from previous tests.

Running unit tests with nose2 and checking testing coverage

Now, run the following command to create all the necessary tables in our test database and use the `nose2` test running to execute all the tests we created. The test runner will execute all the methods for our `InitialTests` class that start with the `test_` prefix and will display the results.

The tests won't make changes to the database we have been using when working on the API. Remember that we configured the `test_messages` database as our test database.

Remove the `api.py` file we created in the previous chapter from the `api` folder because we don't want the tests coverage to take into account this file. Go to the `api` folder and run the following command within the same virtual environment that we have been using. We will use the `-v` option to instruct `nose2` to print test case names and statuses. The `--with-coverage` option turns on test coverage reporting generation:

```
nose2 -v --with-coverage
```

The following lines show the sample output.

```
test_create_and_retrieve_category (test_views.InitialTests) ... ok
test_create_duplicated_category (test_views.InitialTests) ... ok
test_request_without_authentication (test_views.InitialTests) ... ok
test_retrieve_categories_list (test_views.InitialTests) ... ok
test_update_category (test_views.InitialTests) ... ok
----------------------------------------------------
Ran 5 tests in 3.973s
OK
----------- coverage: platform win32, python 3.5.2-final-0 --
Name                    Stmts    Miss   Cover
----------------------------------------
```

```
app.py                        9       0   100%
config.py                    11      11     0%
helpers.py                   23      18    22%
migrate.py                    9       9     0%
models.py                   101      27    73%
run.py                        4       4     0%
status.py                    56       5    91%
test_config.py               12       0   100%
tests\test_views.py          96       0   100%
views.py                    204     109    47%
---------------------------------------------
TOTAL                       525     183    65%
```

By default, `nose2` looks for modules whose names start with the `test` prefix. In this case, the only module that matches the criteria is the `test_views` module. In the modules that match the criteria, `nose2` loads tests from all the subclasses of `unittest.TestCase` and the functions whose names start with the `test` prefix.

The output provides details indicating that the test runner discovered and executed five tests and all of them passed. The output displays the method name and the class name for each method in the `InitialTests` class that started with the `test_` prefix and represented a test to be executed.

The test code coverage measurement report provided by the `coverage` package uses the code analysis tools and the tracing hooks included in the Python standard library to determine which lines of code are executable and have been executed. The report provides a table with the following columns:

- `Name`: The Python module name.
- `Stmts`: The count of executable statements for the Python module.
- `Miss`: The number of executable statements missed, that is, the ones that weren't executed.
- `Cover`: The coverage of executable statements expressed as a percentage.

We definitely have a very low coverage for `views.py` and `helpers.py` based on the measurements shown in the report. In fact, we just wrote a few tests related to categories and users, and therefore, it makes sense that the coverage is really low for the views. We didn't create tests related to messages.

We can run the coverage command with the -m command-line option to display the line numbers of the missing statements in a new Missing column:

```
coverage report -m
```

The command will use the information from the last execution and will display the missing statements. The next lines show a sample output that corresponds to the previous execution of the unit tests:

```
Name                      Stmts   Miss   Cover   Missing
-----------------------------------------------------------
app.py                       9      0    100%
config.py                   11     11      0%   7-20
helpers.py                  23     18     22%   13-19, 23-44
migrate.py                   9      9      0%   7-19
models.py                  101     27     73%   28-29, 44, 46, 48, 50, 52,
54, 73-75, 79-86, 103, 127-137
run.py                       4      4      0%   7-14
status.py                   56      5     91%   2, 6, 10, 14, 18
test_config.py              12      0    100%
tests\test_views.py         96      0    100%
views.py                   204    109     47%   43-45, 51-58, 63-64, 67,
71-72, 83-87, 92-94, 97-124, 127-135, 140-147, 150-181, 194-195, 198,
205-206, 209-212, 215-223, 235-236, 239, 250-253
-----------------------------------------------------------
TOTAL                      525    183     65%
```

Now, run the following command to get annotated HTML listings detailing missed lines:

```
coverage html
```

Open the `index.html` HTML file generated in the `htmlcov` folder with your Web browser. The following picture shows an example report that coverage generated in HTML format:

Module ↓	statements	missing	excluded	coverage
Coverage report: 65%				
app.py	9	0	0	100%
config.py	11	11	0	0%
helpers.py	23	18	0	22%
migrate.py	9	9	0	0%
models.py	101	27	0	73%
run.py	4	4	0	0%
status.py	56	5	0	91%
test_config.py	12	0	0	100%
tests\test_views.py	96	0	0	100%
views.py	204	109	0	47%
Total	**525**	**183**	**0**	**65%**

coverage.py v4.2, created at 2016-09-29 00:22

Click or tap `views.py` and the Web browser will render a Web page that displays the statements that were run, the missing ones and the excluded, with different colors. We can click or tap on the **run**, **missing** and **excluded** buttons to show or hide the background color that represents the status for each line of code. By default, the missing lines of code will be displayed with a pink background. Thus, we must write unit tests that target these lines of code to improve our test coverage:

```
184  class CategoryResource(AuthRequiredResource):
185      def get(self, id):
186          category = Category.query.get_or_404(id)
187          result = category_schema.dump(category).data
188          return result
189
190      def patch(self, id):
191          category = Category.query.get_or_404(id)
192          category_dict = request.get_json()
193          if not category_dict:
194              resp = {'message': 'No input data provided'}
195              return resp, status.HTTP_400_BAD_REQUEST
196          errors = category_schema.validate(category_dict)
197          if errors:
198              return errors, status.HTTP_400_BAD_REQUEST
199          try:
200              if 'name' in category_dict:
201                  category_name = category_dict['name']
202                  if Category.is_unique(id=id, name=category_name):
203                      category.name = category_name
204                  else:
205                      response = {'error': 'A category with the same name already exists'}
206                      return response, status.HTTP_400_BAD_REQUEST
207              category.update()
208              return self.get(id)
209          except SQLAlchemyError as e:
210              db.session.rollback()
211              resp = {"error": str(e)}
212              return resp, status.HTTP_400_BAD_REQUEST
213
214      def delete(self, id):
```

Improving testing coverage

Now, we will write additional unit tests to improve the testing coverage. Specifically, we will write unit tests related to messages and users. Open the existing `api/tests/test_views.py` file and insert the following lines after the last line, within the `InitialTests` class. We need a new `import` statement and we will declare the new `PlayerTests` class. The code file for the sample is included in the `restful_python_chapter_08_02` folder:

```
def create_message(self, message, duration, category):
    url = url_for('api.messagelistresource', _external=True)
    data = {'message': message, 'duration': duration, 'category':
category}
    response = self.test_client.post(
        url,
        headers=self.get_authentication_headers(self.test_user_name,
        self.test_user_password),
        data=json.dumps(data))
```

```
        return response

    def test_create_and_retrieve_message(self):
        """
        Ensure we can create a new message and then retrieve it
        """
        create_user_response = self.create_user(self.test_user_name,
        self.test_user_password)
        self.assertEqual(create_user_response.status_code,
        status.HTTP_201_CREATED)
        new_message_message = 'Welcome to the IoT world'
        new_message_category = 'Information'
        post_response = self.create_message(new_message_message, 15,
        new_message_category)
        self.assertEqual(post_response.status_code,
status.HTTP_201_CREATED)
        self.assertEqual(Message.query.count(), 1)
        # The message should have created a new catagory
        self.assertEqual(Category.query.count(), 1)
        post_response_data =
json.loads(post_response.get_data(as_text=True))
        self.assertEqual(post_response_data['message'],
new_message_message)
        new_message_url = post_response_data['url']
        get_response = self.test_client.get(
            new_message_url,
            headers=self.get_authentication_headers(self.test_user_name,
            self.test_user_password))
        get_response_data = json.loads(get_response.get_data(as_text=True))
        self.assertEqual(get_response.status_code, status.HTTP_200_OK)
        self.assertEqual(get_response_data['message'], new_message_message)
        self.assertEqual(get_response_data['category']['name'],
        new_message_category)

    def test_create_duplicated_message(self):
        """
        Ensure we cannot create a duplicated Message
        """
        create_user_response = self.create_user(self.test_user_name,
        self.test_user_password)
        self.assertEqual(create_user_response.status_code,
        status.HTTP_201_CREATED)
        new_message_message = 'Welcome to the IoT world'
        new_message_category = 'Information'
        post_response = self.create_message(new_message_message, 15,
        new_message_category)
        self.assertEqual(post_response.status_code,
status.HTTP_201_CREATED)
```

```
        self.assertEqual(Message.query.count(), 1)
        post_response_data =
json.loads(post_response.get_data(as_text=True))
        self.assertEqual(post_response_data['message'],
new_message_message)
        new_message_url = post_response_data['url']
        get_response = self.test_client.get(
            new_message_url,
            headers=self.get_authentication_headers(self.test_user_name,
            self.test_user_password))
        get_response_data = json.loads(get_response.get_data(as_text=True))
        self.assertEqual(get_response.status_code, status.HTTP_200_OK)
        self.assertEqual(get_response_data['message'], new_message_message)
        self.assertEqual(get_response_data['category']['name'],
        new_message_category)
        second_post_response = self.create_message(new_message_message, 15,
        new_message_category)
        self.assertEqual(second_post_response.status_code,
        status.HTTP_400_BAD_REQUEST)
        self.assertEqual(Message.query.count(), 1)
```

The preceding code adds many methods to the `InitialTests` class. The `create_message` method receives the desired `message`, `duration`, and `category` (category name) for the new message as arguments. The method builds the URL and the data dictionary to compose and send an HTTP POST method, create a new message, and return the response generated by this request. Many test methods will call the `create_message` method to create a message and then compose and send other HTTP requests to the API.

The class declares the following methods whose names start with the `test_` prefix:

- `test_create_and_retrieve_message`: Tests whether we can create a new `Message` and then retrieve it.
- `test_create_duplicated_message`: Tests whether the unique constraints don't make it possible for us to create two messages with the same message. The second time we compose and send an HTTP POST request with a duplicate message, we must receive an HTTP 400 Bad Request status code (`status.HTTP_400_BAD_REQUEST`) and the total number of `Message` objects retrieved from the database must be 1.

Open the existing `api/tests/test_views.py` file and insert the following lines after the last line, within the `InitialTests` class. The code file for the sample is included in the `restful_python_chapter_08_02` folder:

```python
def test_retrieve_messages_list(self):
    """
    Ensure we can retrieve the messages paginated list
    """
    create_user_response = self.create_user(self.test_user_name,
    self.test_user_password)
    self.assertEqual(create_user_response.status_code,
    status.HTTP_201_CREATED)
    new_message_message_1 = 'Welcome to the IoT world'
    new_message_category_1 = 'Information'
    post_response = self.create_message(new_message_message_1, 15,
    new_message_category_1)
    self.assertEqual(post_response.status_code,
    status.HTTP_201_CREATED)
    self.assertEqual(Message.query.count(), 1)
    new_message_message_2 = 'Initialization of the board failed'
    new_message_category_2 = 'Error'
    post_response = self.create_message(new_message_message_2, 10,
    new_message_category_2)
    self.assertEqual(post_response.status_code,
    status.HTTP_201_CREATED)
    self.assertEqual(Message.query.count(), 2)
    get_first_page_url = url_for('api.messagelistresource',
    _external=True)
    get_first_page_response = self.test_client.get(
        get_first_page_url,
        headers=self.get_authentication_headers(self.test_user_name,
        self.test_user_password))
    get_first_page_response_data =
    json.loads(get_first_page_response.get_data(as_text=True))
    self.assertEqual(get_first_page_response.status_code,
    status.HTTP_200_OK)
    self.assertEqual(get_first_page_response_data['count'], 2)
    self.assertIsNone(get_first_page_response_data['previous'])
    self.assertIsNone(get_first_page_response_data['next'])
    self.assertIsNotNone(get_first_page_response_data['results'])
    self.assertEqual(len(get_first_page_response_data['results']), 2)
    self.assertEqual(get_first_page_response_data['results'][0]['message'],
    new_message_message_1)
    self.assertEqual(get_first_page_response_data['results'][1]['message'],
    new_message_message_2)
    get_second_page_url = url_for('api.messagelistresource', page=2)
    get_second_page_response = self.test_client.get(
        get_second_page_url,
```

```
            headers=self.get_authentication_headers(self.test_user_name,
                self.test_user_password))
        get_second_page_response_data =
        json.loads(get_second_page_response.get_data(as_text=True))
        self.assertEqual(get_second_page_response.status_code,
        status.HTTP_200_OK)
        self.assertIsNotNone(get_second_page_response_data['previous'])
        self.assertEqual(get_second_page_response_data['previous'],
        url_for('api.messagelistresource', page=1))
        self.assertIsNone(get_second_page_response_data['next'])
        self.assertIsNotNone(get_second_page_response_data['results'])
        self.assertEqual(len(get_second_page_response_data['results']), 0)
```

The previous code added a `test_retrieve_messages_list` method to the
`InitialTests` class. This method tests whether we can retrieve the paginated messages
list. First, the method creates two messages and then it makes sure that the retrieved list
includes the two created messages in the first page. In addition, the method makes sure that
the second page doesn't include any message and that the value for the previous page
includes the URL for the first page.

Open the existing `api/tests/test_views.py` file and insert the following lines after the
last line, within the `InitialTests` class. The code file for the sample is included in the
`restful_python_chapter_08_02` folder:

```
    def test_update_message(self):
        """
        Ensure we can update a single field for an existing message
        """
        create_user_response = self.create_user(self.test_user_name,
        self.test_user_password)
        self.assertEqual(create_user_response.status_code,
        status.HTTP_201_CREATED)
        new_message_message_1 = 'Welcome to the IoT world'
        new_message_category_1 = 'Information'
        post_response = self.create_message(new_message_message_1, 30,
        new_message_category_1)
        self.assertEqual(post_response.status_code,
    status.HTTP_201_CREATED)
        self.assertEqual(Message.query.count(), 1)
        post_response_data =
    json.loads(post_response.get_data(as_text=True))
        new_message_url = post_response_data['url']
        new_printed_times = 1
        new_printed_once = True
        data = {'printed_times': new_printed_times, 'printed_once':
        new_printed_once}
        patch_response = self.test_client.patch(
```

```
            new_message_url,
            headers=self.get_authentication_headers(self.test_user_name,
            self.test_user_password),
            data=json.dumps(data))
        self.assertEqual(patch_response.status_code, status.HTTP_200_OK)
        get_response = self.test_client.get(
            new_message_url,
            headers=self.get_authentication_headers(self.test_user_name,
            self.test_user_password))
        get_response_data = json.loads(get_response.get_data(as_text=True))
        self.assertEqual(get_response.status_code, status.HTTP_200_OK)
        self.assertEqual(get_response_data['printed_times'],
new_printed_times)
        self.assertEqual(get_response_data['printed_once'],
new_printed_once)
    def test_create_and_retrieve_user(self):
        """
        Ensure we can create a new User and then retrieve it
        """
        new_user_name = self.test_user_name
        new_user_password = self.test_user_password
        post_response = self.create_user(new_user_name, new_user_password)
        self.assertEqual(post_response.status_code,
status.HTTP_201_CREATED)
        self.assertEqual(User.query.count(), 1)
        post_response_data =
json.loads(post_response.get_data(as_text=True))
        self.assertEqual(post_response_data['name'], new_user_name)
        new_user_url = post_response_data['url']
        get_response = self.test_client.get(
            new_user_url,
            headers=self.get_authentication_headers(self.test_user_name,
            self.test_user_password))
        get_response_data = json.loads(get_response.get_data(as_text=True))
        self.assertEqual(get_response.status_code, status.HTTP_200_OK)
        self.assertEqual(get_response_data['name'], new_user_name)
```

- The previous code added the following two methods to the `InitialTests` class-`test_update_message`-tests whether we can update more than one fields for a message, specifically, the values for the `printed_times` and `printed_once` fields. The code makes sure that both fields have been updated.

- `test_create_and_retrieve_user`: Tests whether we can create a new `User` and then retrieve it.

We just coded a few tests related to messages and one test related to users in order to improve test coverage and notice the impact on the test coverage report.

Now, run the following command within the same virtual environment we have been using:

```
nose2 -v --with-coverage
```

The following lines show the sample output:

```
test_create_and_retrieve_category (test_views.InitialTests) ... ok
test_create_and_retrieve_message (test_views.InitialTests) ... ok
test_create_and_retrieve_user (test_views.InitialTests) ... ok
test_create_duplicated_category (test_views.InitialTests) ... ok
test_create_duplicated_message (test_views.InitialTests) ... ok
test_request_without_authentication (test_views.InitialTests) ... ok
test_retrieve_categories_list (test_views.InitialTests) ... ok
test_retrieve_messages_list (test_views.InitialTests) ... ok
test_update_category (test_views.InitialTests) ... ok
test_update_message (test_views.InitialTests) ... ok

----------------------------------------------------------------
Ran 10 tests in 25.938s
OK
----------- coverage: platform win32, python 3.5.2-final-0 -------
Name                    Stmts   Miss   Cover
----------------------------------------------------
app.py                      9      0   100%
config.py                  11     11     0%
helpers.py                 23      1    96%
migrate.py                  9      9     0%
models.py                 101     11    89%
run.py                      4      4     0%
status.py                  56      5    91%
test_config.py             16      0   100%
tests\test_views.py       203      0   100%
views.py                  204     66    68%
----------------------------------------------------
TOTAL                     636    107    83%
```

The output provided details indicating that the test runner executed 10 tests and all of them passed. The test code coverage measurement report provided by the coverage package increased the Cover percentage of the views.py module from 47% in the previous run to 68%. In addition, the percentage of the helpers.py module increased from 22% to 96% because we wrote tests that used pagination. The new additional tests we wrote executed additional code in different modules, and therefore, there is an impact in the coverage report.

We just created a few unit tests to understand how we can code them. However, of course, it would be necessary to write more tests to provide an appropriate coverage of all the featured and execution scenarios included in the API.

Understanding strategies for deployments and scalability

Flask is a lightweight microframework for the Web. However, as happens with Django, one of the biggest drawbacks related to Flask and Flask-RESTful is that each HTTP request is blocking. Thus, whenever the Flask server receives an HTTP request, it doesn't start working on any other HTTP requests in the incoming queue until the server sends the response for the first HTTP request it received.

We used Flask to develop a RESTful Web Service. They key advantage of these kind of Web Services is that they are stateless, that is, they shouldn't keep a client state on any server. Our API is a good example of a stateless RESTful Web Service with Flask and Flask RESTful. Thus, we can make the API run on as many servers as necessary to achieve our scalability goals. Obviously, we must take into account that we can easily transform the database server in our scalability bottleneck.

Nowadays, we have a huge number of cloud-based alternatives to deploy a RESTful Web Service that uses Flask and Flask-RESTful and make it extremely scalable.

We always have to make sure that we profile the API and the database before we deploy the first version of our API. It is very important to make sure that the generated queries run properly on the underlying database and that the most popular queries do not end up in sequential scans. It is usually necessary to add the appropriate indexes to the tables in the database.

We have been using basic HTTP authentication. We can improve it with a token-based authentication. We must make sure that the API runs under HTTPS in production environments. In addition, we must make sure that we change the following line in the `api/config.py` file:

```
DEBUG = True
```

We must always turn off debug mode in production, and therefore, we must replace the previous line with the following one:

```
DEBUG = False
```

It is convenient to use a different configuration file for production. However, another approach that is becoming extremely popular, especially for cloud-native applications, is to store configuration in the environment. If we want to deploy cloud-native RESTful Web Services and follow the guidelines established in the twelve-factor App, we should store config in the environment.

Each platform includes detailed instructions to deploy our application. All of them will require us to generate the requirements.txt file that lists the application dependencies together with their versions. This way, the platforms will be able to install all the necessary dependencies listed in the file.

Run the following pip freeze to generate the requirements.txt file.

```
pip freeze > requirements.txt
```

The following lines show the contents of a sample generated requirements.txt file. However, bear in mind that many packages increase their version number quickly and you might see different versions in your configuration:

```
alembic==0.8.8
aniso8601==1.1.0
click==6.6
cov-core==1.15.0
coverage==4.2
Flask==0.11.1
Flask-HTTPAuth==3.2.1
flask-marshmallow==0.7.0
Flask-Migrate==2.0.0
Flask-RESTful==0.3.5
Flask-Script==2.0.5
Flask-SQLAlchemy==2.1
itsdangerous==0.24
Jinja2==2.8
Mako==1.0.4
MarkupSafe==0.23
marshmallow==2.10.2
marshmallow-sqlalchemy==0.10.0
nose2==0.6.5
passlib==1.6.5
psycopg2==2.6.2
```

```
python-dateutil==2.5.3
python-editor==1.0.1
pytz==2016.6.1
six==1.10.0
SQLAlchemy==1.0.15
Werkzeug==0.11.11
```

Test your knowledge

1. By default, nose2 looks for modules whose names start with the following prefix:
    1. test
    2. run
    3. unittest

2. By default, nose2 loads tests from all the subclasses of the following class:
    1. unittest.Test
    2. unittest.TestCase
    3. unittest.RunTest

3. The setUp method in a subclass of unittest.TestCase:
    1. Is executed before each test method runs.
    2. Is executed only once before all the tests start their execution.
    3. Is executed only once after all the tests finish their execution.

4. The tearDown method in a subclass of unittest.TestCase:
    1. Is executed after each test method runs.
    2. Is executed before each test method runs.
    3. Is executed after a test method only when it fails.

5. If we declare a get_accept_content_type_headers method within a subclass of unittest.TestCase, by default, nose2:
    1. Will load this method as a test.
    2. Will load this method as the setUp method for each test.
    3. Won't load this method as a test.

Summary

In this chapter, we set up a testing environment. We installed nose2 to make it easy to discover and execute unit tests, and we created a new database to be used for testing. We wrote a first round of unit tests, measured test coverage, and then we wrote additional unit tests to improve test coverage. Finally, we understood many considerations for deployment and scalability.

Now that we have built a complex API with Flask combined with Flask RESTful, and we tested it, we will move to another popular Python Web framework, Tornado, which is what we are going to discuss in the next chapter.

9
Developing RESTful APIs with Tornado

In this chapter, we will work with Tornado to create a RESTful Web API and start working with this lightweight Web framework. We will cover the following topics:

- Designing a RESTful API to interact with slow sensors and actuators
- Understanding the tasks performed by each `HTTP` method
- Setting up a virtual environment with Tornado
- Declaring status codes for the responses
- Creating the classes that represent a drone
- Writing request handlers
- Mapping URL patterns to request handlers
- Making HTTP requests to the Tornado API
- Working with command-line tools – curl and HTTPie
- Working with GUI tools – Postman and others

Designing a RESTful API to interact with slow sensors and actuators

Imagine that we have to create a RESTful API to control a drone, also known as an **Unmanned Aerial Vehicle (UAV)**. The drone is an IoT device that interacts with many sensors and actuators, including digital electronic speed controllers linked to engines, propellers, and servomotors.

The IoT device has limited resources, and therefore, we have to use a lightweight Web framework. Our API doesn't need to interact with a database. We don't need a heavyweight Web framework like Django, and we want to be able to process many requests without blocking the Web server. We need the Web server to provide us with good scalability while consuming limited resources. Thus, our choice is to use Tornado, the open source version of FriendFeed's Web server.

The IoT device is capable of running Python 3.5, Tornado, and other Python packages. Tornado is a Python Web framework and an asynchronous networking library that provides excellent scalability due to its non-blocking network I/O. In addition, Tornado will allow us to easily and quickly build a lightweight RESTful API.

We have chosen Tornado because it is more lightweight than Django and it makes it easy for us to create an API that takes advantage of the non-blocking network I/O. We don't need to use an ORM, and we want to start running the RESTful API on the IoT device as soon as possible to allow all the teams to interact with it.

We will interact with a library that allows us to run the slow I/O operations that interact with the sensors and actuators with an execution that happens outside the **Global Interpreter Lock (GIL)**. Thus, we will be able to take advantage of the non-blocking feature in Tornado when a request needs to execute any of these slow I/O operations. In our first version of the API, we will work with a synchronous execution, and therefore, when an HTTP request to our API requires running a slow I/O operation, we will block the request processing queue until the slow I/O operation with either a sensor or an actuator provides a response. We will execute the I/O operation with a synchronous execution and Tornado won't be able to continue processing other incoming HTTP requests until a response is sent to the HTTP request.

Then, we will create a second version of our API that will take advantage of the non-blocking features included in Tornado, in combination with asynchronous operations. In the second version, when an HTTP request to our API requires running a slow I/O operation, we won't block the request processing queue until the slow I/O operation with either a sensor or an actuator provides a response. We will execute the I/O operation with an asynchronous execution, and Tornado will be able to continue processing other incoming HTTP requests.

We will keep our example simple and we won't use a library to interact with sensors and actuators. We will just print information about the operations that will be performed by these sensors and actuators. However, in our second version of the API, we will write our code to make asynchronous calls in order to understand the advantages of the non-blocking features in Tornado. We will use a simplified set of sensors and actuators—bear in mind that drones usually have more sensors and actuators. Our goal is to learn how to work with Tornado to build a RESTful API; we don't want to become experts in building drones.

Each of the following sensors and actuators will be a resource in our RESTful API:

- A hexacopter, that is, a 6-rotor helicopter
- An altimeter (altitude sensor)
- A blue **LED (Light-Emitting Diode)**
- A white LED

The following table shows the HTTP verbs, the scope, and the semantics for the methods that our first version of the API must support. Each method is composed by an HTTP verb and a scope and all the methods have a well-defined meaning for all sensors and actuators. In our API, each sensor or actuator has its own unique URL:

HTTP verb	Scope	Semantics
GET	Hexacopter	Retrieve the current hexacopter's motor speed in RPMs and its status (turned on or off)
PATCH	Hexacopter	Set the current hexacopter's motor speed in RPMs
GET	LED	Retrieve the brightness level for a single LED
PATCH	LED	Update the brightness level for a single LED
GET	Altimeter	Retrieve the current altitude in feet

Understanding the tasks performed by each HTTP method

Let's consider that `http://localhost:8888/hexacopters/1` is the URL that identifies the hexacopter for our drone.

We have to compose and send an HTTP request with the following HTTP verb (`PATCH`) and request URL (`http://localhost:8888/hexacopters/1`) to set the hexacopter's motor speed in RPMs and its status. In addition, we have to provide the JSON key-value pairs with the necessary field name and the value to specify the desired speed. As a result of the request, the server will validate the provided values for the field, make sure that it is a valid speed and make the necessary calls to adjust the speed with an asynchronous execution. After the speed for the hexacopter is set, the server will return a `200 OK` status code and a JSON body with the recently updated hexacopter values serialized to JSON:

```
PATCH http://localhost:8888/hexacopters/1
```

We have to compose and send an HTTP request with the following HTTP verb (`GET`) and request URL (`http://localhost:8888/hexacopter/1`) to retrieve the current values for the hexacopter. The server will make the necessary calls to retrieve the status and the speed for the hexacopter with an asynchronous execution. As a result of the request, the server will return a `200 OK` status code and a JSON body with the serialized key-value pairs that specify the status and speed for the hexacopter. If a number different than 1 is specified, the server will return just a `404 Not Found` status:

```
GET http://localhost:8888/hexacopters/1
```

We have to compose and send an HTTP request with the following HTTP verb (`PATCH`) and request URL (`http://localhost:8888/led/{id}`) to set the brightness level for a specific LED whose id matches the specified numeric value in the place where `{id}` is written. For example, if we use the request URL `http://localhost:8888/led/1`, the server will set the brightness level for the led whose id matches 1. In addition, we have to provide the JSON key-value pairs with the necessary field name and the value to specify the desired brightness level. As a result of the request, the server will validate the provided values for the field, make sure that it is a valid brightness level and make the necessary calls to adjust the brightness level with an asynchronous execution. After the brightness level for the LED is set, the server will return a `200 OK` status code and a JSON body with the recently updated LED values serialized to JSON:

```
PATCH http://localhost:8888/led/{id}
```

We have to compose and send an HTTP request with the following HTTP verb (`GET`) and request URL (`http://localhost:8888/led/{id}`) to retrieve the current values for the LED whose id matches the specified numeric value in the place where `{id}` is written. For example, if we use the request URL `http://localhost:8888/led/1`, the server will retrieve the LED whose id matches 1. The server will make the necessary calls to retrieve the values for the LED with an asynchronous execution. As a result of the request, the server will return a `200 OK` status code and a JSON body with the serialized key-value pairs that specify the values for the LED. If no LED matches the specified id, the server will return just a `404 Not Found` status:

```
GET http://localhost:8888/led/{id}
```

We have to compose and send an HTTP request with the following HTTP verb (`GET`) and request URL (`http://localhost:8888/altimeter/1`) to retrieve the current values for the altimeter. The server will make the necessary calls to retrieve the values for the altimeter with an asynchronous execution. As a result of the request, the server will return a `200 OK` status code and a JSON body with the serialized key-value pairs that specify the values for the altimeter. If a number different than 1 is specified, the server will return just a `404 Not Found` status:

```
GET http://localhost:8888/altimeter/1
```

Setting up a virtual environment with Tornado

In `Chapter 1`, *Developing RESTful APIs with Django*, we learned that, throughout this book, we were going to work with the lightweight virtual environments introduced in Python 3.3 and improved in Python 3.4. Now, we will follow many steps create a new lightweight virtual environment to work with Tornado. It is highly recommended to read `Chapter 1`, *Developing RESTful APIs with Django*, in case you don't have experience with lightweight virtual environments in Python. The chapter includes all the detailed explanations about the effects of the steps we are going to follow.

First, we have to select the target folder or directory for our virtual environment. The following is the path we will use in the example for macOS and Linux. The target folder for the virtual environment will be the `PythonREST/Tornado01` folder within our home directory. For example, if our home directory in macOS or Linux is `/Users/gaston`, the virtual environment will be created within `/Users/gaston/PythonREST/Tornado01`. You can replace the specified path with your desired path in each command:

```
~/PythonREST/Tornado01
```

We will use the following path in the example for Windows. The target folder for the virtual environment will be the `PythonREST\Tornado01` folder within our user profile folder. For example, if our user profile folder is `C:\Users\Gaston`, the virtual environment will be created within `C:\Users\gaston\PythonREST\Tornado01`. You can replace the specified path with your desired path in each command:

```
%USERPROFILE%\PythonREST\Tornado01
```

Open a Terminal in macOS or Linux and execute the following command to create a virtual environment:

```
python3 -m venv ~/PythonREST/Tornado01
```

In Windows, execute the following command to create a virtual environment:

```
python -m venv %USERPROFILE%\PythonREST\Tornado01
```

The preceding command doesn't produce any output. Now that we have created a virtual environment, we will run a platform-specific script to activate it. After we activate the virtual environment, we will install packages that will only be available in this virtual environment.

If your Terminal is configured to use the `bash` shell in macOS or Linux, run the following command to activate the virtual environment. The command also works for the `zsh` shell:

```
source ~/PythonREST/Torando01/bin/activate
```

If your Terminal is configured to use either the `csh` or `tcsh` shell, run the following command to activate the virtual environment:

```
source ~/PythonREST/Torando01/bin/activate.csh
```

If your Terminal is configured to use either the `fish` shell, run the following command to activate the virtual environment:

```
source ~/PythonREST/Tornado01/bin/activate.fish
```

In Windows, you can run either a batch file in the Command Prompt or a Windows PowerShell script to activate the virtual environment. If you prefer the command prompt, run the following command in the Windows command line to activate the virtual environment:

```
%USERPROFILE%\PythonREST\Tornado01\Scripts\activate.bat
```

If you prefer the Windows PowerShell, launch it and run the following commands to activate the virtual environment. However, notice that you should have scripts execution enabled in Windows PowerShell to be able to run the script:

```
cd $env:USERPROFILE
PythonREST\Tornado01\Scripts\Activate.ps1
```

After you activate the virtual environment, the Command Prompt will display the virtual environment root folder name enclosed in parentheses as a prefix of the default prompt to remind us that we are working in the virtual environment. In this case, we will see (Tornado01) as a prefix for the Command Prompt because the root folder for the activated virtual environment is Tornado01.

We have created and activated a virtual environment. It is time to run many commands that will be the same for either macOS, Linux, or Windows. Now, we must run the following command to install Tornado with pip:

```
pip install tornado
```

The last lines for the output will indicate all the packages that have been successfully installed, including tornado:

```
Collecting tornado
  Downloading tornado-4.4.1.tar.gz (456kB)
Installing collected packages: tornado
  Running setup.py install for tornado
Successfully installed tornado-4.4.1
```

Declaring status codes for the responses

Tornado allows us to generate responses with any status code that is included in the http.HTTPStatus dictionary. We might use this dictionary to return easy to understand descriptions as the status codes, such as HTTPStatus.OK and HTTPStatus.NOT_FOUND after importing the HTTPStatus dictionary from the http module. These names are easy to understand but they don't include the status code number in their description.

We have been working with many different frameworks and micro-frameworks throughout the book, and therefore, we will borrow the code that declares very useful functions and variables related to HTTP status codes from the `status.py` file included in Django REST Framework, that is, the framework we have been using in the first chapters. The main advantage of using these variables for the HTTP status codes is that their names include both the number and the description. When we read the code, we will understand the status code number and their meaning. For example, instead of using `HTTPStatus.OK`, we will use `status.HTTP_200_OK`.

Create a new `status.py` file within the root folder for the recently created virtual environment. The following lines show the code that declares functions and variables with descriptive HTTP status codes in the `status.py` file, borrowed from the `rest_framework.status` module. We don't want to reinvent the wheel and the module provides everything we need to work with HTTP status codes in our Tornado-based API. The code file for the sample is included in the `restful_python_chapter_09_01` folder:

```
def is_informational(code):
    return code >= 100 and code <= 199


def is_success(code):
    return code >= 200 and code <= 299


def is_redirect(code):
    return code >= 300 and code <= 399


def is_client_error(code):
    return code >= 400 and code <= 499


def is_server_error(code):
    return code >= 500 and code <= 599


HTTP_100_CONTINUE = 100
HTTP_101_SWITCHING_PROTOCOLS = 101
HTTP_200_OK = 200
HTTP_201_CREATED = 201
HTTP_202_ACCEPTED = 202
HTTP_203_NON_AUTHORITATIVE_INFORMATION = 203
HTTP_204_NO_CONTENT = 204
HTTP_205_RESET_CONTENT = 205
HTTP_206_PARTIAL_CONTENT = 206
HTTP_300_MULTIPLE_CHOICES = 300
```

```
HTTP_301_MOVED_PERMANENTLY = 301
HTTP_302_FOUND = 302
HTTP_303_SEE_OTHER = 303
HTTP_304_NOT_MODIFIED = 304
HTTP_305_USE_PROXY = 305
HTTP_306_RESERVED = 306
HTTP_307_TEMPORARY_REDIRECT = 307
HTTP_400_BAD_REQUEST = 400
HTTP_401_UNAUTHORIZED = 401
HTTP_402_PAYMENT_REQUIRED = 402
HTTP_403_FORBIDDEN = 403
HTTP_404_NOT_FOUND = 404
HTTP_405_METHOD_NOT_ALLOWED = 405
HTTP_406_NOT_ACCEPTABLE = 406
HTTP_407_PROXY_AUTHENTICATION_REQUIRED = 407
HTTP_408_REQUEST_TIMEOUT = 408
HTTP_409_CONFLICT = 409
HTTP_410_GONE = 410
HTTP_411_LENGTH_REQUIRED = 411
HTTP_412_PRECONDITION_FAILED = 412
HTTP_413_REQUEST_ENTITY_TOO_LARGE = 413
HTTP_414_REQUEST_URI_TOO_LONG = 414
HTTP_415_UNSUPPORTED_MEDIA_TYPE = 415
HTTP_416_REQUESTED_RANGE_NOT_SATISFIABLE = 416
HTTP_417_EXPECTATION_FAILED = 417
HTTP_428_PRECONDITION_REQUIRED = 428
HTTP_429_TOO_MANY_REQUESTS = 429
HTTP_431_REQUEST_HEADER_FIELDS_TOO_LARGE = 431
HTTP_451_UNAVAILABLE_FOR_LEGAL_REASONS = 451
HTTP_500_INTERNAL_SERVER_ERROR = 500
HTTP_501_NOT_IMPLEMENTED = 501
HTTP_502_BAD_GATEWAY = 502
HTTP_503_SERVICE_UNAVAILABLE = 503
HTTP_504_GATEWAY_TIMEOUT = 504
HTTP_505_HTTP_VERSION_NOT_SUPPORTED = 505
HTTP_511_NETWORK_AUTHENTICATION_REQUIRED = 511
```

The code declares five functions that receive the HTTP status code in the code argument and determine to which of the following categories the status code belongs to: informational, success, redirect, and client error or server error categories. We will use the previous variables when we have to return a specific status code. For example, in case we have to return a 404 Not Found status code, we will return status.HTTP_404_NOT_FOUND, instead of just 404 or HTTPStatus.NOT_FOUND.

Creating the classes that represent a drone

We will create as many classes as we will use to represent the different components of a drone. In a real-life example, these classes will interact with a library that interacts with sensors and actuators. In order to keep our example simple, we will make calls to `time.sleep` to simulate interactions that take some time to set or get values to and from sensors and actuators.

First, we will create a `Hexacopter` class that we will use to represent the hexacopter and a `HexacopterStatus` class that we will use to store status data for the hexacopter. Create a new `drone.py` file. The following lines shows all the necessary imports for the classes that we will create and the code that declares the `Hexacopter` and `HexacopterStatus` classes in the `drone.py` file. The code file for the sample is included in the `restful_python_chapter_09_01` folder:

```python
from random import randint
from time import sleep


class HexacopterStatus:
    def __init__(self, motor_speed, turned_on):
        self.motor_speed = motor_speed
        self.turned_on = turned_on


class Hexacopter:
    MIN_SPEED = 0
    MAX_SPEED = 1000

    def __init__(self):
        self.motor_speed = self.__class__.MIN_SPEED
        self.turned_on = False

    def get_motor_speed(self):
        return self.motor_speed
    def set_motor_speed(self, motor_speed):
        if motor_speed < self.__class__.MIN_SPEED:
            raise ValueError('The minimum speed is
{0}'.format(self.__class__.MIN_SPEED))
        if motor_speed > self.__class__.MAX_SPEED:
            raise ValueError('The maximum speed is
{0}'.format(self.__class__.MAX_SPEED))
        self.motor_speed = motor_speed
        self.turned_on = (self.motor_speed is not 0)
        sleep(2)
        return HexacopterStatus(self.get_motor_speed(),
```

```
self.is_turned_on())

    def is_turned_on(self):
        return self.turned_on

    def get_hexacopter_status(self):
        sleep(3)
        return HexacopterStatus(self.get_motor_speed(),
self.is_turned_on())
```

The HexacopterStatus class just declares a constructor, that is, the __init__ method. This method receives many arguments and uses them to initialize the attributes with the same names: motor_speed and turned_on.

The Hexacopter class declares two class attributes that specify the minimum and maximum speed values: MIN_SPEED and MAX_SPEED. The constructor, that is, the __init__ method, initializes the motor_speed attribute with the MIN_SPEED value and sets the turned_on attribute to False.

The get_motor_speed method returns the value of the motor_speed attribute. The set_motor_speed method checks whether the value for the motor_speed argument is in the valid range. In case the validation fails, the method raises a ValueError exception. Otherwise, the method sets the value of the motor_speed attribute with the received value and sets the value for the turned_on attribute to True if the motor_speed is greater than 0. Finally, the method calls sleep to simulate it takes two seconds to retrieve the hexacopter status and then returns a HexacopterStatus instance initialized with the motor_speed and turned_on attribute values, retrieved through specific methods.

The get_hexacopter_status method calls sleep to simulate it takes three seconds to retrieve the hexacopter status and then returns a HexacopterStatus instance initialized with the motor_speed and turned_on attribute values.

Now, we will create a LightEmittingDiode class that we will use to represent each LED. Open the previously created drone.py file and add the following lines. The code file for the sample is included in the restful_python_chapter_09_01 folder:

```
class LightEmittingDiode:
    MIN_BRIGHTNESS_LEVEL = 0
    MAX_BRIGHTNESS_LEVEL = 255

    def __init__(self, identifier, description):
        self.identifier = identifier
        self.description = description
        self.brightness_level = self.__class__.MIN_BRIGHTNESS_LEVEL
```

```
def get_brightness_level(self):
    sleep(1)
    return self.brightness_level

def set_brightness_level(self, brightness_level):
    if brightness_level < self.__class__.MIN_BRIGHTNESS_LEVEL:
        raise ValueError('The minimum brightness level is
{0}'.format(self.__class__.MIN_BRIGHTNESS_LEVEL))
    if brightness_level > self.__class__.MAX_BRIGHTNESS_LEVEL:
        raise ValueError('The maximum brightness level is
{0}'.format(self.__class__.MAX_BRIGHTNESS_LEVEL))
    sleep(2)
    self.brightness_level = brightness_level
```

The `LightEmittingDiode` class declares two class attributes that specify the minimum and maximum brightness level values: `MIN_BRIGHTNESS_LEVEL` and `MAX_BRIGHTNESS_LEVEL`. The constructor, that is, the `__init__` method, initializes the `brightness_level` attribute with the `MIN_BRIGHTNESS_LEVEL` and the `id` and `description` attributes with the values received in the arguments with the same names.

The `get_brightness_level` method calls sleep to simulate, it takes 1 second to retrieve the brightness level for the wired LED and then returns the value of the `brightness_level` attribute.

The `set_brightness_level` method checks whether the value for the `brightness_level` argument is in the valid range. In case the validation fails, the method raises a `ValueError` exception. Otherwise, the method calls `sleep` to simulate it takes two seconds to set the new brightness level and finally sets the value of the `brightness_level` attribute with the received value.

Now, we will create an `Altimeter` class that we will use to represent the altimeter. Open the previously created `drone.py` file and add the following lines. The code file for the sample is included in the `restful_python_chapter_09_01` folder:

```
class Altimeter:
    def get_altitude(self):
        sleep(1)
        return randint(0, 3000)
```

The `Altimeter` class declares a `get_altitude` method that calls `sleep` to simulate it takes one second to retrieve the altitude from the altimeter and finally generates a random integer from 0 to 3000 (inclusive) and returns it.

Finally, we will create a `Drone` class that we will use to represent the drone with its sensors and actuators. Open the previously created `drone.py` file and add the following lines. The code file for the sample is included in the `restful_python_chapter_09_01` folder

```
class Drone:
    def __init__(self):
        self.hexacopter = Hexacopter()
        self.altimeter = Altimeter()
        self.blue_led = LightEmittingDiode(1, 'Blue LED')
        self.white_led = LightEmittingDiode(2, 'White LED')
        self.leds = {
            self.blue_led.identifier: self.blue_led,
            self.white_led.identifier: self.white_led
            }
```

The `Drone` class just declares a constructor, that is, the `__init__` method that creates instances of the previously declared classes that represent the different components for the drone. The `leds` attribute saves a dictionary that has a key-value pair for each `LightEmittingDiode` instance with its id and its instance.

Writing request handlers

The main building blocks for a RESTful API in tornado are subclasses of the `tornado.web.RequestHandler` class, that is, the base class for HTTP request handlers in Tornado. We just need to create a subclass of this class and declare the methods for each supported HTTP verb. We have to override the methods to handle HTTP requests. Then, we have to map the URL patterns to each subclass of `tornado.web.RequestHandler` in the `tornado.web.Application` instance that represents the Tornado Web application.

First, we will create a `HexacopterHandler` class that we will use to handle requests for the hexacopter resource. Create a new `api.py` file. The following lines show all the necessary imports for the classes that we will create and the code that declares the `HexacopterHandler` class in the `drone.py` file. Enter the next lines in the new `api.py` file. The code file for the sample is included in the `restful_python_chapter_09_01` folder:

```
import status
from datetime import date
from tornado import web, escape, ioloop, httpclient, gen
from drone import Altimeter, Drone, Hexacopter, LightEmittingDiode


drone = Drone()
```

```python
class HexacopterHandler(web.RequestHandler):
    SUPPORTED_METHODS = ("GET", "PATCH")
    HEXACOPTER_ID = 1

    def get(self, id):
        if int(id) is not self.__class__.HEXACOPTER_ID:
            self.set_status(status.HTTP_404_NOT_FOUND)
            return
        print("I've started retrieving hexacopter's status")
        hexacopter_status = drone.hexacopter.get_hexacopter_status()
        print("I've finished retrieving hexacopter's status")
        response = {
            'speed': hexacopter_status.motor_speed,
            'turned_on': hexacopter_status.turned_on,
            }
        self.set_status(status.HTTP_200_OK)
        self.write(response)
    def patch(self, id):
        if int(id) is not self.__class__.HEXACOPTER_ID:
            self.set_status(status.HTTP_404_NOT_FOUND)
            return
        request_data = escape.json_decode(self.request.body)
        if ('motor_speed' not in request_data.keys()) or \
            (request_data['motor_speed'] is None):
            self.set_status(status.HTTP_400_BAD_REQUEST)
            return
        try:
            motor_speed = int(request_data['motor_speed'])
            print("I've started setting the hexacopter's motor speed")
            hexacopter_status =
drone.hexacopter.set_motor_speed(motor_speed)
            print("I've finished setting the hexacopter's motor speed")
            response = {
                'speed': hexacopter_status.motor_speed,
                'turned_on': hexacopter_status.turned_on,
                }
            self.set_status(status.HTTP_200_OK)
            self.write(response)
        except ValueError as e:
            print("I've failed setting the hexacopter's motor speed")
            self.set_status(status.HTTP_400_BAD_REQUEST)
            response = {
                'error': e.args[0]
                }
            self.write(response)
```

The `HexacopterHandler` class is a subclass of `tornado.web.RequestHandler` and declares the following two methods that will be called when the HTTP method with the same name arrives as a request on this HTTP handler:

- `get`: This method receives the `id` of the hexacopter whose status has to be retrieved in the `id` argument. If the received id doesn't match the value of the `HEXACOPTER_ID` class attribute, the code calls the `self.set_status` method with `status.HTTP_404_NOT_FOUND` as an argument to set the status code for the response to `HTTP 404 Not Found`. Otherwise, the code prints a message indicating that it started retrieving the hexacopter's status and calls the `drone.hexacopter.get_hexacopter_status` method with a synchronous execution and saves the result in the `hexacopter_status` variable. Then, the code writes a message indicating it finished retrieving the status and generates a `response` dictionary with the `'speed'` and `'turned_on'` keys and their values. Finally, the code calls the `self.set_status` method with `status.HTTP_200_OK` as an argument to set the status code for the response to `HTTP 200 OK` and calls the `self.write` method with the `response` dictionary as an argument. Because `response` is a dictionary, Tornado automatically writes the chunk as JSON and sets the value of the `Content-Type` header to `application/json`.

- `patch`: This method receives the `id` of the hexacopter that has to be updated or patched in the `id` argument. As it happened in the previously explained get method, the code returns an `HTTP 404 Not Found` in case the received id doesn't match the value of the `HEXACOPTER_ID` class attribute. Otherwise, the code calls the `tornado.escape.json_decode` method with `self.request.body` as an argument to generate Python objects for the JSON string of the request body and saves the generated dictionary in the `request_data` variable. If the dictionary doesn't include a key named `'motor_speed'`, the code returns an `HTTP 400 Bad Request` status code. In case there is a key, the code prints a message indicating that it started setting the hexacopter's speed, calls the `drone.hexacopter.set_motor_speed` method with a synchronous execution and saves the result in the `hexacopter_status` variable. If the value specified for the motor speed is not valid, a `ValueError` exception will be caught and the code will return an HTTP 400 Bad Request status code and the validation error messages as the response body. Otherwise, the code writes a message indicating it finished setting the motor speed and generates a `response` dictionary with the `'speed'` and `'turned_on'` keys and their values. Finally, the code calls the `self.set_status` method with `status.HTTP_200_OK` as an argument to set the status code for the response to HTTP 200 OK and calls the `self.write` method with the `response` dictionary as an argument. Since `response` is a dictionary, Tornado automatically writes the chunk as JSON and sets the value of the `Content-Type` header to `application/json`.

The class overrides the `SUPPORTED_METHODS` class variable with a tuple that indicates the class just supports the `GET` and `PATCH` methods. This way, in case the handler is requested a method that isn't included in the `SUPPORTED_METHODS` tuple, the server will automatically return a `405 Method Not Allowed` status code.

Now, we will create a `LedHandler` class that we will use to represent the LED resources. Open the previously created `api.py` file and add the following lines. The code file for the sample is included in the `restful_python_chapter_09_01` folder:

```
class LedHandler(web.RequestHandler):
    SUPPORTED_METHODS = ("GET", "PATCH")

    def get(self, id):
        int_id = int(id)
        if int_id not in drone.leds.keys():
            self.set_status(status.HTTP_404_NOT_FOUND)
            return
        led = drone.leds[int_id]
        print("I've started retrieving {0}'s
status".format(led.description))
        brightness_level = led.get_brightness_level()
        print("I've finished retrieving {0}'s
status".format(led.description))
        response = {
            'id': led.identifier,
            'description': led.description,
            'brightness_level': brightness_level
            }
        self.set_status(status.HTTP_200_OK)
        self.write(response)

    def patch(self, id):
        int_id = int(id)
        if int_id not in drone.leds.keys():
            self.set_status(status.HTTP_404_NOT_FOUND)
            return
        led = drone.leds[int_id]
        request_data = escape.json_decode(self.request.body)
        if ('brightness_level' not in request_data.keys()) or \
            (request_data['brightness_level'] is None):
            self.set_status(status.HTTP_400_BAD_REQUEST)
            return
```

```
try:
    brightness_level = int(request_data['brightness_level'])
    print("I've started setting the {0}'s brightness
    level".format(led.description))
    led.set_brightness_level(brightness_level)
    print("I've finished setting the {0}'s brightness
    level".format(led.description))
    response = {
        'id': led.identifier,
        'description': led.description,
        'brightness_level': brightness_level
        }
    self.set_status(status.HTTP_200_OK)
    self.write(response)
except ValueError as e:
    print("I've failed setting the {0}'s brightness
    level".format(led.description))
    self.set_status(status.HTTP_400_BAD_REQUEST)
    response = {
        'error': e.args[0]
        }
    self.write(response)
```

The `LedHandler` class is a subclass of `tornado.web.RequestHandler`. The class overrides the `SUPPORTED_METHODS` class variable with a tuple that indicates the class just supports the `GET` and `PATCH` methods. In addition, the class declares the following two methods that will be called when the HTTP method with the same name arrives as a request on this HTTP handler:

- `get`: This method receives the `id` of the LED whose status has to be retrieved in the `id` argument. If the received id isn't one of the keys of the `drone.leds` dictionary, the code calls the `self.set_status` method with `status.HTTP_404_NOT_FOUND` as an argument to set the status code for the response to `HTTP 404 Not Found`. Otherwise, the code retrieves the value associated with the key whose value matches the id in the `drone.leds` dictionary and saves the retrieved `LightEmittingDiode` instance in the `led` variable. The code prints a message indicating that it started retrieving the LED's brightness level, calls the `led.get_brightness_level` method with a synchronous execution, and saves the result in the `brightness_level` variable. Then, the code writes a message indicating that it finished retrieving the brightness level and generates a `response` dictionary with the `'id'`, `'description'`, and `'brightness_level'` keys and their values. Finally, the code calls the `self.set_status` method with `status.HTTP_200_OK` as an argument to set the status code for the response to HTTP 200 OK and calls the self.write method with the response dictionary as an argument. Since response is a dictionary, Tornado automatically writes the chunk as JSON and sets the value of the Content-Type header to application/json.

- patch: This method receives the id of the LED that has to be updated or patched in the id argument. As happened in the previously explained get method, the code returns an HTTP 404 Not Found in case the received id doesn't match the any of the keys of the drone.leds dictionary. Otherwise, the code calls the tornado.escape.json_decode method with self.request.body as an argument to generate Python objects for the JSON string of the request body and saves the generated dictionary in the request_data variable. If the dictionary doesn't include a key named 'brightness_level', the code returns an HTTP 400 Bad Request status code. In case there is a key, the code prints a message indicating that it started setting the LED's brightness level, including the description for the LED, calls the drone.hexacopter.set_brightness_level method with a synchronous execution. If the value specified for the brightness_level is not valid, a ValueError exception will be caught and the code will return an HTTP 400 Bad Request status code and the validation error messages as the response body. Otherwise, the code writes a message indicating it finished setting the LED's brightness value and generates a response dictionary with the 'id', 'description', and 'brightness_level' keys and their values. Finally, the code calls the self.set_status method with status.HTTP_200_OK as an argument to set the status code for the response to HTTP 200 OK and calls the self.write method with the response dictionary as an argument. Since response is a dictionary, Tornado automatically writes the chunk as JSON and sets the value of the Content-Type header to application/json.

Now, we will create an AltimeterHandler class that we will use to represent the altimeter resource. Open the previously created api.py file and add the following lines. The code file for the sample is included in the restful_python_chapter_09_01 folder:

```
class AltimeterHandler(web.RequestHandler):
    SUPPORTED_METHODS = ("GET")
    ALTIMETER_ID = 1

    def get(self, id):
        if int(id) is not self.__class__.ALTIMETER_ID:
            self.set_status(status.HTTP_404_NOT_FOUND)
            return
        print("I've started retrieving the altitude")
        altitude = drone.altimeter.get_altitude()
        print("I've finished retrieving the altitude")
```

```
response = {
    'altitude': altitude
    }
self.set_status(status.HTTP_200_OK)
self.write(response)
```

The `AltimeterHandler` class is a subclass of `tornado.web.RequestHandler`. The class overrides the `SUPPORTED_METHODS` class variable with a tuple that indicates the class just supports the `GET` method. In addition, the class declares the `get` method that will be called when the HTTP method with the same name arrives as a request on this HTTP handler.

The `get` method receives the `id` of the altimeter whose altitude has to be retrieved in the `id` argument. If the received id doesn't match the value of the `ALTIMETER_ID` class attribute, the code calls the `self.set_status` method with `status.HTTP_404_NOT_FOUND` as an argument to set the status code for the response to HTTP 404 Not Found. Otherwise, the code prints a message indicating that it started retrieving the altimeter's altitude, calls the `drone.hexacopter.get_altitude` method with a synchronous execution, and saves the result in the `altitude` variable. Then, the code writes a message indicating it finished retrieving the altitude and generates a `response` dictionary with the `'altitude'` key and its value. Finally, the code calls the `self.set_status` method with `status.HTTP_200_OK` as an argument to set the status code for the response to HTTP 200 OK and calls the `self.write` method with the `response` dictionary as an argument. Since `response` is a dictionary, Tornado automatically writes the chunk as JSON and sets the value of the `Content-Type` header to `application/json`.

The following table shows the method of our previously created HTTP handler classes that we want to be executed for each combination of HTTP verb and scope:

HTTP verb	Scope	Class and method
GET	Hexacopter	`HexacopterHandler.get`
PATCH	Hexacopter	`HexacopterHandler.patch`
GET	LED	`LedHandler.get`
PATCH	LED	`LedHandler.patch`
GET	Altimeter	`AltimeterHandler.get`

If the request results in the invocation of an HTTP handler class with an unsupported HTTP method, Tornado will return a response with the HTTP `405 Method Not Allowed` status code.

Mapping URL patterns to request handlers

We must map URL patterns to our previously coded subclasses of
`tornado.web.RequestHandler`. The following lines create the main entry point for the
application, initialize it with the URL patterns for the API, and starts listening for requests.
Open the previously created `api.py` file and add the following lines. The code file for the
sample is included in the `restful_python_chapter_09_01` folder:

```
application = web.Application([
    (r"/hexacopters/([0-9]+)", HexacopterHandler),
    (r"/leds/([0-9]+)", LedHandler),
    (r"/altimeters/([0-9]+)", AltimeterHandler),
], debug=True)


if __name__ == "__main__":
    port = 8888
    print("Listening at port {0}".format(port))
    application.listen(port)
    ioloop.IOLoop.instance().start()
```

The preceding code creates an instance of `tornado.web.Application` named
`application` with the collection of request handlers that make up the Web application.
The code passes a list of tuples to the `Application` constructor. The list is composed of a
regular expression (`regexp`) and a `tornado.web.RequestHandler` subclass
(`request_class`). In addition, the code sets the `debug` argument to `True` to enable
debugging.

The `main` method calls the `application.listen` method to build an HTTP server for the
application with the defined rules on the specified port. In this case, the code specifies `8888`
as the port, saved in the `port` variable, which is the default port for Tornado HTTP servers.
Then, the call to `tornado.ioloop.IOLoop.instance().start()` starts the server
created with the previous call to the `application.listen` method.

As with any other Web framework, you should never enable debugging in
a production environment.

Making HTTP requests to the Tornado API

Now, we can run the `api.py` script that launches Tornados's development server to compose and send HTTP requests to our unsecure and simple Web API. Execute the following command:

```
python api.py
```

The following lines show the output after we execute the previous command. The Tornado HTTP development server is listening at port `8888`:

```
Listening at port 8888
```

With the previous command, we will start the Tornado HTTP server and it will listen on every interface on port `8888`. Thus, if we want to make HTTP requests to our API from other computers or devices connected to our LAN, we don't need any additional configurations.

 If you decide to compose and send HTTP requests from other computers or devices connected to the LAN, remember that you have to use the development computer's assigned IP address instead of `localhost`. For example, if the computer's assigned IPv4 IP address is `192.168.1.103`, instead of `localhost:8888`, you should use `192.168.1.103:8888`. Of course, you can also use the host name instead of the IP address. The previously explained configurations are very important because mobile devices might be the consumers of our RESTful APIs and we will always want to test the apps that make use of our APIs in our development environments.

The Tornado HTTP server is running on localhost (`127.0.0.1`), listening on port `8888`, and waiting for our HTTP requests. Now, we will compose and send HTTP requests locally in our development computer or from other computer or devices connected to our LAN.

Working with command-line tools – curl and httpie

We will start composing and sending HTTP requests with the command-line tools we have introduced in `Chapter 1`, *Developing RESTful APIs with Django*, curl and HTTPie. In case you haven't installed HTTPie, make sure you activate the virtual environment and then run the following command in the terminal or Command Prompt to install the HTTPie package:

```
pip install --upgrade httpie
```

In case you don't remember how to activate the virtual environment that we created for this example, read the following section in this chapter—*Setting up the virtual environment with Django REST Framework.*

Open a Cygwin terminal in Windows or a Terminal in macOS or Linux and run the following command. We will compose and send an HTTP request to turn on the hexacopter and set its motor speed to 100 RPMs:

```
http PATCH :8888/hexacopters/1 motor_speed=100
```

The following is the equivalent curl command. It is very important to use the -H "Content-Type: application/json" option to indicate curl to send the data specified after the -d option as application/json instead of the default application/x-www-form-urlencoded:

```
curl -iX PATCH -H "Content-Type: application/json" -d
'{"motor_speed":100}'
    :8888/hexacopters/1
```

The preceding commands will compose and send the following HTTP request, PATCH http://localhost:8888/hexacopters/1, with the following JSON key-value pair:

```
{
    "motor_speed": 100
}
```

The request specifies /hexacopters/1, and therefore, Tornado will iterate over the list of tuples with regular expressions and request classes and it will match '/hexacopters/([0-9]+)'. Tornado will create an instance of the HexacopterHandler class and run the HexacopterHandler.patch method with 1 as the value for the id argument. As the HTTP verb for the request is PATCH, Tornado calls the patch method. If the hexacopter's speed is successfully set, the method returns an HTTP 200 OK status code and the key-value pairs with the speed and status for the recently updated hexacopter serialized to JSON in the response body. The following lines show an example response for the HTTP request:

```
HTTP/1.1 200 OK
Content-Length: 33
Content-Type: application/json; charset=UTF-8
Date: Thu, 08 Sep 2016 02:02:27 GMT
Server: TornadoServer/4.4.1
{
```

```
    "speed": 100,
    "turned_on": true
}
```

We will compose and send an HTTP request to retrieve the status and the motor speed for the hexacopter. Go back to the Cygwin terminal in Windows or the Terminal in macOS or Linux, and run the following command:

```
http :8888/hexacopters/1
```

The following is the equivalent `curl` command:

```
curl -iX GET -H :8888/hexacopters/1
```

The preceding commands will compose and send the following HTTP request: GET `http://localhost:8888/hexacopters/1`. The request specifies `/hexacopters/1`, and therefore, it will match `'/hexacopters/([0-9]+)'` and run the `HexacopterHandler.get` method with 1 as the value for the `id` argument. As the HTTP verb for the request is GET, Tornado calls the `get` method. The method retrieves the hexacopter's status and generates a JSON response with the key-value pairs.

The following lines show an example response for the HTTP request. The first lines show the HTTP response headers, including the status (200 OK) and the `Content-type` as (`application/json`). After the HTTP response headers, we can see the details of the hexacopter's status in the JSON response:

```
HTTP/1.1 200 OK
Content-Length: 33
Content-Type: application/json; charset=UTF-8
Date: Thu, 08 Sep 2016 02:26:00 GMT
Etag: "ff152383ca6ebe97e5a136166f433fbe7f9b4434"
Server: TornadoServer/4.4.1
{
    "speed": 100,
    "turned_on": true
}
```

After we run the three requests, we will see the following lines in the window that is running the Tornado HTTP server. The output shows the results of executing the print statements that describe when the code started setting or retrieving information and when it finished:

```
I've started setting the hexacopter's motor speed
I've finished setting the hexacopter's motor speed
I've started retrieving hexacopter's status
I've finished retrieving hexacopter's status
```

The different methods we coded in the request handler classes end up calling `time.sleep` to simulate it takes some time for the operations with the hexacopter. In this case, our code is running with a synchronous execution, and therefore, each time we compose and send a request, the Tornado server is blocked until the operation with the hexacopter finishes and the method sends the response. We will create a new version of this API that will use asynchronous execution later and we will understand the advantages of Tornado's non-blocking features. However, first, we will understand how the synchronous version of the API works.

The following image shows two Terminal windows side-by-side on macOS. The Terminal window on the left-hand side is running the Tornado HTTP server and displays the messages printed in the methods that process the HTTP requests. The Terminal window on the right-hand side is running `http` commands to generate the HTTP requests. It is a good idea to use a similar configuration to check the output while we compose and send the HTTP requests:

Now, we will compose and send an HTTP request to retrieve a hexacopter that doesn't exist. Remember that we just have one hexacopter in our drone. Run the following command to try to retrieve the status for an hexacopter with an invalid id. We must make sure that the utilities display the headers as part of the response to see the returned status code:

```
http :8888/hexacopters/8
```

The following is the equivalent `curl` command:

```
curl -iX GET :8888/hexacopters/8
```

The previous commands will compose and send the following HTTP request: `GET` `http://localhost:8888/hexacopters/8`. The request is the same as the previous one we have analyzed, with a different number for the `id` parameter. The server will run the `HexacopterHandler.get` method with 8 as the value for the `id` argument. The `id` is not equal to 1, and therefore, the code will return an HTTP `404 Not Found` status code. The following lines show an example header response for the HTTP request:

```
HTTP/1.1 404 Not Found
Content-Length: 0
Content-Type: text/html; charset=UTF-8
Date: Thu, 08 Sep 2016 04:31:53 GMT
Server: TornadoServer/4.4.1
```

Working with GUI tools – Postman and others

So far, we have been working with two Terminal-based or command-line tools to compose and send HTTP requests to our Tornado HTTP server-cURL and HTTPie. Now, we will work with one of the GUI tools we used when composing and sending HTTP requests to the Django development server and the Flask development server: Postman.

Now, we will use the **Builder** tab in Postman to easily compose and send HTTP requests to `localhost:8888` and test the RESTful API with this GUI tool. Remember that Postman doesn't support curl-like shorthands for localhost, and therefore, we cannot use the same shorthands we have been using when composing requests with curl and HTTPie.

Select **GET** in the drop-down menu at the left-hand side of the **Enter request URL** textbox and enter `localhost:8888/leds/1` in this textbox at the right-hand side of the dropdown. Now, click on **Send** and Postman will display the status (`200 OK`), the time it took for the request to be processed and the response body with all the games formatted as JSON with syntax highlighting (**Pretty** view).

The following screenshot shows the JSON response body in Postman for the HTTP GET request:

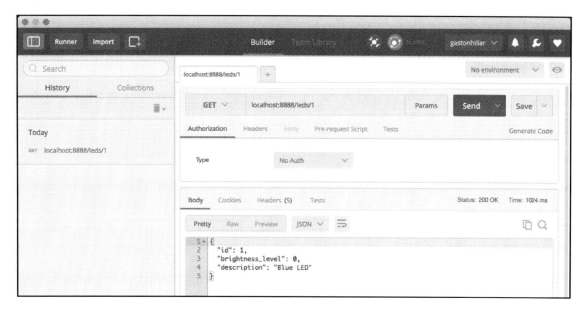

Click on **Headers** on the right-hand side of **Body** and **Cookies** to read the response headers. The following screenshot shows the layout for the response headers that Postman displays for the previous response. Note that Postman displays the **Status** at the right-hand side of the response and doesn't include it as the first line of the Headers, as it happened when we worked with both the cURL and HTTPie utilities:

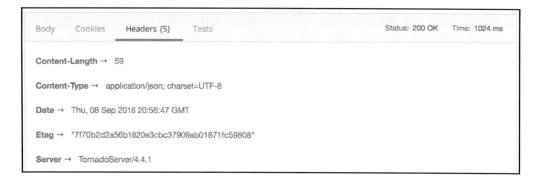

Now, we will use the **Builder** tab in Postman to compose and send an HTTP request to create a new message, specifically, a PATCH request. Follow the next steps:

1. Select **PATCH** from the drop-down menu on the left-hand side of the **Enter request URL** textbox and enter `localhost:8888/leds/1` in this textbox at the right-hand side of the dropdown.
2. Click on **Body** on the right-hand side of **Authorization** and **Headers**, within the panel that composes the request.
3. Activate the **raw** radio button and select `JSON (application/json)` in the dropdown on the right-hand side of the **binary** radio button. Postman will automatically add a `Content-type = application/json` header, and therefore, you will notice the **Headers** tab will be renamed to **Headers (1)**, indicating us that there is one key-value pair specified for the request headers.
4. Enter the following lines in the textbox below the radio buttons, within the **Body** tab:

```
{
    "brightness_level": 128
}
```

The following screenshot shows the request body in Postman:

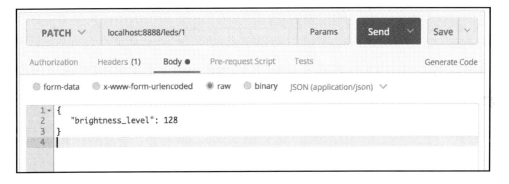

We followed the necessary steps to create an HTTP PATCH request with a JSON body that specifies the necessary key-value pairs to create a new game. Click on **Send** and Postman will display the Status (200 OK), the time it took for the request to be processed, and the response body with the recently added game formatted as JSON with syntax highlighting (**Pretty** view). The following screenshot shows the JSON response body in Postman for the HTTP POST request.

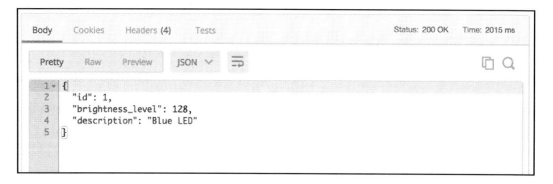

The Tornado HTTP server is listening on every interface on port 8888, and therefore, we can also use apps that can compose and send HTTP requests from mobile devices to work with the RESTful API. For example, we can work with the previously introduced iCurlHTTP app on iOS devices such as iPad Pro and iPhone. In Android devices, we can work with the previously introduced HTTP Request App.

The following screenshot shows the results of composing and sending the following HTTP request with the iCurlHTTP app—GET http://192.168.2.3:8888/altimeters/1. Remember that you have to perform the previously explained configurations in your LAN and router to be able to access the Flask development server from other devices connected to your LAN. In this case, the IP assigned to the computer running the Tornado HTTP server is 192.168.2.3, and therefore, you must replace this IP with the IP assigned to your development computer:

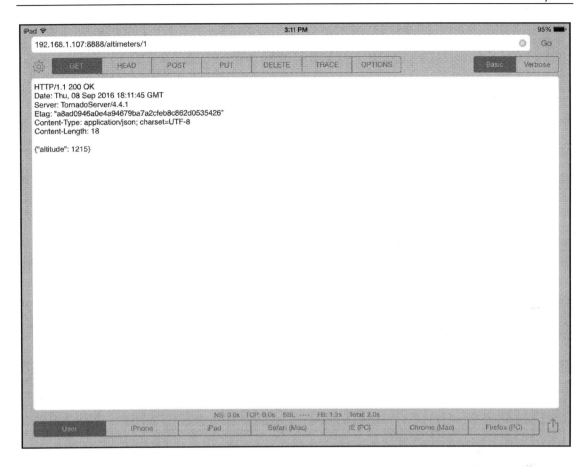

Test your knowledge

1. The main building blocks for a RESTful API in Tornado are subclasses of which the following classes:

   1. `tornado.web.GenericHandler`

   2. `tornado.web.RequestHandler`

   3. `tornado.web.IncomingHTTPRequestHandler`

2. If we just want to support the GET and PATCH methods, we can override the SUPPORTED_METHODS class variable with which of the following values:
    1. ("GET", "PATCH")
    2. {0: "GET", 1: "PATCH"}
    3. {"GET": True, "PATCH": True, "POST": False, "PUT": False}

3. The list of tuples for a the tornado.Web.Application constructor is composed of:
    1. A regular expression (regexp) and a tornado.web.RequestHandler subclass (request_class).
    2. A regular expression (regexp) and a tornado.web.GenericHandler subclass (request_class).
    3. A regular expression (regexp) and a tornado.web.IncomingHTTPRequestHandler subclass (request_class).

4. When we call the self.write method with a dictionary as an argument in a request handler, Tornado:
    1. Automatically writes the chunk as JSON but we have to manually set the value of the Content-Type header to application/json.
    2. Requires us to use the json.dumps method and set the value of the Content-Type header to application/json.
    3. Automatically writes the chunk as JSON and sets the value of the Content-Type header to application/json.

5. A calls to the tornado.escape.json_decode method with self.request.body as an argument in a request handler:
    1. Generates Python objects for the JSON string of the request body and returns the generated tuple.
    2. Generates Python objects for the JSON string of the request body and returns the generated dictionary.
    3. Generates Python objects for the JSON string of the request body and returns the generated list.

Summary

In this chapter, we designed a RESTful API to interact with slow sensors and actuators. We defined the requirements for our API, understood the tasks performed by each HTTP method, and set up a virtual environment with Tornado.

We created the classes that represent a drone and wrote code to simulate slow I/O operations that are called for each HTTP request method, wrote classes that represent request handlers and process the different HTTP requests, and configured the URL patterns to route URLs to request handlers and their methods.

Finally, we started Tornado development server, used command-line tools to compose and send HTTP requests to our RESTful API, and analyzed how each HTTP requests was processed in our code. We also worked with GUI tools to compose and send HTTP requests.

Now that we understand the basics of Tornado to create RESTful APIs, we will take advantage of the non-blocking features combined with asynchronous operations in Tornado in a new version for the API, which is what we are going to discuss in the next chapter.

10
Working with Asynchronous Code, Testing, and Deploying an API with Tornado

In this chapter, we will take advantage of the non-blocking features combined with asynchronous operations in Tornado in a new version for the API we built in the previous chapter. We will configure, write, and execute unit tests and learn a few things related to deployment. We will cover the following topics:

- Understanding synchronous and asynchronous execution
- Working with asynchronous code
- Refactoring code to take advantage of asynchronous decorators
- Mapping URL patterns to asynchronous and non-blocking request handlers
- Making HTTP requests to the Tornado non-blocking API
- Setting up unit tests
- Writing a first round of unit tests
- Running unit tests with `nose2` and checking testing coverage
- Improving testing coverage

Understanding synchronous and asynchronous execution

In our current version of the API, each HTTP request is blocking, as happened with Django and Flask. Thus, whenever the Tornado HTTP server receives an HTTP request, it doesn't start working on any other HTTP request in the incoming queue until the server sends the response for the first HTTP request it received. The methods we coded in the request handlers are working with a synchronous execution and they don't take advantage of the non-blocking features included in Tornado when combined with asynchronous executions.

In order to set the brightness level for both the blue and white LEDs, we have to make two HTTP PATCH requests. We will make them to understand how our current version of the API processes two incoming requests.

Open two Cygwin terminals in Windows or two Terminals in macOS or Linux, and write the following command in the first one. We will compose and send an HTTP request to set the brightness level for the blue LED to 255. Write the line in the first window, but don't press *Enter* yet, as we will try to launch two commands at almost the same time in two windows:

```
http PATCH :8888/leds/1 brightness_level=255
```

The following is the equivalent curl command:

```
curl -iX PATCH -H "Content-Type: application/json" -d
'{"brightness_level":255}' :8888/leds/1
```

Now, go to the second window and write the following command. We will compose and send an HTTP request to set the brightness level for the white LED to 255. Write the line in the second window, but don't press *Enter* yet, as we will try to launch two commands at almost the same time in two windows:

```
http PATCH :8888/leds/2 brightness_level=255
```

The following is the equivalent curl command:

```
curl -iX PATCH -H "Content-Type: application/json" -d
'{"brightness_level":255}' :8888/leds/2
```

Now, go to the first window, press *Enter*. Then, go to the second window and quickly press *Enter*. You will see the following line in the window that is running the Tornado HTTP server:

```
I've started setting the Blue LED's brightness level
```

Then, you will see the following lines that show the results of executing the print statements that describe when the code finished and then started setting the brightness level for the LEDs:

```
I've finished setting the Blue LED's brightness level
I've started setting the White LED's brightness level
I've finished setting the White LED's brightness level
```

It was necessary to wait for the request that changed the brightness level for the blue LED to finish before the server could process the HTTP that changes the brightness level for the white LED. The following screenshot shows three windows on Windows. The window on the left-hand side is running the Tornado HTTP server and displays the messages printed in the methods that process the HTTP requests. The window at the upper-right corner is running the `http` command to generate the HTTP request that changes the brightness level for the blue LED. The window at the lower-right corner is running the `http` command to generate the HTTP request that changes the brightness level for the white LED. It is a good idea to use a similar configuration to check the output while we compose and send the HTTP requests and how the synchronous execution is working on the current version of the API:

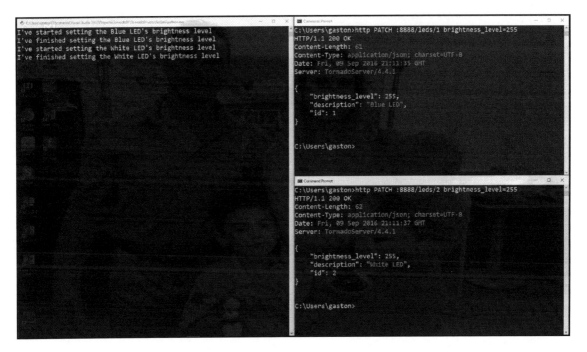

Remember that the different methods we coded in the request handler classes end up calling `time.sleep` to simulate it takes some time for the operations to complete their execution.

As each operation takes some time and blocks the possibility to process other incoming HTTP requests, we will create a new version of this API that will use asynchronous execution, and we will understand the advantages of Tornado's non-blocking features. This way, it will be possible to change the brightness level for the white LED while the other request is to change the brightness level for the blue LED. Tornado will be able to start processing requests while the I/O operations with the drone take some time to complete.

Refactoring code to take advantage of asynchronous decorators

It is extremely difficult to read and understand code split into different methods, such as the asynchronous code that requires working with callbacks that are executed once the asynchronous execution finishes. Luckily, Tornado provides a generator-based interface that enables us to write asynchronous code in request handlers in a single generator. We can avoid splitting our methods into multiple methods with callbacks by using the `tornado.gen` generator-based interface that Tornado provides to make it easier to work in an asynchronous environment.

The recommended way to write asynchronous code in Tornado is to use coroutines. Thus, we will refactor our existing code to use the `@tornado.gen.coroutine` decorator for asynchronous generators in the required methods that process the different HTTP requests in the subclasses of `tornado.web.RequestHandler`.

Instead of working with a chain of callbacks, coroutines use the Python `yield` keyword to suspend and resume execution. By using coroutines, our code is going to be as simple to understand and maintain as if we were writing synchronous code.

We will use an instance of the `concurrent.futures.ThreadPoolExecutor` class that provides us with a high-level interface for asynchronously executing callables. The asynchronous execution will be performed with threads. We will also use the `@tornado.concurrent.run_on_executor` decorator to run a synchronous method asynchronously on an executor. In this case, the methods provided by the different components of our drone to get and set data have a synchronous execution. We want them to run with an asynchronous execution.

Create a new `async_api.py` file. The following lines show all the necessary imports for the classes that we will create and the code that creates an instance of the `concurrent.futures.ThreadPoolExecutor` class named `thread_pool`. We will use this instance in the different methods that we will refactor to make asynchronous calls. The code file for the sample is included in the `restful_python_chapter_10_01` folder:

```
import status
from datetime import date
from tornado import web, escape, ioloop, httpclient, gen
from concurrent.futures import ThreadPoolExecutor
from tornado.concurrent import run_on_executor
from drone import Altimeter, Drone, Hexacopter, LightEmittingDiode


thread_pool = ThreadPoolExecutor()
drone = Drone()
```

Now, we will create an `AsyncHexacopterHandler` class that we will use to handle requests for the hexacopter resource with an asynchronous execution. The lines that are new or changed compared with the synchronous version of this handler named `HexacopterHandler` are highlighted. Open the previously created `async_pi.py` file and add the following lines. The code file for the sample is included in the `restful_python_chapter_10_01` folder:

```
class AsyncHexacopterHandler(web.RequestHandler):
    SUPPORTED_METHODS = ("GET", "PATCH")
    HEXACOPTER_ID = 1
    _thread_pool = thread_pool
    @gen.coroutine
    def get(self, id):
        if int(id) is not self.__class__.HEXACOPTER_ID:
            self.set_status(status.HTTP_404_NOT_FOUND)
            self.finish()
            return
        print("I've started retrieving hexacopter's status")
        hexacopter_status = yield self.retrieve_hexacopter_status()
        print("I've finished retrieving hexacopter's status")
        response = {
            'speed': hexacopter_status.motor_speed,
            'turned_on': hexacopter_status.turned_on,
            }
        self.set_status(status.HTTP_200_OK)
        self.write(response)
        self.finish()

    @run_on_executor(executor="_thread_pool")
```

```
    def retrieve_hexacopter_status(self):
        return drone.hexacopter.get_hexacopter_status()
    @gen.coroutine
    def patch(self, id):
        if int(id) is not self.__class__.HEXACOPTER_ID:
            self.set_status(status.HTTP_404_NOT_FOUND)
            self.finish()
            return
        request_data = escape.json_decode(self.request.body)
        if ('motor_speed' not in request_data.keys()) or \
            (request_data['motor_speed'] is None):
            self.set_status(status.HTTP_400_BAD_REQUEST)
            self.finish()
            return
        try:
            motor_speed = int(request_data['motor_speed'])
            print("I've started setting the hexacopter's motor speed")
            hexacopter_status = yield
            self.set_hexacopter_motor_speed(motor_speed)
            print("I've finished setting the hexacopter's motor speed")
            response = {
                'speed': hexacopter_status.motor_speed,
                'turned_on': hexacopter_status.turned_on,
                }
            self.set_status(status.HTTP_200_OK)
            self.write(response)
            self.finish()
        except ValueError as e:
            print("I've failed setting the hexacopter's motor speed")
            self.set_status(status.HTTP_400_BAD_REQUEST)
            response = {
                'error': e.args[0]
                }
            self.write(response)
            self.finish()
    @run_on_executor(executor="_thread_pool")
    def set_hexacopter_motor_speed(self, motor_speed):
        return drone.hexacopter.set_motor_speed(motor_speed)
```

The AsyncHexacopterHandler class declares a _thread_pool class attribute that saves a reference to the previously created concurrent.futures.ThreadPoolExecutor instance. The class declares two methods with the @run_on_executor(executor="_thread_pool") decorator that makes the synchronous method run asynchronously with the concurrent.futures.ThreadPoolExecutor instance whose reference is saved in the _thread_pool class attribute. The following are the two methods:

- `retrieve_hexacopter_status`: This method returns the results of calling the `drone.hexacopter.get_hexacopter_status` method.
- `set_hexacopter_motor_speed`: This method receives the `motor_speed` argument and returns the results of calling the `drone.hexacopter.set_motor_speed` method with the received `motor_speed` as an argument.

We added the `@gen.coroutine` decorator to both the `get` and `patch` methods. We added a call to `self.finish` whenever we wanted to finish the HTTP request. It is our responsibility to call this method to finish the response and end the HTTP request when we use the `@gen.coroutine` decorator.

The `get` method uses the following line to retrieve the hexacopter status with a non-blocking and asynchronous execution:

```
hexacopter_status = yield self.retrieve_hexacopter_status()
```

The code uses the `yield` keyword to retrieve `HexacopterStatus` from the `Future` returned by `self.retrieve_hexacopter_status` that runs with an asynchronous execution. A `Future` encapsulates the asynchronous execution of a callable. In this case, `Future` encapsulates the asynchronous execution of the `self.retrieve_hexacopter_status` method. The next lines didn't require changes, and we only had to add a call to `self.finish` as the last line after we write the response.

The `get` method uses the following line to retrieve the hexacopter status with a non-blocking and asynchronous execution:

```
hexacopter_status = yield self.retrieve_hexacopter_status()
```

The code uses the `yield` keyword to retrieve the `HexacopterStatus` from the `Future` returned by the `self.retrieve_hexacopter_status` that runs with an asynchronous execution.

The `patch` method uses the following line to set the hexacopter's motor speed with a non-blocking and asynchronous execution:

```
hexacopter_status = yield self.set_hexacopter_motor_speed(motor_speed)
```

The code uses the `yield` keyword to retrieve the `HexacopterStatus` from the `Future` returned by the `self.set_hexacopter_motor_speed` that runs with an asynchronous execution. The next lines didn't require changes, and we only had to add a call to `self.finish` as the last line after we write the response.

Now, we will create an `AsyncLedHandler` class that we will use to represent the LED resources and process requests with an asynchronous execution. The lines that are new or changed compared with the synchronous version of this handler named `LedHandler` are highlighted. Open the previously created `async_pi.py` file and add the following lines. The code file for the sample is included in the `restful_python_chapter_10_01` folder:

```python
class AsyncLedHandler(web.RequestHandler):
    SUPPORTED_METHODS = ("GET", "PATCH")
    _thread_pool = thread_pool

    @gen.coroutine
    def get(self, id):
        int_id = int(id)
        if int_id not in drone.leds.keys():
            self.set_status(status.HTTP_404_NOT_FOUND)
            self.finish()
            return
        led = drone.leds[int_id]
        print("I've started retrieving {0}'s
status".format(led.description))
        brightness_level = yield
        self.retrieve_led_brightness_level(led)
        print("I've finished retrieving {0}'s
status".format(led.description))
        response = {
            'id': led.identifier,
            'description': led.description,
            'brightness_level': brightness_level
            }
        self.set_status(status.HTTP_200_OK)
        self.write(response)
        self.finish()

    @run_on_executor(executor="_thread_pool")
    def retrieve_led_brightness_level(self, led):
        return led.get_brightness_level()
    @gen.coroutine
    def patch(self, id):
        int_id = int(id)
        if int_id not in drone.leds.keys():
            self.set_status(status.HTTP_404_NOT_FOUND)
            self.finish()
            return
        led = drone.leds[int_id]
        request_data = escape.json_decode(self.request.body)
        if ('brightness_level' not in request_data.keys()) or \
            (request_data['brightness_level'] is None):
```

```
                    self.set_status(status.HTTP_400_BAD_REQUEST)
                    self.finish()
                    return
             try:
                    brightness_level = int(request_data['brightness_level'])
                    print("I've started setting the {0}'s brightness
                    level".format(led.description))
                    yield self.set_led_brightness_level(led, brightness_level)
                    print("I've finished setting the {0}'s brightness
                    level".format(led.description))
                    response = {
                        'id': led.identifier,
                        'description': led.description,
                        'brightness_level': brightness_level
                        }
                    self.set_status(status.HTTP_200_OK)
                    self.write(response)
                    self.finish()
             except ValueError as e:
                    print("I've failed setting the {0}'s brightness
     level".format(led.description))
                    self.set_status(status.HTTP_400_BAD_REQUEST)
                    response = {
                        'error': e.args[0]
                        }
                    self.write(response)
                    self.finish()
        @run_on_executor(executor="_thread_pool")
        def set_led_brightness_level(self, led, brightness_level):
             return led.set_brightness_level(brightness_level)
```

The AsyncLedHandler class declares a _thread_pool class attribute that saves a reference to the previously created concurrent.futures.ThreadPoolExecutor instance. The class declares two methods with the @run_on_executor(executor="_thread_pool") decorator that makes the synchronous method run asynchronously with the concurrent.futures.ThreadPoolExecutor instance whose reference is saved in the _thread_pool class attribute. The following are the two methods:

- retrieve_led_brightness_level: This method receives a LightEmittingDiode instance in the led argument and returns the results of calling the led.get_brightness_level method.

- set_led_brightness_level: This method receives a LightEmittingDiode instance in the led argument and the brightness_level argument. The code returns the results of calling the led.set_brightness_level method with the received brightness_level as an argument.

We added the @gen.coroutine decorator to both the get and patch methods. In addition, we added a call to self.finish whenever we wanted to finish the HTTP request.

The get method uses the following line to retrieve the LED's brightness level with a non-blocking and asynchronous execution:

```
brightness_level = yield self.retrieve_led_brightness_level(led)
```

The code uses the yield keyword to retrieve the int from Future returned by self.retrieve_led_brightness_level that runs with an asynchronous execution. The next lines didn't require changes, and we only had to add a call to self.finish as the last line after we write the response.

The patch method uses the following line to retrieve the hexacopter status with a non-blocking and asynchronous execution:

```
hexacopter_status = yield self.retrieve_hexacopter_status()
```

The code uses the yield keyword to retrieve HexacopterStatus from Future returned by self.retrieve_hexacopter_status that runs with an asynchronous execution.

The patch method uses the following line to set the LED's brightness level with a non-blocking and asynchronous execution:

```
yield self.set_led_brightness_level(led, brightness_level)
```

The code uses the yield keyword to call self.set_led_brightness_level with an asynchronous execution. The next lines didn't require changes, and we only had to add a call to self.finish as the last line after we write the response.

Now, we will create an AsyncAltimeterHandler class that we will use to represent the altimeter resource and process the get request with an asynchronous execution. The lines that are new or changed compared with the synchronous version of this handler named AltimeterHandler, are highlighted. Open the previously created async_pi.py file and add the following lines. The code file for the sample is included in the restful_python_chapter_10_01 folder.

```
class AsyncAltimeterHandler(web.RequestHandler):
    SUPPORTED_METHODS = ("GET")
    ALTIMETER_ID = 1
    _thread_pool = thread_pool

    @gen.coroutine
    def get(self, id):
        if int(id) is not self.__class__.ALTIMETER_ID:
```

```
        self.set_status(status.HTTP_404_NOT_FOUND)
        self.finish()
        return
    print("I've started retrieving the altitude")
    altitude = yield self.retrieve_altitude()
    print("I've finished retrieving the altitude")
    response = {
        'altitude': altitude
        }
    self.set_status(status.HTTP_200_OK)
    self.write(response)
    self.finish()


@run_on_executor(executor="_thread_pool")
def retrieve_altitude(self):
    return drone.altimeter.get_altitude()
```

The `AsyncAltimeterHandler` class declares a `_thread_pool` class attribute that saves a reference to the previously created `concurrent.futures.ThreadPoolExecutor` instance. The class declares the `retrieve_altitude` method with the `@run_on_executor(executor="_thread_pool")` decorator that makes the synchronous method run asynchronously with the `concurrent.futures.ThreadPoolExecutor` instance whose reference is saved in the `_thread_pool` class attribute. The `retrieve_altitude` method returns the results of calling the `drone.altimeter.get_altitude` method.

We added the `@gen.coroutine` decorator to the `get` method. In addition, we added a call to `self.finish` whenever we wanted to finish the HTTP request.

The `get` method uses the following line to retrieve the altimeter's altitude value with a non-blocking and asynchronous execution:

```
altitude = yield self.retrieve_altitude()
```

The code uses the `yield` keyword to retrieve the `int` from `Future` returned by `self.retrieve_altitude` that runs with an asynchronous execution. The next lines didn't require changes, and we only had to add a call to `self.finish` as the last line after we write the response.

Mapping URL patterns to asynchronous request handlers

We must map URL patterns to our previously coded subclasses of
`tornado.web.RequestHandler` that provide us asynchronous methods for our request
handlers. The following lines create the main entry point for the application, initialize it
with the URL patterns for the API, and start listening for requests. Open the previously
created `async_api.py` file and add the following lines. The code file for the sample is
included in the `restful_python_chapter_10_01` folder:

```
application = web.Application([
    (r"/hexacopters/([0-9]+)", AsyncHexacopterHandler),
    (r"/leds/([0-9]+)", AsyncLedHandler),
    (r"/altimeters/([0-9]+)", AsyncAltimeterHandler),
],debug=True)


if __name__ == "__main__":
    port = 8888
    print("Listening at port {0}".format(port))
    application.listen(port)
    ioloop.IOLoop.instance().start()
```

The code creates an instance of `tornado.web.Application` named `application` with
the collection of request handlers that make up the Web application. We just changed the
name of the handlers with the new names that have the `Async` prefix.

> As with any other Web framework, you should never enable debugging in
> a production environment.

Making HTTP requests to the Tornado non-blocking API

Now, we can run the `async_api.py` script that launches Tornados's development server to
compose and send HTTP requests to our new version of the Web API that uses the non-
blocking features of Tornado combined with asynchronous execution. Execute the
following command:

```
python async_api.py
```

The following lines show the output after we execute the previous command. The Tornado HTTP development server is listening at port 8888:

```
Listening at port 8888
```

With the previous command, we will start the Tornado HTTP server and it will listen on every interface on port 8888. Thus, if we want to make HTTP requests to our API from other computers or devices connected to our LAN, we don't need any additional configurations.

In our new version of the API, each HTTP request is non-blocking. Thus, whenever the Tornado HTTP server receives an HTTP request and makes an asynchronous call, it is able to start working on any other HTTP request in the incoming queue before the server sends the response for the first HTTP request it received. The methods we coded in the request handlers are working with an asynchronous execution and they take advantage of the non-blocking features included in Tornado, combined with asynchronous executions.

In order to set the brightness level for both the blue and white LEDs, we have to make two HTTP PATCH requests. We will make them to understand how our new version of the API processes two incoming requests.

Open two Cygwin terminals in Windows, or two Terminals in macOS or Linux, and write the following command in the first one. We will compose and send an HTTP request to set the brightness level for the blue LED to 255. Write the line in the first window but don't press *Enter* yet, as we will try to launch two commands at almost the same time in two windows:

```
http PATCH :8888/leds/1 brightness_level=255
```

The following is the equivalent curl command:

```
curl -iX PATCH -H "Content-Type: application/json" -d
'{"brightness_level":255}' :8888/leds/1
```

Now, go to the second window and write the following command. We will compose and send an HTTP request to set the brightness level for the white LED to 255. Write the line in the second window but don't press *Enter* yet, as we will try to launch two commands at almost the same time in two windows:

```
http PATCH :8888/leds/2 brightness_level=255
```

The following is the equivalent curl command:

```
curl -iX PATCH -H "Content-Type: application/json" -d
'{"brightness_level":255}' :8888/leds/2
```

Now, go to the first window, press *Enter*. Then, go to the second window and quickly press *Enter*. You will see the following lines in the window that is running the Tornado HTTP server:

```
I've started setting the Blue LED's brightness level
I've started setting the White LED's brightness level
```

Then, you will see the following lines that show the results of executing the print statements that describe when the code finished setting the brightness level for the LEDs:

```
I've finished setting the Blue LED's brightness level
I've finished setting the White LED's brightness level
```

The server could start processing the request that changes the brightness level for the white LED before the request that changes the brightness level of the blue LED finishes its execution. The following screenshot shows three windows on Windows. The window on the left-hand side is running the Tornado HTTP server and displays the messages printed in the methods that process the HTTP requests. The window on the upper-right corner is running the `http` command to generate the HTTP request that changes the brightness level for the blue LED. The window at the lower-right corner is running the `http` command to generate the HTTP request that changes the brightness level for the white LED. It is a good idea to use a similar configuration to check the output while we compose and send the HTTP requests and check how the asynchronous execution is working on the new version of the API:

Each operation takes some time but doesn't block the possibility to process other incoming HTTP requests thanks to the changes we made to the API to take advantage of the asynchronous execution. This way, it is possible to change the brightness level for the white LED while the other request is to change the brightness level for the blue LED. Tornado is able to start processing requests while the I/O operations with the drone take some time to complete.

Setting up unit tests

We will use `nose2` to make it easier to discover and run unit tests. We will measure test coverage, and therefore, we will install the necessary package to allow us to run coverage with `nose2`. First, we will install the `nose2` and `cov-core` packages in our virtual environment. The `cov-core` package will allow us to measure test coverage with `nose2`.

Make sure you quit the Tornado's HTTP server. Remember that you just need to press *Ctrl +* *C* in the Terminal or command-prompt window in which it is running. We just need to run the following command to install the `nose2` package that will also install the `six` dependency:

```
pip install nose2
```

The last lines for the output will indicate that the nose2 package has been successfully installed:

```
Collecting nose2
Collecting six>=1.1 (from nose2)
  Downloading six-1.10.0-py2.py3-none-any.whl
Installing collected packages: six, nose2
Successfully installed nose2-0.6.5 six-1.10.0
```

We just need to run the following command to install the cov-core package that will also install the coverage dependency:

```
pip install cov-core
```

The last lines for the output will indicate that the django-nose package has been successfully installed:

```
Collecting cov-core
Collecting coverage>=3.6 (from cov-core)
Installing collected packages: coverage, cov-core
Successfully installed cov-core-1.15.0 coverage-4.2
```

Open the previously created async_api.py file and remove the lines that create the web.Application instance named application and the __main__ method. After you remove these lines, add the next lines. The code file for the sample is included in the restful_python_chapter_10_02 folder:

```python
class Application(web.Application):
    def __init__(self, **kwargs):
        handlers = [
            (r"/hexacopters/([0-9]+)", AsyncHexacopterHandler),
            (r"/leds/([0-9]+)", AsyncLedHandler),
            (r"/altimeters/([0-9]+)", AsyncAltimeterHandler),
        ]
        super(Application, self).__init__(handlers, **kwargs)


if __name__ == "__main__":
    application = Application()
    application.listen(8888)
    tornado_ioloop = ioloop.IOLoop.instance()
    ioloop.PeriodicCallback(lambda: None, 500, tornado_ioloop).start()
    tornado_ioloop.start()
```

The code declares an `Application` class, specifically, a subclass of `tornado.web.Application` that overrides the inherited constructor, that is, the `__init__` method. The constructor declares the `handlers` list that maps URL patterns to asynchronous request handlers and then calls the inherited constructor with the list as one of its arguments. We create the class to make it possible for the tests to use this class.

Then, the main method creates an instance of the Application class, registers a periodic callback that will be executed every 500 milliseconds by the `IOLoop` to make it possible to use *Ctrl + C* to stop the HTTP server, and finally calls the `start` method. The `async_api.py` script is going to continue working in the same way. The main difference is that we can reuse the `Application` class in our tests.

Finally, create a new text file named `.coveragerc` within the virtual environment's root folder with the following content. The code file for the sample is included in the `restful_python_chapter_10_02` folder:

```
[run]
include = async_api.py, drone.py
```

This way, the `coverage` utility will only consider the code in the `async_api.py` and `drone.py` files when providing us with the test coverage report. We will have a more accurate test coverage report with this settings file.

 In this case, we won't be using configuration files for each environment. However, in more complex applications, you will definitely want to use configuration files.

Writing a first round of unit tests

Now, we will write a first round of unit tests. Specifically, we will write unit tests related to the LED resources. Create a new `tests` subfolder within the virtual environment's root folder. Then, create a new `test_hexacopter.py` file within the new `tests` subfolder. Add the following lines that declare many `import` statements and the `TextHexacopter` class. The code file for the sample is included in the `restful_python_chapter_10_02` folder:

```
import unittest
import status
import json
from tornado import ioloop, escape
from tornado.testing import AsyncHTTPTestCase, gen_test, gen
from async_api import Application
```

```
class TestHexacopter(AsyncHTTPTestCase):
    def get_app(self):
        self.app = Application(debug=False)
        return self.app

    def test_set_and_get_led_brightness_level(self):
        """
        Ensure we can set and get the brightness levels for both LEDs
        """
        patch_args_led_1 = {'brightness_level': 128}
        patch_args_led_2 = {'brightness_level': 250}
        patch_response_led_1 = self.fetch(
            '/leds/1',
            method='PATCH',
            body=json.dumps(patch_args_led_1))
        patch_response_led_2 = self.fetch(
            '/leds/2',
            method='PATCH',
            body=json.dumps(patch_args_led_2))
        self.assertEqual(patch_response_led_1.code, status.HTTP_200_OK)
        self.assertEqual(patch_response_led_2.code, status.HTTP_200_OK)
        get_response_led_1 = self.fetch(
            '/leds/1',
            method='GET')
        get_response_led_2 = self.fetch(
            '/leds/2',
            method='GET')
        self.assertEqual(get_response_led_1.code, status.HTTP_200_OK)
        self.assertEqual(get_response_led_2.code, status.HTTP_200_OK)
        get_response_led_1_data = \
escape.json_decode(get_response_led_1.body)
        get_response_led_2_data = \
escape.json_decode(get_response_led_2.body)
        self.assertTrue('brightness_level' in
get_response_led_1_data.keys())
        self.assertTrue('brightness_level' in
get_response_led_2_data.keys())
        self.assertEqual(get_response_led_1_data['brightness_level'],
                         patch_args_led_1['brightness_level'])
        self.assertEqual(get_response_led_2_data['brightness_level'],
                         patch_args_led_2['brightness_level'])
```

The `TestHexacopter` class is a subclass of `tornado.testing.AsyncHTTPTestCase`, that is, a test case that starts up a Tornado HTTP Server. The class overrides the `get_app` method that returns the `tornado.web.Application` instance that we want to test. In this case, we return an instance of the `Application` class declared in the `async_api` module, with the `debug` argument set to `False`.

The `test_set_and_get_led_brightness_level` method tests whether we can set and get the brightness levels for both the white and blue LED. The code composes and sends two HTTP `PATCH` methods to set new brightness level values for the LEDs whose IDs are equal to 1 and 2. The code sets a different brightness level for each LED.

The code calls the self.fetch method to compose and send the HTTP `PATCH` request and calls `json.dumps` with the dictionary to be sent to the body as an argument. Then, the code uses `self.fetch` again to compose and send two HTTP `GET` methods to retrieve the brightness level values for the LEDs whose brightness values have been modified. The code uses `tornado.escape.json_decode` to convert the bytes in the response body to a Python dictionary. The method uses `assertEqual` and `assertTrue` to check for the following expected results:

- The `status_code` for the two HTTP `PATCH` responses is HTTP 200 OK (`status.HTTP_200_OK`)
- The `status_code` for the two HTTP `GET` responses is HTTP 200 OK (`status.HTTP_200_OK`)
- The response body for the two HTTP `GET` responses include a key named `brigthness_level`
- The value for the `brightness_level` key in the HTTP `GET` responses are equal to the brightness level set to each LED

Running unit tests with nose2 and checking testing coverage

Now, run the following command to create all the necessary tables in our test database and use the nose2 test running to execute all the tests we created. The test runner will execute all the methods for our `TestHexacopter` class that start with the `test_` prefix and will display the results. In this case, we just have one method that matches the criteria, but we will add more later.

Run the following command within the same virtual environment we have been using. We will use the -v option to instruct nose2 to print test case names and statuses. The --with-coverage option turns on test coverage reporting generation:

```
nose2 -v --with-coverage
```

The following lines show the sample output. Notice that the numbers shown in the report might have small differences if our code includes additional lines or comments:

```
test_set_and_get_led_brightness_level (test_hexacopter.TestHexacopter)
...
I've started setting the Blue LED's brightness level
I've finished setting the Blue LED's brightness level
I've started setting the White LED's brightness level
I've finished setting the White LED's brightness level
I've started retrieving Blue LED's status
I've finished retrieving Blue LED's status
I've started retrieving White LED's status
I've finished retrieving White LED's status
ok

----------------------------------------------------------------
Ran 1 test in 1.311s
OK
----------- coverage: platform win32, python 3.5.2-final-0 -----
Name               Stmts   Miss  Cover
-------------------------------------
async_api.py         129     69    47%
drone.py              57     18    68%
-------------------------------------
TOTAL                186     87    53%
```

By default, nose2 looks for modules whose names start with the test prefix. In this case, the only module that matches the criteria is the test_hexacopter module. In the modules that match the criteria, nose2 loads tests from all the subclasses of unittest.TestCase and the functions whose names start with the test prefix. The tornado.testing.AsyncHTTPTestCase includes unittest.TestCase as one of its superclasses in the class hierarchy.

The output provided details indicating that the test runner discovered and executed one test and it passed. The output displays the method name and the class name for each method in the TestHexacopter class that started with the test_ prefix and represented a test to be executed.

We definitely have a very low coverage for `async_api.py` and `drone.py` based on the measurements shown in the report. In fact, we just wrote one test related to LEDs, and therefore, it makes sense that the coverage has to be improved. We didn't create tests related to other hexacopter resources.

We can run the `coverage` command with the `-m` command-line option to display the line numbers of the missing statements in a new `Missing` column:

```
coverage report -m
```

The command will use the information from the last execution and will display the missing statements. The next lines show a sample output that corresponds to the previous execution of the unit tests. Notice that the numbers shown in the report might have small differences if our code includes additional lines or comments:

```
Name              Stmts   Miss  Cover   Missing
--------------------------------------------------
async_api.py        129     69    47%    137-150, 154, 158-187, 191,
202-204, 226-228, 233-235, 249-256, 270-282, 286, 311-315
drone.py             57     18    68%    11-12, 24, 27-34, 37, 40-41, 59,
61, 68-69
--------------------------------------------------
TOTAL               186     87    53%
```

Now, run the following command to get annotated HTML listings detailing missed lines:

```
coverage html
```

Open the `index.html` HTML file generated in the `htmlcov` folder with your Web browser. The following screenshot shows an example report that coverage generated in HTML format:

Coverage report: 53%	filter...		
Module ↓	*statements*	*missing*	*excluded*	*coverage*
async_api.py	129	69	0	47%
drone.py	57	18	0	68%
Total	**186**	**87**	**0**	**53%**

coverage.py v4.2, created at 2016-09-12 18:04

Click or tap on `drony.py` and the Web browser will render a Web page that displays the statements that were run, the missing ones, and the excluded ones, with different colors. We can click or tap on the **run**, **missing,** and **excluded** buttons to show or hide the background color that represents the status for each line of code. By default, the missing lines of code will be displayed with a pink background. Thus, we must write unit tests that target these lines of code to improve our test coverage.

```
 8
 9  class HexacopterStatus:
10      def __init__(self, motor_speed, turned_on):
11          self.motor_speed = motor_speed
12          self.turned_on = turned_on
13
14
15  class Hexacopter:
16      MIN_SPEED = 0
17      MAX_SPEED = 1000
18
19      def __init__(self):
20          self.motor_speed = self.__class__.MIN_SPEED
21          self.turned_on = False
22
23      def get_motor_speed(self):
24          return self.motor_speed
25
26      def set_motor_speed(self, motor_speed):
27          if motor_speed < self.__class__.MIN_SPEED:
28              raise ValueError('The minimum speed is {0}'.format(self.__class__.MIN_SPEED))
29          if motor_speed > self.__class__.MAX_SPEED:
30              raise ValueError('The maximum speed is {0}'.format(self.__class__.MAX_SPEED))
31          self.motor_speed = motor_speed
32          self.turned_on = (self.motor_speed is not 0)
33          sleep(2)
34          return HexacopterStatus(self.get_motor_speed(), self.is_turned_on())
35
36      def is_turned_on(self):
37          return self.turned_on
38
39      def get_hexacopter_status(self):
40          sleep(3)
41          return HexacopterStatus(self.get_motor_speed(), self.is_turned_on())
42
43
44  class LightEmittingDiode:
```

Improving testing coverage

Now, we will write additional unit tests to improve the testing coverage. Specifically, we will write unit tests related to the hexacopter motor and the altimeter. Open the existing `test_hexacopter.py` file and insert the following lines after the last line. The code file for the sample is included in the `restful_python_chapter_10_03` folder:

```
def test_set_and_get_hexacopter_motor_speed(self):
    """
    Ensure we can set and get the hexacopter's motor speed
    """
    patch_args = {'motor_speed': 700}
    patch_response = self.fetch(
        '/hexacopters/1',
        method='PATCH',
        body=json.dumps(patch_args))
    self.assertEqual(patch_response.code, status.HTTP_200_OK)
    get_response = self.fetch(
        '/hexacopters/1',
        method='GET')
    self.assertEqual(get_response.code, status.HTTP_200_OK)
    get_response_data = escape.json_decode(get_response.body)
    self.assertTrue('speed' in get_response_data.keys())
    self.assertTrue('turned_on' in get_response_data.keys())
    self.assertEqual(get_response_data['speed'],
                     patch_args['motor_speed'])
    self.assertEqual(get_response_data['turned_on'],
                     True)

def test_get_altimeter_altitude(self):
    """
    Ensure we can get the altimeter's altitude
    """
    get_response = self.fetch(
        '/altimeters/1',
        method='GET')
    self.assertEqual(get_response.code, status.HTTP_200_OK)
    get_response_data = escape.json_decode(get_response.body)
    self.assertTrue('altitude' in get_response_data.keys())
    self.assertGreaterEqual(get_response_data['altitude'],
                            0)
    self.assertLessEqual(get_response_data['altitude'],
                         3000)
```

The previous code added the following two methods to the `TestHexacopter` class whose names start with the `test_` prefix:

- `test_set_and_get_hexacopter_motor_speed`: This tests whether we can set and get the hexacopter's motor speed.
- `test_get_altimeter_altitude`: This tests whether we can retrieve the altitude value from the altimeter.

We just coded a few tests related to the hexacopter and the altimeter in order to improve test coverage and notice the impact on the test coverage report.

Now, run the following command within the same virtual environment we have been using:

```
nose2 -v --with-coverage
```

The following lines show the sample output. Notice that the numbers shown in the report might have small differences if our code includes additional lines or comments:

```
test_get_altimeter_altitude (test_hexacopter.TestHexacopter) ...
I've started retrieving the altitude
I've finished retrieving the altitude
ok
test_set_and_get_hexacopter_motor_speed
(test_hexacopter.TestHexacopter) ... I've started setting the hexacopter's
motor speed
I've finished setting the hexacopter's motor speed
I've started retrieving hexacopter's status
I've finished retrieving hexacopter's status
ok
test_set_and_get_led_brightness_level (test_hexacopter.TestHexacopter)
... I've started setting the Blue LED's brightness level
I've finished setting the Blue LED's brightness level
I've started setting the White LED's brightness level
I've finished setting the White LED's brightness level
I've started retrieving Blue LED's status
I've finished retrieving Blue LED's status
I've started retrieving White LED's status
I've finished retrieving White LED's status
ok
----------------------------------------------------------------------
Ran 3 tests in 2.282s
OK
----------- coverage: platform win32, python 3.5.2-final-0 ---
Name            Stmts   Miss   Cover
-----------------------------------
async_api.py      129     38    71%
drone.py           57      4    93%
-----------------------------------
TOTAL             186     42    77%
```

The output provided details indicating that the test runner executed 3 tests and all of them passed. The test code coverage measurement report provided by the `coverage` package increased the `Cover` percentage of the `async_api.py` module from 47% in the previous run to 71%. In addition, the percentage of the `drone.py` module increased from 68% to 93% because we wrote tests that worked with all the components for the drone. The new additional tests we wrote executed additional code in the two modules, and therefore, there is an impact in the coverage report.

If we take a look at the missing statements, we will notice that we aren't testing scenarios where validations fail. Now, we will write additional unit tests to improve the testing coverage further. Specifically, we will write unit tests to make sure that we cannot set invalid brightness levels for the LEDs, we cannot set invalid motor speeds for the hexacopter, and we receive an HTTP 404 Not Found status code when we try to access a resource that doesn't exist. Open the existing `test_hexacopter.py` file and insert the following lines after the last line. The code file for the sample is included in the `restful_python_chapter_10_04` folder:

```python
    def test_set_invalid_brightness_level(self):
        """
        Ensure we cannot set an invalid brightness level for a LED
        """
        patch_args_led_1 = {'brightness_level': 256}
        patch_response_led_1 = self.fetch(
            '/leds/1',
            method='PATCH',
            body=json.dumps(patch_args_led_1))
        self.assertEqual(patch_response_led_1.code,
status.HTTP_400_BAD_REQUEST)
        patch_args_led_2 = {'brightness_level': -256}
        patch_response_led_2 = self.fetch(
            '/leds/2',
            method='PATCH',
            body=json.dumps(patch_args_led_2))
        self.assertEqual(patch_response_led_2.code,
status.HTTP_400_BAD_REQUEST)
        patch_response_led_3 = self.fetch(
            '/leds/2',
            method='PATCH',
            body=json.dumps({}))
        self.assertEqual(patch_response_led_3.code,
status.HTTP_400_BAD_REQUEST)

    def test_set_brightness_level_invalid_led_id(self):
        """
        Ensure we cannot set the brightness level for an invalid LED id
        """
```

```
            patch_args_led_1 = {'brightness_level': 128}
            patch_response_led_1 = self.fetch(
                '/leds/100',
                method='PATCH',
                body=json.dumps(patch_args_led_1))
            self.assertEqual(patch_response_led_1.code,
    status.HTTP_404_NOT_FOUND)

    def test_get_brightness_level_invalid_led_id(self):
        """
        Ensure we cannot get the brightness level for an invalid LED id
        """
        patch_response_led_1 = self.fetch(
            '/leds/100',
            method='GET')
        self.assertEqual(patch_response_led_1.code,
    status.HTTP_404_NOT_FOUND)

    def test_set_invalid_motor_speed(self):
        """
        Ensure we cannot set an invalid motor speed for the hexacopter
        """
        patch_args_hexacopter_1 = {'motor_speed': 89000}
        patch_response_hexacopter_1 = self.fetch(
            '/hexacopters/1',
            method='PATCH',
            body=json.dumps(patch_args_hexacopter_1))
        self.assertEqual(patch_response_hexacopter_1.code,
        status.HTTP_400_BAD_REQUEST)
        patch_args_hexacopter_2 = {'motor_speed': -78600}
        patch_response_hexacopter_2 = self.fetch(
            '/hexacopters/1',
            method='PATCH',
            body=json.dumps(patch_args_hexacopter_2))
        self.assertEqual(patch_response_hexacopter_2.code,
        status.HTTP_400_BAD_REQUEST)
        patch_response_hexacopter_3 = self.fetch(
            '/hexacopters/1',
            method='PATCH',
            body=json.dumps({}))
        self.assertEqual(patch_response_hexacopter_3.code,
        status.HTTP_400_BAD_REQUEST)

    def test_set_motor_speed_invalid_hexacopter_id(self):
        """
        Ensure we cannot set the motor speed for an invalid hexacopter id
        """
        patch_args_hexacopter_1 = {'motor_speed': 128}
```

```
        patch_response_hexacopter_1 = self.fetch(
            '/hexacopters/100',
            method='PATCH',
            body=json.dumps(patch_args_hexacopter_1))
        self.assertEqual(patch_response_hexacopter_1.code,
        status.HTTP_404_NOT_FOUND)

    def test_get_motor_speed_invalid_hexacopter_id(self):
        """
        Ensure we cannot get the motor speed for an invalid hexacopter id
        """
        patch_response_hexacopter_1 = self.fetch(
            '/hexacopters/5',
            method='GET')
        self.assertEqual(patch_response_hexacopter_1.code,
        status.HTTP_404_NOT_FOUND)

    def test_get_altimeter_altitude_invalid_altimeter_id(self):
        """
        Ensure we cannot get the altimeter's altitude for an invalid
altimeter id
        """
        get_response = self.fetch(
            '/altimeters/5',
            method='GET')
        self.assertEqual(get_response.code, status.HTTP_404_NOT_FOUND)
```

The previous code added the following seven methods to the TestHexacopter class whose
names start with the test_ prefix:

- test_set_invalid_brightness_level: This makes sure that we cannot set an
  invalid brightness level for an LED through an HTTP PATCH request.
- test_set_brightness_level_invalid_led_id: This makes sure that we
  cannot set the brightness level for an invalid LED ID through an HTTP PATCH
  request.
- test_get_brightness_level_invalid_led_id: This makes sure that we
  cannot get the brightness level for an invalid LED ID.
- test_set_invalid_motor_speed: This makes sure that we cannot set an
  invalid motor seed for the hexacopter through an HTTP PATCH request.
- test_set_motor_speed_invalid_hexacopter_id: This makes sure that we
  cannot set the motor speed for an invalid hexacopter ID through an HTTP PATCH
  request.

- `test_get_motor_speed_invalid_hexacopter_id`: This makes sure that we cannot get the motor speed for an invalid hexacopter ID.
- `test_get_altimeter_altitude_invalid_altimeter_id`: This makes sure that we cannot get the altitude value for an invalid altimeter ID.

We coded many tests that will make sure that all the validations work as expected. Now, run the following command within the same virtual environment we have been using:

```
nose2 -v --with-coverage
```

The following lines show the sample output. Notice that the numbers shown in the report might have small differences if our code includes additional lines or comments:

```
I've finished retrieving the altitude
ok
test_get_altimeter_altitude_invalid_altimeter_id
(test_hexacopter.TestHexacopter) ... WARNING:tornado.access:404 GET
/altimeters/5 (127.0.0.1) 1.00ms
    ok
test_get_brightness_level_invalid_led_id
(test_hexacopter.TestHexacopter) ... WARNING:tornado.access:404 GET
/leds/100 (127.0.0.1) 2.01ms
    ok
test_get_motor_speed_invalid_hexacopter_id
(test_hexacopter.TestHexacopter) ... WARNING:tornado.access:404 GET
/hexacopters/5 (127.0.0.1) 2.01ms
    ok
test_set_and_get_hexacopter_motor_speed
(test_hexacopter.TestHexacopter) ... I've started setting the hexacopter's
motor speed
    I've finished setting the hexacopter's motor speed
    I've started retrieving hexacopter's status
    I've finished retrieving hexacopter's status
    ok
test_set_and_get_led_brightness_level (test_hexacopter.TestHexacopter)
... I've started setting the Blue LED's brightness level
    I've finished setting the Blue LED's brightness level
    I've started setting the White LED's brightness level
    I've finished setting the White LED's brightness level
    I've started retrieving Blue LED's status
    I've finished retrieving Blue LED's status
    I've started retrieving White LED's status
    I've finished retrieving White LED's status
    ok
test_set_brightness_level_invalid_led_id
(test_hexacopter.TestHexacopter) ... WARNING:tornado.access:404 PATCH
/leds/100 (127.0.0.1) 1.01ms
```

```
    ok
    test_set_invalid_brightness_level (test_hexacopter.TestHexacopter) ...
I've started setting the Blue LED's brightness level
    I've failed setting the Blue LED's brightness level
    WARNING:tornado.access:400 PATCH /leds/1 (127.0.0.1) 13.51ms
    I've started setting the White LED's brightness level
    I've failed setting the White LED's brightness level
    WARNING:tornado.access:400 PATCH /leds/2 (127.0.0.1) 10.03ms
    WARNING:tornado.access:400 PATCH /leds/2 (127.0.0.1) 2.01ms
    ok
    test_set_invalid_motor_speed (test_hexacopter.TestHexacopter) ... I've
started setting the hexacopter's motor speed
    I've failed setting the hexacopter's motor speed
    WARNING:tornado.access:400 PATCH /hexacopters/1 (127.0.0.1) 19.27ms
    I've started setting the hexacopter's motor speed
    I've failed setting the hexacopter's motor speed
    WARNING:tornado.access:400 PATCH /hexacopters/1 (127.0.0.1) 9.04ms
    WARNING:tornado.access:400 PATCH /hexacopters/1 (127.0.0.1) 1.00ms
    ok
    test_set_motor_speed_invalid_hexacopter_id
(test_hexacopter.TestHexacopter) ... WARNING:tornado.access:404 PATCH
/hexacopters/100 (127.0.0.1) 1.00ms
    ok
    ----------------------------------------------------------------------
    Ran 10 tests in 5.905s
    OK
    ----------- coverage: platform win32, python 3.5.2-final-0 -----------
    Name            Stmts   Miss  Cover
    ----------------------------------------
    async_api.py      129      5    96%
    drone.py           57      0   100%
    ----------------------------------------
    TOTAL             186      5    97%
```

The output provided details indicating that the test runner executed 10 tests and all of them passed. The test code coverage measurement report provided by the `coverage` package increased the `Cover` percentage of the `async_api.py` module from 71% in the previous run to 97%. In addition, the percentage of the `drone.py` module increased from 93% to 100%. If we check the coverage report, we will notice that the only statements that aren't executed are the statements included in the main method for the async_api.py module because they aren't part of the tests. Thus, we can say that we have 100% coverage.

Now that we have a great test coverage, we can generate the `requirements.txt` file that lists the application dependencies together with their versions. This way, any platform in which we decide to deploy the RESTful API will be able to easily install all the necessary dependencies listed in the file.

Run the following `pip freeze` to generate the `requirements.txt` file:

```
pip freeze > requirements.txt
```

The following lines show the content of a sample generated `requirements.txt` file. However, bear in mind that many packages increase their version number quickly and you might see different versions in your configuration:

```
cov-core==1.15.0
coverage==4.2
nose2==0.6.5
six==1.10.0
tornado==4.4.1
```

Other Python Web frameworks for building RESTful APIs

We built RESTful Web Services with Django, Flask, and Tornado. However, Python has many other Web frameworks that are also suitable for building RESTful APIs. Everything we learned throughout the book about designing, building, testing, and deploying a RESTful API is also applicable to any other Python Web framework we decide to use. The following list enumerates additional frameworks and their main Web page:

- **Pyramid**: http://www.pylonsproject.org/
- **Bottle**: http://bottlepy.org/
- **Falcon**: https://falconframework.org/

As always happens with any Python Web framework, there are additional packages that might simplify our most common tasks. For example, it is possible to use Ramses in combination with Pyramid to create RESTful APIs by working with **RAML (RESTful API Modeling Language)**, whose specification is available at http://github.com/raml-org/raml-spec. You can read more details about Ramses at http://ramses.readthedocs.io/en/stable/getting_started.html.

Test your knowledge

1. The `concurrent.futures.ThreadPoolExecutor` class provides us:
    1. A high-level interface for synchronously executing callables.
    2. A high-level interface for asynchronously executing callables.
    3. A high-level interface for composing HTTP requests.

2. The `@tornado.concurrent.run_on_executor` decorator allows us to:
    1. Run an asynchronous method synchronously on an executor.
    2. Run an asynchronous method on an executor without generating a Future.
    3. Run a synchronous method asynchronously on an executor.

3. The recommended way to write asynchronous code in Tornado is to use:
    1. Coroutines.
    2. Chained callbacks.
    3. Subroutines.

4. The `tornado.Testing.AsyncHTTPTestCase` class represents:
    1. A test case that starts up a Flask HTTP Server.
    2. A test case that starts up a Tornado HTTP Server.
    3. A test case that doesn't start up any HTTP Server.

5. If we want to convert the bytes in a JSON response body to a Python dictionary, we can use the following function:
    1. `tornado.escape.json_decode`
    2. `tornado.escape.byte_decode`
    3. `tornado.escape.response_body_decode`

Summary

In this chapter, we understood the difference between synchronous and asynchronous execution. We created a new version of the RESTful API that takes advantage of the non-blocking features in Tornado combined with asynchronous execution. We improved scalability for our existing API and we made it possible to start executing other requests while waiting for the slow I/O operations with sensors and actuators. We avoided splitting our methods into multiple methods with callbacks by using the `tornado.gen` generator-based interface that Tornado provides to make it easier to work in an asynchronous environment.

Then, we set up a testing environment. We installed nose2 to make it easy to discover and execute unit tests. We wrote a first round of unit tests, measured test coverage, and then we wrote additional unit tests to improve test coverage. We created all the necessary tests to have a complete coverage of all the lines of code.

We built RESTful Web Services with Django, Flask, and Tornado. We have chosen the most appropriate framework for each case. We learned to design a RESTful API from scratch and to run all the necessary tests to make sure that our API works without issues as we release new versions. Now, we are ready to create RESTful APIs with any of the Web frameworks with whom we have been working throughout this book.

Exercise Answers

Chapter 1, Developing RESTful APIs with Django

Q1	2
Q2	1
Q3	3
Q4	1
Q5	3

Chapter 2, Working with Class-Based Views and Hyperlinked APIs in Django

Q1	1
Q2	2
Q3	3
Q4	3
Q5	1

Chapter 3, Improving and Adding Authentication to an API With Django

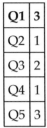

Q1	3
Q2	1
Q3	2
Q4	1
Q5	3

Chapter 4, Throttling, Filtering, Testing, and Deploying an API with Django

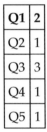

Q1	2
Q2	1
Q3	3
Q4	1
Q5	1

Chapter 5, Developing RESTful APIs with Flask

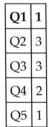

Q1	1
Q2	3
Q3	3
Q4	2
Q5	1

Chapter 6, Working with Models, SQLAlchemy, and Hyperlinked APIs in Flask

Q1	1
Q2	2
Q3	3
Q4	3
Q5	1

Chapter 7, Improving and Adding Authentication to an API with Flask

Q1	3
Q2	1
Q3	3
Q4	1
Q5	2

Chapter 8, Testing and Deploying an API with Flask

Q1	1
Q2	2
Q3	1
Q4	1
Q5	3

Chapter 9, Developing RESTful APIs with Tornado

Q1	2
Q2	1
Q3	3
Q4	3
Q5	2

Chapter 10, Working with Asynchronous Code, Testing, and Deploying an API with Tornado

Q1	2
Q2	3
Q3	1
Q4	2
Q5	1

Index

drone
   classes, creating for representation 340
duplicate code
   eliminating, with model serializers 58

E

endpoints
   configuring 208
   for API, working with 97
Enter request URL textbox 218, 355

F

Falcon
   reference 392
Field Filters 171
fields, for resource
   updating, with PATCH method 273, 274
Filters button 171
Flask API
   HTTP requests, making to 210
Flask-RESTful
   used, for setting up virtual environment 196
Flask
   used, for setting up virtual environment 196

G

generic class based views
   using 95
generic classes
   using 94
generic pagination class
   coding 275, 278, 279
Global Interpreter Lock (GIL) 332
GUI tool
   reference link 23

H

HTTP methods
   DELETE 75
   GET 75
   PATCH 75
   POST 75
   PUT 75
   tasks 9

tasks performing 334
tasks, performing 194
HTTP requests, making to Flask API
   about 210
   curl, working with 211
   Httpie, working with 211
   Postman, working with 218
HTTP requests
   creating, to Tornado API 351
   curl, working with 36
   httpie, working with 36
   making, to API 36
   making, to Flask API 210
   making, to Tornado non-blocking API 374
HTTP verbs
   DELETE 9
   GET 8
   POST 8
   PUT 8

I

IoT (Internet of Things) 192

L

Light-Emitting Diode (LED) 333
lightweight virtual environments
   working with 11
limitations, API usage
   authenticated users 152
   unauthenticated users 152

M

message
   required attributes 193
migrations
   default value, setting for new required field 139
   running 250
   running, for user table generation 296, 298, 299
model serializers
   used, for eliminating duplicate code 58
models
   creating 20, 200
   deserializing, by creating schemas 236
   relationships, declaring with 78
   security-related data, adding 131

Printed in Great Britain
by Amazon